# The Epochal Nature of Process in Whitehead's Metaphysics

# THE EPOCHAL NATURE OF PROCESS IN WHITEHEAD'S METAPHYSICS

F. Bradford Wallack

State University of New York Press

Albany

Grateful acknowledgement is made to the Macmillan Publishing Co., Inc. for permission to reprint the following material:

1. 3000 words from *Adventures in Ideas* by Alfred North Whitehead. Copyright 1933 by Macmillan Publishing Co., Inc., renewed 1961 by Evelyn Whitehead.
2. 2500 words from *Modes of Thought* by Alfred North Whitehead. Copyright 1938 by Macmillan Publishing Co., Inc., renewed 1966 by T. North Whitehead.
3. 2200 words from *Science and the Modern World* by Alfred North Whitehead. Copyright 1925 by Macmillan Publishing Co., Inc., renewed 1953 by Evelyn Whitehead.
4. 16,000 words from *Process and Reality,* corrected edition, by Alfred North Whitehead edited by David Ray Griffin and Donald W. Sherburne. Copyright 1929 by Macmillan Publishing Co., Inc., renewed 1957 by Evelyn Whitehead. Copyright 1978 by The Free Press, a Division of Macmillan Publishing Co., Inc.
5. 350 words from *Religion in the Making* by Alfred North Whitehead. Copyright 1926 by Macmillan Publishing Co., Inc., renewed 1954 by Evelyn Whitehead.

Published by
State University of New York Press, Albany

© 1980 State University of New York

For information, address State University of New York
Press, State University Plaza, Albany, N.Y., 12246


Library of Congress Cataloging in Publication Data

Wallack, F    Bradford, 1943-
   The epochal nature of process in Whitehead's
metaphysics.

   Bibliography: p.
   Includes index.
   1. Whitehead, Alfred North, 1861-1947—Metaphysics.
2. Metaphysics. 3. Time. I. Title.
B1674.W354W34      110       79-22898
ISBN 0-87395-404-1

To M. W. whose enduring love has seen it through everything.

# Contents: An Overview

# Detailed Contents

# List of Abbreviations

| | |
|---|---|
| *AE* | *The Aims of Education* |
| *AI* | *Adventures of Ideas* |
| *CN* | *The Concept of Nature* |
| *ESP* | *Essays in Science and Philosophy* |
| *FR* | *The Function of Reason* |
| *IS* | *The Interpretation of Science* |
| *MT* | *Modes of Thought* |
| *PNK* | *An Enquiry Concerning the Principles of Natural Knowledge* |
| *PR* | *Process and Reality: An Essay in Cosmology* |
| *Prel* | *The Principle of Relativity* |
| *RM* | *Religion in the Making* |
| *S* | *Symbolism: Its Meaning and Effect* |
| *SMW* | *Science and the Modern World* |
| *WhA* | *Alfred North Whitehead: An Anthology* |

| | |
|---|---|
| *PS* | *Process Studies* |
| *TS* | *Tulane Studies*, Volume X (1961) |
| *SJP* | *The Southern Journal of Philosophy*, Volume 7, Number 4 (1969-70) |
| *RW* | *The Relevance of Whitehead*, ed. Ivor Leclerc |
| *KEP* | *Alfred North Whitehead: Essays on his Philosophy*, ed. George L. Kline |
| *LLP-W* | *The Philosophy of Alfred North Whitehead*, ed. Paul Arthur Schilpp |

| | |
|---|---|
| *PICP* | *The Philosophical Impact of Contemporary Physics*, Milic Capek |
| *BMP* | *Bergson and Modern Physics*, Milic Capek |
| *CST* | *The Concepts of Space and Time*, ed. Milic Capek |
| *R* | *The Special Theory of Relativity*, David Bohm |
| *CC* | *Causality and Chance in Modern Physics*, David Bohm |
| *QT* | *Quantum Theory*, David Bohm |
| *E* | *Experience and Conceptual Activity*, J. M. Burgers |

# Preface

With this book I offer my own interpretation of Whitehead's thought. His philosophy abounds in paradoxical expression. Its actual entity is both actual and potential; both cause and effect; both subject and object; both indeterminate and determinate; both perishable and immortal; both real and apparent; both private and social; both whole and part; both a concrescence and a transcendence; both a process of becoming and an immobile, unchanging quantum; both a continuous transition and a discontinuous atomic succession; both a sequence of phases and a phaseless whole; both passage and arrest; both divisible and undivided; both extensive and indivisible; both past and present; both temporal and beyond time: there seems to be no end of contradiction. Yet Whitehead's works have always impressed me as knowledgeable and profound. Then there must be a way of resolving these contradictions and interpreting the actual entity in a sensible, credible way. This book is the conclusion of my struggle with Whiteheadian paradox.

It focuses on Whiteheadian time, which was the key to my understanding the actual entity. For a contradiction to hold, both an assertion and its denial must be true at the same time. But twentieth century physics has shown that there is no absolute definition for "the same time": spatio-temporal relationships depend upon the perspective of those whom they affect, and are differently defined from different perspectives. Whiteheadian time, an epochal theory of time, is consonant with relativity physics; and the actual entity was inspired by quantum mechanics. The purpose of this book is to explain and justify Whitehead's theory of time as the appropriate theory for his conception of actual entities whose principles of creation are in keeping with the principles of modern physics.

My research into Whitehead's philosophy has led me to disagree with most of the prevalent views about it. It seems to me that many Whiteheadians have compounded the difficulties of understanding Whitehead either by a misunderstanding of the actual entity or a coy reluctance even to state exactly what they think an actual entity to be. I have recorded my dissent from the positions of several Whiteheadians on important points as they occur. But I do not here investigate their reasons for their views; I have concentrated my efforts on Whitehead rather than his interpreters.

There are other omissions from the book which I should mention. Whitehead proposes that his cosmology be an alternative to that of scientific materialism. This book concerns Whitehead's conception of scientific materialism, not the actual merits or deficiencies of scientific materialism. My intention is only to show that Whitehead should not be interpreted as supporting the very premises of the scientific materialist cosmology that he pointedly rejects. Similarly, in this book there is almost no comparison of Whitehead with other thinkers, and little comparison of his epochal theory of time with other modern theories of time.

Certain issues even in Whitehead's discussion of time have been omitted. Most importantly, there is no mention of Whiteheadian durations, presented durations, strain loci, or his method of extensive abstraction yielding abstractive sets. Such topics, in their relevance to time, are necessary for Whitehead's practical extension of his philosophy, his provision for a foundation for time measurement that can serve science; but they are less important for a rendering of the metaphysics.

I am much indebted to Dr. Michael J. B. Jackson for help with this work. His fairness and willingness to advise on every detail gave me the courage to turn a pandemonium into a structured text. And my gratitude extends to William D. Eastman, Director of the State University of New York Press, for bringing this work to publication. His serious interest in Whitehead and infinite patience with me have made this book possible.

The Whiteheadian cosmology would still escape me were it not for the discussions about it with Michael Wallack. His argument and criticisms are all that have made this interpretation of Whitehead become credible; his kindness, interest, and participation have made it a pleasure.

And acknowledgement must surely be given to both Parmenides and Heraclitus. I nowhere mention them myself, but I am under the distinct impression that they have had a guiding hand in my exploration of this subject. For, Whiteheadian time is here trimmed down to the dialectics of the one and the many, the occasional and the continuous.

# Introduction

A study of Whiteheadian time, that is, epochal process in Whitehead's metaphysics, inevitably brings in many other features of the philosophy. For example, in an article on time Whitehead finds it necessary to explain time in terms of six other concepts derived from his philosophy: supersession, prehension, incompleteness, objective immortality, simultaneity, and epochs.[1] These concepts in turn are special to Whitehead's philosophy and themselves need explanation by reference to other of its points. The philosophy consequently has a weblike structure so that the whole of it must somehow be understood before any individual sentence can be seen to make sense.

The interdependence of each concept and the whole philosophy is often displayed in single sentences, making comprehension slow and difficult. For this reason, there can be no simple or direct approach to the study of Whiteheadian time. Just as every actuality in Whitehead's "cosmic epoch" essentially refers to all other actualities, so no conception in his philosophy can be isolated from its context there and still be understandable. "Any knowledge of the finite always involves a reference to infinitude."[2] Whiteheadian time must be unraveled from the rest of the complex and very unwieldy metaphysics without too much loss of comprehension, and explained by its context in that metaphysics without too much obscurity—a delicate task of balancing.

The difficulties of either describing or illustrating in ordinary English any new concept, such as epochal time, that claims applicability to modern physics are legion. Whitehead, who has made the effort, is very perplexing and obscure indeed. In fact, it is widely believed to be impossible, as Milic Capek suggests:

In this respect the contemporary revolution in physics is more far-reaching than the so-called Copernican revolution in the sixteenth century; the heliocentric universe was in principle as imaginable as the universe of Ptolemy. But today it is obvious that the objective substrate of physical phenomena cannot be described in imaginative terms. . . . Abstract mathematical constructs seem to be today the only way, not to reach, but to *represent* the structure of the transphenomenal plane.[3]

And since ordinary English is riddled with substantialist assumptions, such as those of enduring matter, simple location, and absolute spacetime, our difficulties are even more acute: modern physics is not only unimaginable but untranslatable into ordinary English as it is. These difficulties are compounded by that of penetrating the Whiteheadian vocabulary without converting it into ordinary substantialist English.

We may ordinarily think of time as a fine line separating all the present from all the past and future; or we may think of it as a unique linear sequence of moments which are empty in themselves but which we fill up with events. In the same vein, we may think of it as a single empty cosmic container filled with the whole universe of all events. Or we may think of it as a series of points or numbers that mark events. Or perhaps we think of it as a perfectly running cosmic machine which clocks imitate. When time is characterized thus, as a huge, perhaps boundless, container, or as a series of containers, or a series of lines or points or numbers, or as a cosmic clock, it is absolute and unique. It is absolute in that it is independent of all things and events; and its uniqueness lies in the fact of its universality, that it is one and the same time that contains or separates or marks all things alike, the same uniform progression everywhere. Absolute time is a single temporal series, everywhere flowing at the same rate. Such time would be a container though it contained nothing and no one; it would flow or progress though nothing participated in it. In the words of Henri Bergson: "Common sense believes in a single time, the same for all beings and all things."[4] Our common sense notion of time is a notion of absolute time.

This conception of an absolute time is one of the premises of the scientific materialist cosmology that Whitehead rejects. "The uniqueness of the temporal series is presupposed in the materialist philosophy of nature."[5] Whitehead intends that his own cosmology replace that of scientific materialism, which has been the cosmological framework of science until very recent times. At one point Whitehead attributes its origin to Alexandrian scholars:

The materialistic theory . . . is a purely intellectual rendering of experience which has had the luck to get itself formulated at the dawn of scientific thought. It has dominated the language and the imagination of science since science flourished in Alexandria, with the result that it is now hardly possible to speak without appearing to assume its immediate obviousness.[6]

Then scientific materialism, or simply materialism, was an entrenched body of beliefs held by almost everyone in Western culture until Whitehead's day. An alternative to any of its basic presuppositions, such as absolute time, was unimagined and thought to be unimaginable. "Can alternative temporal series be found in nature? A few years ago such a suggestion would have been put aside as being fantastically impossible."[7]

Whitehead's account of scientific materialism is surveyed in the course of this book in order to show how he contrasts it with his own cosmology of process. Whitehead intends that all the conceptions of his philosophy be divested of materialist connotation. For example, he rarely even uses the term "time" because of its absolute and substantial signification, but prefers such terms as "epoch," "quantum," "process," "becoming," "transition," and "passage": "I definitely refrain at this stage from using the word 'time,' since the measurable time of science and of civilised life generally merely exhibits some aspects of the more fundamental fact of the passage of nature."[8]

Whitehead's entire vocabulary is devised with the same intention, namely, to free thought from its materialist presumptions. "My point is that a further stage of provisional realism is required in which the scientific scheme is recast, and founded upon the ultimate concept of *organism*."[9] Whitehead's philosophy is the "philosophy of organism."[10] Just as materialism penetrated language, thought, and imagination far beyond its service as a framework for science, so Whitehead expects the same extended application for his philosophy of organism, his cosmology of process.

> The field is now open for the introduction of some new doctrine of organism which may take the place of the materialism with which, since the seventeenth century, science has saddled philosophy. . . . The concrete fact, which is the organism, must be a complete expression of the character of a real occurrence. Such a displacement of scientific materialism, if it ever takes place, cannot fail to have important consequences in every field of thought.[11]

Modern physics has abandoned the materialist cosmology, including the absolute spacetime presupposed by classical or Newtonian physics: "In the first place, the development of natural science has gradually discarded every single feature of the original commonsense notion. Nothing whatever remains of it. . . ."[12] Just as classical physics presupposed the materialist cosmology,

Whitehead contends that modern physics presupposes his process cosmology. The two cosmologies, materialism and organism, are everywhere contrasted in this work, as in Whitehead's works, so that not only the original Whiteheadian vocabulary but also its adequacy as a conceptual framework for modern physics can be more easily appreciated.

> The old foundations of scientific thought are becoming unintelligible. . . . If science is not to degenerate into a medley of *ad hoc* hypotheses, it must become philosophical and must enter upon a thorough criticism of its own foundations.[13]

For Whitehead, scientific materialism has its basis in substantialism, or belief in substance. It is on this basis that I use the term "scientific materialism" to include substantialism and dualism as well, since dualism is belief in two substances (matter and mind).

> The materialistic starting point is from independently existing substances, matter and mind. . . . The organic starting point is from the analysis of process as the realisation of events disposed in an interlocked community.[14]

Scientific materialism might more appropriately be termed "substantialism" to name its direct opposition to Whiteheadian process. But "substantialism" is not commonly Whitehead's usage whereas "materialism" or "scientific materialism" is; so these terms will be used here, keeping in mind they encompass "substantialism" and "dualism."

Scientific materialism is, of course, the cosmology behind "the famous mechanistic theory of nature,"[15] the clock-work universe articulated in classical physics. Illustrating the fallacy of simple location, Whitehead characterizes the materialist conception of nature as a "fixed routine" of "brute matter," because value and purpose are absent:

> There persists, however, throughout the whole period the fixed scientific cosmology which presupposes the ultimate fact of an irreducible brute matter, or material, spread throughout space in a flux of configurations. In itself such a material is senseless, valueless, purposeless. It just does what it does do, following a fixed routine imposed by external relations which do not spring from the nature of its being. It is this assumption that I call 'scientific materialism.'[16]

This passage brings out another important contrast between materialism and organism emphasized in this book: for Whiteheadian organism, every concrete occurrence in nature is invested with final causation, that is, autonomous decision among alternative possibilities for the sake of realizing some end, whereas materialism accepts only efficient causation, the effects of which can be predetermined. It is for this reason that "materialism" is so named: it envisions a vacuous material existence, a pure matter devoid of aim, value, and meaning. Internal decision has no credence whatever with materialism, which admits only actions that are determined by external forces alone. Thus, in addition to absolute spacetime, substance, and dualism, materialism signifies the "brute matter" of classical mechanics, all action of which is conducted strictly by efficient causation alone.

Whitehead's vocabulary may indeed seem at first unnecessarily contrived or laboriously obscure beyond even possible understanding. Whitehead believes, however, that only by changing the language can one redirect thought. "Every science must devise its own instruments. The tool required for philosophy is language."[17] And he points out that no language, neither his own nor any other's, substitutes for experience or provides an understanding of experience without effort. "But no language can be anything but elliptical, requiring a leap of the imagination to understand its meaning in its relevance to immediate experience."[18] Whitehead's philosophy and its language, then, should be judged in the widest context of our experience with its great variety of aims, including knowledge of ourselves as well as nature. Even though Whitehead's language is relatively obscure and untried, it should not be rejected simply because it does not coincide with the tenets and language of materialist beliefs and philosophies that have helped to formulate our present language and thought. Nor should it be rejected simply because it does not satisfy positivistic linguistic criteria drawn from materialist science and its reflection in ordinary language.

> An old established metaphysical system gains a false air of adequate precision from the fact that its words and phrases have passed into current literature. . . . It is, therefore, no valid criticism on one metaphysical school to point out that its doctrines do not follow from the verbal expression of the facts accepted by another school.[19]

If Whitehead rejects scientific materialism and the absolute spacetime ingredient in it, how does he propose to replace it? The chapters following expound Whitehead's answer, an epochal theory of time for a cosmology of process. I try to gradually elucidate Whitehead's theory throughout the course of this book, introducing the Whiteheadian ideas one at a time in the order of their increasing dependence upon other Whiteheadian terms. Thus, the actual entity I explain first because it is defined by ideas accessible to anyone; whereas the extensive continuum is the subject of the last chapter because its explication depends upon terms special to the philosophy. As I define and interpret the Whiteheadian conceptions necessary to this exposition, I contrast them with those of materialism and materialist assumptions about them on the part of some interpreters of Whitehead. Each chapter is provided with both an introduction and a conclusion, all of which taken together will summarize this book.

# 1

# The Actual Entity

*Thus, then, in accordance with the likely account, we must declare that this cosmos has verily come into existence as a living creature endowed with soul and reason owing to the forethought of God.*

Plato, *Timaeus* 30B

## INTRODUCTION

Just what the actual entity is and what it refers to are of utmost importance to any discussion of Whitehead's philosophy, since the philosophy is about actual entities and their interrelationships. "In the three notions—actual entity, prehension, nexus—an endeavor has been made to base philosophical thought upon the most concrete elements in our experience."[1] This chapter defines the actual entity and provides examples of those things that it refers to. This chapter's thesis is that the actual entity is *any concrete existent whatsoever.*

Many Whiteheadians have interpreted Whitehead so as to limit the application of his basic ontological category of existence—his actual entity— to just two kinds of existents: subatomic entities, such as electrons, protons, photons, and the like, and human percipient experience. In so doing, they have silently reintroduced the materialist and dualist foundations of previous philosophies and our present language, thereby seriously undermining Whitehead's professed intentions to replace them with his own philosophy and language, so I shall argue.

There is good evidence to show that Whitehead intended his basic conceptions to apply to anything concretely existing, not only the small, the short, or the allegedly simple. Given Whitehead's definitions, descriptions, and examples of actual entities, I argue that they cannot correctly be interpreted as necessarily only of one size, duration, quality, character, intensity, or degree of complexity or palpability. They cannot rightly be identified exclusively with entities of subatomic scale or with human percipient experiences or both: there are not only one or two kinds of existences.

Another important misconception among interpreters of Whitehead is the view that Whitehead's actual entities, like the atoms of Democritus, are simple rather than composite. It is often suggested that these absolutely simple entities are to be contrasted with Whitehead's "nexūs," which are composite, being related sets of actual entities. I shall try to show that Whitehead has argued that there is only one kind of real togetherness. Insofar as a nexus is really a togetherness, it forms also an actual entity in the Whiteheadian cosmology. It is a set of actual entities comprising another actual entity. And since every actual entity is itself a real composite of other actual entities, it is also from this perspective a nexus. The implications of these views are discussed at length throughout the rest of this work.


## ACTUALITY

*RES VERAE.* Whitehead does not offer a great many examples of actual entities. However, the examples that he does give show that the term "actual entity" has the broadest possible reference: namely, to all things. ". . . Descartes uses the phrase *res vera* in the same sense as that in which I have used the term 'actual.' It means 'existence' in the fullest sense of that term, beyond which there is no other."[2] Actual entities are the existences, any real or true and concrete existences whatsoever, of any kind, in any proportion and complexity that existence is. Actual entities are the "Final Realities" or "*Res Verae*,"[3] this latter expression being the Latin for "true things" or "real things." By "final" Whitehead cannot mean small, short, simple, or impalpable; rather, he means "actual" or "concrete": there is nothing more concrete than the actual entity. Its actuality or concreteness is that which existence has; there is not a more actual or more concrete substance or substratum behind or beyond the actual entities from which they derive their actuality or concreteness.

In the following passage, Whitehead defines actual entities as "real things," and says explicitly that they differ qualitatively and that they are complex. In giving examples of actual entities he chooses two "things" of extreme difference in every way: God and a trivial puff.

'Actual entities'—also termed 'actual occasions'—are the final real things of which the world is made up. There is no going behind actual entities to find anything more real. They differ among themselves: God is an actual entity, and so is the most trivial puff of existence in far-off empty space. But, though there are gradations of importance, and diversities of function, yet in the principles which actuality exemplifies all are on the same level. The final facts are, all alike, actual entities; and these actual entities are drops of experience, complex and interdependent.[4]

This passage expresses several of the points that I shall discuss in this chapter: that all actual entities are not necessarily small, short, and impalpable; that they are complex and not simple; that they are ontologically equal. Then there are not actual entities of fundamentally different kinds, such as minds and bodies, or atoms and societies, or subatomic particles and organisms. There is only one genus of actual entity. "The presumption that there is only one genus of actual entities constitutes an ideal of cosmological theory to which the philosophy of organism endeavors to conform."[5] Since everything concretely existing from the most trivial puff of existence to God is an actual entity, and ontologically equal as such, then Ivor Leclerc's assertion is antithetical to Whitehead's: "All compounds, and bodies in particular, are derivative entities, of a different ontological status from that of actual entities."[6] This is exactly what Whitehead's conception of the actual entity denies. For Whitehead, all actual entities are on the same ontological level and in that sense all are of a kind inasmuch as all share the same nature as concrete existences. Then let us say that there is only one genus of actual entity but many types, the types distinguished by their differences in size, duration, quantity, quality, intensity, degree of complexity and palpability, and so on. To differ in any of these ways or in other ways is not to differ in existence.

*Particular things, sensible objects.* For examples of actual entities in between the most insignificant puff and God, Whitehead provides examples of "particular things" taken from Locke's philosophy: a bird, a beast, a tree, a plant, a leaf, a crow, a sheep, a grain of sand.[7] And he later adds to this list "the child's idea of its mother."[8] The idea is not the actual entity, but the idea on the part of the child, the child's experience. Some interpreters of Whitehead suggest that Whitehead is to be most instructively compared to ancient atomists, Democritus or Lucretius, or to the Leibniz of the Monadology. Yet Whitehead most often compares his own philosophy to Locke's:

The first point to notice is that in some of his statements Locke comes very near to the explicit formulation of an organic philosophy of the type being developed here. . . . His true topic is the analysis of the types of experience enjoyed by an actual entity.[9]

Whitehead feels the most affinity with Locke. He repeatedly advises us that the actual entity is comparable to Locke's "particular thing," "particular existent," and "exterior thing." In fact, Whitehead is willing to substitute his own term "actual entity" for Locke's "particular thing." Here for example:

The context [in Locke's *Essay*] shows that it is not the impossibility of an 'idea' of any particular thing which is the seat of the difficulty; it is solely their number. This notion of a direct 'idea' (or 'feeling') of an actual entity is a presupposition of all common sense . . . .[10]

This substitution of "actual entity" for Locke's "particular thing" in the second sentence is clear indication that Whitehead wishes us to apply his term "actual entity" where Locke applies "particular thing." And here too Whitehead speaks of the equivalence of Locke's conception and his own:

But later (III, III, 2), when discussing general terms . . . [Locke] adds paranthetically another type of ideas which are practically what I term 'objectified actual entities' and 'nexūs.' He calls them 'ideas of particular things'; and he explains why, in general, such ideas cannot have their separate names. The reason is simple and undeniable: there are too many actual entities.[11]

The qualification "practically" in this passage should not be read so as to obliterate Whitehead's intended comparison between his actual entities and Locke's particular things. Whatever difference in meaning Whitehead may have had in mind between his term "actual entities" and Locke's term "particular things," he is willing to substitute his own term for Locke's in the very same paragraph ("there are too many actual entities," he says, referring to all the particular things that might be separately named). Thus, Whitehead intends his term to refer to the same "particular things" that Locke lists, such as birds, beasts, plants, and sand. So, Whitehead's qualification "practically" alerts us to the fact that the terms of the two philosophers are not, however, precisely equivalent in meaning. The terms *refer* to the same things, namely concrete existences, but have somewhat different *meanings*.

The actual entities of this last passage are described as "objectified," which is to say, as "felt." A bird, a beast, a plant, a grain of sand are (felt as) these things to us: we regard them or feel them to be these familiar things, whereas they may be "objectified" or felt very differently by some other creature. What is a grain of sand to us may be a brick to an ant; what is objectified as a sheep to us may be objectified as a soup to a bacterium. Similarly, Whitehead regards Locke's examples as a list of actual entities *and* nexūs. This is one of the many instances where Whitehead does not trouble to distinguish actual entities from nexūs, since an actual entity in any case composes a nexus of antecedent actual entities, and since any actual entity can be seen as a nexus of its component actual entities. A bird is both an actual bird entity, for example, and a nexus of cell entities. The bird is also another nexus from another perspective: it is a series of actual bird entities that make up the bird's life-time or history.

> In other words, an 'exterior thing' is either one 'actual entity,' or is a 'society' with a 'defining characteristic.' For the organic philosophy, these 'exterior things' (in the former sense) are the final concrete actualities. The individualized substance (of Locke) must be construed to be the historic route constituted by some society of fundamental 'exterior things,' stretching from the first 'thing' to the last 'thing.'[12]

Thus, actual entities are comparable to Locke's "exterior things," the historic routes of which amount to Whiteheadian nexūs or "societies" and Lockean "substances." Because Whitehead considers the examples taken from Locke as examples of both actual entities and nexūs, to deny that they are possible examples of actual entities is to eliminate Whitehead's own comparison of his own philosophy with Locke's.

Just as the actual entity is comparable to Locke's "particular thing," "particular existent," and "exterior thing," because these terms all refer to actual concrete existences, so the actual entity is comparable to Descartes' "object" and Newton's "sensible object." Descartes uses the sun as an example of an object; so the sun is used by Whitehead as an example of an actual entity in his discussion of Descartes' and Locke's correspondence theory of truth. "Both Descartes and Locke, in order to close the gap between idea representing and 'actual entity represented,' require this doctrine of 'the sun itself existing in the mind.'"[13] Then for Whitehead, in this example, the sun itself is an actual entity which "exists" in the mind as the idea representing it. Similarly, Whitehead equates actual entities with Newton's "sensible objects": "We may expand Newton's phrase, and state that the common sense of mankind conceives that all its notions ultimately refer to actual entities, or as Newton terms them, 'sensible objects.'"[14]

These comparisons seem to me incontrovertible evidence that Whitehead intends his term "actual entity" to refer to any concrete existent whatsoever.

But there is more. There are innumerable places where Whitehead speaks simply of "things" instead of using his term "actual entities." We have seen that he has defined actual entities as "final real things." Numerous passages declare this equation again and again.

> The most general term 'thing'—or, equivalently, 'entity'—means nothing else than to be one of the 'many' which find their niches in each instance of concrescence. Each instance of concrescence *is itself* the novel individual 'thing' in question.[15]

And again we meet the *res verae,* or "really real things": "I hold that these unities of existence, these occasions of experience, are the really real things which in their collective unity compose the evolving universe, ever plunging into the creative advance."[16] And again: "Apart from 'potentiality' and 'givenness,' there can be no nexus of actual things in process of supersession by novel actual things."[17] And so on.

*Logical subjects.* Further evidence for the generality of application of Whitehead's "actual entity" can be found in his discussion of "logical subjects" of propositions and the conditions under which these logical entities come into existence. For, it is actual entities that are the logical subjects of propositions; and logical subjects of propositions are all actual entities. "These actual entities are the logical subjects of the proposition. . . . The logical subjects are, nevertheless, in fact actual entities which are definite in their realized mutual relatedness."[18] Anything to which it is possible to refer, anything about which a proposition is possible, is an actual entity. Whitehead explains that actual entities are transformed into logical subjects (in this case, the term "actualities" is used instead of "actual entities"): "Thus the actualities, which were first felt as sheer matter of fact, have been transformed into a set of logical subjects with the potentiality for realizing an assigned predicative pattern."[19] This is a clear statement that logical subjects necessarily refer to actual entities.

Whitehead explains that every proposition presupposes certain definite settled actual entities in the experience of the judging subject; these presupposed actual entities are the logical subjects. "Every proposition presupposes those actual entities which are its logical subjects."[20] To judge the truth or falsity of a proposition, the judging subject must be acquainted with the presupposed actual entities. Whitehead asks us to consider the utterance, "Socrates is mortal":

Thus in one meaning of the phrase 'Socrates is mortal,' the logical subjects are one singular *IT* (Socrates) and the actual entities of this actual world, forming a society amid which mortality is realizable and including the former '*IT*.' In the other meaning, there are also included among the logical subjects the actual entities forming the Athenian society. These actual entities are required for the realization of the predicative pattern 'Socratic and mortal' and are the definitely indicated logical subjects.[21]

In one meaning, then, this utterance may be understood as the proposition "It is mortal." That is, it may be uttered without intended reference to the historical Socrates, and judged on the basis of its place in a logical scheme where no particular facts about the historical Socrates are taken into account. (Whitehead is thinking of the logic text example, All men are mortal; Socrates is a man; therefore, Socrates is mortal.) But the utterance may also be taken as the proposition, "It is Socratic and mortal."[22] In this case, Whitehead explains, "Thus, 'Socratic,' as here used, refers to a society of actual entities realizing certain general systematic properties such that the Socratic predicate is realizable in that environment."[23] Then in this case, Whitehead says, "The word 'Socratic' means 'realizing the Socratic predicate in Athenian society.'"[24] It refers to a particular historically definite set of actual entities. And included among the logical subjects referred to by the proposition are the "actual entities forming the Athenian society." This proposition requires the actual entities that have made up Athenian society, including Socrates, for its meaning. Then very many actual entities are "the definitely indicated logical subjects" of this one proposition, not only those realizing Socrates, but those forming the Athenian society of his environment.

The only things which cannot be logical subjects of propositions are those things not in existence. Whitehead uses the proposition "Caesar crossed the Rubicon" to make this point. This is a proposition for us, but it could not have been a proposition for Hannibal, since Hannibal predates Caesar. Caesar could not have been the logical subject of any proposition in Hannibal's day because Caesar was no actual entity in Hannibal's day.

Evidently new propositions come into being with the creative advance of the world. For every proposition involves its logical subjects; and it cannot be the proposition which it is, unless those logical subjects are the actual entities which they are. Thus no actual entity can feel a proposition, if its actual world does not include the logical subjects of that proposition. The proposition 'Caesar crossed the Rubicon' could not be felt by Hannibal in any occasion of his existence on earth.[25]

In this passage Whitehead also refers to Hannibal as an actual entity. Thus, not only are all logical subjects actual entities, but all those who "feel" (or "entertain" as we say) propositions. Hannibal did not feel that particular proposition about Caesar, but nevertheless he is an actual entity inasmuch as he feels any proposition at all. This is so whether or not the proposition be true.

> But its own truth, or its own falsity, is no business of a proposition. That question concerns only a subject entertaining a propositional feeling with that proposition for its datum. Such an actual entity is termed a 'prehending subject' of the proposition.[26]

Then all subjects "entertaining a propositional feeling" are actual entities, as well as all logical subjects of propositions, regardless of whether the proposition be true or false. Propositions need not be judged true or false to be what they are, so that even an untrue proposition is nevertheless a proposition about actual entities, its logical subjects. And propositions need not even be verbal statements in Whitehead's view; and in fact they are not fully expressed in words: ". . . a verbal statement is never the full expression of a proposition."[27] For, propositions need not even be consciously entertained. "Propositional feelings are not, in their simplest examples, conscious feelings."[28] And as we have seen, even the propositions consciously entertained are ultimately based on a wide background of actual entities omitted from statement.

Without straying too far afield, as a further discussion of Whitehead's theory of judgment would require, we may use this brief discussion to further the claim that actual entities are, in Whitehead's examples, a very diverse collection which may be extended to all concrete existences. For we see that propositions being either true or false must refer to determinate actual entities, even while they make an incomplete abstraction from them. A proposition as an abstraction contains a "logical subject" which is a bare "it" together with the "predicative pattern" of characteristics. These bare logical subjects are themselves actual entities; therefore, these bare indicative feelings are included in the scope of what Whitehead refers to as "actual entities." But at the other end of the continuum of examples, Whitehead has asserted that these bare indicative feelings arise from determinate actual entities. And to illustrate this point, he refers to the "actual entities forming the Athenian society." And finally, the subject judging the proposition is also referred to as an actual entity. We have then, as examples of actual entities, featureless indicative feelings or bare logical subjects, judging subjects (presumably all sapient creatures, perhaps all sentient creatures), and the entities that propositions refer to.

*Examples.* Some specific examples of actual entities have been given; but a survey of a few of Whitehead's works yields more. Right after the trivial puff come the subatomic entities: "This epoch is characterized by electronic and protonic actual entities, and yet more ultimate actual entities which can be dimly discerned in the quanta of energy."[29] These entities may seem to endure a long time; ". . . each electron and each proton has a long life. . . ."[30] But these are the subatomic particles, not the subatomic entities making up the particles. It is not a subatomic particle with its long life-history that is considered an actual entity, but only the individual entities making up the particle. A subatomic particle is a society of actual subatomic entities. "Also each electron is a society of electronic occasions, and each proton is a society of protonic occasions."[31] The subatomic particles considered as long-lived enduring things are societies; but they are societies of the actual subatomic entities. But these cannot be the only actual entities since Whitehead names a variety of others.

For example, in the following passage Whitehead regards the organs of the human body as actual entities:

When we perceive a contemporary extended shape which we term a 'chair,' the sense-data involved are not necessarily elements in the 'real internal constitution' of this chair-image: they are elements—in some way of feeling—in the 'real internal constitutions' of those antecedent organs of the human body *with* which we perceive the 'chair.' The *direct* recognition of such antecedent actual entities, *with* which we perceive contemporaries, is hindered.[32]

In this example, "antecedent organs *with* which we perceive" are actual entities; that is, eyes in the case of seeing the chair or hands in the case of touching it, to name only two types of organs involved in perception. Antecedent nerve cells involved in perception may be named as well: "Thus the 'eye as experiencing such-and-such sights' is passed on as a datum, from the cells of the retina, through the train of actual entities forming the relevant nerves, up to the brain."[33] Then the relevant nerves involved in sense-perception are actual entities. Here we have clear examples of actual entities as organs and nerves.

Rocks and stones seem to be favorites among philosophers for illustrating their thoughts on existence; and they are a natural choice for demonstrating arguments one way or another about concrete reality. And we find Whitehead discussing a specific rock of his acquaintance in order to illustrate the nature of his actual entity:

> The real internal constitution of an actual entity progressively constitutes a decision conditioning the creativity which transcends that actuality. The Castle Rock at Edinburgh exists from moment to moment, and from century to century, by reason of the decision effected by its own historic route of antecedent occasions. And if, in some vast upheaval of nature, it were shattered into fragments, that convulsion would still be conditioned by the fact that it was the destruction of *that* rock.[34]

Then a moment of the Castle Rock is an actual entity. It is an actual Castle Rock occasion.

A moment of the Castle Rock is an unmistakably large actual entity compared to a moment of an electron. And some other examples of actual entities that Whitehead uses are on rather a grand scale too. In saying that an actual entity is more than a complex of eternal objects, he uses Rome and Europe for illustration:

> One actual entity has a status among other actual entities, not expressible wholly in terms of contrasts between eternal objects. For example, the complex nexus of ancient imperial Rome to European history is not wholly expressible in universals. . . . But it involves more. For it is the nexus of *that* Rome with *that* Europe. . . . In part we are conscious of such physical feelings, and of that particularity of the nexus between particular actual entities. This consciousness takes the form of our consciousness of particular spatial and temporal relations between things directly perceived. But, as in the case of Rome and Europe, so far as concerns the mass of our far-reaching knowledge, the particular nexus between the particular actualities in question is only indicated by constructive reference to the physical feelings of which we are conscious.[35]

Here Whitehead treats both Rome and Europe as actual entities; they are "particular actual entities" or "particular actualities" just like any other real concrete existents. He explains that they are in a nexus together; but this does not prevent *that* Rome and *that* Europe from being actual entities, a Rome entity and a Europe entity, in their own right; and he refers to them as such.

Another example using Europe may be documented. This time one specific actual entity referred to is "the history of the European races in North

America." Whitehead points out that this actual entity cannot be understood without reference to other actual entities which he names.

> Every detail in the process of being actual involves its own gradation in reference to the other details. . . . You cannot fully understand the history of the European races in North America, without reference to the double failure of Spanish domination over California in the nineteenth century, and over England in the sixteenth century.[36]

In this example, an actual entity is called "the process of being actual." The different wording need not obscure the fact that Whitehead is talking about actual entities.

In the same way, Whitehead thinks that any topic of study will exemplify actual entities. And, more specifically, he mentions the subject matters of geology, Shakespearean sonnets, and Bach fugues to show the diversity of things that might be studied.

> The whole understanding of the world consists in the analysis of process. . . . The point is that every individual thing infects any process in which it is involved, and thus any process cannot be considered in abstraction from particular things involved. . . . The distinctions between various sciences, and various topics for study, illustrate this point. No one would study geology as a preparation for appreciation of the sonnets of Shakespeare or the fugues of Bach. The things discussed in geology are so different from the sonnets and so different from fugues.[37]

Here the actual entities under consideration are called "things" which are inextricable aspects of processes.

Going well beyond Rome, Europe, and even rocks, Whitehead mentions the nebulae in the following illustration of actual entities, and indicates a galaxy as well:

> The contrast of finitude and infinity arises from the fundamental metaphysical truth that every entity involves an indefinite array of perspectives, each perspective expressing a finite characteristic of that entity. . . . The entity is then experienced in a wider finite perspective, still presupposing the inevitable background which is the universe in its relation to that entity. For example, consider this lecture hall. We each have an immediate finite experience of it. In order to understand this hall, thus experienced, we widen the analysis of its obvious relations. The hall is part of a building; the building is in Cambridge, Mass.; Cambridge,

Mass., is on the surface of the Earth; the Earth is a planet in the solar system; the solar system belongs to a nebula; this nebula belongs to a spatially related system of nebulae; these nebulae exhibit a system with a finite temporal existence.[38]

The word "entity" appears in this passage rather than the full phrase "actual entity." Whitehead in fact allows that there are four main types of entities:

> In conclusion, there are four main types of entities in the universe, of which two are primary types and two are hybrid types. The primary types are actual entities and pure potentials (eternal objects); the hybird types are feelings and propositions (theories).[39]

My choice among these for Whitehead's meaning in the foregoing passage, wherein nebulae are cited as entities, is actual entities because the entities cited there are real concrete existences. Also, it is actual entities that afford a multiplicity of perspectives upon them by way of being felt by diverse other actual entities. It should not be surprising that such things as planets and stars are counted as actual entities, since we have already seen Whitehead using the sun and the "things discussed in geology" to illustrate his conception of actual entities.

However, Whitehead most often picks out a human experience to illustrate the actual entity. So much so in fact, that the actual entity may equally be called an "occasion of experience:" ". . . I have termed each individual act of immediate self-enjoyment an 'occasion of experience'. . . . But the basis of all experience is this immediate stage of experiencing, which is myself now."[40] A human being viewed historically is a stream of experiences, occasions of experience, or "living occasions" as Whitehead says here: "The enduring personality is the historic route of living occasions which are severally dominant in the body at successive instants."[41]

One example using specific human experience that Whitehead develops is the hearing of a sound. "The audition of this note is a feeling. This feeling has first an auditor, who is the subject of the feeling."[42] A subject in Whitehead's philosophy is always an actual entity. The foregoing discussion of logical subjects established that subjects entertaining propositional feelings are actual entities. But in fact subjects entertaining any feeling whatsoever are actual entities. "A feeling cannot be abstracted from the actual entity entertaining it. This actual entity is termed the 'subject' of the feeling."[43] In the example of hearing a note, then, the auditor is the subject entertaining the sound, and as such is an actual entity. Thus, we are asked to consider a specific audition of a particular sound just as we were asked to consider the

Castle Rock in order to learn Whitehead's view of the nature of actual entities.

Similarly for other cases of sense-perception: a viewer is subject of a sight; a sniffer is subject of a smell; a taster is subject of a flavor; a sentient body is subject of a texture or an ache; and as such all are actual entities. The experiences of sense-perceptions, seeing, hearing, touching, tasting, and smelling, are naturally very important actual entities for people; and accordingly they figure very importantly in Whitehead's philosophy where they are addressed in his theory of presentational immediacy. In fact, Whitehead allows that an animal body is constructed so as to provide percipient experience of this sort for the animal.

> According to this interpretation, the human body is to be conceived as a complex 'amplifier. . . .' In principle, the animal body is only the more highly organized and immediate part of the general environment for its dominant actual occasion, which is the ultimate percipient.[44]

However, occasions of sense-perception are not by any means the only authentic actual entities that Whitehead admits of in his philosophy, nor are they even the only types of human percipient experience that he employs.

The type of human experience that most recurs in Whitehead's works is what he calls "perception of causal efficacy" or "perception in the mode of causal efficacy."[45] A memory is such a perception. "Memory is an example of perception in this mode."[46] Then for Whitehead, memory is a kind of perception. This may seem peculiar; but Whitehead's philosophy is distinguished by this unusual doctrine. Memory is a human percipient experience, although in a different mode, just as are the sense-perceptions. And among memories of particular importance to Whitehead for illustrating the nature of actual entities is the recent past.

> Actuality is the self-enjoyment of importance. But this self-enjoyment has the character of the self-enjoyment of the one self. The most explicit example of this is our realization of those other actualities, which we conceive as ourselves in our recent past, fusing their self-enjoyment with our immediate present.[47]

In this passage, both the present remembering occasion and the past or remembered occasions are actual entities, or what he here terms "actualities."

It is the general case that perception in the mode of causal efficacy is perception of past or antecedent actual entities. "Thus there is, in the mode of causal efficacy, a direct perception of those antecedent actual occasions which are causally efficacious both for the percipient and for the relevant events in the present locus."[48] Any antecedent experiences whatsoever remembered (that is, perceived in the mode of causal efficacy) in the present and affecting the present are actual entities. And present experiences, such as myself now, are actual entities as well. Then it may be said that any experience, whether percipient in the mode of causal efficacy or percipient in the mode of presentational immediacy (sense-perception), is an actual entity. For it is real concrete existence just as are the stones and the stars.

Because both past and present human experiences are actual entities, it is not surprising that Whitehead is willing to regard the ego, the soul, and the mind of previous philosophers as actual entities. "For each time he pronounces 'I am, I exist,' the actual occasion, which is the ego, is different. . . ."[49] And in respect of the soul and the mind he says: "In the philosophy of organism 'the soul' as it appears in Hume, and 'the mind' as it appears in Locke and Hume, are replaced by the phrases 'the actual entity' and 'the actual occasion,' these phrases being synonymous."[50]

Similarly, both past and present knowing experiences are actual entities. Whitehead speaks of the stream of occasions of a man's knowing the Greek language.

> That set of occasions, dating from his first acquirement of the Greek language and including all those occasions up to his loss of any adequate knowledge of that language, constitutes a society in reference to knowledge of the Greek language.[51]

Occasion's of a person's knowledge of the Greek language, then, are all actual entities, or actual knowledgeable-in-Greek occasions—as well as are all the occasions of his/her ignorance of Greek or of anything else.

> If we are considering the society of successive actual occasions in the historic route forming the life of an enduring object, some of the earlier actual occasions may be without knowledge, and some of the later may possess knowledge. In such a case, the unknowing man has become knowing.[52]

Then both knowing and unknowing experiences of a person are actual entities. For, they are real concrete existences.

*Two paradigms.* It is human experiences that are the most important examples of actual entities since it is only through our own experiences that we can know actual entities at all. Our experience as a product of nature, knowledgeable and unknowledgeable, is the richest source of material at our disposal for suggesting what nature is capable of. Whitehead's equation of "actual entity" with "occasion of experience" or "unity of emotion" and the like is not just self-indulgence or pleasing metaphor, but, for him, truth. Lower orders of actual entities are lower by comparison to the human.

> In describing the capacities, realized or unrealized, of an actual occasion, we have, with Locke, tacitly taken human experience as an example upon which to found the generalized description required for metaphysics. But when we turn to the lower organisms we have first to determine which among such capacities fade from realization into irrelevance, that is to say, by comparison with human experience which is our standard.[53]

Then a human experience is not only an exemplary actual entity but the standard by which to judge the nature of all actual entities. The lower organisms including subatomic particles must be interpretable under the same principles that describe human experiences, since all these are equally actual entities.

> It is the accepted doctrine in physical science that a living body is to be interpreted according to what is known of other sections of the physical universe. This is a sound axiom; but it is double-edged. For it carries with it the converse deduction that other sections of the universe are to be interpreted in accordance with what we know of the human body.[54]

The "accepted doctrine" in physical science Whitehead calls "scientific materialism." It is just this doctrine that Whitehead's philosophy of organism reverses. Whitehead points out that materialism has acquired its force by its refusal to admit extraneous considerations into its materialistic, mechanistic theory of nature. None but independent, solitary substances and the mechanics of their interaction enter into its principles. But Whitehead believes that his organic theory of nature can acquire the same force by not admitting materialistic and mechanistic principles even for the subatomic particles and inorganic bodies.

> The strength of the theory of materialistic mechanism has been the demand, that no arbitrary breaks be introduced into nature, to eke out the collapse of an explanation. I accept this principle. But if you start from the immediate facts of our psychological experience, as surely an empiricist should begin, you are at once led to the organic conception of nature. . . .[55]

For materialism all things are to be explained on the basis of the principles operating for inorganic physical existence, conceived as autonomous substance; for organism all things are to be explained on the basis of the principles by which living organisms and human experiences are created.

Whitehead remarks that his philosophy of organism is derived from modern physics:

> It is equally possible to arrive at this organic conception of the world if we start from the fundamental notions of modern physics, instead of, as above, from psychology and physiology. In fact by reason of my own studies in mathematics and mathematical physics, I did in fact arrive at my convictions in this way.[56]

For this reason, Whitehead is himself sure that his organic theory of nature applies to the modern conceptions regarding physical existence, because it was derived therefrom. And he puts forward his own experiences to testify that his organic theory applies equally to human experience, its standard.

Thus, the fact that Whitehead's conception of concrete existence is derived from modern physics does not mean that it fails to apply to things not considered in physics. And the fact that he uses human experience as a model for all concrete existence does not mean that he regards all concrete existences as human. His concern is to point out the common nature of all concrete existences, conceived as on a scale of increasing complexity from the subatomic occasions to occasions of human experience. Materialism has failed to fully explain human nature; but perhaps organism can succeed in explaining the less complex natures by the human. All concrete existences are actual entities; but these two types of existences, the subatomic entities and human experiences, are of special importance to Whitehead, serving as paradigm actual entities, for good reason.

If there can be seen to be something in common between two types of actualities as diverse as these, then it is the more easily granted that there is something in common between *any* two actualities whatsoever. The philosophy of organism is an attack against the bifurcation of nature into bodies and minds, that is, dualism.

> What I am essentially protesting against is the bifurcation of nature into two systems of reality, which, insofar as they are real, are real in different senses. One reality would be the entities such as electrons which are the study of speculative physics. This would be the reality which is there for knowledge; although on this theory it is never known. For what is known is the other sort of reality, which is the byplay of the mind. Thus there would be two natures, one is the conjecture and the other is the dream.[57]

If there is something in common between any two things whatsoever, however we choose to select our things, then Whitehead has accomplished his task. For reality can only be bifurcated into two or more substances, such as matter and mind, when nothing can be found in common between them. In Whitehead's philosophy what is common to both matter and mind is that both are prehendable and both occur in every actuality in existence.

Thus, the actual entity, being the conception of what every concrete existent has in common, is most tested in the two extreme cases of subatomic occasions and conscious human experience—extreme in their degree of mentality. For if it adequately describes features shared by such extremely diverse types of existences as these, the one inorganic and unthinking, the other conscious and knowledgeable, then it is the more likely to be adequate as the general description of the nature of any concrete existent whatsoever, as intended.

> An occasion of experience which includes a human mentality is an extreme instance, at one end of the scale, of those happenings which constitute nature. . . . We should either admit dualism, at least as a provisional doctrine, or we should point out the identical elements connecting human experience with physical science.[58]

It is natural, then, that interpreters of Whitehead see analogies for actual entities coming from both directions, subatomic particles and human experience, its two paradigms.[59] Neither source of analogies can exclude the other, since the conception of an actual entity must be appropriate to both. And if the two paradigm cases are indeed capable of unification under the one conception, then Whitehead has unified matter and mind.

*Metaphysical generality.* A cosmology is an attempt to make explicit and coherent the general assumptions of a natural philosophy or physics. It is an interpretation of the universe, its composition and its laws, that a physics implies. Newton introduced his physics with a *Scholium*; this is the Newtonian cosmology. The assumptions and definitions for the usage of Newtonian physics are clarified and defended in this introductory material, the *Scholium* and Definitions, in Newton's *Principia*. "The *Timaeus* of Plato, and the *Scholium* of Newton . . . are the two statements of cosmological theory which have had the chief influence on Western thought."[60]

The Newtonian cosmology itself embodied and clarified for physics scientific materialism, otherwise known as "the classical concept of the material world" and "the famous mechanistic theory of nature."[61] The authors of this seventeenth century cosmology were Galileo, Descartes, Newton, and Locke; *Process and Reality: An Essay in Cosmology* attempts "an enterprise of the same kind" responsible to twentieth century knowledge.[62] Consequently, Whitehead intends that his cosmology be adequate for interpreting modern physics, both relativity theory and quantum mechanics; and it must be adequate for modern science if it is to be judged adequate at all. "A philosophic system should present an elucidation of concrete fact from which the sciences abstract."[63]

But Whitehead's work is more comprehensive than cosmology, and attempts to show that the principles of modern physics and those of all experience belong in one coherent system of ideas. In this way, his cosmology extends into metaphysics: as cosmology it must be adequate for interpreting physics; as metaphysics it must be adequate for interpreting all experience. "Speculative philosophy is the endeavor to frame a coherent, logical, necessary system of general ideas in terms of which every element of our experience can be interpreted."[64] In stating that "every element of our experience" should be interpretable in the terms of his philosophy, Whitehead certainly means *every* element, those drawn from ordinary living (such as perceiving and remembering) as well as those drawn from all human undertakings (all the sciences, arts, and religion), not only modern physics. "Also, it must be one of the motives of a complete cosmology to construct a system of ideas which brings the aesthetic, moral, and religious interests into relation with those concepts of the world which have their origin in natural science."[65] The "complete cosmology" is metaphysics.

The Whiteheadian cosmological ideas cannot just happen to be applicable to other kinds of experience besides those drawn from modern physics. They *must* be so applicable if they are to be accounted true, confirmed, or successful. "A metaphysical description takes its origin from one select field of interest. It receives its confirmation by establishing itself as adequate and as exemplified in other fields of interest."[66] For, the Whiteheadian scheme postulates one nature, the same for both subatomic particles and human beings. Thus, the origins of the Whiteheadian cosmology lie in the particular discipline of physics; but the scope of its generalizations must comprehend human experience taken from every field and including ordinary living, if it is to be successful. This is the scope of metaphysics.

The actual entity is Whitehead's construction of the common (that is, generic) character of *all* things whatsoever, so that it is necessarily adequate as a general description of *any* thing whatsoever. "The metaphysical characteristics of an actual entity—in the proper general sense of 'metaphysics'—should be those which apply to all actual entities."[67] It must be so general as to encompass the common nature of an occasion in the life of an electron, a rock, a star, a vegetable, an animal, a person, God, and all things else. "The description of the generic character of an actual entity should include God, as well as the lowliest actual occasion, though there is a specific difference between the nature of God and that of any occasion."[68] There must be no confusion as to what the actual entity is: all concrete existences are actual entities *because* all have a common nature. There is only one genus of actual entity ontologically speaking because there is only one nature.

The generality of the conception of the actual entity precludes its exclusive identification with some particular type of thing, say, palpable bodies, or human abstract thought, or invisible subatomic particles, or only those things that happen to have names in the vocabulary of English speaking peoples, and so on. It includes nothing of specific content or quality, but is, rather the general principles by which all things function. The qualitative differences among things, small and large, short and long, compact and diffuse, heavy and light, dim and bright, bitter and sweet, dull and eventful, deep and shallow, smooth and jagged, conscious and unconscious, organic and inorganic, trivial and important, good and evil, do not amount to a difference in their general nature as actual entities.

Similarly, evidence for concrete existence from every quarter must be taken account of in a metaphysics, no matter how far afield from physics, as long as it is indeed evidence. It cannot appeal only to the concrete existence of special interest to particular parties, whether physicists or philosophers, poets or painters, or ordinary people. Whitehead welcomes evidence from both modern physics and common sense, two sources that are often considered to be antithetical.

> For subsequent empiricists the pleasure of the dogma has overcome the metaphysical rule of evidence: that we must bow to those presumptions, which, in despite of criticism, we still employ for the regulation of our lives. Such presumptions are imperative in experience.[69]

Whitehead claims for his actual entity a unity of principles derived from the most disparate types of sources, the objects of science and the objects of common sense.

There must be no confusion of the idea "actual entity" with actual entities. Actual entities are the real concrete existences; the description of their generic character is a conception, "the actual entity." This conception of "the actual entity" is exemplified by any given actual entity, or real concrete existent. Actual entities should not be replaced by the conception. For example, William A. Christian writes, "When we see a table we do not see actual entities. . . . Nor do we, in the act of seeing a table, experience our *seeing* it as itself an actual occasion."[70] But Whitehead's actual entities include such things as tables, occasions of human sense-perception, and organs of the human body involved in sense-perception. It is not actual entities that we do not see, but the *conception* of actual entity; it is not actual entities that we do not experience seeing, but the *conception* of actual entity.

*Grades of occasions.* Whitehead takes account of the qualitative differences among actual entities by grading them. He groups them into four major grades:

> In the actual world we discern four grades of actual occasions, grades which are not to be sharply distinguished from each other. First, and lowest, there are the actual occasions in so-called 'empty space'; secondly, there are the actual occasions which are moments in the life-histories of enduring non-living objects, such as electrons or other primitive organisms; thirdly, there are the actual occasions which are moments in the life-histories of enduring living objects; fourthly, there are the actual occasions which are moments in the life-histories of enduring objects with conscious knowledge.[71]

These grades are not ontological distinctions between kinds of actual entities, such as bodies and minds, or between actual entities and something else, such as reality and appearance. Rather, they are the major orders of complexity of actual entities. The innumerable types of actual entities, differing in all the ways that concrete existences differ, involve gradations of complexity that may be classified in these four ways.

The lowest grade of actual entity is the least complex, and consequently has the least experience: "The simplest grade of actual occasions must be conceived as experiencing a few sensa, with the minimum of patterned contrast."[72] Organic actual entities are a step up in complexity of experience from those inorganic.

"But the transition from without to within the body marks the passage from lower to higher grades of actual occasions."[73] The highest grade of actual entity (excepting God) is capable of a very rich experience, one conscious and knowledgeable.

There is nothing exact about these grades, and many types of actual entities would fall between the grades, or alternate between them. For example, organisms that are part living and part non-living would not belong solely to either grade. Different types of actual entities partake of these grades only more or less. "It is obvious that a structured society may have more or less 'life,' and that there is no absolute gap between 'living' and 'non-living' societies."[74] There are graduations in the order of complexity of actual entities between the four major grades.

In fact, Whitehead's theory is that even live enduring objects are not entirely living. That is, the life-history even of a living creature (a "living society" of creature occasions) includes non-living actual entities. "A 'living society' is one which includes some 'living occasions.' Thus a society may be more or less 'living,' according to the prevalence in it of living occasions."[75] There is no living creature, no live enduring object, no living society, that does not incorporate societies of non-living actual entities. "We do not know of any living society devoid of its subservient apparatus of inorganic societies."[76] This is partly because life, strictly speaking, cannot itself be the defining characteristic of a society at all; so that there is no such thing as an entirely living society, an entirely living enduring object, or an entirely living creature.

The root fact is that 'endurance' is a device whereby an occasion is peculiarly bound by a single line of physical ancestry, while 'life' means novelty. . . . This amounts to the doctrine that an organism is 'alive' when in some measure its reactions are inexplicable by *any* tradition of pure physical inheritance. . . . It follows from these considerations that in abstraction from its animal body an 'entirely living' nexus is not properly a society at all, since 'life' cannot be a defining characteristic. It is the name for originality, and not for tradition.[77]

Strictly speaking, then, the life-history of even a living creature (a live enduring object) is not all of the same grade. The creature's life includes both entirely living actual entities, classified as a higher grade, and non-living actual entities on a lower grade. Likewise, the life-history of a conscious and knowledgeable person includes many actual sleep occasions. A person as conscious and knowledgeable is an actual entity of the highest grade; but a sleeping person cannot share the same characteristics. More than one grade of actual entities mingle in a person's life, that is, the person considered historically, considered as a society or enduring object. Also, every single live actual entity incorporates societies of non-living actual entities in its make-up.

Whitehead alternatively calls the grades of actual entities "types" or "modes."

Also the differences between actual occasions, arising from the characters of their data, and from the narrowness and widths of their feelings, and from the comparative importance of various stages, enable a classification to be made whereby these occasions are gathered into various types. From the metaphysical standpoint these types are not to be sharply discriminated; as a matter of empirical observation, the occasions do seem to fall into fairly distinct classes.[78]

Thus, as the complexity of their data and the use of their mentality increases, along with the breadth and intensity of their feelings, the experience of the actual entities is enriched.

And Whitehead does not even stick to the division of four major grades of actual entities, but also acknowledges six: "A rough division can be made of six types of occurrences in nature."[79] In the following passage, for example, he distinguishes five or six grades of actual entities, calling the grades "modes of natural existence." He affirms not only the blurring of the different grades into one another, but the relativity of time-span of the different actual entities, depending on the scale of observation.

> The sharp-cut scientific classifications are essential for scientific method. But they are dangerous for philosophy. Such classification hides the truth that the different modes of natural existence shade off into each other. There is the animal life with its central direction of a society of cells, there is the vegetable life with its organized republic of cells, there is the cell life with its organized republic of molecules, there is the large-scale inorganic society of molecules with its passive acceptance of necessities derived from spatial relations, there is the infra-molecular activity which has lost all trace of the passivity of inorganic nature on a larger scale.
>
> In this survey some main conclusions stand out. One conclusion is the diverse modes of functioning which are produced by diverse modes of organization. The second conclusion is the aspect of continuity between these different modes. There are border-line cases, which bridge the gap. But span of existence is merely relative to our habits of human life. For infra-molecular occurrences, a second is a vast period of time. A third conclusion is the difference in the aspects of nature according as we change the scale of observation.[80]

This passage affords a number of examples of actual entities: moments in the life-histories of animals; moments in the life-histories of vegetables; moments in the life-histories of cells; moments in the life-histories of large-scale inorganic enduring objects; infra-molecular moments.

*List of examples.* The examples of actual entities so far uncovered are listed for the convenience of seeing their diversity in one place: God, a trivial puff of existence, a bird, a beast, a tree, a plant, a leaf, a crow, a sheep, a grain of sand, a child's idea of its mother, the sun, Socrates, mortal occasions, Athenian occasions, Caesar, the Rubicon, Caesar's crossing the Rubicon, Hannibal, electronic occasions, protonic occasions, quanta of energy, organs of the human body, nerve cells, the Castle Rock at Edinburgh, ancient imperial Rome, Europe, the history of the European races in North America, the failure of Spanish domination over California, the failure of Spanish domination over England, the things discussed in geology, Shakespearean sonnets, Bach fugues, a lecture hall, a building, Cambridge, Mass., the earth's surface, the earth, the solar system, a nebula, a system of nebulae, living occasions, an auditor, an ultimate percipient, ourselves in our recent past, our immediate present, the ego, the soul, the mind, occasions of a man's knowledge of Greek, knowing occasions of a man, unknowing occasions of a man, human experience, lower organisms, occasions in so-called "empty space," occasions of enduring non-living objects, primitive organisms, occasions of animal life, occasions of vegetable life, occasions of cell life, occasions of large-scale inorganic nature, and infra-molecular occurrences. Clearly an actual entity is not necessarily something small, short, simple, and impalpable. And clearly, major works of Whitehead have not been available to Edward Pols, who believes: ". . . we cannot give any concrete examples of actual entities."[81]

This is not an exhaustive list of all the examples of actual entities that Whitehead uses, of course, but it should be sufficient to question the conventional interpretations of Whitehead which allow that only occasions of subatomic proportions or human percipient experiences or only these two kinds and God be actual entities. The list compiles clearer examples, principally those taken from passages wherein "actual entity" or "actual occasion" appear, so that it is obvious that the examples are indeed examples of actual entities. But it could be considerably lengthened by taking examples from contexts that use some other synonymous expression. Whitehead has named the actual entity differently in different works, and also differently in the same work, depending on the capacities he wishes to emphasize. Some synonyms have already been indicated, such as "actual occasion," "actuality," and "thing"; but the plethora of expressions, all signifying the nature of actual entities, might be appreciated by a list of them too.

Here, then, is the actual entity in various capacities, all of which are met with in this book: *"res vera,"* "final fact," "complete fact," "fully realized fact," "individual fact," "individual," "really real thing," "atomic actuality," "concrete actuality," "concretion," "concrescence," "occurrence," "natural existence," "unity of existence," "particular existence," "creature," "organism," "organization," "composition," "event," "process," "process of concrescence," "process of fusion," "process of being actual," "process of the becoming of actuality," "process of becoming," "process of activity," "activity," "activity of concern," "happening," "occasion of experience," "act of experience," "drop of experience," "emergent value," "prehensive unification," "feeler," "pulsation of actuality," "natural pulsation," "becoming," "act of becoming," "epochal becoming," "epoch," "microscopic process," "macroscopic process," "subject," "object," "superject," "one," "many," "being."

All of these terms apply to every concrete existent; but each emphasizes a different aspect of that existence. For example, the terms "organism" and "creature" emphasize both a dependence upon an environment of others and an independence as a living and self-directed whole; the words "individual" and "emergent value" suggest decisive agents; "act of experience" and "prehensive unification" emphasize the fact that an actual entity in some way feels and acknowledges itself and others; "act of becoming" and "process of concrescence" suggest that an actual entity comes into being; "process of becoming" and "epochal becoming" emphasize an evolution and growth; "activity of concern" and "subject" suggest that an actual entity is the source of its own inner quality of life; "final fact" and "object" emphasize a creation of nature on the same footing with other creations of nature; "pulsation of actuality" and "event" suggest that an actual entity is not a static enduring substance; "organization" and "composition" emphasize both complexity and unity; and the word "being" suggests that the actual entity is intended to replace the notion of "substance" in philosophy.

And the term "actual occasion" emphasizes the spatiotemporal extensiveness of the actual entity.

> (vi) the term 'actual occasion' is used synonymously with 'actual entity';
> but chiefly when its character of extensiveness has some direct relevance
> to the discussion, either extensiveness in the form of temporal
> extensiveness, that is to say, 'duration', or extensiveness in the form of
> spatial extension, or in the more complete signification of spatio-
> temporal extensiveness.[82]

Because this book largely concerns Whiteheadian time, or better, Whiteheadian timespace, hereafter "actual occasion," often shortened to "occasion," will oftentimes be used instead of "actual entity." There is only one concrete existent that cannot be designated as an actual occasion, and that is God. God is the only actual entity who is not also an actual occasion. "The term 'actual occasion' will always exclude God from its scope."[83] This is because God is non-temporal, in fact, the only non-temporal actual entity.[84]

*Whitehead misinterpreted.* Despite Whitehead's definitions and examples of actual occasions, despite his doctrine that human experience is a paradigm for actual occasions, a number of his interpreters insist that actual occasions can only be occurrences on the subatomic scale; microscopic entities, microphysical vibrations, quanta, or other usually unspecified extremely small, brief, and impalpable occurrence. Edward Pols tells us: "But it is quite clear that one must go well below the order of the molecule to arrive at an actual occasion: even an electron is thought of as a 'route' or 'society' of actual occasions."[85] An electron is indeed a route or society of actual occasions: it is a route of actual electronic occasions. And Robert M. Palter also thinks that the subatomic particles are the only actual entities: "The ultimate organisms are those not decomposable into other organisms; these Whitehead calls *primates* and tentatively identifies with electrons and protons."[85a] And Abner Shimony believes as well: "Whitehead's conception is of the actual occasion as a microscopic entity."[86] Richard Rorty says the same thing: "The most obvious and dramatic difference between process philosophy and common sense is that the units of actuality, for process philosophy, are no longer such macroscopic objects. They are replaced by sub-microscopic unrepeatable entities."[86a] Such interpretations of the actual occasion as something only and necessarily small have no foundation in Whitehead's philosophy. Dorothy Emmet realized this sort of interpretation is a problem: "But the difficulty still remains in conceiving the atomic occasion, even if it be a process of becoming . . . occupying about the dimensions of a quantum vibration. . . ."[87] This difficulty is not Whitehead's, but the difficulty of imposing a modern version of atomism on his philosophy. Whitehead in fact made every effort to oppose this modern atomism since it is a vestige of scientific materialism. His actual occasions are atomic without being the simple, minute, indestructible bits of matter out of which everything visible and palpable is composed.

The assumption that Whitehead's cosmology is but a new and interesting, a colorful and poetic atomism created for our literary delight trivializes Whitehead's work. Martin Jordan, for example, describes Whitehead as a poet of quantum physics:

It should be acknowledged that Whitehead's occasions are far removed in scale from the activities of humankind, which at best provide mere parallels for apt description. The occasions as conceived are atomistic and perishing. They correspond as a concept with the pulses or minute rhythms of nature which have not only in the past suggested themselves to poetic minds but have emerged in various guises as scientific entities.[88]

But Jordan's view, that Whitehead's actual entities are nothing but "scientific entities" poetically described, has serious, even fatal, consequences for Whitehead's philosophy if it is accepted. For according to Whitehead, a metaphysics must be adequate to describe the broadest possible range of experience. Jordan sees only "scientific entities" as in need of adequate description. Furthermore, it is difficult to see how Whitehead's use of conceptions taken from less than real human experiences *could* be adequate to describe the really real "scientific entities." If only the "scientific entities" are really real, as Jordan assumes, than what use is there in describing them, as Whitehead does, as having a mental pole, conceptual prehensions, subjective aims, and so on? Whitehead intentionally uses language evoking human experience to characterize actual occasions, which is part of his attack on scientific materialism and dualism. He speaks of "feeling," "lures for feeling," "subjective aims," "subjective immediacy," "satisfaction," "concern," "freedom," "decision," "self-functioning," "attainment of an ideal," "enjoyment," "propositions," "intellectual feeling," "standpoint," "perspective," "privacy," "conceptual prehension," "valuation," "intensification of experience," "society," "creativity," "personal order," "real potentiality," "subjects," "mental operations," "mental pole," "objectification," and so on. If all actual entities were vibrations of subatomic scale, whose mentality is negligible, there would be no point in elaborating a philosophical position especially to take account of even their negligible mentality. Whitehead's attribution of mentality, decision, final causation and the like to all actual entities is not because of a merely sentimental attachment to human tendencies and expression but is because of its increasing evidence in entities in an ascending scale of complexity to human beings. If human experience, even a great variety of human experience, cannot be credited with actuality, then there is no point in Whitehead's language not to mention his philosophy. So on Jordan's account Whitehead's conceptual scheme is mere poetic excess. For, what reason, other than poetic excess, can be given by interpreters such as Jordan for the application of such a humanistic language to electrons, protons, photons, and the like?

Jordan's description, therefore, contains the misguided presumption that the philosophy of organism is only metaphor. For Jordan, the "activities of humankind" while not themselves actual occasions serve somehow as "parallels for apt description" of the atomic occasions. However, human activities cannot very well serve as parallels or anything else if they have no actuality in the terms of the philosophy. For if human activities are less real than Jordan's atomic occasions, it is hardly apt to use concepts drawn from human activity to describe quantum physical entities. Subatomic occasions are not *like* occasions of human experience if there are no actual human occasions of experience. Then on Jordan's account, Whitehead may be regarded as a poet making meaningless metaphor.

However, Whitehead's claim to metaphysics is not mere pretence. He holds that the test of the truth of a metaphysics is that its principles apply to all things, from whatever field "things" are taken for consideration. If his actual entities denoted only subatomic scale vibrations, he would have no reason to regard his metaphysics as true, and he would have no reason to suppose he had written a metaphysics rather than a poem on physics. But in fact he demonstrates the general applicability of his ideas, including his conception of the actual entity, to many fields of interest and study, and including ordinary human experience, on every page by discussing the relevance of his philosophy to many aspects of life, thought, and science (not only physics). He readily compares his ideas to other philosophies using examples taken from ordinary human experience. Indeed, without this broad applicability, even Whitehead would agree that his work ought to be considered no more than a literary physics: "In default of extended application, a generalization started from physics, for example, remains merely an alternative expression of notions applicable to physics."[89] Every section of Whitehead's works testify to this "extended application."

There is more mischief yet in Jordan's assertions. He suggests that the "minute rhythms" of today are conceptually the same as those theorized by ancient atomists and classical scientific materialists. In other words, atoms, Newtonian bits of matter, and modern quanta are all substantially the same in Jordan's view, the modern quanta being merely a revised edition of the Newtonian bits of matter, being now rhythmic and short-lived. This is a misinterpretation of modern physics. The discoveries in quantum physics are revolutionary precisely because they cannot be handled in classical or ancient terms: the quanta and other microphysical events do not behave like atoms or material particles conceived as substances. Jordan not only misinterprets Whitehead, but modern physics; and in so doing makes of Whitehead not the poet of quantum physics, but of some revised edition of atomism. Jordan's conception may be of Whitehead as a poet of a revised Newtonian physics. But it is not the Whitehead of this book. I have discussed implications of Jordan's view at such length because they apply to many other interpreters of Whitehead as well.


## NEXUS

*Complex unity.* Having explained something of what Whitehead means by "actual entity," what he intends it to refer to, the rest of this book is devoted to explicating its constitution in order to arrive at an understanding of its epochal nature. To begin with, an actual entity is always complex: "An actual entity is not merely one; it is also definitely complex."[90] So that, although an "actual entity" refers only to one thing, that thing is invariably complex. It is one by virtue of its unity of components, not by virtue of an absolute simplicity. Its oneness can not be "mere" or absolutely indivisible (as opposed to undivided); it is the oneness of union.

Different types of actual occasions are complex to different degrees; but none are not complex. An actual occasion may be less complex, and there may be a least complex type of actual occasion; and in the same way an actual occasion may be more simple, and there may be a simplest type of actual occasion. But none have absolute simplicity. Simplicity is relative to our standard of judgment regarding comparative complexities. "We may doubt whether 'simplicity' is ever more than a relative term, having regard to some definite procedure of analysis. I hold this to be the case. . . ."[91]

Actual occasions are complex because they are composite. There is nothing that is actual that is not also composite, and nothing composite even in thought that does not refer to the composite nature of actual occasions.

> In the philosophy of organism it is assumed that an actual entity is composite. 'Actuality' is the fundamental exemplification of composition; all other meanings of 'composition' are referent to this root-meaning. But 'actuality' is a general term, which merely indicates this ultimate type of composite unity: there are many composite unities to which this general term applies.[92]

Then compositeness is the essential nature of every actual entity, so much so that composition is taken as the very meaning of actual entity. When composition is referred to in the definition of actual entity, it is called "actuality." So "actuality" is the synonymous term for "actual entity" used to signify its compositeness, just as "actual occasion" is used to signify its spatiotemporality. "'Actuality' is in its essence 'composition.'"[93] Composite unity is "ultimate" because all actualities are ultimately composite, complex. An absolutely simple actuality is a contradiction in terms. There is no more ultimate type of actual entity that is not composite, for then it would be no actuality either. Composite unity is already ultimate.

The use of "actuality" to mean the composite nature of an actual entity can be seen again here: "An actuality is a complex unity, which can be analyzed as a process of feeling its own components. This is the doctrine that each actuality is an occasion of experience, the outcome of its own purposes."[94] It is clear that "actuality" does not refer only to a nexus, but refers to an actual entity. For it is the actual entity that is an "occasion of experience" and a "process of feeling its own components"; it is the actual entity that has purposes. That Whitehead views the actual entities as composite must not be ignored or denied: "The actual entity is composite and analysable; . . . ."[95] And the foregoing passages defining actuality as the compositeness of actual entities show that not only are all actual entities conceived as composite, but all compositions are those constituting actual entities. This rule is repeated here: "There is no general fact of composition not expressible in terms of the composite constitutions of the individual occasions."[96]

This doctrine of actuality repudiates atomism. One expression of atomism is to be found in Lucretius:

> The first-beginnings, therefore, are of solid singleness, made of these smallest parts closely packed and cohering together, not compounded by the gathering of the parts, but strong rather by their eternal singleness, and from these nature allows nothing to be torn away or diminished any longer, but keeps them as seeds for things. Besides, unless there is to be a smallest something, each littlest body will consist of infinite parts . . . you must yield and confess that there are things which no longer consist of any parts and are of the smallest possible nature. And since these exist, you must also confess that the first-beginnings are solid and everlasting.[97]

We have seen that Whitehead's actual entity is not "of the smallest possible nature," although it includes the smaller natures too. Nor is it a "solid singleness"; rather, it is a complexity. All actual entities are composite, and there is nothing composite that is not the constitution of an actual entity. Ivor Leclerc's atomism cannot be maintained of Whitehead's philosophy: "Ultimately there must be simples as constituents. These simples must be the ultimate elements of all compounds."[98]

*Subatomic organisms.* This doctrine of actuality means that Whitehead considers that elementary particles are not elementary in virtue of absolute simplicity, but in virtue of least complexity. For this reason, he calls even occasions of subatomic proportions "organisms" to emphasize that they have a measure of the same complex nature as living creatures and we ourselves. "Biology is the study of the larger organisms; whereas physics is the study of the smaller organisms."[99] His writing nowhere concedes an absolute simplicity on the part of subatomic occasions or any other lower or primitive organisms, just as here he speaks only of "less complex organisms": "But the whole point of the modern doctrine is the evolution of the complex organisms from antecedent states of less complex organisms."[100]

If occasions of elementary particles are composite, it cannot be because they are composed of another organism or actual occasion, for they are the least composite of things. They are composed not of other entire occasions but of their aspects. In this way, they are able to be affected by other occasions. And this is Whitehead's view. An elementary occasion is composite not because it literally contains smaller occasions yet, since there are none smaller, but because it is affected by aspects of its environment; it is modifiable. Whitehead explains at length that this is the very idea that distinguishes his organic philosophy from scientific materialism:

> The doctrine which I am maintaining is that the whole concept of materialism only applies to very abstract entities, the products of logical discernment. The concrete enduring entities are organisms, so that the plan of the *whole* influences the very characters of the various subordinate organisms which enter into it. In the case of an animal, the mental states enter into the plan of the total organism and thus modify the plans of the successive subordinate organisms until the ultimate smallest organisms, such as electrons, are reached. Thus an electron within a living body is different from an electron outside it, by reason of the plan of the body. The electron blindly runs either within or without the body; but it runs within the body in accordance with its character within the body; that is to say, in accordance with the general plan of the body, and this plan includes the mental state. But the principle of modification is perfectly general throughout nature, and represents no property peculiar to living bodies . . . this doctrine involves the abandonment of the traditional scientific materialism, and the substitution of an alternative doctrine of organism.[101]

Thus, the subatomic, elementary, ultimate, and smallest occasions have the same nature as have larger organisms inasmuch as they are modified according to the plans of the organisms that make up their environment. Their "very characters" are influenced inasmuch as they are internally affected by other actualities, the other organisms. The passage again shows that Whitehead treats the elementary particles such as electrons no differently than other actual occasions: he calls them "organisms" as he calls all actual occasions, and has no special category to single them out except to say that they are the "ultimate smallest." Even the fact that electrons "blindly run" does not distinguish them from other organisms by any ontological degree. For example, people too are known to blindly run: "It is said that 'men are rational.' This is palpably false: they are only intermittently rational—merely liable to rationality."[102]

The passage shows that Whitehead considers the distinguishing feature of the philosophy of organism to be that the "principle of modification" that we recognize for living creatures holds as well for the elementary particles and all other things and creatures. It holds "throughout nature." The passage is another expression of the metaphysical generality of Whitehead's conceptions, and the importance of their applicability to the two paradigm cases (one a living experience, the other a subatomic occasion) if scientific materialism is to be unseated.

*Nexūs within.* Aspects of actual occasions enter into the internal constitution of another actual occasion. In so doing, the former and the latter occasions form a new actual occasion together, and the former occasions become bound together therein as a nexus with respect to the new occasion. This is the way in which actual occasions are composite: each is composed of others. And these others comprising the constitution of the one occasion are in a nexus with it. "In this sense, an organism is a nexus."[103] Then an organism is not only an actual occasion, but a nexus.

This may seem confusing. But Whitehead's thesis that actual occasions are composite is not supported without this corollary that an actual occasion composes a nexus of occasions. As tortuous as Whitehead's writing is, this idea can be discerned. "(i) actual entities form a system, in the sense of entering into each other's constitutions. . . ."[104] Then actual occasions may be said to be in, within, inside of, contained in, and included in the actual occasions whose constitutions they enter. And so they are: "The principle of universal relativity directly traverses Aristotle's dictum, 'A substance is not present in a subject.' On the contrary, according to this principle an actual entity *is* present in other actual entities."[105] This principle must be carefully adhered to.

In fact, an actual occasion would have no actual content but for the occasions composing it. "There can only be evidence of a world of actual entities, if the immediate actual entity discloses them as essential to its own composition."[106] So there is only evidence of an actual world inasmuch as that world enters into the constitution of the occasion whose world it is. The philosophy of organism postulates interdependent occasions, thereby protesting philosophies of independent substances. The interdependence is a fact of the internal constitutions of every occasion being composed of other occasions. "The coherence, which the system seeks to preserve, is the discovery that the process, or concrescence, of any one actual entity involves the other actual entities among its components."[107] It is important to realize that actual occasions have no actual content otherwise. If they are not composed of other occasions, then all that is left for them to be composed of in the philosophy of organism is eternal objects. "An actual entity cannot be described, even inadequately, by universals; because other actual entities do enter into the description of any one actual entity."[108] An actual occasion might also be conceived as composed of parts of itself. But in the philosophy of organism, these parts are derived from other actual occasions.

It may be that certain subatomic occasions cannot be said to literally contain or include other occasions, though perhaps they may be said to include some energy of other occasions. However, any occasion only includes those aspects of other occasions that affect it. This is so of an occasion of any size or duration whatsoever. It is only certain aspects of other occasions that are important to the occasion they compose, not the entire other occasions. For example, if I am conscious of holding a stone in my hand, I am also unconscious of very many other things. My conscious experience includes many aspects of my cells and the stone, and we are a nexus together in respect of these aspects, but it excludes many aspects of the same cells and stone not relevant to it. Aspects of my cells and the stone not affecting my conscious experience may be said not to be included in my conscious experience. And so with every occasion. Some aspects of other occasions are included in its experience, and other aspects even of the same occasions are not. An actual occasion includes other actual occasions, but not in their entirety. It is this inclusion that makes a nexus of the other occasions; it is necessarily an inclusion for which they had the potentiality.

Similarly, those occasions composing the constitution of a given occasion only become a nexus there in respect of those aspects relevant to the given occasion and from which the given occasion is derived. "The Grouping of Occasions is the outcome of some common function performed by those occasions in the percipient experience."[109] The constituent occasions of the percipient experience are grouped only with respect to their common function there, a function for which the occasions had the potentiality. The same occasions will be involved in many other occasions and nexūs in their performance of other functions. For example, my cells and the stone's minerals are involved in multitudes of actual occasions and nexūs of occasions besides the one occasion of my conscious experience of them.

This is why Whitehead is most often not very concerned to clarify whether he is speaking of an occasion or a nexus: any occasion will be composed of a nexus and will itself become a member of this nexus or of another nexus upon its joining other occasions and entering into the experience of yet another occasion. In Whitehead's expression, occasions both include and transcend the nexūs that compose them:

The actual entities of the actual world are bound together in a nexus of these feelings. Also in the creative advance, the nexus proper to an antecedent actual world is not destroyed. It is reproduced and added to, by the new bonds of feeling with the novel actualities which transcend it and include it.[110]

Then once a nexus is formed, it becomes a stubborn fact that future occasions will have to take account of as the objective constitution of antecedent occasions; the fact is that the occasions comprising the nexus are involved in each successive member of it in a specific way. The occasion of my holding a stone is a fact of life affecting my future; and the fact of the involvement of other occasions in this one is also an unalterable fact. The other occasions are bound together in this one in a particular way which influences how future occasions can experience them, occasions of both my future and theirs.

Every nexus is a component nexus, first accomplished in some later phase of concrescence of an actual entity, and ever afterwards having its status in actual worlds as an unalterable fact, dated and located among the actual entities connected in itself.[111]

And so we find Whitehead speaking of nexūs in just the same way that he speaks of actual occasions:

There are thus real individual facts of the togetherness of actual entities, which are real, individual, and particular, in the same sense in which actual entities and the prehensions are real, individual, and particular. Any such particular fact of togetherness among actual entities is called a 'nexus' (plural form is written nexūs). The ultimate facts of immediate actual experience are actual entities, prehensions, and nexūs.[112]

The nexus, like the actual occasion, is a "particular fact of togetherness" and a "fact of immediate experience." For many purposes, "actual occasion" and "nexus" need not be discriminated since both are involved in each other.

Whitehead's formal explanation of a nexus, that it is a set of related actual entities, Category XIV of his Explanations, does not bring out very well the fact that a nexus originates in an actual occasion and is a component there and in other occasions later on.[113] But foregoing passages cited here have shown it. And there are others. For example, Whitehead says that occasions are bound into a nexus by internal relations: "The 'extensive' scheme is nothing else than the generic morphology of the internal relations which bind the actual occasions into a nexus, and which bind the prehensions of any one actual occasion into a unity, coordinately divisible."[114] Internal relations are those within an actual occasion. A nexus is a set of related occasions, the relationships taking place within an occasion and by virtue of it. It is the very constitution of an actual occasion, being the way in which some other occasions have become together and composed the one. It is Whitehead's explanation of the "actual world" that brings out the fact that nexūs originate in and constitute actual occasions. For, "An actual world is a nexus; and the actual world of one actual entity sinks to the level of a subordinate nexus in actual worlds beyond that actual entity."[115] Being a nexus, the actual world is naturally comprised of actual occasions, members of the nexus. "Thus the actual world is built up of actual occasions."[116] The actual world is the full constitution of an actual occasion as derived from other occasions. "The actual world is the 'objective content' of each new creation."[117] It is clear, then, following this line of thought, that any actual occasion is composed of other actual occasions, though not in their entirety, and that the act of composition binds the other occasions into a nexus. The nexus is then a fact just as much as is the occasion.

*Togetherness.* The point is, a nexus is not a group, aggregate, or class of occasions mutually external and independent. A group of occasions independent and external with respect to one another in every way has no existence in the Whiteheadian philosophy. A group of occasions can only be a group in point of their togetherness in an actual occasion. We have seen that the very meaning of actuality is composition and that the very example of a composition is an actual occasion (not a group of occasions mutually independent). This must not be lost sight of in a discussion of nexūs; for it means that nexūs are not themselves compositions outside of occasions within which they are bound and within which they are again experienced thereafter. A nexus is a fact of composition only inasmuch as it is a fact about an actual occasion. There are not two kinds of compositions: one for actual occasions, the other for nexūs. If actual occasions are bound together at all, they are bound as component aspects of another occasion. ". . . the connectedness of things is nothing else than the togetherness of things in occasions of experience."[118] Whitehead acknowledges only the one internal genus of binding, connectedness, composition, organization, group, nexus,—in fine, togetherness—just as he acknowledges only one genus of actual entity. A nexus does not have a different kind of binding from that of the constitution of an actual occasion. This is what Whitehead asserts in the following "togetherness passage," indicating a nexus by the phrase "stream of experience":

There is a togetherness of the component elements of individual experience. This 'togetherness' has that special peculiar meaning of 'togetherness in experience.' It is togetherness of its own kind, explicable by reference to nothing else. For the purpose of this discussion it is indifferent whether we speak of a 'stream' of experience, or of an 'occasion' of experience. With the former alternative there is togetherness in the stream, and with the latter alternative there is togetherness in the occasion. In either case, there is the unique 'experiential togetherness.'

The consideration of experiential togetherness raises the final metaphysical question: whether there is any other meaning of 'togetherness.' The denial of any alternative meaning, that is to say, of any meaning not abstracted from the experiential meaning, is the 'subjectivist' doctrine. This reformed version of the subjectivist doctrine is the doctrine of the philosophy of organism.[119]

This important statement, having so many ramifications throughout the philosophy, may be the most important to be cited in this book. It is Whitehead's denial of the scientific materialist interpretation of nature as bifurcated and his substitution of his own doctrine. For materialism, ever the "contrary doctrine" to the philosophy of organism, objects have one kind of togetherness as bodies or groups and subjects have another kind of togetherness as minds or experiences. Nature is bifurcated into ontologically separate and unrelatable external and internal realities, "the disjunction of the components of subjective experience from the community of the external world." It is just this bifurcation and dualism that the reformed subjectivist principle denies in prohibiting two kinds of togetherness, one kind applying to occasions, the other kind applying to nexūs. There is only the one kind of togetherness for all nature; everything that there is, including every togetherness of occasions, is to be found within the experience of individual occasions. "Finally, the reformed subjectivist principle must be repeated: that apart from the experiences of subjects there is nothing, nothing, nothing, bare nothingness."[120]

Whitehead states that this principle answers "the final metaphysical question." The dualist answer, proposing objective togetherness for nexūs and subjective togetherness for actual entities, "creates the insurmountable difficulty for epistemology." A dualist interpretation of Whitehead provides this answer and this difficulty in providing that larger occasions are a kind of togetherness of smaller occasions that is unlike any experience of the smaller occasions—that a nexus of occasions is unified in a different way than an occasion is unified. An ontological distinction between nexūs and actual occasions is created in keeping with an ontological distinction between objects and subjects. This makes it impossible for larger occasions to have any affect on smaller ones, since a larger occasion, being one kind of group of smaller occasions, is outside their possible experience which is another kind of unity altogether. But for Whitehead, there are no nexūs that are not also the compositions of actual occasions, and consequently components of their experience. Nexūs must be experienced just as are the actual occasions. ". . . the whole universe consists of elements disclosed in the analysis of the experiences of subjects."[121] This includes nexūs.

*Examples.* For examples of nexūs, then, actual entities may be given, each one being composed of a nexus of other actual entities. So the foregoing list of actual entities is also a list of nexūs. I have noted that Whitehead regards Locke's "particular things" as (objectified) actual entities *and* nexūs. Similarly, both the subjects entertaining propositions and the logical subjects of the propositions are actual entities *and* nexūs. In fact, a subject entertaining or judging a proposition and the proposition's logical subjects form a nexus together as well. "Every proposition presupposes some general nexus with an indicative relational system. This nexus includes its locus of judging subjects and also its logical subjects."[122] Further examples of nexūs will be found in the section "Societies" of Chapter 2. For, every society is a nexus (although every nexus is not a society). Societies are nexūs of certain types, whereas actual entities are composed of nexūs and contribute to them.

Whitehead is oftentimes unconcerned to discriminate the actual entities and the nexūs of actual entities. For example, in the togetherness passage given above, he says that, "it is indifferent whether we speak of a 'stream' of experience, or of an 'occasion' of experience." The same equality of treatment is expressed here:

> In other words, just as, for some purposes, one atomic actuality can be treated as though it were many coordinate actualities, in the same way, for other purposes, a nexus of many actualities can be treated as though it were one actuality. This is what we habitually do in the case of the span of life of a molecule, or of a piece of rock, or of a human body.[123]

This indifference and this reciprocity of treatment is borne throughout the philosophy so that establishing what is an actual entity and what is a nexus, both in general principle and in regard to any particular example that Whitehead gives, can be very difficult and uncertain. How can Whitehead be indifferent to the difference between an occasion and a stream (nexus) of occasions? How can a lifetime be both a nexus of numerous occasions and one actual occasion? How can occasions be composed of the very nexus that together they comprise? Only a grasp of the Whiteheadian principles will shed any light on this baffling, dubious, elusive, most strange issue.

*Whitehead misinterpreted.* The reformed subjectivist principle is ignored by a number of interpreters of Whitehead. Again we have Ivor Leclerc presenting Whitehead as an atomist:

> . . . the truly active entities must be identified with the ultimate constituents, those which are not themselves composite. . . . Whitehead's 'actual entities,' like the 'monads' of Leibniz and Kant, are such ultimate acting entities. Thus this position, like that of material atomism, makes a basic distinction in status among entities between those comprising the ultimate constituents, which are 'simple,' in the sense of not being composites, and those which are composites.[124]

Leclerc has forgotten that there is only one kind of togetherness, which is that of experience: his "simples" have no experience of compositeness, and no experience of the compositions (for they are simple). The compositions that they make up are outside their experience. But we have seen that Whitehead thinks that even the smallest types of actual entities are internally modified by the larger bodies in which they exist. Leclerc creates an ontological distinction between occasions and nexūs, echoing a dualism between subjects that experience and objects that aggregate, an ontology and dualism that Whitehead emphatically rejects. And Abner Shimony imputes the same atomism to Whitehead: "Whitehead conceives of the nexus in a reductionist manner, as the totality of its constituent occasions."[125]

And David Ray Griffin writes: "It is by virtue of this distinction between *two basic types of organization* that Whitehead accounts for those things which manifestly are devoid of the power of self-determination, without positing a dualism between *two kinds of actual entities.*"[126] But the same dualism has crept into Griffin's account. One type of organization that Griffin allows for is a "mere aggregate." This is the conception of a nexus of actual occasions that is unlike the togetherness of occasions in experience, the very conception Whitehead denies. "On the one hand [macroscopic societies] can form a mere aggregate, such as a rock. This type of thing, although it is *composed* of partially self-determining organisms, itself has no power of self-determination."[127] Griffin holds that rocks have no self-determination, while molecules and electrons do: ". . . the electron, proton, or molecule has a significant degree of unity of response to its environment. . . ."[128] Then the rock is no actual occasion at all, but a composition of smaller things which are the experiencing and self-determining actual occasions. The compositeness which is the rock is no experiential togetherness and Whitehead's reformed subjectivism has been violated.

Griffin had meant to distinguish the more regnal and imperial societies from the more democratic and republican. But in so doing he created an impassable dualism between occasions and nexūs that is typical of atomistic or modern day materialist interpreters of Whitehead. Truly there are many kinds of societies and nexūs—physical, chemical, nuclear, biological, sociological, and many types within the broader kinds—but none are such that they are not within an occasion's experience; none are not components constituting an occasion. The occasion they compose need not be conceived as larger than they; it may be another member of the same society or nexus, the same atom, molecule, strand, cell, stem, flock, tribe, culture, committee, or species. To be a nexus, each member occasion must feel the antecedent members as one with itself. Just as there is only one genus of actual entity, but many types and several grades of this one genus, so there is only one (internal experiential) kind of togetherness, but many types and styles of this one kind. "The ontological principle can be expressed as: All real togetherness is togetherness in the formal constitution of an actuality."[129]

## CONCLUSION

This chapter has seen that the actual entity is most fairly interpreted as *Any concrete existent whatsoever.* Existence is not a factor of one or two particular sizes, time-spans, qualities, intensities, degrees of complexity or accessibility to human sense-perception. The actual entity can no more be identified solely with events of subatomic proportions than time can be identified solely with intervals of $10^{-24}$ seconds. It can no more be assigned one or two sizes or temporal durations than sizes can only be inches or microns, times can only be Tuesdays or springtimes, spaces can only be rooms or boxes, quantities can only be tens or bushels. "Remember that the human concepts of one inch in length, and of one second in time, as being reasonable basic quantities, are purely relevant to human life."[130]

Thus, questions as to the "correct size" and "correct time-span" of actual occasions are absurd, as are the proposals that actual occasions are necessarily of a certain specific size, that they are necessarily small for example. Asking what is the size and time-span for all occasions alike is tantamount to asking, "How big are things?" and "How long are times?" Or, more abstractly, considering the actual occasion as a metaphysically general conception, it is to ask, "What size is quantity?" and "What length is time?" No one asks these questions, yet sizes and time-spans for the actual occasion are seriously proposed and pondered. "It is a curious thing that Whitehead never asks himself, 'How big is an actual occasion?'"[131] Happily Nathaniel Lawrence answers his own query thus: "I do not see how one can avoid the implication that actual occasions come in different sizes according to their type."[132] And indeed, even occasions of one type may vary in size. Even the photons are not all of a size. "Quanta themselves vary continuously in size."[133]

Subatomic occasions and conscious human experiences are paradigm cases of actual occasions for the purpose of explicating Whitehead's philosophy, in particular, for the purpose of demonstrating that the Whiteheadian theories are applicable to any concrete existent whatsoever, concrete existences being conceived as on a scale of increasing complexity from subatomic particles to conscious human experience. The various grades of occasions are the major levels of complexity; there is no zero complexity. Occasions of the lowest grade are nevertheless capable of modification, just as are the larger and more complex occasions. Some aspect of larger occasions is included in smaller occasions; some aspect of smaller occasions is included in larger occasions. Aspects of other actual occasions enter into the nature, the internal constitution, the objective content, the feeling, of any given actual occasion, of any grade and type whatsoever. Actual occasions are all ontologically equal, fulfilling the same nature as actual occasions, though affording specific differences.

Aspects of other occasions entering into the constitution of a given occasion form a nexus therein in respect to these aspects, and with the given occasion itself, once this occasion becomes a new member of the same nexus by entering into the constitution of another occasion succeeding itself. And so it goes on. An occasion becomes a new member of the same nexus to which its ancestors belong when it, like its ancestors, has helped to create descendents in whom it is felt as an ancestor. Every nexus of occasions is a nexus by virtue of aspects of its member occasions having been bound together as components of a given occasion. Each member of a nexus has bound together aspects of the preceding members, and is only a member itself by virtue of its successors binding it together with its antecedents. Consequently, a nexus is experienced by its members; there can be no nexus outside the experience of actual occasions. That is to say, there is no way in which actual occasions are together that is not experienced by some actual occasion.

This doctrine of one kind of togetherness, experiential togetherness, is one expression of the reformed subjectivist principle. It is this that primarily distinguishes Whiteheadian organism from scientific materialism with its inherent dualism wherein knowing subjects and the objects of knowledge, or consciousness and the external world, or autonomous organisms and aggregates of material particles are not together. Ann L. Plamondon articulates this distinction between organism and materialism delineated in this chapter:

> A doctrine of materialism entails that all relationships are external. This is to say that what a thing (bit of material) is does not depend on its relationships to other things (bits of material); the relationships of a thing are not constitutive of it. The application of this doctrine to the formation of higher levels of order out of lower levels results in an aggregate view of the higher order. This means that when higher levels are formed out of lower levels of order there is no modification of the lower levels to a pattern of the higher level. There is no modification of this kind because such modification requires that the relationships of the lower orders be constitutive of them. . . . There can be no new order if what the lower orders are is independent of the relationships into which they enter.[134]

Organism requires that the relationships of the lower orders be constitutive of the lower order occasions. These relationships also create other orders of occasions; and the lower order occasions are constitutive of these as well, as they also modify the lower order occasions. Organism requires in fact that relationships among any occasions be constitutive of some occasion. This occasion need not be larger than those occasions whose aspects constitute it. Every actual occasion, however miniscule and insignificant, is a system of relationships to other occasions (and therein a nexus), even ultimately relating to all other occasions.

# 2

# Prehension

*Here it is. Whatever has a native power, whether of affecting anything else, or of being affected in ever so slight a degree by the most insignificant agents, even on one solitary occasion, is a real being. In short, I offer it as the definition of beings that they are potency, and nothing else.*

Plato, *Sophist* 247D

## INTRODUCTION

This chapter takes a look at some of the principles governing the interior life of an actual occasion and the interrelationships among occasions. Most importantly, an occasion is always a process, no matter how dull and inert it may appear. It is a process of synthesizing other occasions, then contributing itself to the synthesis of others. This is the causal efficacy of occasions: they act on one another effecting syntheses, new occasions, which, if they conform to the old in important ways, continue the society or nexus of which the old are a part. All the occasions of a society or nexus are connected by their causal efficacy of one another, the antecedent ones efficacious of their successors. These societies, chains or trains or successions of occasions, replace the substantial enduring bodies of materialist conjecture. It is only this causal efficacy of occasions of a society or nexus that produces the spatiotemporal ordering among occasions. Where occasions have no causal relationships, they have no spatiotemporal relationships either; none are above or below another, none before or after. Each society or nexus is a spacetime system; the Whiteheadian cosmos is a plurality of these spacetime systems that are joined wherever their paths cross.

The interior world of every occasion is full of feeling. It is the feeling of being acted upon, and of guiding that action. This is Whitehead's way of describing the causal efficacy that produces each new occasion. The new occasion feels its antecedents in process of creating it. The very experience of an occasion is that of converting cause into effect. The fact that this conversion is within an occasion, within its experience and providing its experience, is another remarkable feature of the Whiteheadian philosophy. This, and the fact that causal efficacy includes final causations, that is, purposes, goals, aims, hopes, intentions, anticipations, and the like, enlarge our conventional notion of causation. This chapter is the story of causal efficacy and what it means for a new cosmological design. The Whiteheadian view of things as processes of becoming which experience and develop the efficacy of other things is always to be contrasted with materialism wherein autonomous enduring substances, abiding in an enduring absolute time and space, make no substantial impression upon one another. "The new view is entirely different. The fundamental concepts are activity and process. . . . For the modern view process, activity, and change are the matter of fact."[1]

## THE NATURE OF ACTUALITY

*The stuff of substance.* The actual occasions are the things that concretely exist. But the nature of things is unlike enduring, self-sufficient substance; rather, it is process. The term "thing" is misleading in its substantialist connotation. Things are not the static, enduring, material stuff they may appear to be. "Secondly, each actual entity is itself only describable as an organic process . . . and is not describable in terms of the morphology of a 'stuff.'"[2]

The predominant conception of nature in Western tradition has been materialism, the conception of nature as made of stuff.

> The Ionian philosophers asked, What is nature made of? The answer is couched in terms of stuff, or matter, or material—the particular name chosen is indifferent—which has the property of simple location. . . .[3]

The stuff or material has the permanence and independence of substance. A substance is conceived as an autonomous, independent, self-sufficient, enduring, unchanging, permanent, impervious existence that is consequently describable and intelligible without reference to anything else. The idea of substance is the idea of simple existence: it is the idea that an existent thing, "' . . . requires nothing but itself in order to exist.'"[4] The stuff or material of nature has been conceived as deriving these characteristics from the fact that it is a substance. The idea that something should require "nothing but itself" may seem preposterous and incredible to us. But this idea has only been displaced in very recent times, and by dint of the esoteric researches of modern physics. The idea has been but common sense, ". . . so obvious that people do not know what they are assuming because no other way of putting things has ever occurred to them."[5] Matter has always been known to change its shape, character, quality, and appearance; but a constant substance was always believed to underlie all its changing conditions so that regardless of what it went through, it was still there, still essentially unaffected, still the basic matter that it had been but with a new face.

For Whitehead this idea of an enduring and impervious substantial existence is "sheer error":

> But in metaphysics the concept is sheer error. This error does not consist in the employment of the word 'substance'; but in the employment of the notion of an actual entity which is characterized by essential qualities, and remains numerically one amidst the changes of accidental relations and of accidental qualities.[6]

A substance endures "numerically one"; all the changes to which it is susceptible do not affect its essential, abiding, material, independent existence. It cannot arise, it cannot perish; it ever remains its one same self, while putting on new appearances. For Whitehead, there is no such thing, and for this reason he avoids even the term "substance" in his philosophy and substitutes "actual entity." "The notion of 'substance' is transformed into that of 'actual entity'. . . ."[7]

An actual occasion is a process of the becoming of other occasions into the one, and a perishing of the one again into the becoming of many successors. The relationships among occasions, so far from being external, accidental, and unessential to what the occasions are, constitute the occasions. The relations among occasions, being made within them, are an integral part of their internal nature. That is to say, relationships are inevitably internal: ". . . the concept of internal relations requires the concept of substance as the activity synthesizing the relationships into its emergent character."[8] This is the only concept of substance Whitehead endorses, substance conceived as a "synthesizing activity." The substance of materialism cannot change into something else; but an occasion changes into other occasions. Substances are impervious to one another, unchanged in any essential way by the other; but actual occasions evolve new orders of occasions by promoting certain effects they have upon one another. "The aboriginal stuff, or material, from which materialistic philosophy starts is incapable of evolution. This material is in itself the ultimate substance."[9]

Then the actual occasion is neither substantial, nor requires, confirms, presupposes, or derives from an underlying substantial existence, a basic material substrate. An occasion has no more actuality beyond its synthesis of relationships to other occasions, and the qualities and characteristics that accrue therefrom. "The contrary doctrine is that an actual entity . . . is the outcome of whatever can be ascribed to it in the way of quality or relationship."[10] This is the reason actual entities were introduced as "final"; they are the "final real things." There is no more, no further reality to be ascribed to them than their constitution exhibits. They are not also enduring, autonomous, impervious, mutually exclusive, and numerically one above and beyond what they are as actual occasions. Thus, actual occasions are party to a radical relativity unknown to enduring substances. "For the philosophy of organism, the percipient occasion is its own standard of actuality. If in its knowledge other actual entities appear, it can only be because they conform to its standard of actuality."[11]

Where matter had been thought to change in condition but not in substance, actual occasions perish and create new occasions. Instead of the changed matter is a new actual occasion; instead of a play of changing qualities in a substantial material is a succession of actual occasions. We have seen that the existence of actual occasions is not validated by, or increased or decreased in proportion to, diminishing size or longevity; the varying qualities, complexities, and palpabilities of things do not alter their claim to existence. But what these things are as particular concrete existences, what particular qualities, characters, and complexities they manifest, never goes so far as to predicate an underlying substance by means of which alone they are able to exist. There is evidence of an existence where there is some quality, character, and palpability; but there is no substance underlying, behind, or supporting the existence. "The obvious commonsense notion has been entirely destroyed, so far as concerns its function as the basis for all interpretation."[12]

*Substance-quality, subject-predicate.* Whitehead's abandonment of substance as employed in materialist philosophies and as implicated in ordinary English speech and thought explains why the language of his own works seems so very oblique and circuitous. The fact is, we expect Whitehead to be speaking of substances. This presumption, embodied in our own language and thought, may give us the impression that Whitehead is trying to discuss substances but does not know how to write, or that he has invented a new language for speaking about substances in order to be fanciful and hyperbolic. But Whitehead is not speaking of substances at all, but of processes that concresce as organisms.

The philosophy of organism . . . differs by the abandonment of the subject-predicate forms of thought, so far as concerns the presupposition that this form is a direct embodiment of the most ultimate characterization of fact. The result is that the 'substance-quality' concept is avoided; and that morphological description is replaced by description of dynamic process.[13]

It obviously takes some doing to avoid subject-predicate language and thought and still write in English. But Whitehead's works show his strong effort to create new language descriptive of process. He insists that his philosophy is not understood, not even expressible, in subject-predicate phraseology. "If the subject-predicate form of statement be taken to be metaphysically ultimate, it is then impossible to express this doctrine of feelings and their superject."[14] Taking the subject-predicate form of statement as the true expression of reality, the qualities of an occasion would not necessarily relate the occasion to any other occasion: an occasion's characteristics would not necessarily show that the occasion had any connection with any other. But for Whitehead, an occasion's qualities are a consequence of its feeling other occasions and their qualities.

The subject-predicate way of thinking assumes not only substance, but a dualism of substances, matter and mind, mutually exclusive. An independent mind is substantialized and qualities predicated of it. Materialist philosophies, so far from solving the metaphysical and epistemological problems of independently existing substances with accidental qualities inhering in them and an unbridgeable dualism of matter and mind, create the problem. Whitehead considers that his philosophy with its description of organic process solves the problem in providing that not only qualities inhere in substances, but substances inhere in one another.

The perceptive constitution of the actual entity presents the problem, How can the other actual entities, each with its own formal existence, also enter objectively into the perceptive constitution of the actual entity in question? This is the problem of the solidarity of the universe. The classical doctrines of universals and particulars, of subject and predicate, of individual substances not present in other individual substances, of the externality of relations, alike render this problem incapable of solution. The answer given by the organic philosophy is the doctrine of prehensions, involved in conrescent integrations, and terminating in a definite, complex unity of feeling.[15]

Whitehead's language so thoroughly avoids implying substance that the substantialism imposed on his philosophy by materialist interpreters is deflected by its devious and obscure phraseology (devious and obscure if Whitehead is taken to be—ineptly—writing about substances). The philosophy has a way of knocking substance right out from under us, just as quantum mechanics disabuses us of enduring particles and relativity pulls the rug of absolute spacetime out from under us. This defiance of substance is a positive achievement of the Whiteheadian terminology, its contribution to thought by way of remolding language, not an ineptitude. Milic Capek reminds us, "The required radical revision of the traditional forms of thought cannot be realized without sustained and vigorous effort."[16]

*Inexplicable creativity.* The concrete things which are the actual entities are not substances, then, but creative processes. Processes are creative because they create new actual entities. A process is a process of the becoming of a new actual occasion. "Creativity" names the general phenomenon that actual occasions become and enter into the becoming of other occasions; "process" names this creative fact about the particular actual occasions. "'Creativity' is the universal of universals characterizing ultimate matter of fact."[17] Therefore, any particular case of matter of fact fulfills the description, "That the actual world is a process, and that the process is the becoming of actual entities."[18] So creativity is the fact that process applies to all occasions; process is the fact that an occasion comes into being, becomes, out of an actual world of other occasions.

Whitehead does not explain or justify by argument either process or creativity. Quite the contrary: "Nature is a process. . . . There can be no explanation of this characteristic of nature."[19] Nor does he see this lack of explanation or justification as a defect; for Whitehead, no philosophy can explain or justify concrete existence or the nature of concrete existence. Rather, philosophy *describes*: "The explanatory purpose of philosophy is often misunderstood . . . . philosophy is explanatory of abstraction, and not of concreteness."[20] If creativity and process are to be believed as the nature of matter of fact, then they must be observed. For Whitehead, creativity and process are indeed the observed nature of things. It is not this nature, but the ideas and principles drawn from it that need explaining. "All philosophy is an endeavor to obtain a self-consistent understanding of things observed."[21]

It is for this reason that creativity is the "universal of universals" and the "ultimate principle" of the philosophy; it is not itself explained but is used to explain. It is simply the observed nature of actualities that they create other actualities; that they are consequently, creatures. ". . . the individual fact is a creature, and creativity is the ultimate behind all forms, inexplicable by forms, and conditioned by its creatures."[22] There can be no explanation that appeals to principles more fundamental than creativity; it is already the ultimate principle.

Creativity is really the fact of cause. It is not itself cause, since the actual occasions are the causes, but the fact that there is causation at all. Whitehead does not often use the terms "cause" or "causation" since they are replete with materialist connotations. They imply determinism wherein predeterminable efficient causes are the sole sources of effects; and they imply mechanism wherein external forces are to explain every effect. Whitehead substitutes "causal efficacy" for the causation of materialism to bring out his own conception of cause the better, a conception of cause as indeterminant and acting through internal relations. "Creativity" is the fact of cause, but of cause conceived as causal efficacy, indeterminate, immanent. Whitehead here explains his conception of creativity, avoiding materialist terminology, and pointing out that this conception is intended to replace that of substance:

> 'Creativity' . . . is that ultimate principle by which the many, which are the universe disjunctively, become the one actual occasion, which is the universe conjunctively. It lies in the nature of things that the many enter into complex unity. . . . The 'creative advance' is the application of this ultimate principle of creativity to each novel situation which it originates. . . . The ultimate metaphysical principle is the advance from disjunction to conjunction, creating a novel entity other than the entities given in disjunction. . . . In their natures, entities are disjunctively 'many' in process of passage into conjunctive unity. This Category of the Ultimate replaces Aristotle's category of 'primary substance.'[23]

Thus, creativity is the presupposition of the philosophy of organism just as substance has been the presupposition of materialist philosophies as well as Aristotle. This is Whitehead's general characterization of the general nature of existence. Aspects of many occasions become one occasion; aspects of the one occasion effect many occasions. This creativity of occasions is not to be explained or justified: it simply "lies in the nature of things." The truth of this description of things can only be verified by experience, by observation, by testing its adequacy for oneself: "The sole appeal is to intuition."[24]

*Energy and activity.* Then Whitehead's answer to the Ionian philosophers, asking what is nature made of, is that nature is made of creative process. No matter how passive, unchangeable, unaffectable, complacent, and inefficacious a thing may seem to us, this is not its ultimate character according to the philosophy of organism. For, even the fact that a thing is able to seem anything at all to us, however uneventful and inert it does seem, means that it has been in relationship with us so much as to seem anything at all. The most dull and unperturbable rock we see, for example, has been a cause of our seeing it; it has been able to reflect light and appear grey, green, or blue. The rock has innumerable powers besides: it is able to respond to the gravitational force of the planet as a whole, which in turn is in relationship with the stars; it has relationships with the surrounding climate, atmosphere, and life, being able to be worn away, broken, rotted, and eaten by roots and lichen; it is a cause of nutrition in plants and animals that partake of it; it has relationships with us if we sit on it three feet above ground, in preventing us from sitting there two feet off the ground; it is a cause of our feeling warm or cold if we touch it in sun or shade; it is a cause of obstructing us if we trip on it. "The 'stone' has a reference to its past, when it could have been used as a missile if small enough, or as a seat if large enough. A 'stone' has certainly a history, and probably a future."[25]

These are some of the obvious activities of a rock; a microscopic examination would reveal countless more. It has a plentitude of causal powers with respect to its environment, and powers both beneficial and injurious with respect to people. All things are similarly engaged in relationships and actively engaging in more. Nothing is so static as to be incapable of relationship with its environment. Rocks and chairs are activities. "[A chair] gradually changes, even throughout its solid wooden parts. At the end of a million years in a cave, it becomes fragile, and dissolves at a touch. A slow, imperceptible change is always in progress."[26] If rocks and chairs are activities, what is not? The Whiteheadian philosophy asks that we conceive all things as energy, active and creative. "In the language of physical science, the change from materialism to 'organic realism'—as the new outlook may be termed—is the displacement of the notion of static stuff by the notion of fluent energy."[27]

Substance has been totally replaced by creative process; it has not been revised, qualified, or amended, but discarded and replaced. The Whiteheadian conception is not that there are substances which are also in process and creative; there are not substances which may or may not also act on one another. There is no substance, no stuff, no substantial endurance at all. These are high abstractions which make living and thinking easier, but they are not reality. "The behavior apart from the things is abstract, and so are the things apart from their behavior."[28] Things are their behavior, their activities, and their behavior is them. The conception of substance is the conception of a thing apart from its behavior. As a self-sufficient enduring material, the behavior is acted upon it, the only action of its own being to self-subsist. Whitehead denies that there is any such thing as a mere material concretely existing. "But what has vanished from the field of ultimate scientific conceptions is the notion of vacuous material existence with passive endurance, with primary individual attributes, and with accidental adventures."[29] Similarly, mere mind has vanished from the philosophical field. "There is no such independent item in actuality as 'mere concept' . . . the notion of 'mere concept', or of 'mere realization', apart from relevant emotional derivation, which is its emotional origin, is fallacious."[30]

Whitehead does not view the creative processes as divided into physical activities and mental activities. That is, there are not physical actual occasions and mental actual occasions. The differences among types of occasions, and types of their activities, can be accounted for without resorting to a dualism of substances, a mere material and a mere mind.

> According to this account of the World of Activity there is no need to postulate two essentially different types of Active Entities, namely, the purely material entities and the entities alive with various modes of experiencing. The latter type is sufficient to account for the characteristics of that World, when we allow for variety of recessiveness and dominance among the basic factors of experience, namely consciousness, memory, and anticipation. This conclusion has the advantage of indicating the possibility of the emergence of Life from the lifeless material of this planet—namely, the gradual emergence of memory and anticipation.[31]

Again, human experience is taken as the model for all occasions, the non-human occasions enjoying some type of experience but to a lesser degree, very many even to a negligible degree. What is emotion in human experience is energy in microphysical occasions. Negligible humanity, negligible consciousness, negligible mentality and thought, negligible memory and anticipation nevertheless fuel energetic occasions. "The key notion from which such construction [of systematic metaphysical cosmology] should start is that the energetic activity considered in physics is the emotional intensity entertained in life."[32] Energy is in the infra-molecular what emotion is in animals: the activity of the different types of creature.

*Emotion and experience.* Human experience is characterized by emotion more than anything else. This is another point wherein the Whiteheadian philosophy diverges from many traditional philosophies. Human beings are primarily emotional and not primarily conscious, or ideational, or knowledgeable, or perceptive. Emotion is fundamental in human experience because this is what all people share with other animal natures and, in the form of energy, ultimately with all actual existences. "The basis of experience is emotional."[33] It is what we have in common with the rest of nature that is fundamental for Whitehead, not what is unique to us. "Clear, conscious discrimination is an accident of human existence. It makes us human. But it does not make us exist. It is of the essence of our humanity. But it is an accident of our existence."[34] And so Whitehead declares himself to be primarily a "unity of emotions"; he is essentially a feeler, whereas Descartes had been essentially a doubter (thinker).

> I find myself as essentially a unity of emotions, enjoyments, hopes, fears, regrets, valuations of alternatives, decisions—all of them subjective reactions to the environment as active in my nature. My unity—which is Descartes' 'I am'—is my process of shaping this welter of material into a consistent pattern of feelings.[35]

Similarly, every actual occasion may be considered an experience on a scale of more or less, a scale continuous from the human to the microphysical. "But this complete experience is nothing other than what the actual entity is in itself, for itself. . . . Process is the becoming of experience."[36]

But there is more than emotion in Whitehead's description of his experience, his unity of emotion. For example, there are valuations, decisions, unity, and shaping. These are witness to the final causation that unifies the experience into a whole of its disparate emotional ingredients. With no dualism between physical and mental occasions, there is no dualism of causation either. The dualism of causation embodied in ordinary language and thought and articulated in philosophies, wherein final causes such as purposes, aims, intentions, and ideals are delegated to human mental actions and to God, and efficient causes such as force, power, attraction, and repulsion are delegated to the merely material bodies, is sustained by the dualism of substances. With dualism, final causes and efficient causes never even apply to the same things. Just as, with dualism, matter and mind could make no substantial impression upon one another, both independent and without inherent relationship to the other, so efficient and final causation could never join, the one to affect the work of the other. Whitehead considers that if there were really a bifurcation of the merely material from the merely mental, and a bifurcation in their corresponding causes, nothing that was merely material could ever be influenced by final causes. And if this were the case, then people, for example, would not even be able to direct their own merely material bodies.

In fact we are *directly* conscious of our purposes as *directive* of our actions. Apart from such direction no doctrine could in any sense be acted upon. The notions entertained mentally would have no effect upon bodily actions. Thus what happens would happen in complete indifference to the entertainment of such notions.[37]

Every occasion is a consequence of both efficient and final causes. ". . . the creativity is endowed with the double character of final causation, and efficient causation."[38] Every experience, in fact every emotion, shows that both types of causation have been at work; the enjoyments, hopes, fears, regrets, valuations, and decisions Whitehead names all show a mingling of efficient and final causation. Occasions of the past bringing on these reactions are their efficient causes; but the reactions would not be what they are but for some ideal entertained, some aim pursued, some possibility imagined. An enjoyment must be wanted, something hoped or feared must be imagined as a possibility, a valuation must be intended, a decision and a shaping must be purposeful. And so for all experience to different degrees; it is not only emotional but purposeful. It involves final aims as well as the objects giving rise to it.

*Metaphysical generality.* Actual occasions are activities; their activity is that of engaging relationships with other occasions, and synthesizing them so as to form a compatible whole. Each engagement is called a "prehension." Then prehensions are the "Concrete Facts of Relatedness."[39] The actual occasion may be defined in terms of prehension: "In Cartesian language, the essence of an actual entity consists solely in the fact that it is a prehending thing. . . ."[40] Just as the conception of the actual occasion has the utmost generality, so also has prehension. It is metaphysically general, comprehending all relationships. "Accordingly, on the Leibnizian model, I use the term 'prehension' for the general way in which the occasion of experience can include, as part of its own essence, any other entity, whether another occasion of experience or an entity of another type."[41] A prehension is any way an occasion includes, or relates to, aspects of other occasions, any way at all.

The engaging of each relationship, being an action, is a causal action, a cause and effect transition. Just as occasions are all the concrete existences, prehensions are all the cause and effect transactions among them. Prehension encompasses both efficient and final causation; it encompasses the entire range of cause and effect activity such as is signified in verbs. Naturally, then, there are many ways of approaching, defining, exemplifying, and describing prehension just as there are many approaches to the actual occasion. But the metaphysical generality of the conception, encompassing any cause and effect transition whatsoever, is best expressed by terms which least favor specific types of causes and least suggest a dualism of types of causes. That is to say, it is best described in the most general terms for causal activity available: relating, transforming, transmuting, transacting, apprehending, originating, acting, reacting, absorbing, appropriating, growing, possessing, grasping, taking, making, taking account of, having to do with.[42] Whitehead frequently prefers to depict prehension chemically, as absorption.[43] And he just as frequently speaks of it as appropriation, which keeps in view a taking and a grasping action.[44] This is in fact the root meaning of "prehension": "Whitehead proclaimed the doctrine that the acting of substances is a grasping, a prehending (in the original etymological sense) of other substances."[45] But "appropriation" adds something to "grasping": it is a taking and making one's own, an internalizing what was external. And so it is equally well described as possessing: "Just as Descartes said, 'this body is mine'; so he should have said, 'this actual world is mine.' My process of 'being myself' is my origination from my possession of the world."[46] All the types of actual occasions that there are, from subatomic particles, to proteins, to plants, to people, to planets, are busily active engaging all types of relationships, each relationship being one cause and effect transition in which the occasion is involved: physical, chemical, neural, biological, biophysical, biochemical, electrical, nuclear, physiological, psychological, personal, cultural, familial, sociological, political, legal, economical, religious, aesthetic, geological, geophysical, astronomical, ecological, and so on. Chemical bonds are not the only relationships; physical forces do not afford the only examples of cause and effect transitions.

*Concrescence.* New occasions come into concrete existence upon synthesizing their prehensions of other occasions. This is to say that an occasion effects its own concretion through prehension: "Accordingly I have adopted the term 'prehension,' to express the activity whereby an actual entity effects its own concretion of other things."[47] Coming into being is a concrescing, the being once become is concrete. Concrescing is becoming concrete by virtue of prehensions' growing together. The word is chosen for its root meaning, "growing together":

The word Concrescence is a derivative from the familiar latin verb, meaning 'growing together'. It also has the advantage that the participle 'concrete' is familiarly used for the notion of complete physical reality. Thus Concrescence is useful to convey the notion of many things acquiring complete complex unity.[48]

All told, concrescence means becoming concrete by growing together. It is the prehensions that grow together. Various and disparate cause and effect transitions mutually adjust so as to compatibly compose one actual occasion together. To say the same thing in another way, relationships among occasions grow together so as to compose a new occasion. As the relationships grow together, the new occasion concresces. The growth is completed as all the relationships are synthesized. The new occasion is then concrete, its prehensions concrete facts of relatedness, the occasions prehended bound together as a nexus. This nexus is only a nexus in repect to those aspects of its occasions prehended by, in relationship with, the new occasion. That is, it is only in respect of their causally efficacious aspects for the new occasion that the prehended occasions are a nexus.

In summary, to prehend is to relate to, a prehension is a relationship; and a relationship is a consequence of a cause and effect transition between occasions. A concrescence is a togetherness of prehensions. An occasion is a composition and a nexus in respect to the aspects of other occasions composing it; it is a concrescence in respect to the prehensions composing it, that is, in respect to its relationships with occasions having grown together. We have seen that an occasion is nothing else than what can be ascribed to it in the way of relationship. Whitehead repeats the same dictum this way: "An actual occasion is nothing but the unity to be ascribed to a particular instance of concrescence. This concrescence is thus nothing else than the 'real internal constitution' of the actual occasion in question."[49]

*The analysis of a feeling.* Prehensions are either positive or negative. Positive prehensions are called "feelings." Negative prehensions, therefore, ". . . are said to 'eliminate from feeling'."[50] Here Whitehead explains that a single feeling is a single cause and effect transition, a single act of causal efficacy.

A simple physical feeling is an act of causation. The actual entity which is the initial datum is the 'cause,' the simple physical feeling is the 'effect', and the subject entertaining the simple physical feeling is the actual entity 'conditioned' by the effect. This 'conditioned' actual entity will also be called the 'effect.' All complex causal action can be reduced to a complex of such primary components. Therefore simple physical feelings will also be called 'causal' feelings.[51]

This may seem confused: a feeling described as "causal" and "an act of causation" at the same time that it is called an "effect" along with the entire occasion. But this is Whiteheadian causal efficacy, wherein causes are immanent in their effect. A feeling is not only a cause, but a cause becoming an effect; it is the act of the cause creating its effect. Being an act, it cannot be only a cause alone or an effect alone, but the transition relating both. It is the activity of a cause creating, becoming, an effect. This entire activity is within, immanent in, its subject occasion, which is being effected by the concrescence of many feelings. It is just this causally efficacious activity that makes for experience. With the concrescence of feelings, a whole new integral experience is created, a new feeling subject, a new actual occasion. An occasion always has many feelings, not just one; for it is a concrescence of feelings. A single feeling cannot concresce since there is then nothing for it to grow together with. An occasion is always the togetherness of aspects of many occasions, and its relationship with each one is a prehension. There is no such thing as an occasion with only one prehension. This would mean the single prehension was an actual occasion itself rather than a part of one; and it would mean there had been no concrescence, no growing together, of prehensions. But prehensions are not themselves occasions; only a concrescence of prehensions is an occasion.

An occasion is always a complex of many prehensions. But more than this, even a single feeling is complex, as an analysis of a feeling shows:

A feeling—i.e., a positive prehension—is essentially a transition effecting a concrescence. Its complex constitution is analysable into five factors which express what that transition consists of, and effects. The factors are: (i) the 'subject' which feels, (ii) the 'initial data' which are to be felt, (iii) the 'elimination' in virtue of negative prehensions, (iv) the 'objective datum' which is felt, (v) the 'subjective form' which is *how* that subject feels that objective datum.[52]

This analysis shows again that a feeling is a cause and effect transition, such that it includes *both* cause and effect. Causes are the "initial data which are to be felt." These are the aspects of the other occasions which come to compose the one occasion upon being felt by it. The "objective datum" is what the subject actually feels in feeling the aspects of other occasions. And the subject occasion is the complete effect of all the feelings together. Each feeling contributes its one cause and effect transition to the whole, and the synthesis of the whole lot of feelings achieves the integral, complex effect which is the subject.

*Subjective form.* One of the factors in feeling seen in the analysis of a feeling is subjective form. This factor is the factor of final causation ingredient in every single feeling. Final and efficient causes do not act separately or with respect to separate kinds of things. Every single cause and effect transition is both efficient and final; that is, it has both its determinant and its intentional features. Data are the efficient factors in a feeling, subjective form its final factor. The entire feeling is causally efficacious, efficiently and finally causally efficacious of one subject. It is one causally efficacious part of a total subject, which is a concrescence of many such parts.

Subjective forms may be viewed as reactions guided by final causation, subjective reactions that the feeling has to its data. "Thus an actual entity, on its subjective side, is nothing else than what the universe is for it, including its own reactions. The reactions are the subjective forms of the feelings, elaborated into definiteness through stages of process."[53] This means that the subjective form is inseparable from the objective datum, since this datum is characterized by the way in which the feeling has reacted to it, the way in which it has felt it. "The subjective form cannot be absolutely disjoined from the pattern of the objective datum."[54]

Subjective forms are such as these: ". . . emotions, valuations, purposes, adversions, aversions, consciousness, etc."[55] Their final causation derives from the subjective aim of the entire subject occasion in which the feeling with its subjective factor concresces. "The emotional pattern in the subjective form of any one feeling arises from the subjective aim dominating the entire concrescent process."[56] The subjective aim is the final cause of the entire subject. ". . . the 'subjective aim' at 'satisfaction' constitutes the final cause, or lure, whereby there is determinate concrescence. . . ."[57] Then the subjective aim, responsible for the final causation of the subject occasion in its entirety, is effective through its influence upon every subjective form of every feeling of the subject.

A feeling can be genetically described in terms of its process of origination, with its negative prehensions whereby its many initial data become its complex objective datum. In this process the subjective form originates, and carries into the feeling its own history transformed into the way in which the feeling feels. The way in which the feeling feels expresses how the feeling came into being. It expresses the purpose which urged it forward, and the obstacles which it encountered, and the indeterminations which were dissolved by the originative decisions of the subject.[58]

The "originative decisions" of the subject spring from its subjective aim; the subjective forms express this aim, the purposes and decisions of the total subject, in every feeling. All the disparate feelings of a subject, and all their different subjective forms, are obliged to become congruous as they concresce, since all share the very same subjective aim of the one subject and must compose one subject. The feelings need not be alike to belong to one subject, and in fact experience is enriched if they contrast; but they cannot be incompatible. Incompatibility is eliminated by negative prehension.

*Negative prehension.* Each feeling, or positive prehension, includes negative prehensions as well, as the analysis of a feeling shows. A subject occasion not only is definitely effected in a certain way, but it definitely is not effected in other ways. "But the negative prehensions which consist of exclusions from contribution to the concrescence can be treated in their subordination to the positive prehensions."[59] An aspect of an antecedent occasion must be prehended by a subject occasion before *it*, that aspect, can be eliminated from feeling. There is no definite elimination but for definite prehension of what is to be eliminated. For this reason, we find negative prehension included in positive prehension. "A negative prehension is the definite exclusion of that item from positive contribution to the subject's own real internal constitution. This doctrine involves the position that a negative prehension expresses a bond."[60] An occasion is not only definitely what it *is,* but also very definitely not what it is *not.* And just as it has a hand in becoming what it is, how it feels, how it is effected, through the final causation of its subjective aim, so it has a hand in not becoming what it is not through negative prehension. "Now to be definite always means that all the elements of a complex whole contribute to some *one* effect, to the exclusion of others. The creative process is a process of exclusion to the same extent as it is a process of inclusion."[61]

Then a negative prehension, like its positive counterpart, has a datum, but it has barred its transition to effect. "A negative prehension holds its datum as inoperative in the progressive concrescence of prehensions constituting the unity of the subject."[62] However, the negative prehension, like its positive counterpart, will still have a subjective form: "The negative prehensions have their own subjective forms which they contribute to the process."[63] These subjective forms are reactions to what is not. They are integrated with the other feelings of the subject, so that the subjective forms of the positive prehensions are affected even by those of the negative prehensions. "Thus the negative prehensions, involved in the production of any one feeling, are not independent of the other feelings. The subjective forms of feelings depend in part on the negative prehensions."[64] Whatever is felt, is felt in conjunction with what is not felt; and whatever is the reaction to what is felt, is combined with a reaction to what is not felt. There is no feeling of something that is not also a feeling that it is not something else.

*Inextricable feelings.* All the factors of a feeling are interdependent, as are all the feelings of an occasion, as are all occasions. "It will be presupposed that all entities or factors in the universe are essentially relevant to each other's existence."[65] There is no way of extricating an occasion from its environment of other occasions (part of which compose it) and still know what the occasion is. "For you cannot abstract the universe from any entity, actual or non-actual, so as to consider that entity in complete isolation."[66] This is because an occasion *is* its feelings of aspects of other occasions. Similarly, there is no way of extricating a feeling from its subject occasion and still know what the feeling is. "The partial nature of a feeling, other than the complete satisfaction, is manifest by the impossibility of understanding its generation without recourse to the whole subject."[67] Without the occasion of which it is a part, one feeling among others, a feeling is nonsense: "A particular feeling divorced from its subject is nonsense."[68]

The data of a feeling, then, will be inseparable from that feeling, which is in turn inseparable from its subject. The initial data are the antecedent occasions that are prehended. "In a simple physical feeling, the initial datum is a single actual entity. . . ."[69] This datum cannot be understood without the feeling of it. There is no such thing as an isolated datum, a datum understandable and interpretable in separation from its context in the subject of which it is a part. "Thus, just as the 'feeling as one' cannot bear the abstraction from it of the subject, so the 'data as one' cannot bear the abstraction from it of every feeling which feels it as such."[70] A datum is a datum only of those particular feelings feeling it, and the particular subjects of those feelings, and nothing otherwise.

The inextricability of all the feelings of one subject, and all the factors of the feelings—their subjective forms, negative prehensions, and data both initial and objective—means that these feelings and factors express what the subject is and nothing else. Each feeling is a part of the subject, it is a partial subject. "The prehensions in disjunction are abstractions; each of them is its subject viewed in that abstract objectification."[71] A feeling is the subject considered in one part, from one perspective. Thus, Whitehead speaks of prehensions as "quasi-actualities" at one point.[72] They are not themselves actualities but partial actualities. "Each ultimate unit of fact is a cell-complex, not analysable into components with equivalent completeness of actuality."[73] The component prehensions have not the actuality of their subject, but the partial, quasi-actuality of belonging to it. Thus, as I have argued, there can be no subject with only one prehension.

To emphasize the inextricable bond that unites all of an occasion's feelings together and prohibits their independent isolation and their abstraction from their subject, Whitehead calls the subjects of the feelings "feelers":

> The feelings are inseparable from the end at which they aim; and this end is the feeler. The feelings aim at the feeler, as their final cause. The feelings are what they are in order that their subject may be what it is. . . . Thus the feeling would be wrongly abstracted from its own final cause. This final cause is an inherent element in the feeling, constituting the unity of that feeling. An actual entity feels as it does feel in order to be the actual entity which it is.[74]

The extrication of a feeler and its feeling is inconceivable.

This is understandable in ordinary terms. No concretely existing thing has but one cause. It is a unity of numerous causes. A rock has not come into being by virtue of one cause only. Nor has my seeing it. More than an eye, a brain, a rock, a ground, and a photon are causally involved in an occasion of my seeing a rock. All its aspects and causes are inextricable; all are the occasion partially, and that is all they are. They are neither understandable nor describable in isolation from their context in the occasion. This is because there is no cause but that it has had effect. "The reason why the cause is objectively in the effect is that the cause's feeling cannot, as a feeling, be abstracted from its subject which is the cause."[75] A rock is only a seen rock if it is one cause of sight; a food is only a nutritive food if it is a cause of nutrition; an orchestra is only a musical orchestra if it is a cause of music. The causes are immanent in their effect; none are understandable or describable without their effect. Similarly, in reverse, an effect cannot be extricated from its causes. A statue is only a statue if it is an effect of human artisanship; an erosion is only erosion if it is an effect of wind and water; a day is only a day if it is an effect of earth and sun.

*Immanence and final causation.* Thus the analysis of a feeling reveals two most important features of causal efficacy that are not found in the materialist conception of causation: immanence and final causation. The materialist conception of causation is that of strictly efficient cause determining the behavior of mere material. It is the conception of causes as external forces acting on enduring bodies. In the words of Einstein: "The great achievements of mechanics . . . contributed to the belief that it IS possible to describe all natural phenomena in terms of simple forces between unalterable objects."[76] The forces and the bodies too are conceived as external to each other, and final causation does not enter into their behavior.

But we have seen that Whiteheadian causal efficacy is very different. An occasion is a concrescence of its many feelings; the data of the feelings, their efficient causes, are immanent in the feelings and inextricable from them as is the final causation provided by their mutual subjective aim. Causal efficacy cannot be reduced to a simple formula of one cause, a force instigated by one thing, determining an action of another thing, both things and the force external and unessential to one another's substantial subsistence. A single Whiteheadian feeling is only partially causal of an occasion, and it is also partially an effect of its initial data and partially an effect of the occasion's final cause. A feeling is a partial occasion and not an accident that happened to one nor a superfluous action executed by an enduring body. "A prehension reproduces in itself the general characteristics of an actual entity: it is referent to an external world, and in this sense will be said to have a 'vector character'; it involves emotion, and purpose, and valuation, and causation."[77]

The vector character of feeling indicates its combination of immanence and final causation. "Feelings are 'vectors'; for they feel what is *there* and transform it into what is *here*."[78] The data are what are there and the subject is what is here: the data are not complete, efficient determinants of what the subject is because final causation enters into their transition. The data determine the available content of a subject, but not its reactions, its style of reception, or its usage. "In the phraseology of physics, this primitive experience is 'vector feeling,' that is to say, feeling from a beyond which is determinate and pointing to a beyond which is to be determined."[79] The beyond is not completely determined by the before; final causation in the present is required to complete the picture. The data have direction and efficacy; but they do not by themselves determine their effect which is the completed subject except as they acquire its purposes in their transition from cause to effect. "The vector character of the datum is this causal efficacy."[80]

Then feelings are vectors in their transference of aspects of antecedent occasions to a present occasion experiencing them.

The operations of an organism are directed towards the organism as a 'superject,' and are not directed from the organism as a 'subject.' The operations are directed *from* antecedent organisms and *to* the immediate organism. They are 'vectors' in that they convey the many things into the constitution of the single superject.[81]

The aspects of the antecedent organisms conveyed into the present experiencing subject are objects with respect to it. Whiteheadian causal efficacy entails an object-to-subject structure of nature, the many objects transforming into the one subject.

> Immanence is at once the doctrine of the unity of nature, and of the unity of each human life. The conclusion follows that our consciousness of the self-identity pervading our life-thread of occasions, is nothing other than knowledge of a special strand of unity within the general unity of nature. It is a locus within the whole, marked out by its own peculiarities, but otherwise exhibiting the general principle which guides the constitution of the whole. This general principle is the object-to-subject structure of experience. It can be otherwise stated as the vector-structure of nature. Or otherwise, it can be conceived as the doctrine of the immanence of the past energizing in the present.[82]

This passage speaks again of human experience as the standard by which we may know the general principles of all occasions. And it shows again the way in which one occasion also composes a nexus. The "life-thread" of occasions of this passage is the "stream of experience" of the togetherness passage. The occasions of this thread compose a "special strand" of unity, which unity is considered a single locus within the whole of nature. Just as its objects are immanent in their subject as the data of its feelings, so is the nexus which is thereby formed with the subject and these antecedent occasions it has prehended. In prehending its objects, aspects of antecedent occasions, a subject is in relationship with them and this is a nexus. The subject, composed of this nexus, its relations to antecedent occasions, occupies a single locus, a single spatiotemporal unit. Thus, a locus is no empty moment or empty space, and neither is it defined by only one thing, but encompasses a nexus and an occasion. "A feeling is the agency by which other things are built into the constitution of its one subject in process of concrescence. Feelings are constitutive of the nexus by reason of which the universe finds its unification ever renewed by novel concrescence."[83] Thus, we see feelings constituting not only an occasion, but a nexus within it, immanent in it.

*Merits of the terminology.* The merits of the Whiteheadian terminology for expressing the organic philosophy are evident from this discussion of feeling. Immanence of cause in effect and a factor of final causation are more readily suggested in the term "causal efficacy" than in "causation" with its mechanistic and deterministic connotations. A feeling has been described by Whitehead as one cause and effect transition, including both cause and effect, and in all amounting to the subject in part. Here is a comparable description of a feeling, but without so much as using the terms "cause," "causation," or "effect":

> Each actual entity is conceived as an act of experience arising out of data. It is a process of 'feeling' the many data, so as to absorb them into the unity of one individual 'satisfaction.' Here 'feeling' is the term used for the basic generic operation of passing from the objectivity of the data to the subjectivity of the actual entity in question. Feelings are variously specialized operations, effecting a transition into subjectivity.[84]

A transition from objectivity to subjectivity, a subjectivity that is an experience by virtue of its many feelings culminating in a satisfaction, this is the Whiteheadian way of depicting causation, far removed from the classical materialist description that Einstein helped to replace: "In the kinetic theory of matter and in all its important achievements we see the realization of the general philosophical program: to reduce the explanation of all phenomena to the interaction between particles of matter."[85]

The term "experience" allows for the participation of final causation in a material content, and suggests the individuality and uniqueness accorded each subject, whereas "effect" does not. Also, an experience is evidently a complex occurrence arising out of many causes, whereas an effect is not necessarily so in our customary conception of it. An experience cannot be accounted for without all of its aspects taken together; and no one aspect of it makes any sense outside of its context in that experience. But in the materialist conception each cause has a determinate effect such that there is no indetermination making room for final causation.

The Whiteheadian conception of prehension echoes Leibniz' theory of imperceptible perceptions.[86] It allows for the immanence of cause in effect, and suggests the partial nature of its activity in relation to a prehending subject. A prehension and a feeling are evidently nothing in and by themselves without a prehender and a feeler; whereas cause and effect in our conception need not be experienced and integrated with other causes and effects to be what they are. The terms "prehension" and "feeling" suggest purposeful activity, guided process, informed experience, self-fulfilling action that are part and parcel of a unified experience rather than external forces perpetrated on permanent particles of matter. All told, "feeling" is the appropriate term for conveying the ideas of immanence and final causation that causal efficacy requires. "The word 'feeling' has the merit of preserving this double significance of subjective form and of the apprehension of an object."[87] The Whiteheadian vocabulary is well designed to accommodate the Whiteheadian ideas. Its plethora of neologisms is every indication that new ideas are at hand; ". . . an outcry as to neologisms is a measure of unconscious dogmatism."[88]

## THE RELATIVITY OF OCCASIONS

*The principle of process.* The Categories of Explanation are the cohesive framework of principles and definitions that systematize the Whiteheadian metaphysical ideas. Three of these principles stand out especially as formulations of causal efficacy: the principle of process, the ontological principle, and the principle of relativity. Because these principles describe causal efficacy they are also the key principles of Whiteheadian time. Time and causal efficacy are aspects of one another. "The idea of temporal transition can never be wholly disengaged from that of 'causation'. This latter notion is merely a special way of considering direct immanence of the past in its future."[89]

The ontological principle maintains that there can be no time but that of actual occasions. It specifies actual occasions be the only temporal units, as opposed to instants of an absolute time external to the occasions. "There is nothing to which the term 'temporal' can refer except the actual occasion itself."[90] And the principle of relativity maintains that there be a succession of actual occasions. These successions are the nexūs and societies that form all the spacetime systems of our cosmic epoch, and, blending together as they cross paths, give us the impression of an absolute and instantaneous spacetime. And the principle of process maintains that an occasion be a unification of temporal sequences of other occasions: its past arising from antecedent occasions is part of its present. So the ontological principle places time within the occasion, the principle of relativity sees to its continuation in sequences of occasions, and the principle of process sees that sequences also converge in one occasion. The three principles are compressed in this one passage: "Supersession is a three-way process. Each occasion supersedes other occasions, it is superseded by other occasions, and it is internally a process of supersession, in part potential and in part actual."[91] Time is the supersession of occasions, and has the three key

characteristics: relativity in being superseded by other occasions, ontology in itself superseding other occasions, and process in unifying supersessions.
The principle of process is stated in this way:

> (ix) That *how* an actual entity *becomes* constitutes *what* that actual entity *is*; so that the two descriptions of an actual entity are not independent. Its 'being' is constituted by its 'becoming.' This is the 'principle of process.'[92]

That an occasion's being is constituted by its becoming reiterates the immanence of cause in effect that distinguishes causal efficacy. An occasion comes into being out of its causes, efficient and final; efficient causation is its becoming, final causation is the how of its becoming. That an occasion should be constituted by its becoming shows that it is a process and not a substance. This principle insures that an occasion is nothing over and above its becoming: it is the antithesis of substantial subsistence. An occasion is not an enduring thing which happens to change qualities or become unessentially affected. It is not something already there which is then acted upon: it *is* this action of causal efficacy that brings it into being. Its process of becoming is what it is and all it is.

*The ontological principle.* That causal efficacy is the very heart of the philosophy is evidenced in the ontological principle wherein actuality is defined by its causal efficacy. It reads:

> (xviii) That every condition to which the process of becoming conforms in any particular instance has its reason *either* in the character of some actual entity in the actual world of that concrescence, *or* in the character of the subject which is in process of concrescence. This category of explanation is termed the 'ontological principle.' It could also be termed the 'principle of efficient, and final, causation.' This ontological principle means that actual entities are the only *reasons*; so that to search for a *reason* is to search for one or more actual entities. It follows that any condition to be satisfied by one actual entity in its process expresses a fact either about the 'real internal constitutions' of some other actual entities, or about the 'subjective aim' conditioning that process.[93]

Then here is the principle of efficient and final causation, that is, causal efficacy. Every characteristic of an occasion is a consequence of the efficient causation of antecedent occasions (occasions of its actual world) or of its own final causation (its subjective aim). Therefore, everything about an occasion to be explained is a fact about antecedent, efficacious occasions or about itself. "Every explanatory fact refers to the decision and to the efficacy of an actual thing."[94] There is no character of an occasion that is not caused or explained by some character of an occasion, another or itself. In the plural, the principle means that actual occasions are the causes and reasons for everything. Then efficient and final causes are not the powers of two different kinds of actuality, such as a mere material and a mere mind, or matter and God; but all that is effective has its source in actual occasions.

This includes time. The temporality of an occasion is to be explained only by reference to its antecedents and to its own inner purpose, not by reference to an independent absolute time outside the occasion. "According to the ontological principle there is nothing which floats into the world from nowhere. . . . It is either transmitted from an actual entity in the past, or belongs to the subjective aim of the actual entity to whose concrescence it belongs."[95] Temporal duration of a present occasion depends upon past occasions and its own subjective aim. The ontological principle means that an occasion only develops inasmuch as it supersedes other occasions, its efficacious antecedents.

The ontological principle affords another definition of actuality: "The philosophy of organism extends the Cartesian subjectivism by affirming the 'ontological principle' and by construing it as the definition of 'actuality.'"[96] The ontological principle so construed as to yield a definition of actuality reads thus: ". . . that actual occasions form the ground from which all other types of existence are derivative and abstracted. . . ."[97] And all other types of existence are derived by and for actual occasions. In other words, actuality as defined by the ontological principle is that which is causally efficacious; or, that which is caused is a factor of actuality. Causal efficacy is both efficient *and* final. Both what is caused and what causes are actual occasions or factors thereof. Then actuality is defined by its causal efficacy; but we have found it before to be defined as that which is composite. And in fact there are a number of definitions of actuality extant in the philosophy. For example, an actuality is that which is self-realizing, as well as that which is concrete; and it means definiteness, as well as decision amid potentiality; and it is also the characterization of creativity.[98] These various definitions of actuality are a natural reflection of the complex, multifaceted nature of actual occasions. The manifold descriptions of actual occasions abounding in the philosophy inundate this book as well. But it is certain that however actuality be defined and however the actual occasion be described, it may be experienced. ". . . nothing is to be received into the philosophical scheme which is not discoverable as an element in subjective experience. This is the ontological principle."[99] The ontological principle has turned into the reformed subjectivist principle. And since the ontological principle is the principle of causal efficacy, this means that causal efficacy must be discoverable in subjective experience. For Whitehead, we have direct experience of causation; for we, as actual human occasions, are a consequence of the causal efficacy of others and ourselves..

*The observation of efficacy.* Thus, these principles and definitions have the advantage of avoiding an irreparable dualism of substance and of causation, but they were not conceived solely to perform this unification for philosophy. They are speculations based on experience. The experience in particular is this: that nothing has been observed which was found to be utterly incapable of causing or of being affected. Causal efficacy is the observed nature of every occasion observed, by that very observation: the occasion has had sufficient efficacy upon us so as to be observed. Observed occasions have at least that causal efficacy: observability, palpability. The degree of palpability among occasions differs vastly; but nonetheless, some degree is warranted. Just as there may be a least complex type of occasion, but none simple, so there may be a least palpable type of occasion, but none impalpable. It may have reflected light, left a track, absorbed a stain, made a sound, produced an odor, attracted a current, repulsed a particle; whatever be its efficacy, it cannot *be* without it. The more and the less palpable have their different styles of efficacy, but all have some. "Sometimes we see an elephant, and sometimes we do not. The result is that an elephant, when present, is noticed."[100]

Whether occasions are observed to affect one another or to affect our own perception of them, they are observed. Occasions that are not ordinarily palpable to our sense-perceptions are led into palpability by ingenious experiments. The experiments show that the ordinarily invisible ones do have some type of efficacy such that we may claim they concretely exist. This fact, that nothing whatever has been observed utterly inefficacious or utterly unaffectable in every way, is what Whitehead is saying here:

> But the philosophy of organism attributes 'feeling' throughout the actual world. It bases this doctrine upon the directly observed fact that 'feeling' survives as a known element constitutive of the 'formal' existence of such actual entities as we can best observe.[101]

*The principle of relativity.* The principle of relativity is the other side of the ontological principle. All the categories of explanation are interrelated.

But these two principles, along with two others, ". . . state different aspects of one and the same general metaphysical truth."[102] The principle of relativity is as follows:

> (iv) That the potentiality for being an element in a real concrescence of many entities into one actuality is the one general metaphysical character attaching to all entities, actual and non-actual; and that every item in its universe is involved in each concrescence. In other words, it belongs to the nature of a 'being' that it is a potentiality for every 'becoming.' This is the 'principle of relativity.'[103]

The observed efficacy of all occasions just mentioned is formulated in this principle. It states that all entities are creative such that they contribute to the becoming of new occasions. There is no occasion utterly inefficacious, inert, uncreative; there is no occasion so lacking in potentiality that it does not concresce with others into new occasions. The principle of relativity is the principle of the real potentiality of every entity. Every entity in existence is endowed with real potentiality for further creation beyond itself; it has the capacity to engage in any other process and thereby partially effect a new occasion. "It asserts that the notion of an 'entity' means 'an element contributory to the process of becoming.' We have in this category the utmost generalization of the notion of 'relativity.'"[104]

Then what the principle of relativity does is to universalize the efficacy of each entity. Every occasion potentially effects every other occasion. Each occasion is efficacious for a plurality of occasions, not just one. If it exists at all, it is potentially efficacious for all other existences to come. Its efficacy never ends. It differs in different occasions and is negligible in some and eliminated in others through negative prehension. But it goes on to concresce in occasion after occasion, whatever be its fate therein. Each occasion comes to have universal efficacy as it effects further and further occasions. An entity is a real potentiality for *every* becoming, not just one. There is no occasion coming into being with which it is impossible to relate. Any occasion has the potentiality to engage in relationship with any other occasion coming into being. This universalization of efficacy makes of an occasion a field. The occasion has a real potentiality for every becoming in its neighborhood. It cannot contribute to the becoming of its own contemporaries, that is, occasions for which it has no causal efficacy; but for all occasions of its neighborhood becoming after itself it has real potentiality for partially effecting them. Each occasion is a field of potential efficacy; and it acts to partially effect each occasion becoming in its field.

*The rescue from monism.* The real potentiality addressed in the principle of relativity makes all the difference between this organic philosophy and substance philosophies. Substances are already actual; not so the actual occasions. Occasions achieve actuality upon the satisfaction of their concrescence; and having become actual, they become also real potentials for subsequent concrescence. Whitehead regards all substance philosophies, whether they afford one substance or a plurality of substances, as monistic. For, all substance philosophies assume that the subject-predicate type of statement conveys the basic truth about reality: ". . . every respectable philosophy of the subject-predicate type is monistic."[105] A quality is predicated of a substance that is already actual in every respect, with no chance of its essentially becoming another kind of thing. A monistic universe is that wherein all substance, whether one or many, is wholly actual, already fully realized. The Whiteheadian universe is characterized rather by potentiality. "The alternative is a static monistic universe, without unrealized potentialities; since 'potentiality' is then a meaningless term."[106]

The ontological principle alone does not prevent the actual occasions from terminating in one entirely actual, static, completed, timeless occasion. The ontological principle stipulates that whatever occasions there are have their causes, efficient and final, in occasions. But all the occasions could theoretically have their effect upon one single occasion; it is possible that all be felt by one and the same hypothetical actual occasion. This final occasion would have its causes in these occasions, and in itself as *causa sui*. The ontological principle has not been violated, and a final, completely actual, static occasion reigns in a monistic universe.

There is nothing in the ontological principle to prevent there being such a last occasion, a final actuality wherein no further creation occurred, no potentiality was channeled into new concrescence. The fact that whatever conditions there are owe their causes and reasons to factors of occasions does not itself discourage the monism of a last condition. "A mere system of mutually prehensive occasions is compatible with the concept of a static timeless world."[107] It is the principle of relativity that secures the continued succession of occasions. "The principle of relativity is the axiom by which the ontological principle is rescued from issuing in an extreme monism."[108] For, all occasions have the real potentiality for entering into the becoming of new occasions. It is the principle of relativity that realizes a plurality of successions of occasions.

In this way, a final, static, timeless, wholly actual monistic universe is prohibited. For even such a hypothetical last occasion must become a cause, not simply of itself, but potentially of every other occasion of the universe— its universe in this case. This occasion must have the capability of entering into the new becomings of all the other occasions of the universe, as they must also have the capability of entering into a new becoming with this one occasion. All occasions have the real potentiality for entering into the becoming of every other occasion. This includes God. God does not escape the principle of relativity. "But the principle of universal relativity is not to be stopped at the consequent nature of God. This nature itself passes into the temporal world according to its gradation of relevance to the various concrescent occasions."[109]

A hypothetical final occasion must become available as a potential cause for, and constituent in, all other occasions, which in this case have constituted it. These occasions must themselves be processes such that they may concresce into new occasions. They too must be potential causes not only of one occasion but of all other occasions as well. All occasions have potential efficacy for any and all, not just one. "It follows that every item of the universe, including all the other actual entities, is a constituent in the constitution of any one actual entity. This conclusion has already been employed under the title of the 'principle of relativity.'"[110] Every occasion is a potential constituent of every other occasion, and an actual constituent of some other occasions. Its causal efficacy is never finished.

*Subjective immediacy and objective immortality.* Actual occasions become and perish. "This is the doctrine that the creative advance of the world is the becoming, the perishing, and the objective immortalities of those things which jointly constitute *stubborn fact.*"[111] In perishing occasions acquire objective immortality; that is, their real potentiality for effect is immortal. Once an occasion has come into being, its efficacy for further creation thereafter is immortal. It is a contributing cause of occasion after occasion, forever. Objective immortality is that ". . . whereby what is divested of its own living immediacy becomes a real component in other living immediacies of becoming."[112] There are a virtual infinity of living immediacies beyond that of any one occasion and in which it may become a component.

Living immediacy is enjoyed by an occasion as a subject; immortality is its fate as an object. Immediacy refers to the self-functioning capacity of a subject, its inherent final causation, and the mortality of this.

(xxi) An entity is actual, when it has significance for itself. By this it is meant that an actual entity functions in respect to its own determination. . . . (xxiii) That this self-functioning is the real internal constitution of an actual entity. It is the 'immediacy' of the actual entity. An actual entity is called the 'subject' of its own immediacy.[113]

Because the self-functioning, final causation of an occasion terminates with its satisfaction, immediacy also refers to the mortality of the occasion *qua* subject. The subject enjoys its present experience once and once only; and the occasion is the subject that it is once and once only. Its present, and the present subject, is immediate because it does not endure but perishes. Immediacy is not to be confused with brevity, momentariness, or short-lived experience. It is the duration of self-functioning, whatever it be. Subjective immediacy or living immediacy perish upon the subject's complete concrescence and is lost and gone forever; it need not have been short-lived, but it cannot live beyond concrescence. "Completion is the perishing of immediacy. . . ."[114] Subjective immediacy, then, is the perishable, mortal self-determination, self-functioning state of a subject.

But the loss of subjectivity is the gain of objectivity. The occasion loses final causation and gains efficient causation as it is turns from subject to object. "Actuality in perishing acquires objectivity, while it loses subjective immediacy. It loses the final causation which is its internal principle of unrest, and it acquires efficient causation whereby it is a ground of obligation characterizing the creativity."[115] And the occasion, *qua* object, is immortal. "The creature perishes *and* is immortal. The actual entities beyond it can say, 'It is mine.'"[116]

Objective immortality must not be identified with substantial endurance. It is immortal inasmuch as it has real potentiality for partially effecting subsequent occasions. It has manifold potentialities such that its engagement in the processes of different subsequent occasions activates and actualizes different potentialities; it cannot even be identified with one of its potentialities but must be identified with all. An objectively immortal occasion does not endure a singular object, numerically one; it has a different effect in every occasion prehending it and succeeding it. Its influence is spread about. And the object *is* this influence; it *is* its efficacy in successors, not a singular enduring thing that may happen to have influence on other things. It is the object's efficacy in subsequent creation that is immortal, not the self-same object itself.

An occasion becomes not one object, but many, as many objects as occasions in which it has effect. For, the occasion *qua* object *is* that which succeeding occasions prehend and constitute themselves of. An occasion as object is its multiple efficacy in a virtual infinity of occasions succeeding its own creation. It is the principle or relativity that describes a perished occasion as a multiple object; the occasion is a potential for *every* becoming thereafter. The occasion is an object for each becoming it enters into. No object endures the same through all succeeding occasions; but its efficacy for each new successor differs according to its particular real potentiality for that successor and according to its efficacy in the successor's antecedents from which the successor prehends the object. A succeeding occasion must prehend an object as a part of its own antecedents and not otherwise. We must look at the remains of ancient Rome through modern air pollution, which affects it and us. Ancient Rome, the living imperial city, has not endured. Its effects are scattered throughout the world. These effects are it, are all we know of ancient Rome. There is no substantial Rome above and beyond its efficacy today. Its effects today are devoid of its ancient living immediacy, the Rome that perished. But all its effects in subsequent experience taken together are the immortal Rome, Rome as multiple objects for prehension, Rome as objective.

It can be seen that Whitehead intends no ontological distinction between subjects and objects. It is the subject that, upon perishing, becomes objects. It is the objects that, upon concrescing in one occasion, constitute a subject. "The word 'object' thus means an entity which is a potentiality for being a component in feeling; and the word 'subject' means the entity constituted by the process of feeling, and including this process."[117] Then "object" and "subject" do not designate two disjunctive kinds of substances, the one known, the other knowing, since they change places in becoming. A subject becomes an object for another subject, and objects united together by one aim become a subject. "Thus subject and object are relative terms."[118] And objects are relative to their particular efficacy for subjects. An object's effect depends upon the subject; it differs in differing subjects according as which of its real potentialities is utilized there. An object has the potential to partially effect *any* other occasion. This means that it has diverse real potentialities such that no succeeding occasion could fail utterly to engage it in relationship, either positively or negatively. An electron has some efficacy for an elephant, as has an elephant for an electron. But what the objects are for the diverse subjects differs with the subjects.

*Microscopic and macroscopic process.* We have seen that a subject occasion is a process: it is a process of feeling, a process of becoming, a process of concrescence, a creative process. But Whitehead describes objects as in process also. The transformation of objects into the constitution of new subjects is one side of process, the becoming of subjects is another side. He calls these two sides of process "two kinds of fluency."[119] There is the fluency of subjects coming into being, and the fluency of the immortal careers of objects as they transform into aspects of subjects. Unfortunately, however, Whitehead also calls the two sides of process two "species" of process, the "microscopic process" and the "macroscopic process."

There are two species of process, macroscopic process, and microscopic process. The macroscopic process is the transition from attained actuality to actuality in attainment; while the microscopic process is the conversion of conditions which are merely real into determinate actuality. The former process effects the transition from the 'actual' to the 'merely real'; and the latter process effects the growth from the real to the actual. The former process is efficient; the latter process is teleological.[120]

Thus, the efficient causation of objects and the final causation of subjects are treated as two species of process which might be thought to apply to two different kinds of things, small things and large things, or occasions and societies. But there are not two species of actual occasions so that one species of process does not apply to one of the species of occasions. Both species of process apply to all occasions coming into being. There is no macroscopic process outside of the microscopic becoming of occasions. Macroscopic process applies to the becoming of occasions as does the microscopic, but refers to the efficient side of the becoming, that deriving from its objects, rather than the final side deriving from the subject. The terms are unfortunate, however, in their implication of size. "Microscopic process" seems to imply the becoming of a small thing; "macroscopic process" is likely to imply the becoming of a large thing, or perhaps the becoming of a society.

However, this is not Whitehead's intention. Microscopic and macroscopic are meant to suggest privacy, internality, subjectivity, togetherness, unity, and singularity on the one hand, and publicity, externality, objectivity, disjunction, plurality, and multiplicity on the other hand. The microscopic process is subjective; the macroscopic process is objective, and constitutes the objective content of the subject.

In the philosophy of organism it is held that the notion of 'organism' has two meanings, interconnected but intellectually separable, namely, the microscopic meaning and the macroscopic meaning. The microscopic meaning is concerned with the formal constitution of an actual occasion, considered as a process of realizing an individual unity of experience. The macroscopic meaning is concerned with the givenness of the actual world, considered as the stubborn fact which at once limits and provides opportunity for the actual occasion.[121]

The terms "microscopic" and "macroscopic," then, refer to subjectivity and objectivity, both of which are aspects of each occasion, not to smallness and largeness, or simplicity and complexity. Microscopic and macroscopic are "two meanings of 'organism'" that are "intellectually separable" aspects of process: not actually separate processes applying to two separate kinds of things or two different sizes of actualities. These two species of process are two sides of the one process of becoming. Similarly, "microcosmic" and "macrocosmic" do not refer to size or to the distinction between occasions and societies. "The initial fact is macrocosmic, in the sense of having equal relevance to all occasions; the final fact is microcosmic, in the sense of being peculiar to that occasion."[122] A microcosmic fact is a unique, individual, and mortal fact. A macrocosmic fact is a fact of plural, immortal, creative efficacy for the indefinite future.

Subjects are microscopic and microcosmic in their self-absorption, self-functioning, self-creation, and mortality: they are relevant to themselves rather than others. They prehend others but are unprehended. Objects are macroscopic and macrocosmic in their other-directedness, other-functioning, other-creation, and immortality: their relevancy is for others rather than themselves. And subjects are microscopic in that their immediacy is exhausted in the one occasion; objects are macroscopic in that their potentiality is not exhausted by any one subject in which they have effect but extends to an infinity of subjects beyond in which they will have efficacy.

*Whitehead misinterpreted.* The Whiteheadian terminology in this case lends itself to an atomistic interpretation of occasions. V. C. Chappell writes: "The composite sort of process Whitehead calls 'macroscopic,' or the 'process of transition'; the unit sort he calls 'microscopic,' or the 'process of concrescence.'"[123] And Chappell speaks of "macroscopic becoming" referring to the becoming of a large and composite thing.[124] Chappell distinguishes microscopic and macroscopic process on the basis of size and alleged simplicity: as though microscopic process were the coming into being of allegedly simple and elementary particles; and as though the macroscopic process were the coming into being of the compounds (or societies) of these. In fact Chappell thinks that the distinction between these two processes as supposedly applying to two different kinds of actualities, the simple and the compound, accounts for the epochal theory of time: "And this . . . is just the epochal theory of time."[125] But there is no such thing in Whitehead as "macroscopic becoming." There is only macroscopic process, which is one meaning of organism, not the becoming of a special kind of organism, large and complex.

And David Ray Griffin too identifies macroscopic process with large and compound things, societies of simpler things. He speaks of "macroscopic societies" and "macroscopic things": "[Whitehead] does this with his idea of two basic ways in which enduring objects can be organized into macroscopic societies. . . . On the other hand, some macroscopic things have self-determination."[126] But microscopic and macroscopic do not distinguish occasions from societies of occasions; macroscopic process is not the becoming of "macroscopic things." Microscopic process is that of final causation, and macroscopic process is efficient, which means that Griffin's "macroscopic societies" come into being only by virtue of efficient causation. This is the scientific materialist conception of societies and their causation, a conception that wrongs every Whiteheadian society.

And Ivor Leclerc tells us:

> ['Vacuous actuality'] is a generalization from entities which are not *actual* entities. These entities are the macroscopic objects presented to us in sense perception, the 'physical bodies' of common sense. . . .
> Whitehead rejects the view that they are *actual* entities; they are, he holds, entities constituted by *multiplicities* of actual entities. Now for practical everyday purposes we habitually treat a multiplicity as one single thing; and for practical purposes this is perfectly legitimate. The trouble is, however, that because of this habitual treatment, we are apt to overlook the fact that the single entity constituted by a multiplicity is an *abstract* entity.[127]

Thus, Leclerc says that the "macroscopic objects" and "physical bodies" of our acquaintance are not actual entities, but multiplicities of presumably elementary particles. He is using "macroscopic" to mean large and compound; and he is using "actual" to mean not only concrete but also small and simple. This is the reason he cannot regard the large scale bodies as actual entities, though Whitehead includes them in his list of grades of actual entities. On this view, the "us" that he refers to ("objects are presented to 'us' in sense-perception") and the "we" ("'we' overlook") are also "abstract entities" since we are also large scale, compound "physical bodies." Being "abstract entities" and not ourselves at any moment actual entities, then, there is no possibility of sense-perception for us, or of any other type of prehending, such as "overlooking a fact" or "habitually treating" anything.

For Whitehead, however, the large scale material bodies of our acquaintance are actual occasions at any moment in their life-histories. Neither these moments nor the life-histories they comprise are abstract.

If all microscopic processes are those of allegedly elementary particles and consequently all that comes into being are supposedly elementary particles, then all the large bodies of our acquaintance, elephants, Rome, trees, stars, chairs, rocks, and we ourselves can only be illusion on the part of elementary particles. The identification of actuality with small and simple entities relegates the rest of reality to the status of illusion on the part of such small and simple actual entities. The aggregating elementary entities must become, apparently, illusions of large and complex bodies and illusions of large creatures such as ourselves with such illusions: for the elementary entities cannot themselves become the large and complex bodies or societies, for they are small and simple. Such distortions of meaning amount to a travesty of the Whiteheadian philosophy.

## SOCIETIES

*Social classification.* The interrelatedness of all occasions by virtue of their prehensions of one another, so that all successor occasions are constituted of aspects of their predecessors, makes occasions social. "Every actual entity is in its nature essentially social. . . ."[128] This sociability means that an occasion belongs to a nexus and is also composed of the antecedent members of the nexus whose aspects have caused and constituted it. There are two types of nexūs, the non-social and the social, including the personal. The non-social nexus is a chaos: "A non-social nexus is what answers to the notion of 'chaos.'"[129] And the social nexus is a society. "A 'society,' in the sense in which that term is here used, is a nexus with social order. . . ."[130]

Just as Whitehead distinguishes grades of occasions, he distinguishes types of societies based on increasing degrees of complexity. For example, he posits the extensive continuum, which includes both extensive and geometrical societies; and structured societies, both specialized and unspecialized; enduring objects; and both corpuscular and non-corpuscular societies.[131] Both the grade of occasion and the type of society it belongs to are classifications according to types of order. "We now pass on to the general notion of a *Society.* This notion introduces the general consideration of types of order, and the genetic propagation of order."[132] The higher the grade of occasion, the more complex; the higher the type of society, the more complex a structure it sustains and transmits from one member to another. A complex society should also be sufficiently stable so that it lasts as a society, continuing to reproduce its complex structure through very many member occasions. "Thus the problem for Nature is the production of societies which are 'structured' with a high 'complexity', and which are at the same time 'unspecialized'. In this way, intensity is mated with survival."[133]

A society is a succession of like occasions: all members of the society have some specific character or characters in common with their fellows, which characteristics define the society. But a society is not what might be thought of as simply a class of like occasions, because the likeness has to be inherited through the membership as successors prehend their predecessors. It is the causal efficacy of like occasions that creates societies. When the important defining characteristics which make the society what it is no longer appears in, or no longer has importance for, succeeding occasions, that society has come to an end.

The point of a 'society,' as the term is here used, is that it is self-sustaining; in other words, that it is its own reason. Thus a society is more than a set of entities to which the same class-name applies: that is to say, it involves more than a merely mathematical conception of 'order.' To constitute a society, the class-name has got to apply to each member, by reason of genetic derivation from other members of that same society. The members of the society are alike because, by reason of their common character, they impose on other members of the society the conditions which lead to that likeness.[134]

*The coordination of societies.* An occasion may be a member of numerous societies; and members of numerous societies may be aspects of its own constitution. There are societies of societies of societies, all intimately related.

The Universe achieves its values by reason of its coordination into societies of societies, and in societies of societies of societies. Thus an army is a society of regiments, and regiments are societies of men, and men are societies of cells, and of blood, and of bones, together with the dominant society of personal human experience, and cells are societies of small physical entities such as protons, and so on, and so on.[135]

A structured society is one that includes other entire societies. These wider, inclusive societies are the environment of the more specialized societies subordinated to them. These more specialized and more complex societies depend for their survival upon the wider and less complex societies that make up their environment.

> The notion of a society which includes subordinate societies and nexūs with a definite pattern of structural inter-relations must be introduced. Such societies will be termed 'structured.' A structured society as a whole provides a favourable environment for the subordinate societies which it harbours within itself. Also the whole society must be set in a wider environment permissive of its continuance.[136]

The subordinate and more specialized societies can only be within or included in the wider societies if they are a real part of them. The societies are all interrelated and coordinated so that the functioning of one affects that of the others.

> But there is no society in isolation. Every society must be considered with its background of a wider environment of actual entities, which also contribute their objectifications to which the members of the society must conform. . . . Thus we arrive at the principle that every society requires a social background, of which it is itself a part.[137]

Human beings require the social background of their cultures, and mammalian animals, and land animals, and vertebrates, sense-perceiving animals, living creatures, molecules, an oxygen atmosphere, a watered earth, electromagnetic occasions, and green plants, for example, to be what they are and survive.

The many types of societies are within one another, pervading one another, and coordinated with one another because members of one society prehend and "conform to" antecedent members of other societies, as well as their own. Societies cross paths as they jointly contribute to the constitution of individual occasions; the societies are therein modified just as are the occasions. Societies are no more dissociated from one another than are occasions. Just as occasions of one type influence each other as members of the same society, so do occasions of different types that make up the different types of societies. "It follows from this doctrine that the character of an organism depends on that of its environment. But the character of an environment is the sum of the characters of the various societies of actual entities which jointly constitute that environment. . . ."[138]

Thus, societies of occasions of all grades and types and sizes and temporal durations are coordinated, and this because the members of one society prehend members of others. But prehending members of different societies does not involve sharing all the important characteristics of those societies, though some characteristics will be shared inasmuch as they are positively efficacious. Occasions of one society are modified by their prehensions of those of others; but they need not be so modified as to forfeit the defining characteristics of their membership in one society, as long as it is still extant. For example, "Also the functionings of inorganic matter remain intact amid the functionings of living matter."[139] They remain intact, so that the member occasions of the inorganic societies perpetuate their defining characteristics, as do the organic societies, though each nevertheless affects the other to some extent. Thus, for example, "The molecules within an animal body exhibit certain peculiarities of behaviour not to be detected outside an animal body."[140] The molecules amid all the societies making up an animal body are modified; nevertheless, they retain the characteristics defining them as members of specific molecular societies.

There would be no coordination of societies, then, but that occasions of different grades and types prehend one another so that aspects of one type of occasion are ingredient in another type. In the following passage, for example, Whitehead speaks of a cell as having aspects in a molecule, as well as in "some subtler entity." Then the lower grade occasion, the molecule, prehends the higher grade living cell: the cell consequently is an aspect of the molecule's constitution, however insignificant.

It is true that each molecule is affected by the aspect of this pattern [of the complete living organism] as mirrored in it, so as to be otherwise than what it would have been if placed elsewhere. . . . In the same way, in a magnetic field soft iron exhibits magnetic properties which are in abeyance elsewhere. . . . It would, however, be entirely in consonance with the empirically observed action of environments, if the direct effects of aspects as between the whole body and its parts were negligible. We should expect transmission. In this way the modification of total pattern would transmit itself by means of a series of modifications of a descending series of parts, so that finally the modification of the cell changes its aspect in the molecule, thus effecting a corresponding alteration in the molecule—or some subtler entity.[141]

Similarly, a city has affect upon any person in it, just as a person has affect upon the city. But their modifications of one another are transmitted through intermediate occasions.

Therefore, societies are coordinated in occasions: they are necessarily coordinated at those occasions wherein they are prehended, as the occasions form a nexus with all the antecedent occasions, of whatever society, they prehend. The result of the coordination of societies for people is "a peculiar richness of inheritance": "In a living body of a high type there are grades of occasions so coordinated by their paths of inheritance through the body, that a peculiar richness of inheritance is enjoyed by various occasions in some parts of the body."[142] And these occasions enjoying a rich experience derived from many grades of occasions available in the body return their effect to the other bodily occasions as well. "In its turn, this culmination of bodily life transmits itself as an element of novelty throughout the avenues of the body."[143] This rich inheritance and returned influence could not be enjoyed but that the occasions involved prehend occasions of different grades from different societies. And new societies only evolve by the combination of characteristics of present societies in the same occasions. Here again Whitehead speaks of societies merging in one occasion: "Thus in an animal body the presiding occasion, if there be one, is the final node, or intersection, of a complex structure of many enduring objects."[144] Thus, we see a single occasion as the intersection of enduring objects, which are societies. It is clear as can be, then, that Whitehead does not regard societies as mere collections of occasions that are extrinsic to the nature of the occasions.

*The electromagnetic society.* One of the very widest societies that includes and supports many subordinate societies is the electromagnetic society. Every high grade occasion, and in fact occasions of every grade, are beholden to the orderly conduct of electromagnetic occasions. Their order is that characterizing the electromagnetic society: it is adequate for the production of the electromagnetic occasions. "Thus our present epoch is dominated by a society of electromagnetic occasions."[145] New types of occasions gradually evolved from the interchange of such types of less complex societies. And having evolved, they create their own societies inasmuch as they reproduce themselves in succession and not the types of occasions they evolved from. Whitehead explains that the electromagnetic society is pervaded by more special societies which are productive of the more special, that is, more complex and higher grade, occasions:

> But in its turn, this electromagnetic society would provide no adequate order for the production of individual occasions realizing peculiar 'intensities' of experience unless it were pervaded by more special societies, vehicles of such order. The physical world exhibits a bewildering complexity of such societies, favouring each other, competing with each other.[146]

This statement is a direct denial of the atomist conception of societies that is often attributed to Whitehead. For atomism, the higher grade occasions would be mere compilations, mere multiplicities of electromagnetic occasions and the like less complex occasions. But Whitehead says that the electromagnetic society is only one of many types and that it alone does not provide the order adequate for producing more complex occasions enjoying a richer experience. That is, the electromagnetic society alone does not create the more complex, higher grade occasions. More specialized societies are required to produce the more specialized occasions. The higher grade occasions gradually evolved from less complex occasions, and evolved their own societies to recreate themselves. They cannot be directly produced by the least complex of occasions at this stage of their development. The atomist conception that electromagnetic occasions, or other subatomic occasions, can directly add up to, directly create, the occasions of high grade such as ourselves has no foundation in Whitehead's philosophy.

Whitehead mentions that the electromagnetic society is characterized by variations in physical quantities. "We here arrive at the notion of physical quantities which vary from individual to individual. . . ."[147] This indicates that all the ways in which electromagnetic occasions can differ are quantifiable, so that if there were only the electromagnetic society, there would only be quantitative differences among (electromagnetic) occasions. The defining characteristics of the electromagnetic society are quantitative, whereas the defining characteristics of other societies are qualitative. All the defining characteristics familiar to us, such as leafy, smelly, salty, bony, damp, hand-crafted, plastic, or leather characteristics help define other entire societies; none of these specific qualitative characteristics of societies can be credited to the electromagnetic society. For, such specific qualitative characteristics first come into being with the coming into being of the more complex occasions.

*Enduring objects.* One type of society that Whitehead discusses is called "enduring object." And its type of order is called "personal":

> Now, for the sake of simplicity, consider a society of the 'personal' type. Such a society will be a linear succession of actual occasions forming a historical route in which some defining characteristic is inherited by each occasion from its predecessors. A society of this sort is an 'enduring object.'[148]

Personal order, then, defines a society of serial occasions, one occasion arising from one antecedent occasion. Two conditions are required for a serial order to be personal. The first is that any member occasion must inherit from absolutely all members of the society that are past with respect to it, and none that are future; that is, it must succeed all its predecessors and precede all its successors. The second condition is that a member's relationship to other members must be transitive. This is to say that the occasions which a given member succeeds, its successors must also succeed; and the occasions which it precedes, its predecessors must also precede. If occasion *O* precedes *P, Q,* and *R,* then occasion *N,* which precedes *O,* must also precede *P, Q,* and *R.* And if occasion *O* succeeds *L, M,* and *N,* then occasion *P,* which succeeds *O,* succeeds also *L, M,* and *N.*[149] In this case the alphabet represents an enduring object.

An enduring object, being a linear, single file, serially ordered society, is obviously the model for absolute time. The entire universe is believed to be one enduring object uniformly transpiring in one absolute time which is believed to be one single file sequence of instants. Here Whitehead says that the notion of absolute time is indeed a generalization of the personal order of enduring objects, and that this common sense notion of time has been discredited only recently by modern physics.

There is a prevalent misconception that 'becoming' involves the notion of a unique seriality for its advance into novelty. This is the classic notion of 'time,' which philosophy took over from common sense. Mankind made an unfortunate generalization from its experience of enduring objects. Recently physical science has abandoned this notion.[150]

The personal order of enduring objects distinguishes this type of society from, for example, the electromagnetic society. A member of an enduring object has to inherit from absolutely all preceding members from the beginning of the society and has to be predecessor of all subsequent members to the end of the society. But this is not the case for members of the electromagnetic society: all its members are not aligned in one single file succession from the beginning to the end of the society. For this reason, this society has been described as a wide society providing background and environment for the more specialized societies such as the enduring objects. In the following passage, Whitehead explains that he thinks that light starts out as an enduring object and ends joining the wider, non-personal electromagnetic society.

In speaking of a society . . . 'membership' will always refer to the actual occasions such as the life of an electron or of a man. These latter societies are the strands of 'personal' order which enter into many societies; generally speaking, whenever we are concerned with occupied space, we are dealing with this restricted type of corpuscular societies; and whenever we are thinking of the physical field in empty space, we are dealing with societies of the wider types. It seems as if the careers of waves of light illustrate the transition from the more restricted type to the wider type.[151]

This passage also shows that the life of an electron as well as the life of a man are enduring objects. They are in fact paradigm enduring objects for the Whiteheadian philosophy since the electronic occasions and the human occasions of which they are comprised are paradigm actual occasions. As a member of an enduring object, one electronic occasion supersedes in linear succession the predecessor electronic occasions of its society. It is the entire linear succession, the enduring object, that is what we ordinarily mean by "electron" or "subatomic particle," not a single electronic occasion. This is the reason an enduring object is so named: it refers to what we ordinarily regard as substantial objects enduring through time, although they are in fact personal societies. A human body, of course, is a construction of very many enduring objects, and relies upon its environment of wider societies as well. But a person is also a single enduring object taking only his or her presiding occasion, what we ordinarily call his or her "mind," into account. "There is also an enduring object formed by the inheritance from presiding occasion to presiding occasion. This endurance of the mind is only one more example of the general principle on which the body is constructed."[152] What we ordinarily think of as a person's mind, then, is an enduring object, as well as what we think of as a personality, or simply, a person:

> . . . a more important character of order would have been that complex character in virtue of which a man is considered to be the same enduring person from birth to death. Also in this instance the members of the society are arranged in a serial order by their genetic relations. Such a society is said to possess 'personal order.'[153]

Then one presiding human occasion and one occasion of human personality are each single actual occasions; and the serial successions of these are the enduring objects we ordinarily think of as a mind or a person. Therefore, "electrons," the subatomic particles, as well as "minds" or persons are Whiteheadian personal societies. As societies they are apparent life-time endurances. That is, each such personal society appears to be one object enduring for life-time—an enduring object. "These enduring objects and 'societies,' analysable into strands of enduring objects, are the permanent entities which enjoy adventures of change throughout time and space."[154]

It must be clear that neither the occasions of an enduring object nor their orderly, serial propagation are mere appearances. What is an appearance is endurance, the apparent endurance of numerically one and the same actual occasion through time. What is an appearance is the identification of the successive occasions of an enduring object as one occasion.

In other words, a society must exhibit the peculiar quality of endurance. The real actual things that endure are all societies. They are not actual occasions. It is the mistake that has thwarted European metaphysics from the time of the Greeks, namely, to confuse societies with the completely real things which are the actual occasions.[155]

In saying that the things that endure are not actual occasions but societies (that is, enduring objects), Whitehead cannot mean that societies are not comprised of actual occasions, or that only entities of subatomic scale are actual occasions, or that all enduring things are societies only of subatomic entities. The emphasis is on endurance: "The real actual things that *endure* are all societies," not actual occasions. An actual occasion does *not* "exhibit the peculiar quality of endurance" but a society *does*. A personally ordered, serial society (enduring object) is what appears to us as one enduring thing when it is in fact a succession of actual occasions. Whitehead is not suggesting that actual occasions are necessarily small and short-lived, only that they are replaced by their fellows in succession, whatever be their own proportions.

*Material bodies.* A corpuscular society is a combination of coordinated enduring objects. "A nexus which (i) enjoys social order, and (ii) is analysable into strands of enduring objects may be termed a 'corpuscular society.'"[156] The material bodies of our acquaintance and including ourselves are corpuscular societies in that they and we are not only one enduring object, but many—all coordinated so as to form one corpuscular society. We do not ordinarily perceive or consider a single enduring object, just as we do not ordinarily perceive or consider a single actual occasion, but rather, we perceive and consider many. "What we normally consider is the wider society in which many strands of enduring objects are to be found, a 'corpuscular society.'"[157]

One example of a corpuscular society that Whitehead gives is that formed by the relationship of a person and a chair that he or she sees. Whitehead calls this corpuscular society the "real chair." Aspects of the seen chair and the person prehending it form a nexus together, which constitutes the person's percipient occasions. The chair itself is already one corpuscular society (although, in respect of some characteristics it is also one enduring object just as is a rock) and the person is another (although the person too is one enduring object in respect of his or her presiding occasions alone). Perception of the chair creates new percipient occasions, and these occasions and the chair occasions combined are another corpuscular society coordinated with the corpuscular societies that the chair and person already are. They are new members of the societies of the chair and person, the chair having faded somewhat from reflecting light and the person having perceived, now combined as the society which is the real chair as seen by the person.

> This prehension, in the particular example considered, will be termed the prehension of a 'chair-image'. . . . If there be a 'real chair,' there will be another historical route of objectifications from nexus to nexus in this environment. The members of each nexus will be mutually contemporaries. Also the historical route will lead up to the nexus which is the chair-image. The complete nexus, composed of this historical route and the chair-image, will form a 'corpuscular' society. This society is the 'real chair.'[158]

Thus the chair considered as an enduring object (historical route of occasions) forms a nexus with the person's percipient occasions that include chair images: this nexus is another corpuscular society, the real chair.

A material body may be both a corpuscular society and an enduring object. "Also each of these enduring objects, such as tables, animal bodies, and stars, is itself a subordinate universe including subordinate enduring objects."[159] As subordinate universes that combine many enduring objects, these material bodies are corpuscular societies. But Whitehead says that they are also themselves enduring objects. Then a table is a serial, single file succession of actual table occasions; an animal body, including a person, is a linear succession of actual animal occasions; a star is a personally ordered succession of actual star occasions. Because these material bodies are enduring objects whose member occasions succeed one another in single file procession, they afford examples of rather large scale actual occasions, as large as stars. A star as one enduring object is a succession of star occasions. It is the enduring object that we ordinarily mean by "star," just as an enduring object of electronic occasions is what we ordinarily mean by "electron."

And the material bodies of our acquaintance are not only both enduring objects and corpuscular societies, but they are structured societies as well inasmuch as they provide environments for still other societies.

These material bodies belong to the lowest grade of structured societies which are obvious to our gross apprehensions. They comprise societies of various types of complexity—crystals, rocks, planets, and suns. Such bodies are easily the most long-lived of the structured societies known to us, capable of being traced through their individual life-histories.[160]

And these material bodies are also enduring objects inasmuch as they have individual life-histories. The member occasions of these life-histories or enduring objects are again rather large scale: crystal occasions, rock occasions, planet occasions, sun occasions. It is evident that material bodies may themselves be more than one type of society, and these may be comprised of relatively large scale occasions which are themselves members of more than one society. Occasions of many types are members of societies of many types: membership in one society does not preclude membership in another. A man may be a musician, a male animal, and an American; he may be both a mind and an environment for bacteria.

These structured societies mentioned are only those directly palpable to us, directly impinging upon our "gross apprehensions"; there are many more beyond these less directly palpable. For example, "Molecules are structured societies, and so in all probability are separate electrons and protons."[161] Then electrons are enduring objects, corpuscular societies, and structured societies as well, just as are all other material bodies. "The societies of enduring objects—electrons, protons, molecules, material bodies—at once sustain that order and arise out of it."[162] As enduring objects, electrons are linear successions of electronic occasions. As corpuscular societies, electrons are nexūs of quanta, photons—waves of light. Each electron is a society of the societies of quanta.

Thus the quanta are, themselves, in their own nature, somehow vibratory; but they emanate from the protons and electrons. Thus there is every reason to believe that rhythmic periods cannot be dissociated from the protonic and electronic entities.[163]

The society of quanta is at times corpuscular, at times non-corpuscular: "Thus the train of waves starts as a corpuscular society, and ends as a society which is not corpuscular."[164] Thus, electrons are several types of societies, just as are every material body.

More examples of material bodies are listed here: "The most general examples of such societies are the regular trains of waves, individual electrons, protons, individual molecules, societies of molecules such as inorganic bodies, living cells, and societies of cells such as vegetable and animal bodies."[165] It can be seen that these examples are not all equally material. And indeed, Whitehead stresses that enduring objects may be more or less material:

> We must remember the extreme generality of the notion of an enduring object—a generic character inherited through a historic route of actual occasions. Some kinds of enduring objects form material bodies, others do not. But just as the difference between living and non-living occasions is not sharp, but more or less, so the distinction between an enduring object which is an atomic material body and one which is not is again more or less.[166]

Similarly, a society may be more or less corpuscular; or it may pass from a corpuscular society to a non-corpuscular society as does the train of light waves. "A society may be more or less corpuscular, according to the relative importance of the defining characteristics of the various enduring objects compared to that of the defining characteristic of the whole corpuscular nexus."[167] And a nexus may be only more or less an enduring object too: "The notion of an 'enduring object' is, however, capable of more or less completeness of realization."[168] Then a material body is necessarily comprised of enduring objects; but an enduring object is not necessarily material. A train of waves, an electron, a proton are enduring objects; but they are not as material as a molecule, inorganic body, live cell, vegetable body, and animal body. And all live material bodies are necessarily nexūs of enduring objects; but not all enduring objects are living. The inorganic personal societies are enduring objects; whereas the organic personal societies may be called "enduring creatures"—or "enduring personalities" if they are human.[169]

*The three-fold character of occasions.* This proliferation of societies is still within actual occasions. It is to be remembered that occasions, nexūs, and societies are not mutually exclusive, not ontologically distinct kinds of actualities. Occasions comprise the nexūs and societies, and antecedent nexūs and societies compose occasions. The immanence of past nexūs and societies in occasions is testified in every section of Whitehead's works. I have alluded to it as the immanence of the actual world in actual occasions, of data in feeling, of objects in subjects. The actual occasion cannot be adequately described without taking into account the antecedent nexus or society causing it. Here Whitehead states that (objectifications of) antecedent members of a nexus constitute any given member:

> (ii) That this end is concerned with the gradations of intensity in the satisfaction of actual entities (members of the nexus) in whose formal constitutions the nexus (i.e., antecedent members of the nexus) in question is objectified.[170]

Any given occasion, then, is internally constituted of aspects of the antecedent members of the nexus it belongs to, those aspects objectified by it. In other words, the nexus up to that point is immanent in the member occasion. And if the nexus be social, then the antecedent society is immanent in each succeeding member of the society. "The self-identity of a society is founded upon the self-identity of its defining characteristic, and upon the mutual immanence of its occasions."[171] It is the mutually relevant aspects of antecedent members of a society that constitute each succeeding member in their likeness.

The reason for the immanence of the antecedent society in each successive member occasion is quite clear: if it were not immanent it would be gone altogether. There would be no way the antecedent society could be presently effective but that aspects of it were immanent in each present occasion. "It is gone, and yet it is here."[172] Antecedent members of a nexus or society are past, gone: at least, they have perished subjectively. They are objectively immortal only in that, as objects, they are constituting present subjects, concrescing into novel occasions that are the new members of the same nexus or society. "Causal efficacy is the hand of the settled past in the formation of the present."[173] It is aspects of the antecedent members of the nexus or society that are the objective content of each new member. "The past has an objective existence in the present which lies in the future beyond itself."[174] A present occasion has no objective content otherwise than what is derived from its past.

It is clear, for example, that each and every occasion of our past is gone; yet we are today a culmination of our past lives. Aspects of the antecedent members of our personal society, an enduring personality, are with us today and with all others whom we have affected, immanent in our and their present existence, and not otherwise surviving. Our every present occasion is an inheritance from all its predecessors and advances our personal society by one new member.

Given the immanence of occasions in their successors, every occasion is always describable in three ways:

Thus an actual entity has a threefold character: (i) it has the character 'given' for it by the past; (ii) it has the subjective character aimed at in its process of concrescence; (iii) it has the superjective character, which is the pragmatic value of its specific satisfaction qualifying the transcendent creativity.[175]

This is to say, an actual occasion is necessarily something with a past, present, and future. It is an individual and novel concrescence of its feelings of antecedents, and it becomes a member of the very nexus of which its antecedents are a member when it has been prehended. These descriptions are mutually compatible and equally necessary for an understanding of what an actual occasion is. There is no time or place when or where an occasion is one of these things without being the others: an individual, a descendent of its antecedents, and a potential predecessor. If an occasion comes into being at all, it comes into being with the potentiality for membership in the nexus to which its antecedents belong, with the potentiality for contributing to concrescences succeeding itself, and with a novel unification of aspects of its antecedents. Inasmuch as an occasion becomes, so do also its objective content (the antecedent nexus comprising its actual world), its subjective reaction as a unique comprehension of its world, and its real potentiality for partially effecting other occasions.

I have stressed the threefold character of actual occasions here because Whiteheadian immanence is not generally taken very seriously or given very much credibility; the actual occasion is widely believed to possess these characteristics only one at a time, in which case it would not have a threefold character but one character at different times, as though it endured through time changing characters. But for Whitehead, if an occasion exists at all, it has an objective content derived from the past, its own subjective reaction to it, and a potential efficacy or inherent creativity for the future—all immanent in any given occasion. There is no occasion existing at any time or place that does not reveal this threefold nature. And of course, the very possibility of observing it reveals its potential efficacy for occasions beyond itself, e.g., the present occasion of observation. An occasion's threefold character means that it is to be described as having an aim and synthesis of its own, as having prehended or related to its antecedents, and as prehendable to its successors.

*The retreat of scientific materialism.* Just as the personal order of enduring objects suggested to Western people an absolute time, the enduring objects themselves suggest substance. Whitehead remarks that the scientific materialist concept of impervious substance, enduring numerically one, comes from the appearance of a single, persisting, quiet stone, which is in fact a society of stone occasions (enduring object) the members of which have been identified or transmuted into one seemingly enduring thing.

> Thus the imaginations of men are dominated by the quiet extensive stone with its relationships of positions, and its quality of colour— relationships and qualities which occasionally change. . . .
>
> Thus in framing cosmological theory, the notion of continuous stuff with permanent attributes, enduring without differentiation, and retaining its self-identity through any stretch of time however small or large, has been fundamental. The stuff undergoes change in respect to accidental qualities and relations; but it is numerically self-identical in its character of one actual entity throughout its accidental adventures. The admission of this fundamental metaphysical concept has wrecked the various systems of pluralistic realism.
>
> This metaphysical concept has formed the basis of scientific material-ism.[176]

Scientific materialists of today impose this view of an undifferentiated substantial endurance that remains numerically one on the modern day subatomic occasions, the energy units researched in high energy physics. It does not matter that these so-called "elementary" occasions of subatomic proportions are of shorter duration than the quiet stone of our daily acquaintance: the materialist view is the same, that of a permanent substance "retaining its self-identity through any stretch of time however small or large." Even if an occasion of subatomic scale have a temporal duration of only $20^{-24}$ seconds, if it is independent of others, unaffectable by others, in principle isolatable, completely simple, undifferentiated, and numerically one, then it is a scientific materialist enduring substance and not a Whiteheadian actual occasion. An actual occasion does not endure unaffectable and numerically one even for $20^{-24}$ seconds. It becomes; it perishes. And it becomes both one and many, the one being itself a unity of many, the many being the occasions of its actual world immanent in it; and it perishes into many objects, the many aspects of its unity that are efficacious for others.

Materialists derived their belief in substance from the appearance of the quiet stone, but have since been shown contrary evidence. "But the interpretation of the stone, on which the whole concept [of scientific materialism] is based, has proved to be entirely mistaken."[177] Materialists must impose their view on occasions of subatomic scale because the larger material bodies have been found to evolve, to be highly complex, active, agitated. "The stone is now conceived as a society of separate molecules in violent agitation."[178] And even the atom has been found to be affectable, alterable, rhythmic, complex, multiple, and in process. "The atom is only explicable as a society with activities involving rhythms with their definite periods."[179] So materialism was found equally unsubstantiated as regards the atom as the stone. "But this materialistic concept has proved to be as mistaken for the atom as it was for the stone."[180] The last resort of scientific materialism, therefore, is the subatomic occasions, the least complex of occurrences. The materialist conception of subatomic occasions is of enduring, however briefly, numerically one, minuscule bits of material. "Again the concept shifted its application: protons and electrons were conceived as materialistic electric charges whose activities could be construed as locomotive adventures."[181] But locomotive adventures, motion through absolute time and space, are unintelligible to quantum theory.

Materialists of today are faced with quanta that do not retain their self-identity and do not move, but become and perish; they are confronted with quanta that can be treated as either one particle or as a wave of many particles. Then the evidence again is that the materialist concept of enduring substance is as unsubstantiated in regard to the occurrences of subatomic scale as it is for the atom and the stone.

> . . . but again there is evidence that the concept may be mistaken. The mysterious quanta of energy have made their appearance, derived, as it would seem, from the recesses of protons, or of electrons. Still worse for the concept, these quanta seem to dissolve into the vibrations of light.[182]

David Bohm's description of the retreat of scientific materialism with the advance of modern science parallels that of Whitehead:

> Early scientists, for example, supposed that atoms were absolutely permanent entities, the basic 'building blocks' of the universe, so that the ever-changing appearances of large-scale matter were regarded as nothing but consequences of the underlying movements of its permanent atomic constituents. But then the atoms were seen to be constituted of moving structures of 'elementary particles' (electrons, protons, and neutrons) with the result that atoms could be altered, transformed into other atoms, built up and torn down, etc. It was then assumed, however, that there is something else that is absolutely permanent, i.e., the elementary particles. But as we have seen, nuclear

and other processes have been discovered, in which even these particles are transformed into each other and annihilated and created, with the liberation and absorption of corresponding amounts of energy. So once again the search for absolutely permanent entities and substances has been foiled.[183]

*Whitehead misinterpreted.* And yet, Whitehead is taken to be materialist and atomist, his atoms the modern subatomic entities, his cosmology the very representation of scientific materialism in the modern day—the scientific materialism that has relocated substance in the subatomic entities. His nexūs are considered nothing more than ununified, uncreative, static aggregates or collections; his societies nothing more than ineffective compounds of unknowable, impalpable, minuscule bits of substance enduring numerically one. John W. Lango repeats a version of the modern day scientific materialism, that which has resorted to the subatomic particles, attributing it to Whitehead.

> . . . those entities which are perceived by the senses are always societies of actual entities, and never an individual actual entity, simply because some societies are large enough to be perceived, whereas their component actual entities are too small. For example, a stone, which is seen lying on the ground, is composed of actual entities which cannot be seen.[184]

When a society is taken to be a mere collection without internally constituting any occasion, then the antecedent part of the society cannot be immanent in, and creative of, its succeeding member occasions.

Almost everywhere in the literature on Whitehead is the same insistence on simple, uniform, in principle isolatable, numerically one actual occasions all of one (small) type; societies of occasions are obliged to be mere aggregates of this one small, impalpable type of occasion; the third and fourth, if not the second grades of occasions are ignored and treated as societies of the small and allegedly simple occasions; large scale occasions spanning any appreciable area and temporal duration are not to exist; and the small occasions are treated as mere material whose existence is only posited on the conditon that a veritable lack of palpable qualities can be asserted of them, and so on. In Lango's words:

> But the fundamental entities of Whitehead's ontology—the actual entities—are pretty hypothetical, postulated by his metaphysics, but not known in any other way. We cannot observe an actual entity with our

senses; we cannot infer an actual entity with empirical theories; we cannot consciously apprehend an actual entity through introspection. We must therefore obtain an understanding of actual entities through speculation, by using metaphors derived from the *societies* of actual entities that we can observe, infer, or introspect.[185]

Of course, Lango does not provide evidence for his views; as indeed he cannot. They have no foundation in the Whiteheadian philosophy.

In spite of the thoroughgoing relativity of his occasions, wherein each one is what it is only in virtue of its relation to and context among what others are; in spite of the becoming and perishing of occasions, which is a becoming together with other occasions and not a creation of an enduring numerically one entity, and a perishing which is the real potentiality of multiple future effects; in spite of his ontological commitment to actual occasions and actual occasions only, so that these are the only source and substance of experience and existence; in spite of universal relativity, wherein each occasion can engage any other occasion whatsoever in relationship no matter how small or large the occasion be; in spite of his conception of causal efficacy requiring that occasions be internally constituted of their predecessors and inextricable from them, their data; in spite of the immanence of antecedent nexūs and societies in successive members which is the very way in which nexūs and societies are formed and continued; in spite of his examples of large organisms such as animals modifying electrons and molecules within them; in spite of his recognition of types of societies based on the types of their member occasions participating in a variety of types of order; in spite of the coordination of societies by means of their prehension in single occasions; in spite of an occasion's membership in more than one nexus and society; in spite of the third and fourth and sometimes fifth and sixth grades of occasions including living creatures and man; in spite of his enduring objects, wherein relatively large scale occasions may reproduce themselves in a stable, serial order; in spite of his repeated requests that we consult our experience wherein a mere material and a vacuous actuality are not to be found; in spite of everything, Whitehead is treated as scientific materialist in one version or another.

Ivor Leclerc says in no uncertain terms that Whitehead's metaphysics is another illustration of scientific materialism, or what he calls here "material atomism":

> With the introduction of the doctrine of material atomism towards the end of the first quarter of the seventeenth century, there entered modern thought a fundamental metaphysical position which soon came

to receive widespread adherence and by the end of the century was dominant. . . . It seemed that Whitehead might have abandoned it in *Science and the Modern World*, but the presupposition of this position exerted itself fully when he came to elaborate his metaphysics in *Process and Reality*.

This metaphysical position is that the ultimate physical existent or substance in the strict sense of the term is to be identified with the final constituents of compounds, and that consequently no compound entity can be a substance.[186]

It would be otiose to add that this view is incongruous with the Whitehead of this book. It stands simply as a testament to the lingering dominion of scientific materialism, the dogged persistence of common sense notions.

And such views, outrageous as I think them to be, are not the exception among interpreters of Whitehead; rather, they are typical. Edward Pols will not recognize even a paradigm actual occasion, human experience. "But there are no Whiteheadian monads or actual occasions that define something as complex as a man. The continuity of a man is, then, not that of an entity (or genuine subject) but that of a 'society.'"[187] Certainly the continuity of a man over his life-time is that of a society (an enduring object enjoying personal order); but this society is a society of actual man occasions, among others. The man's life as an enduring object cannot be a society only of subatomic occasions; then he would be nothing but a subatomic particle, the life-time of a society of subatomic occasions. And Richard H. Overman states the view this way: "We must . . . remember that an animal body is a structured society of occasions, not a single actual occasion."[188] But an animal body is more than a structured society; it is a corpuscular society and an enduring object of presiding occasions. The animal is also an actual occasion at each moment of its occurrence as an animal. Overman continues: "If we are to avoid serious logical errors, we must distinguish carefully between the several grades of actual occasions discussed by Whitehead and the several grades of *aggregations* of occasions."[189] But the Whiteheadian societies are even classified according the grade of their member occasions. Overman then lists aggregations of occasions; his list of *aggregations* corresponds to Whitehead's list of grades of *occasions*. Hardly any interpreter of Whitehead will allow that there be occasions on the scale of vegetables and animals. There is no basis for Overman's distinction between occasions and aggregates except that it is in keeping with scientific materialism.

Robert M. Palter makes an ontological category of societies: "Electrons, atoms, and living things all belong to a single ontological category, namely, all are 'societies' of one kind or another."[190] But there is only one ontological category, that of the actual occasion. It is only the materialist conception of societies as nothing more than mere aggregates of microphysical entities that might require an ontological distinction between them and these entities. Donald W. Sherburne informs us again of Whitehead's atomism and its consequence for the material bodies of our acquaintance:

> Actual entities play the role in Whitehead's system that atoms play in the philosophy of Democritus and monads play in the philosophy of Leibniz—i.e., actual entities are for Whitehead the ultimate building blocks of the universe, the ultimately and finally real sort of existence from which all other modes of existence are derived. . . .
>
> Our concern, rather, will be with the conglomerations of actual entities which Whitehead terms 'societies' or 'nexūs' which answer to our everyday experience of trees, houses and persons in the macroscopic world.[191]

These actual entities, as usual, belong to the microcosmic world, and there is no possibility of our experiencing them. And there is no possibility that societies, conceived as mere aggregates of these entities, can constitute single occasions or have any real efficacy in single occasions: it is only the entities that comprise the societies, the societies compose no entities. But for Whitehead, there is no such thing as a society that does not also compose its member occasions: each succeeding member is a composition of the antecedent society. But interpreters of Whitehead think nothing of attributing some version of scientific materialism to Whitehead. Materialism has retreated to the subatomic scale occurrences and interpreters of Whitehead have typically retreated with it. But the imposition of material-ism on Whitehead's philosophy can hardly be said to count as an interpretation of it.

## CONCLUSION

This chapter has shown that the actual occasion is defined by its causal efficacy and not by its size, temporal duration, or degree of palpability or complexity, though these differences make for different grades of occasions. An actual occasion is that which has been effected by actual occasions and that which has had effect, not that which is small, simple, short, impalpable, and so on. The chapter has shown that occasions of larger and longer spans of existence come into being and perish on the same principles as small and brief occasions; although all processes of becoming are called "microscopic," yet all do not yield small occasions.

The chapter has shown that the theory of nexūs and societies does not require an ontological distinction between the small and simple and the large and compound aggregates of these; on the contrary, the theory of nexūs as prehended occasions constituting successive member occasions is devised to bridge just such a bifurcation of actualities. Societies, the social nexūs, are aspects of the very internal character of occasions, an integral part of what occasions are and the reason they are social beings. When a sequence of occasions share in the same type of order because they impose upon successors the order they have themselves acquired by prehension, they are a society. Thus, the relationship between members of one society is a strengthened version of the relationship that there is between any causally connected occasions. As J.M. Burgers says: "The causal relationship which becomes effective within a society is thus an intensification of the primary relationship between single processes."[192] The members of a society are all alike in those important respects that have caused them to come into being as members. Societies considered as mere aggregates cannot cause their likenesses, their defining characteristics, to be reproduced.

The scientific materialist interpretation of occasions and their societies, wherein societies cannot in any way internally constitute occasions, has been shown untenable as an interpretation of the Whiteheadian cosmology. And the scientific materialist conception of the entire universe as a single enduring thing, proceeding in a single linear sequence of instants—a substantial universe marking absolute time—has been shown to be replacable by Whitehead's creative advance. "In these lectures the term 'creative advance' is not to be construed in the sense of a uniquely serial advance."[193] There is not one temporal sequence for a monolithic universe, then, but many. Whitehead's "cosmic epoch" is not a single substance enduring numerically one, but is instead populated by a plurality of nexūs and societies. The cosmic epoch is a structured society, or society of societies. "Here the phrase 'cosmic epoch' is used to mean that widest society of actual entities whose immediate relevance to ourselves is traceable."[194] Neither actual occasions nor societies nor the entire cosmic epoch correspond to the materialist conception of these. Victor Lowe understands the untenability of scientific materialism for interpreting Whitehead, and sees the Whiteheadian cosmology as a viable alternative to it.

In all of Whitehead's later writings one can see that a strong motive for metaphysical exposition is his belief that the educated man's implicit conception of the universe has not responded to the advance from the seventeenth-century physics of inert matter to the late nineteenth-century physics of energetic vibrations described in terms of vectors. He sees that, whereas a number of philosophic systems have been produced in the modern period, it is not any system of philosophy, but the success of the materialistic ideas of science, which has shaped the philosophy unconsciously held by mankind. No epistemology and no philosophy of religion, but only a new and equally scientific set of ideas about nature and nature's relation to human experience, can hope to get this philosophy displaced.[195]

The Whiteheadian enduring objects are linear, single-file successions of occasions, each successor prehending and thereby appropriating or absorbing aspects of the antecedent members of the succession. Enduring objects are spacetime systems. The cosmic epoch is a plurality of spacetime systems.

There is no necessity that temporal process, in this sense, should be constituted by one single series of linear succession. Accordingly, in order to satisfy the present demands of scientific hypothesis, we introduce the metaphysical hypothesis that this is not the case. We do assume (basing ourselves upon direct observation), however, that temporal process of realisation can be analysed into a group of linear serial processes. Each of these linear series is a space-time system.[196]

Each linear serial process is an enduring object; a group of them is a corpuscular society. Enduring objects converge in any occasion prehending antecedent members of more than one enduring object, thereby coordinating them. Since spacetime systems are the spatiotemporal dimensions of the enduring objects, these converge in and are coordinated by individual occasions also. The converging of enduring objects means that the antecedents of any one occasion are not limited only to the members of one society, one enduring object. As J. M. Burgers says parenthetically: "(We cannot exlude that there may be more than one immediately preceding process since there is no unique serial development of processes but rather ramifications and convergences.)"[197] And in fact, it is the convergences of members of different enduring objects in one occasion that enriches the experience of that occasion.

In the following passage Whitehead speaks in a general way about the temporal character of his universe:

The actual temporal world can be analyzed into a multiplicity of occasions of actualization. . . . Call each such occasion an 'epochal occasion. . . .' These epochal occasions are the creatures. The reason for the temporal character of the actual world can now be given by reference to the creativity and the creatures. For the creativity is not separable from its creatures. Thus the creatures remain with the creativity. Accordingly, the creativity for a creature becomes the creativity with the creature, and thereby passes into another phase of itself. It is now the creativity for a new creature. Thus there is a transition of the creative action, and this transition exhibits itself, in the physical world, in the guise of routes of temporal succession.

This protean character of the creativity forbids us from conceiving it as an actual entity. For its character lacks determinateness. It equally prevents us from considering the temporal world as a definite actual creature. For the temporal world is an essential incompleteness. It has not the character of a definite matter of fact, such as attaches to an event in past history, viewed from a present standpoint.[198]

This chapter has accomplished something if it has made this passage intelligible. The actual occasions, with regard to their temporality, are epochal occasions. They are creative, so that they do not remain engaged with only one set of relationships, but reproduce themselves anew ("passing into another phase of themselves") by engaging new relationships. Their creativity insures their transition into new epochal occasions.

And Whitehead distinguishes his "protean" conception of temporality from the scientific materialist conception of absolute time in saying that neither time nor the universe are single actual entities. Whitehead's theory of prehensions is prohibitive of a static monism. Universal relativity requires that all things become other things. The nature of an occasion is not a particular quality or character or essence the possessing of which distinguishes it from societies or from other substances. Its nature is prehension, that is, causal efficacy: the ability to transform and be transformed into something else. In the words of David Bohm:

> . . . nothing has yet been discovered which has a mode of being that remains eternally defined in any given way. . . . Thus we conclude that the notion that all things can become other kinds of things implies that a complete and eternally applicable definition of any given thing is not possible in terms of any finite number of qualities and properties.[199]

# 3

# Potentiality

*You would exclaim loudly that you know no other way by which anything can come into existence than by participating in the proper essence of each thing in which it participates, and therefore you accept no other cause of the existence of two than participation in duality, and things which are to be two must participate in duality, and whatever is to be one must participate in unity, and you would pay no attention to the divisions and additions and other such subtleties, leaving those for wiser men to explain.*

Plato, *Phaedo* 101C

## INTRODUCTION

The Whiteheadian cosmos is through and through potentiality: potentiality that is actualizing, perishing, and actualizing anew. Potentiality is not actuality, but neither is it nothing at all: it is the aim for achieving new definite actuality; it is the lure for the satisfaction of actuality; it is the reaching for the togetherness of feelings that forms a novel being. If and when a particular aim is fulfilled, so is the potentiality for that particular actuality. But actuality, once in creation, does not then subsist since real potentiality for creation beyond itself is inherent in its nature; everything created is also creative of other things. Substantial existence and potential existence occasionally actualized are antithetical. Here Whitehead speaks of the difference between his conception of the potentiality inherent in all things, and the universe of substantial actualities:

The notion of potentiality is fundamental for the understanding of existence, as soon as the notion of process is admitted. If the universe be interpreted in terms of static actuality, then potentiality vanishes. Everything is just what it is. Succession is mere appearance, rising from the limitation of perception. But if we start with process as fundamental, then the actualities of the present are deriving their characters from the process, and are bestowing their characters upon the future. Immediacy is the realization of the potentialities of the past, and is the storehouse of the potentialities of the future. Hope and fear, joy and disillusion, obtain their meaning from the potentialities essential in the nature of things. We are following a trail in hope, or are fleeing from the pursuit in fear. The potentialities in immediate fact constitute the driving force of process.[1]

The actual past is gone, past. There is nothing to fear or hope, nothing to follow or flee in the actualities that are past. It is the very real potentialities of the past for the present and in the present that are to be feared or hoped for, followed or fled, in the present.

The time-span, or temporal duration, of an occasion is its present; it covers both its potentiality and its actualization, its entire process of concrescence from the initiation of its subjective aim in God to its satisfaction as an individual actuality. It is an occasion's present moment of existence as a subject, from the beginning of the potentiality for that subject, to its completion as a new actual occasion. Just as actual occasions are intended to replace substances which are ever the same things, their time-spans replace instants which are also ever actual. Instants are the units of absolute time, world-wide and instantaneous, necessary to classical physics; epochs, the time-spans of actual occasions, are the units of Whiteheadian time, consonant with modern physics. Thus, Whiteheadian time is relative time. This is to say that neither a single occasion nor a sucession of occasions are calibrated in instants; rather the occasion, being one epoch, replaces the instant and a plurality of interrelated spacetime systems replaces the one subsisting absolute spacetime. Therefore, no absolute time, time in the sense of a succession of instants, passes for a subject during its becoming. In this chapter I show that an epoch cannot be treated as a miniature Newtonian universe proceeding in absolute time, nor can all occasions be described as inhabiting a single cosmic container of absolute spacetime, which is the original Newtonian universe.

Just as occasions are not all of one size or complexity, they are not all of one duration. Their time-spans vary depending on what the occasions are. And what the occasions are depends on what subjective aim lured their predecessors into creating them. This chapter explains subjective aims and their variety, and the resulting variation in time-spans. Because a time-span is the duration of a subjective aim, it is a potentiality that becomes actualized, just as is the occasion. Time is no more a substantial enduring substance than are the actual occasions. The epoch is the unit of Whiteheadian time, embracing both the potentiality for time and its actuality. A potential epoch becomes an actual epoch, just as a potential occasion (a subject) becomes an actual occasion. An epoch cannot be understood as an instant, instantaneously actual, nor can instants be applied to it as though it were itself an entity residing in absolute spacetime.

## MENTALITY

*Conceptual prehension.* Whitehead distinguishes immortal objects from eternal objects. The former are occasions which have perished subjectively and are currently creating new occasions; the latter are the characteristics occasions have in common with one another considered in abstraction from the occasions themselves. The prehension of actual occasions is called "physical prehension"; the prehension of eternal objects, "conceptual prehension." "Prehensions of actual entities—i.e., prehensions whose data involve actual entities—are termed 'physical prehensions'; and prehensions of eternal objects are termed 'conceptual prehensions.'"[2] Immortal objects and eternal objects are not two different kinds of actualities, but are the actualities and their forms.

Eternal objects are necessary to Whitehead's philosophy as the forms of definiteness of the actual occasions. "The definiteness of fact is due to its forms. . . ."[3] Occasions can be alike in specific ways if they share the same forms of definiteness. Members of a society all partake of some of the very same forms of definiteness which they press upon their successors. "In particular each historic route of like occasions tends to prolong itself, by reason of the weight of uniform inheritance derivable from its members."[4] But the likeness shared by all members of a society is prehended in abstraction from the occasions themselves: conceptual prehension is prehension of form alone. Whitehead calls these forms that occasions share "eternal objects" because they are permanent and unchanging. "In the philosophy of organism it is not 'substance' which is permanent, but 'form.'"[5]

Immortal objects do not remain the same, numerically one and the same object forever, but contribute different aspects of themselves to different successive concrescences which transform them in accordance with their own requirements for compatibility. But eternal objects do remain the same. For, eternal objects *are* the common characteristics of occasions; they *are* the forms that occasions share; they *are* the likenesses between occasions; they *are* the definite characters and qualities that occasions share; they *are* the order that characterizes a society. Therefore, again they are nothing outside of occasions. Here in an earlier formulation Whitehead expresses this idea; eternal objects make occasions comparable because they *are* the factors of them which can "be again":

> Thus the theory of objects is the theory of the comparison of events. Events are only comparable because they body forth permanences. We are comparing objects in events whenever we can say, 'There it is again.' Objects are the elements in nature which can 'be again.'[6]

Eternal objects are, of course, a remodeling of the Platonic forms.[7] They might easily be mistaken for the "universals" of previous philosophers, but Whitehead does not use the same distinction between universals and particulars. For the Whiteheadian particulars become universalized by the principle of relativity. Each actual occasion is a potentiality for the becoming of all actual occasions. And Whitehead's "universals," his eternal objects, are particular in being the specific characters of individual occasions. Traditional universals are distinct, e.g., blue and red are distinct from one another, and so they are particular in this sense; but they do not depend on individuals for their distinctness. The Platonic forms depend on no actualities; they may inhere in nothing. Thus, both universality and particularity are common to both Whitehead's actual occasions and eternal objects.[8]

*Ingression.* Antecedent occasions that are positively prehended are objectified by and for the subject prehending them. And eternal objects of antecedent occasions that are conceptually prehended ingress in the subject prehending them. "An actual entity as felt is said to be 'objectified' for that subject. Only a selection of eternal objects are 'felt' by a given subject, and these eternal objects are then said to have 'ingression' in that subject."[9] The antecedent occasions, having been objectified, contribute to the subject's internal constitution and are inextricable from it. Objectified antecedent occasions are occasions *as felt,* as experienced, by their successors. Eternal objects are the means whereby the antecedent occasions are objectified; how an antecedent occasion is felt depends on what eternal objects have been selected to objectify it. Positively prehended antecedent occasions are objectified by eternal objects; prehended eternal objects, having ingression in an occasion for this purpose of objectification, are exhibited therein.

"Objectification" and "ingression" are terms for the immanence of aspects of past occasions and their characteristics in their successors.

The functioning of one actual entity in the self-creation of another actual entity is the 'objectification' of the former for the latter actual entity. The functioning of an eternal object in the self-creation of an actual entity is the 'ingression' of the eternal object in the actual entity.[10]

No antecedent occasion is an absolute object, the same for all subjects; it is only eternal objects of the antecedent occasions that are the same for all subjects. This is the reason Whitehead does not use the expression "immortal objects" as I have done when referring to perished, antecedent occasions. He speaks instead of their objective immortality. Any antecedent occasion is efficacious for myriad subjects; its objectivity is its efficacy, not its self-identity as a persisting object. There is no absolute description of an object, no privileged perspective from which alone it is defined; for, the perished occasion is nothing above and beyond its myriad subsequent effects. In other words, there are no immortal objects and no substantial objects in the common sense understanding of these terms. There are successive objectifications. An object is always the state of an antecedent occasion as prehended by one successor and nothing substantial on its own. Similarly, an eternal object always has ingression in occasions and has no reality otherwise. "For realization means ingression in an actual entity, and this involves the synthesis of all ingredients with data derived from a complex universe."[11] Both occasions and eternal objects are required for there to be any actuality at all; neither exists in separation. Here Whitehead says that occasions necessarily participate in eternal objects: "The actual cannot be reduced to mere matter of fact in divorce from the potential."[12] And here he says that eternal objects necessarily ingress in actual occasions: "Thus the endeavor to understand eternal objects in complete abstraction from the actual world results in reducing them to mere undifferentiated nonentities."[13]

*Objectification.* The analysis of a feeling revealed both initial data, which are to be felt, and the objective datum, which is felt. This objective datum is a unity of aspects of antecedent occasions objectified for the subject. By being objectified, the aspects of antecedents are accommodated under a single perspective that the subject has of them. "Thus the initial data are felt under a 'perspective' which is the objective datum of the feeling."[14] It is the subject's perspective on its antecedents that makes the subject what it is. The antecedents exercise efficient causation in creating the new subject; but this causation is only efficacious in the specific way that it is given the subject's aim and interest. A plant may grow given water; iron may rust. A forest may be poetry to one person, lumber to another. "The actual entity which is the initial datum is the actual entity perceived, the objective datum is the 'perspective' under which that actual entity is perceived, and the subject of the simple physical feeling is the perceiver."[15]

Perception on the human level is one kind of prehension made conscious. Thus, Whitehead speaks of perception and perspective on the part of a perceiver referring to one type of prehension and objectification that higher animals are capable of. Prehension and objectification are the general terms for a causally efficacious transition and its resultant construct of the data, namely, the resultant objective datum. Given that objectifications amount to perspective in people, it can easily be seen why Whitehead regards objectifications as the efficient causes rather than simply the antecedent occasions. Our own attitude shapes what we see at least as much as what we see effects us. "The 'objectifications' of the actual entities in the actual world, relative to a definite actual entity, constitute the efficient causes out of which *that* actual entity arises. . . ."[16]

What causes a subject to be what it is is not only its antecedents, but its own perspective of them which is in fact inextricable from both it and them, though these may be intellectually discriminated. We can analyze a subject's feeling and discern initial data available to it as distinct from the objective datum that the subject has admitted into feeling; but the subject cannot be in fact extricated from its own feeling. "For the subject is at work in the feeling, in order that it may be the subject with that feeling."[17] Oxygen may sustain an astronaut, and kill a cyanobacterium. Children may gladden one person, threaten another. The antecedents alone, whether children or oxygen, are not efficient causes without the subject's particular way of prehending them. It is how the subject prehends its antecedents that causes it to be what it is.

Objectification is accomplished by way of the subject selecting certain eternal objects from among all those available ingressed in its antecedents and by which the antecedents are to be exemplified for it. "In a feeling the actual world, selectively appropriated, is the presupposed datum, not formless but with its own realized form selectively germaine, in other words 'objectified.'"[18] Antecedent occasions exhibit a spectrum of eternal objects; a subject conceptually prehending them chooses which among them are to have ingression in itself as the way in which its objective datum are displayed for it. The subject decides how its antecedents will be exemplified, conceived, described, viewed, and interpreted for itself on the basis of its own purposes in synthesizing them.

In other words, each actuality is prehended by means of some element of its own definiteness. This is the doctrine of the 'objectification' of actual entities. Thus the primary stage in the concrescence of an actual entity is the way in which the antecedent universe enters into the constitution of the entity in question, so as to constitute the basis of its nascent individuality.[19]

*Subjective and objective species.* A successor reproduces or reenacts its antecedent if an eternal object of its subjective form is the same as one of its antecedent's subjective form. Subjective forms (being forms) are eternal objects: "The subjective form in abstraction from the feeling is merely a complex eternal object."[20] But the subjective forms, of course, are not in fact in abstraction from feelings; they are the forms of the feelings. When an antecedent's subjective form is adopted by a successor as its own subjective form and as the eternal object with which it objectifies the antecedent, then the antecedent has been recreated.

When there is re-enaction there is one eternal object with two-way functioning, namely, as partial determinant of the objective datum, and as partial determinant of the subjective form. In this two-way role, the eternal object is functioning relationally between the initial data on the one hand and the concrescent subject on the other.[21]

Thus, the data is partially objectified by the same subjective form that characterizes the subject's feeling. "Thus the cause passes on its feeling to be reproduced by the new subject as its own, and yet as inseparable from the cause. There is a flow of feeling."[22] This flow of feeling means that a new occasion is sympathetic with the old. It feels what its antecedent felt. "In the language appropriate to the higher stages of experience, the primitive element is *sympathy*, that is, feeling the feeling *in* another and feeling conformally *with* another."[23]

The eternal objects that can be subjective forms are subjective eternal objects, and the eternal objects that characterize objective data are objective. In the case of reenaction of successive occasions discussed here, where an eternal object functions as both an element of a subjective form and as a determinant of an objective datum, the eternal object is relational. It is only the subjective species of eternal object that can function relationally in this sense, as having the two-way role of both subjective form and objectification. "The eternal object can then function both subjectively and relatively. It can be a private element in a subjective form, and also an agent in the objectification."[24] Objective eternal objects are relational only in the sense that they relate the occasions in which they obtain ingression. They relate both prehending and prehended occasions in that both exhibit the same eternal objects; a successor objectifies its antecedents by means of eternal objects having ingression in the antecedents. But objective eternal objects can never be subjective forms. "Its sole avocation is to be an agent in objectification. It can never be an element in the definiteness of a subjective form."[25]

For an example of reenaction by way of the relational functioning of the subjective species of eternal object, an angry man will do. There is an occasion of a man's anger at an insult; anger is the subjective form of his feeling of the data. He objectifies the data as insulting to him and feels angry. There is reenaction of his occasion of anger when its successor objectifies this feeling with the same form of anger and appropriates the same form for its own subjective form as well. The succeeding and sympathetic occasion is angry like the antecedent about the insult to the antecedent. The same subjective eternal object, of anger, is the determinant of both the objective datum and the subjective form of the successor. The successor has felt its antecedent as angry and has responded with anger itself.

> In our experience, as in distinct analysis, physical feelings are always derived from some antecedent experient. Occasion *B* prehends occasion *A* as an antecedent subject experiencing a sensum with emotional intensity. Also *B*'s subjective form of emotion is conformed to *A*'s subjective form. Thus there is a vector transmission of emotional feeling of a sensum from *A* to *B*. In this way *B* feels the sensum as derived from *A* and feels it with an emotional form also derived from *A*. This is the most primitive form of the feeling of causal efficacy.[26]

*Examples.* The objective species of eternal objects include the numbers: "Eternal objects of the objective species are the mathematical Platonic forms."[27] The subjective species of eternal objects include the emotions:

> A member of the subjective species is, in its primary character, an element in the definiteness of the subjective form of a feeling. It is a determinate way in which a feeling can feel. It is an emotion, or an intensity, or an adversion, or an aversion, or a pleasure, or a pain.[28]

And these same subjective eternal objects are relational when they ingress as elements of objective data as well as subjective forms.

Whitehead considers the "sensa" or "sense-data" of previous philosophies correspond to eternal objects of his philosophy. "In the first place, those eternal objects which will be classified under the name 'sensa' constitute the lowest category of eternal objects."[29] And he gives these examples of sense-data: "These qualities, such as colours, sounds, bodily feelings, tastes, smells, together with the perspectives introduced by extensive relationships, are the relational eternal objects whereby the contemporary actual entities are elements in our constitution."[30] These sense-data are relational eternal objects, then; this means that they are eternal objects of the subjective species characterizing both the subjective form and objective datum of a subject. We may have difficulty understanding how a color, for example, or a smell, are subjective forms. It is easy to understand them as forms of objective data: we perceive a ruby as red, we perceive a rose as fragrant. But we do not ordinarily imagine that we feel red or fragrant about these things. Yet Whitehead proposes that we do. "The intellect fastens on smell as a datum: the animal experiences it as a qualification of his subjective feelings. . . . The experience starts as that smelly feeling, and is developed by mentality into the feeling of that smell."[31] The same holds for color:

> We are so used to considering the high abstraction, 'the stone as green,' that we have difficulty in eliciting into consciousness the notion of 'green' as the qualifying character of an emotion. . . . The separation of the emotional experience from the presentational intuition is a high abstraction of thought.[32]

Sense-data, then, are relational eternal objects with roles in both objective data and subjective form.

Locke's "ideas of particular things" supply further examples of eternal objects. Just as Locke's "particular things" serve as examples of actual occasions and nexus, Locke's "ideas of particular things" are given by Whitehead as examples of the eternal objects characterizing the occasions. "These 'eternal objects' are Locke's ideas as explained in his *Essay*. . . ."[33] And the examples from Locke are whiteness, hardness, sweetness, thinking, motion, man, elephant, army, drunkenness.[34] And Whitehead also uses heat as an example of an eternal object. "The quality of 'being hot' is an abstraction. . . . But in the real physical world, the quality of 'being hot' can only appear as a characteristic of concrete things which *are* hot."[35] And more examples of eternal objects are contained here:

The words electron, proton, photon, wave-motion, velocity, hard and soft radiation, chemical elements, matter, empty space, temperature, degradation of energy, all point to the fact that physical science recognizes qualitative differences between occasions in respect to the way in which each occasion entertains its energy.[36]

Each way of entertaining or characterizing energy is one eternal object. The quantity and speed of water in a stream are intellectually distinguishable (conceptually prehendable) in abstraction from the water, though they are not in fact abstracted therefrom. They are eternal objects by which the water flow is characterized. Also, the water's quantity and speed are intellectually distinguishable from each other though they are not in fact separated in the water. All factors of an occasion of water are inextricable.

The defining characteristics of any nexus and society are also examples of eternal objects. For, the common characters of members of a nexus or society taken in abstraction are eternal objects. "Such a nexus is called a 'society,' and the common form is the 'defining characteristic' of the society. . . . The common element of form is simply a complex eternal object exemplified in each member of the nexus."[37] The antecedent society imposes its common character on each new occasion that is to become a member of it. Every likeness between any two occasions is an eternal object; and the likeness is proof that the occasions are members of the same nexus, the antecedent members of which was efficacious in creating them.

All these examples of eternal objects, plus all the common characters of nexūs and societies that we care to think of, show that Whitehead intends his conception of actual occasion to cover the full range of concrete existences. For, eternal objects ingress in actual occasions. It may obtain ingression by characterizing either an objective datum or a feeling; either way it is a form of definiteness for an individual occasion. Subjective forms are necessarily those of individual occasions. "[A member of the subjective species] defines the subjective form of feeling of one actual entity."[38] And objective eternal objects are those objectifying the data for an individual occasion. "An eternal object of the objective species . . . is always, in its unrestricted realization, an element in the definiteness of an actual entity, or a nexus, which is the datum of a feeling belonging to the subject in question."[39] Nexūs and societies can be said to exhibit or participate in eternal objects only if it is their members that are meant. A subject may objectify an antecedent nexus or society; but this objectification is by way of eternal objects that are conceptually prehended in antecedent occasions and chosen for characterizing the antecedent nexus or society in the subject's experience. The eternal objects relate two occasions because they have ingression in both.

It is evident, then, that Whitehead has rather large scale occasions in mind when he considers emotions, pleasures, pains, aversions, adversions, colors, sounds, tastes, smells, hardness, thought, drunkenness, heat, and elephantness to be the forms of their definiteness. Occasions that may be characterized in these ways have relatively large scale spatiotemporal proportions in comparison to the subatomic occasions. Neither a subatomic occasion nor a society of subatomic occasions, such as the electromagnetic society or an enduring object such as a subatomic particle, may have most of these qualities. No subatomic occasion nor any subatomic particle is drunken, hard, in pain, colored, hot, or thoughtful. Also, these characteristics do not apply only to human percipient occasions, nor have they only the spatiotemporal dimensions that an occasion of human vision has. A sound requires rather longer to be heard than a sight to be seen; an elephant has not the same spatiotemporal dimension as an occasion of human pain; a thought cannot come into being at the same rate as a visual perception; the time-span required for a man to become drunk far exceeds that required for a color to register with his brain. Also, occasions of rather high grade are required even to conceptually prehend many of these eternal objects and complexes of eternal objects. In short, the examples of eternal objects show that Whitehead does not intend his actual occasions to be only of subatomic scale, or only of the scale of the specious present of human vision, or only on a scale of dimension between these two types of occasions.

*Real potentiality.* Objects are both stubborn fact and real potentiality. The real potentiality of objects has been treated in the discussions of the principle of relativity and objective immortality. It becomes very important in considering Whiteheadian time; for time is just as much potentiality as occasions are. It is very important that potentiality be taken for what it is and not confused with nothingness. In comparison with nothing, potentiality has actuality. But it is not an actuality. It is rather the state of incomplete or indeterminate actuality, actuality in becoming. "This indetermination, rendered determinate in the real concrescence, is the meaning of 'potentiality.' It is a *conditioned* indetermination, and is therefore called a '*real* potentiality.'"[40] The potentiality of objects is very real because they have very specific capacities for very definite effects.

Whitehead describes real potentiality as a sort of being without being actual. The not-being of potentiality is a sort of being.

Events become and perish. In their becoming they are immediate and then vanish into the past. They are gone; they have perished; they are no more and have passed into not-being. . . . [Plato] wrote in the *Sophist,* not-being is itself a form of being. He only applied this doctrine to his eternal forms. He should have applied the same doctrine to the things that perish.[41]

Surely this seems the end of any hope for intelligibility for Whitehead's philosophy. Where not-being is a sort of being, surely the point of making distinctions is lost, anything can be said of anything. But I hope that this chapter's discussion of potentiality will bring out Whitehead's intentions and show that the philosophy is intelligible, once his conception of potentiality is distinguished from non-being and from actuality. Potentiality and actuality, while not the same, are not mutually exclusive, since potentiality is itself a sort of being. But most importantly, the potentiality of perished occasions enjoying objective immortality is very real: it is not nothing. "When they perish, occasions pass from the immediacy of being into the not-being of immediacy. But that does not mean they are nothing. They remain stubborn fact. . . ."[42]

Real potentiality includes eternal objects as well as the efficacy of antecedent occasions: this is the reason eternal objects are objects. "The data are potentials for feeling; that is to say, they are objects."[43] The data for feeling may be antecedent occasions in the case of physical prehension or eternal objects in the case of conceptual prehension. The general nature of all objects is their real potentiality for actualization, in the case of immortal objects, or realization, in the case of eternal objects, in further occasions. Thus, eternal objects, like immortal objects, obey the principle of universal relativity and contribute to processes beyond, potentially to every becoming. "A conceptual feeling is feeling an eternal object in the primary metaphysical character of being an 'object,' that is to say, feeling its *capacity* for being a realized determinant of process."[44] Both actual entities and eternal objects are entities (things, existences, beings) in this sense, i.e., in the sense that they are objects. ". . . it is the one general metaphysical character of all entities of all sorts, that they function as objects."[45]

Thus, actual entities are called "entities" for the same reason eternal objects are called "objects": they have real potentiality for the creation of other occasions, their content in the case of antecedent occasions, their form in the case of eternal objects. Whitehead distinguishes four types of objects: "There are four main types of objects, namely, 'eternal objects,' 'propositions,' 'objectified' actual entities and nexūs."[46] Eternal objects are always objects because they are potentialities and never actualities; for this reason they may be called 'non-actual' as long as this does not mean non-existing.[47] Actual entities *qua* objects are real potentialities in their immortal efficacy for becoming; without being actual, they are a sort of being, and they are the concrete stubborn facts as felt by subjects. Actual entities *qua* subjects are real potential occasions until they have concresced; but they are actual too inasmuch as they are actually self-functioning, and actually enjoying immediate experience. All objects are real potentialities; only subjects become actual.

*Pure potentiality*. Whitehead calls eternal objects not only the forms of definiteness, but "Pure Potentials for the Specific Determination of Fact."[48] They are pure potentials because they do not in themselves reveal in which occasions they have ingression, nor do they in their own nature evoke specific occasions. Occasions are affected by their participation in forms, for by way of them they become definitely formed as they are, occasions having a particular character. But eternal objects are permanently and eternally the same and remain unaffected by their concourse in actualities. Ingression in billions of particular occasions leaves no impression on them. So there is no way to tell, just by conceptually prehending them alone, what occasions they have informed, "An eternal object is always a potentiality for actual entities; but in itself, as conceptually felt, it is neutral as to the fact of its physical ingression in any particular actual entity of the temporal world."[49]

Thus, for example, a pleasure, a pain, an ideal, a purpose, an elephant, a drunkard, a color, a sound, a smell may be conceptually prehended completely devoid of their contexts in specific pleasant or pained occasions, occasions vitalized by an ideal or purpose, elephants or drunkards, or colored, sonorous, or odoriferous occasions. We may prehend the forms without the occasions; nevertheless the forms are never actually without the occasions. It is just their pure potentiality, while ingressed, that enables them to be conceptually prehended in abstraction from any particular actuality. "The datum of a conceptual feeling is an eternal object which is referent (*qua* possibility) to any actual entities, where the *any* is absolutely general and devoid of selection."[50] In fact, this is the reason the prehension of eternal objects is conceptual rather than physical: they do not themselves disclose any actuality. This does not mean that prehended eternal objects are not in actualities, only that they are prehended in abstraction from the actualities they are in. "Now an eternal object, in itself, abstracts from all determinate actual entities, including even God. It is merely referent to *any* such entities, in the absolutely general sense of *any*."[51]

Subjects may choose which among all the eternal objects they prehend shall ingress in their own feeling, either as elements in subjective form or objective data.

> The actualities *have* to be felt, while the pure potentialities *can* be dismissed. So far as concerns their functionings as objects, this is the great distinction between an actual entity and an eternal object. The one is stubborn matter of fact; and the other never loses its 'accent' of potentiality.[52]

Eternal objects afford real alternatives for subjects to become something of what they choose. For they can be entertained without reprisal in actuality. Their pure potentiality permits them to be conceptually prehended without obligation to ingress and exhibit them. "The physical feeling is feeling a real fact; the conceptual feeling is valuing an abstract possibility."[53]

The possibility of conceptual prehension is also the possibility for final causation. The subject selects among all the eternal objects it prehends those which are to have ingression in its own nature. "Thus the selection is a selection of relevant eternal objects whereby what is a datum from without is transformed into its complete determination as a fact within."[54] A subject does not choose all of its antecedents; but it chooses its own perspective on them, and it chooses how it is affected by them. "These eternal objects determine *how* the world of actual entities enters into the constitution of each one of its members via its feelings."[55] This how has been a choice. It could have been otherwise. Thus, the decisiveness of subjects, as agents in their own creation, is enabled by the pure potentiality of eternal objects. "'Actuality' is the decision amid 'potentiality.'"[56] It is just this potentiality that distinguishes mentality from physical nature.

> Mentality involves conceptual experience, and is only one variable ingredient in life. The sort of functioning here termed 'conceptual experience' is the entertainment of possibilities for ideal realization in abstraction from any sheer physical realization. The most obvious example of conceptual experience is the entertainment of alternatives.[57]

Mentality allows for entertainment without obligation and the free choice to decide among possibilities; but along with these come responsibility. For the subject is responsible for its choice and decision, since it had alternatives. And once made, the choice is irrevocable: the subject has become a concrete occasion of that definite type, it has that definite character which is inextricable from it, though it may be conceptually prehended. "The definiteness of the actual arises from the exclusiveness of eternal objects in their function as determinants. If the actual entity be *this*, then by the nature of the case it is not *that* or *that*."[58]

While the analysis of eternal objects discloses no actual occasion, it does disclose other eternal objects.[59] Just as Whitehead envisions a hierarchy of societies of occasions, he envisions a hierarchy of eternal objects. In other words, the eternal objects too must be coordinated since they are the defining characters of societies which are coordinated. The graded relevance of occasions and diverse societies to one another in part reflects the pre-established coordination and graded relevance of all eternal objects to one another, a coordination and relevancy due to God's agency.

*General potentiality.* Whitehead has reason to discriminate even a third type of potentiality, namely, general potentiality, which is: ". . . the bundle of possibilities, mutually consistent or alternative, provided by the multiplicity of eternal objects. . . ."[60] Then there are three meanings of potentiality: the real potentiality of all objects, the pure potentiality of eternal objects, and the general potentiality of the multiplicity of eternal objects evaluated by God.

The general potentiality of the universe accounts for the creative evolution of novel occasions without novel eternal objects. By the ontological principle, this general potentiality, like everything else, must have its cause and reason in some actuality. That actuality is God.

Everything must be somewhere; and here 'somewhere' means 'some actual entity.' Accordingly the general potentiality of the universe must be somewhere; since it retains its proximate relevance to actual entities for which it is unrealized. This 'proximate relevance' reappears in subsequent concrescence as final causation regulative of the emergence of novelty. This 'somewhere' is the non-temporal actual entity. Thus 'proximate relevance' means 'relevance as in the primordial mind of God.'[61]

The "final causation regulative of the emergence of novelty" of this passage refers to the subjective aims of occasions. The eternal objects of the subjective aims are relevant lures for feeling for the occasions in becoming. The general potentiality of the universe is the fact that subjective aims, already evaluated by God, are available for occasions to fulfill.

Whitehead is answering the question, Where is the relevancy of certain eternal objects such that a subject lured by them will become one compatible whole? Whitehead's answer is God. God has provided that certain eternal objects be ordered among themselves and compatible with one another such that they afford an appropriate and relevant subjective aim for a subject prehending them. "Accordingly the differentiated relevance of eternal objects to each instance of the creative process requires their conceptual realization in the primordial nature of God."[62] God has evaluated and selected the eternal objects of an occasion's subjective aim in advance of the occasion so that its aim for these eternal objects is a real possibility for it, so that it not be lured by an impossible and irrelevant conjugation of eternal objects. "This final entity is the divine element in the world, by which the barren inefficient disjunction of abstract potentialities obtains primordially the efficient conjunction of ideal realization."[63]

The subjective aim of an occasion is not necessarily that of its direct antecedents. If all subjective aims were exactly the same, all occasions would be exactly alike. But the fact is, the antecedent world and the aims of that world are not exactly reduplicated; there is an evolution of novel occasions. However, while novel occasions come into being, there is no such thing as a novel eternal object coming into being: ". . . but there are no novel eternal objects."[64] Not even God creates new eternal objects for new occasions. "[God] does not create eternal objects; for his nature requires them in the same degree that they require him."[65] This is the reason for the eternality of eternal objects; none ever change, none are novel. It is the same eternal objects that recur again and again in new occasions; none are made up just for the occasion. "The eternal objects are the same for all actual entities."[66]

For there to be a novel eternal object, one would have to suppose that an eternal object never before realized suddenly appeared out of nowhere as an occasion's novel character. But the Whiteheadian cosmology does not countenance sheer invention out of nothing. Its ontological principle requires that eternal objects, like all other features of actual occasions, have their causes and reasons in actual occasions. They cannot be created out of nothing, not even by God. "The definite ingression into a particular actual entity is not to be  conceived as the sheer evocation of that eternal object from 'not-being' into 'being'. . . ."[67] Eternal objects are not suspended in some kind of unreality awaiting prehension: none are uningressed. They are selected by a subject for ingression from among those that are there, having ingression in some antecedent occasions somewhere, and including God. A. H. Johnson contradicts Whitehead's dictum that there are no novel eternal objects: "There is 'change' in the sense that an eternal object is now exemplified in an actual entity whereas previously it was not exemplified in any actual entity."[68] If it were not exemplified in any actual entity, then it does not exist, by Whitehead's account.

*A plenum of occasions.* It must be clear that potentiality, real, pure and general is not "non-being." Occasions neither come into being out of nothing nor perish into nothing. For the Whiteheadian cosmology, there is no "non-being." Our ordinary substantialist frame of mind inclines us to think that whatever is not fully actual, wholly and completely and concretely realized, is *not,* is nothing at all. Substantialism leaves no room for potentiality. For example, Rasvihary Das writes:

> . . . it is extremely difficult to understand what Whitehead means when he speaks of 'settled fact' or 'objective immortality.' His settled fact seems to be no fact, and his objective immortality appears to be enjoyed by actual entities only when they are no longer actual and are reduced to nothing.[69]

But we have seen that perishing is not vanishing; it is only with respect to their self-functioning and their subjective immediacy that occasions perish. Having perished, an occasion is both stubborn fact and real potentiality for myriad specific effects in occasions to come. The perished occasion becomes many objects for many subjects as each new subject objectifies it in its own way. The perished occasion enjoys the objective immortality of its status as objects in the experience of many successive subjects. Such an occasion, though gone and not actual subjectively, is not "no fact" and "nothing." For Whitehead there is no "nothing." "It is a natural figure of speech, but only a figure of speech, to conceive a slighter actuality as being an approach towards nonentity. But you cannot approach nothing; for there is nothing to approach."[70] "Nothing" does not exist: the existence of "nothing" is a contradiction in terms.

Potentiality is potentiality for and of actual occasions; it is not itself an actual occasion nor does it belong to a separate ontological category any more than objects are a separate ontological category from subjects. And certainly "nothingness" is no category of being, for Whitehead. Lewis S. Ford has a problem with the ontological category of potentiality: "The problem turns on the being to be assigned that which is in becoming."[71] The being to be assigned a subject is that of potentiality, which is neither complete actuality nor nothing at all; it is the process of actualization. A subject is emerging from its objects or objectifications which are its efficient causes. These objects, the real potentialities of actual, concrete stubborn facts, have the relevant potentiality for becoming that subject, which is not yet an actual and concrete fact.

Thus, there is no empty space or empty time: there is no space and no time where and when there is no occasion or occasions and potential occasions. Space and time are special properties of the extension of the occasions themselves. The universe is a plenum of occasions creating new occasions. "Descartes' doctrine of the physical world as exhibiting an extensive plenum of actual entities is practically the same as the 'organic' doctrine."[72] The universe is a plenum of occasions both actual and potential. It is not a plenum of static, ever-actual, already completed, fully actualized occasions without potentiality, occupying otherwise empty spaces and times. Spaces and times are the spatial and temporal dimensions of the occasions.

## SATISFACTION

*Subjective aim.* The subjective aim of a subject lures all its feelings to concresce as one united occasion.

> This doctrine of the inherence of the subject in the process of its production requires that in the primary phase of the subjective process there be a conceptual feeling of subjective aim: the physical and other feelings originate as steps towards realizing this conceptual aim through their treatment of initial data.[73]

Both antecedent occasions (the data of physical feelings) and eternal objects are prehended. Physical nature and its form have this in common: both are prehendable. The general potentiality of the universe, by means of subjective aims, insures the possibility of the unity of antecedent occasions and eternal objects for new occasions succeeding them. It provides that antecedent occasions and eternal objects are potentially compatible for a new creation, such that they might be bound together as the achievement of a subjective aim.

> It is now obvious that blind prehensions, physical and mental, are the ultimate bricks of the physical universe. They are bound together within each actuality by the subjective aim which governs their allied genesis and their final concrescence.[74]

The subjective aim, then, is the final cause that "controls the becoming of a subject."[75] It lures the diverse feelings into ingressing certain eternal objects appropriate to all the feelings as a unity. It is by virtue of sharing one subjective aim that all the different feelings coalesce. They aim at and are thereby lured into one united feeling—a single feeler. The subject is nothing more than this subjective aim shared by many feelings, enabling them to concresce into one feeling. "The feeling is an episode in self-production, and is referent to its aim. This aim is certain definite unity with its companion feelings."[76] Thus, the subject *is* the unity of feelings. There is not both a subject and an aim; there is not an already actual subject which also happens to have an aim; there is not a subject over and above the feelings it has. The subject *is* the shared aim of fellow feelings. It is constituted by this aim of the feelings to concresce; in other words, it is constituted by its own process of self-creation. "The immediacy of the concrescent subject is constituted by its living aim at its own self-constitution."[77]

The subjective aim is the lure to be something. Whatever concrete existent there is has been aimed at. The subjective aim controls *what* the new occasion is to be.

On one side, the one becomes many; and on the other side, the many become one. But *what* becomes is always a *res vera*, and the concrescence of a *res vera* is the development of a subjective aim.[78]

A subject's definite character is the set of related eternal objects which its feelings had aimed at realizing in concrescing. It is important to recognize that the subjective aim determines what being shall arise from a becoming. For, then it is the more readily seen that differing subjective aims will require differing spatiotemporal dimensions for their actualization. Not all subjective aims are alike; not all are those of subatomic occasions or of occasions of human visual perception. Subjective aims are the aims at all the beings there are, in all the varieties of character and all the variations of spatiotemporal extent that there are. Whatever concrete *being*, whatever *existent*, whatever *self*, whatever *thing* comes into being demonstrates the fulfillment of a subjective aim to do so.

The actual entity, in becoming itself, also solves the question as to *what* it is to be. Thus process is the stage in which the creative idea works towards the definition and attainment of a final end. . . . The determinate unity of an actual entity is bound together by the final causation towards an ideal progressively defined. . . . The ideal, itself felt, defines what 'self' shall arise from the datum; and the ideal is also an element in the self which thus arises.[79]

*God.* All the conceptual prehensions of all the eternal objects of all subjective aims taken together are God's primordial nature. That is, the general potentiality of the universe is an expression of God's intention for each actual occasion. "But the initial stage of its aim is an endowment which the subject inherits from the inevitable ordering of things, conceptually realized in the nature of God."[80] Subjective aims begin in God and by way of guiding the mutual adjustment of prehensions through stages of their concrescence end as the achievement of the particular and individual actual occasions.

Subjective aims have their natural origin in God inasmuch as God has provided that the eternal objects aimed at are appropriate and relevant candidates for ingression in one occasion together. He has evaluated them and ordered them according to their capacities for ingression together in particular occasions.

> In what sense can unrealized abstract form be relevant? What is its basis of relevance? 'Relevance' must express some real fact of togetherness among forms. . . . So if there be relevance of what in the temporal world is unrealized, the relevance must express a fact of togetherness in the formal constitution of a non-temporal actuality. . . . This is the ultimate, basic adjustment of the togetherness of eternal objects on which creative order depends. . . . Its status as an actual efficient fact is recognized by terming it the 'primordial nature of God.'[81]

A tree does not become a human being; an occasion of a sheep has not the subjective aim of an electronic occasion; a vegetable does not come into being a stone. The subjective aims of antecedent occasions creating successors are appropriate to them.

Thus, the final causes of all occasions are all God, since all subjective aims originate in God. "In this sense, God can be termed the creator of each temporal actual entity."[82] The subjective aim of each occasion is an aim of God's as well. God is just as much the guide of concrescence as is the subjective aim. "In this sense God is the principle of concretion; namely, he is that actual entity from which each temporal concrescence receives that initial aim from which its self-causation starts."[83] However, one conceptual prehension of the eternal objects belonging to a subjective aim is not a prehension of God's before his prehension of another. Before and after, earlier and later cannot be applied to God or within God since he is non-temporal. God's initiation of subjective aims is not in time. No subjective aim marks a past or future part of God. God does not become and perish with occasions. "In the case of the primordial actual entity, which is God, there is no past."[84] Therefore, there is no society of God, no nexus of God occasions; God is not an enduring object or a structured society; there is no succession, no historical route of God. God is ever concrescing.[85]

God's initiation of a subjective aim for a subject means that its direct antecedents and the eternal objects ingressed in these antecedents are not the sole source of the efficient causation creating the subject. "The antecedent environment is not wholly efficacious in determining the initial phase of the occasion which springs from it."[86] The antecedent occasions comprising a subject's actual world, then, do not determine even the subject's initial phase of creation. The subjective aim of the subject founded in God is required. It is God and the actual world combined that initiate an occasion. "If we prefer the phraseology, we can say that God and the actual world jointly constitute the character of the creativity for the initial phase of the novel concrescence."[87] It may be that an eternal object belonging to a subject's subjective aim is not to be found in its immediate antecedents, the occasions comprising its actual world. But such an eternal object has ingression in some occasion somewhere in the antecedent universe relative to the subject, and has relevance to this subject on account of God's arrangement. "Apart from God, eternal objects unrealized in the actual world would be relatively non-existent for the concrescence in question."[88] God can furnish a subjective aim with an eternal object from the remotest of antecedent occasions. The range of eternal objects available for subjective aims is that of the general potentiality of the universe. For this reason, Whitehead speaks of the general potentiality of the universe as having relevance to each occasion: "Transcendent decision includes God's decision. He is the actual entity in virtue of which the *entire* multiplicity of eternal objects obtains its graded relevance to each stage of concrescence."[89]

God is responsible not only for the order in the universe, but the novelty. "Apart from the intervention of God, there could be nothing new in the world, and no order in the world."[90] While there may be no novel eternal objects, there may be novel combinations, novel sets of eternal objects never before realized. That new conjugations of eternal objects will make possible, realistic, and relevant goals for subjects to achieve shows God's handiwork in evaluating all possible combinations of eternal objects. Eternal objects are all realized in some occasions somewhere; but not all possible combinations. "Apart from God, there could be no relevant novelty."[91] Thus, subjective aims of successive subjects need not be the same as those of their antecedents. The real possibility of new combinations of eternal objects serving subjective aims is a fact: the general potentiality of the universe pre-established by God.

And God's purpose in evaluating all eternal objects so that they afford appropriate subjective aims for forthcoming occasions is the intensification of experience. "In this function, as in every other, God is the organ of novelty, aiming at intensification."[92] All subjective aims are arranged so as to intensify experience within the limits of possibility; all have this ultimate purpose, God's purpose, in common. In other words, the intensification of experience is God's subjective aim. "'Order' and 'novelty' are but the instruments of his subjective aim which is the intensification of 'formal immediacy.'"[93]

*Subjective ends.* However, a subjective aim is not only God's, but a subject's. The aim may begin in God, but it is completed and fulfilled by a subject, if it be completed and fulfilled at all.

The mental pole introduces the subject as a determinant of its own concrescence. The mental pole is the subject determining its own ideal of itself by reference to eternal principles of valuation autonomously modified in their application to its own physical objective datum.[94]

The fact that a subjective aim is an aim of a particular subject and not only God is shown in the subject's modification of the aim in the course of its development.

The subjective aim would not be a subject's final cause but that it is the subject's aim to fulfill; otherwise it is only God's final cause. If subjective aims could not be modified and belonged only to God, then actual occasions would simply be God and nothing else. They would have no individuality and decisiveness owing to themselves alone, and they would have no responsibility for their own inner quality of life. But an occasion *is* a final cause of its concrescence. The occasion chooses how it reacts by selecting eternal objects for its subjective forms. "To be *causa sui* means that the process of concrescence is its own reason for the decision in respect to the qualitative clothing of feelings."[95] It is the modification of the subjective aim, that is to say, its use by the subject in adapting its actual world to itself, that attests to the individuality and individual responsibility of the subject. In Whitehead's words, modifying the subjective aim is the subject's "final decision"; it is not God's decision.

Further, in the case of those actualities whose immediate experience is most completely open to us, namely, human beings, the final decision of the immediate subject-superject, constituting the ultimate modification of subjective aim, is the foundation of our experience of responsibility, of approbation or of disapprobation, of self-approval or of self-reproach, of freedom, of emphasis.[96]

If this were not so, if all occasions had only the aim of God and nothing else, there would not even be recognizable differences among occasions: all would be recognizable only as God. There would only be God's primordial nature in existence. But as it is, both occasions and God are creative; both are final causes. "All actual entities share with God this characteristic of self-causation."[97] God initiates the subject; but the subject develops itself from there. "Thus the initial stage of the aim is rooted in the nature of God, and its completion depends on the self-causation of the subject-superject."[98]

Thus, a subjective aim suffers successive modifications as the subject decides how it is to be fulfilled. The subjective aim includes many relevant alternatives for the subject; these are eliminated as the subject realizes only one of the alternatives. Whitehead describes the subjective aim as simplified by the subject through phases of its process of concrescence.

This basic conceptual feeling suffers simplification in the successive phases of the concrescence. It starts with conditioned alternatives, and by successive decisions is reduced to coherence. The doctrine of responsibility is entirely concerned with this modification. In each phase the corresponding conceptual feeling is the 'subjective end' characteristic of that phase. The many feelings, in any incomplete phase, are necessarily compatible with each other by reason of their individual conformity to the subjective end evolved for that phase.[99]

In view of the fact that a subjective aim is modified by the subject fulfilling it, then, Whitehead has termed each stage of modification the "subjective end" of that stage. It is that part of the subjective aim realized by a subject at any stage. The subjective aim lures feelings into a new concrescence; the subject decides how all the feelings as a whole react to their new unification.

*Actualization.* A subject's fulfillment of its subjective aim in the way that it has chosen Whitehead calls its "satisfaction." ". . . the 'subjective aim' at 'satisfaction' constitutes the final cause, or lure, whereby there is determinate concrescence; and that attained 'satisfaction' remains as an element in the content of creative purpose."[100] Thus, satisfaction refers to the fact that a process of concrescence is completed, that the subjective aim of an occasion to be whatever it be has been met.

With the achievement of its subjective aim a subject becomes a concrete actual occasion. It is satisfied upon exhibiting certain eternal objects which are elements of its subjective aim as its own; it is satisfied having that definite character, the eternal objects, aimed at. Satisfaction refers to concretion as opposed to the process of concrescence by which it arrived. "This satisfaction is the attainment of something individual to the entity in question."[101] With the satisfaction of its lure for feeling, the subject is a particular concrete actual entity distinct from all others and comparable to others and prehendable. Thus, concrescence and satisfaction are not synonymous. Concrescence is the growing together of feelings; it is the process of the becoming of an occasion rather than the concrete occasion having become. Concrescence is the development of a subjective aim, whereas satisfaction is the attainment of the subjective aim. Concrescence concludes in satisfaction. ". . . the concrescence issues in one concrete feeling, the satisfaction."[102]

The process of concrescence is indeterminate; the emerging occasion is still a potentiality deciding on how it is to be satisfied, how it is to be unified as one concrete existent with one complex experience. But the satisfaction is completely determinate since all decisions have been made and all feelings unifed accordingly.

This process of the integration of feeling proceeds until the concrete unity of feeling is obtained. In this concrete unity all indetermination as to the realization of possibilities has been eliminated. The many entities of the universe, including those originating in the concrescence itself, find their respective roles in this final unity. This final unity is termed the 'satisfaction.' The 'satisfaction' is the culmination of the concrescence into a completely determinate matter of fact.[103]

Concrescence proceeds through several stages or phases, the data of feeling accounting for one phase and the subject's decisions as to how to handle its data account for other phases. The satisfaction accounts for another phase entirely, the final phase of the concrescence.

(xxv) The final phase in the process of concrescence, constituting an actual entity, is one complex, fully determinate feeling. This final phase is termed the 'satisfaction.' It is fully determinate (a) as to its genesis, (b) as to its objective character for the transcendent creativity, and (c) as to its prehension—positive or negative—of every item in its universe.[104]

The term "satisfaction" is not meant to imply that the process of concrescence necessarily concludes pleasantly, enjoyably, or that the concrete occasion it produces is necessarily good. On the contrary, an occasion may attain satisfaction as something bad, ugly, painful, or evil. Evil occasions come into being too; their evil is in their having evil effect upon successors. "A novelty has emerged into creation. The novelty may promote or destroy order; it may be good or bad."[105] The process of concrescence actualizes potentiality, for good or for evil; satisfaction is the concrete actuality achieyed. "The process of self-creation is the transformation of the potential into the actual, and the fact of such transformation includes the immediacy of self-enjoyment."[106]

*Abruptness of satisfaction.* The satisfaction of a subject completes its process of becoming abruptly. What was not an actuality before is one now; a particular concrete existent never before among us has appeared. The occasion abruptly exhibits the definiteness that it has become. Satisfaction is abrupt because the ingression of eternal objects is abrupt. "This abrupt synthesis of eternal objects in each occasion is the inclusion in actuality of the analytical character of the realm of eternality."[107] The eternal objects of the subjective aim abruptly ingress in the subject upon its fulfilling the aim, and the subject is now that actual occasion for which its antecedents and its feeling had the potentiality.

However, the eternal objects belonging to a subjective aim abruptly ingressing in an occasion with its satisfaction is not an instantaneous or even a brief occurrence; it is not an occurrence at all since the actual occasions are the occurrences. A process of concrescence is the construction of one occurrence; participation in eternal objects is not a separate occurrence within it. Real potentials are actualized, pure potentials are realized;[108] the actualization and realization are what occur, not what happens to things that have already occurred. Something comes into being realizing some definite character; its character is not other than what it has become as though it could occur to it later, but occurs with it.

When the subjective aim is fulfilled, and the eternal objects belonging to it are abrupty realized, the process of concrescence halts.

> . . . the attainment of a peculiar definiteness is the final cause which animates a particular process; and its attainment halts its process, so that by transcendence it passes into its objective immortality as a new objective condition added to the riches of definiteness attainable, the 'real potentiality' of the universe.[109]

Similarly, Whitehead says that becoming ceases upon the completion of concrescence, that the process of concrescence terminates with determinate satisfaction.[110] And here he speaks of time as standing still upon an occasion's arrival at satisfaction.

In the conception of the actual entity in its phase of satisfaction, the entity has attained its individual separation from other things; it has absorbed the datum, and it has not yet lost itself in the swing back to the 'decision' whereby its appetition becomes an element in the data of other entities superseding it. Time has stood still—if only it could.[111]

Thus, there is cessation and termination of concrescence with the fulfillment of its final cause, the subjective aim: subjective immediacy perishes and objective immortality begins. Satisfaction brings the subject to a halt and a standstill, and its time-span too.

The time-span, or temporal duration, of a process of concrescence begins with the initiation of its subjective aim in God and ends with its satisfaction with itself. "The factor of temporal endurance selected for any one actuality will depend upon its initial 'subjective aim.'"[112] The time-span is the temporal duration required for a subjective aim to be fulfilled; it is the unit of time in which a subject becomes, from its initiation to its complete coming into being as a new actual occasion. The time-span of an occasion is not that of its satisfaction as though this were a separate occurrence added to becoming, but that of the entire process of concrescence including its satisfaction.

*The spatialization of time.* Whiteheadian time, the succession of epochal occasions, each epoch being the duration required to fulfill its subjective aim, should be contrasted with absolute time. Classical physics was governed by absolute spacetime; but modern physics requires epochal time such as Whitehead describes. Absolute time is best described by Newton, its greatest exponent: "Absolute, true, and mathematical time, of itself, and from its own nature, flows equably without relation to anything external."[113] Here is the conception of time as a substantial movement, flowing ever at the same rate for all things alike, and independent of all things. Newton's definition and descriptions of absolute time seem for all the world obvious, indubitable. "The flowing of absolute time is not liable to any change. . . . The order of the parts of time is immutable."[114] This conception of time seems so reasonable, so intelligible it is hard to imagine doing without it. Yet it has no validity today, if modern physics has validity. "But at last the Newton cosmology has broken down,"[115] writes Whitehead, and he points out that its doctrine of an instantaneous action is unintelligible.

There is a fatal contradiction inherent in the Newtonian cosmology. . . .
Now assuming this Newtonian doctrine, we ask— What becomes of

velocity, at an instant? Again we ask— What becomes of momentum at an instant? These notions are essential for Newtonian physics, and yet they are without any meaning for it.[116]

The Newtonian "mathematical flow" was the flow of instants or instantaneous spaces, that is, spaces at successive instants. The instants and the spaces were conceived as substances, actualities just as substantial as the material bodies occupying them. "Thus bits of space and time were conceived as being as actual as anything else, and as being 'occupied' by other actualities which were the bits of matter. This is the Newtonian 'absolute' theory of space-time. . . ."[117] The autonomous and substantial flow of absolute time, because it was thought to be a substance, then, amounts to the substantialization, reification, or hypostatization of an idea of time.[118] Whitehead, naturally, has his own term for this confusion. He calls it the "fallacy of misplaced concreteness": it is the error of mistaking the abstract for the concrete. For Whitehead, Newtonian time is an example of this fallacy.[119] Time, instead of being a part of the nature of actualities, is conceived as a substantial actuality on its own, requiring nothing but itself in order to exist. "The Newtonian description of matter abstracts matter from time. It conceives matter 'at an instant'. So does Descartes' description. If process be fundamental such abstraction is erroneous."[120] Absolute time would flow right along at the same rate even if there were no matter and no universe at all. In Einstein's expression: "The idea of the independent existence of space and time can be expressed drastically in this way: If matter were to disappear, space and time alone would remain behind (as a kind of stage for physical happening)."[121]

The flow of instants or instantaneous spaces could also be treated as one whole, a static spacetime container that all matter occupied, a place and instant of cosmic size; ". . . the succession of instantaneous spaces is tacitly combined into one persistent space."[122] Absolute time, then, lent itself to spatialization, the conception of a static ("persisting") space. Absolute time is absorbed into absolute and timeless space. In the words of Milic Capek, ". . . the . . . tendency prevailed: to subordinate time to space, and even to deny the objective status of time entirely."[123] So the flow of absolute time was easily eliminated entirely, being regarded as itself only an accidental quality of a substantial, enduring space. ". . . the habit of spatializing time is only one mode of the tendency to eliminate time, the tendency which is as old as philosophy."[124] Capek traces the spatialization of time, and consequently its elimination, to the beginnings of Western thought.

Such spatialization of time is only a particular form of another perennial illusion which can be traced to the very dawn of Western thought: the belief that becoming can be reduced to being, process to substance, time to the timeless, *events* to *things.*[125]

But the awareness that time was regularly eliminated by way of spatializing it, and the analysis of its consequences, originated with Bergson. "Bergson's lasting merit is to point out the distortions which spatializing habits cause in our representation of time."[126]

Absolute time is so readily spatialized that even Newton, for whom time was an equable flow, speaks of time as being, like space, a place. "For times and spaces are, as it were, the places as well of themselves as of all other things."[127] This may well be expected of Newton, the world's leading proponent of absolute time. But the practice of spatializing time goes on today.

The persistence of our linguistic habits merely reflect the obstinacy of the underlying mental habits; we are all unconsciously Newtonians . . . and the classical idea of world-wide instants, containing simultaneous spatially separated events, still haunts the subconscious even of relativistic physicists; though verbally rejected, it manifests itself, like a Freudian symbol, in a certain conservatism of language. . . . The task of an epistemologist in contemporary physics is therefore a little like that of the psychoanalyst: to detect the remnants of classical thought beneath the verbal denials and conscious rejections.[128]

Capek's psychoanalysis is well taken. For example, calling time the "fourth dimension" spatializes it. Hans Reichenbach agrees: "Calling time the fourth dimension gives it an air of mystery. One might think that time can now be conceived as a kind of space and try in vain to add visually a fourth dimension to the three dimensions of space."[129] And there is much more in the way of spatialization of time.

Expressions like 'Reimannian *space*' or 'curvature of *space*' abound, and not only in popular expositions. . . . How stubborn this tendency is to believe in a processless container is evidenced by the fact that even now physicists continue to speak about motion of bodies *in* non-Euclidian space.[130]

The most striking manifestation of the unconscious tendency to eliminate time by spatializing it is the expression "spacetime" itself, with its emphasis on space. As Whitehead remarks: "This survival of fragments of older doctrines is also exemplified in the modern use of the term space-time."[131] Thus, "spacetime" is a concession to absolute time. Therefore, ". . . it is more accurate to speak of *time-space* than of space-time."[132]

So unconsciously assumed, so ingrained in our ordinary thinking and language, is absolute spacetime that even contemporary physicists might be found adhering to it. "The presuppositions of yesterday's physics remain in the minds of physicists, although their explicit doctrines taken in detail deny them."[133] The reification of time did not end with Einstein; the spatialization of time did not stop with Bergson; the elimination of time has not heeded Whitehead: our common sense conceptions still predominate, even with many physicists and philosophers. It is possible to study modern physics and come away from it just as Newtonian as without studying it, so complete is our acceptance of common sense. Similarly, it is also possible to study Whitehead and come away from it just as scientific materialist as without studying it. A mastery of the Whiteheadian vocabulary does not necessarily mean an understanding of its contribution to thought.

*Instantaneousness.* Absolute time, then, is the conception of a uniform and universal flow or succession of instants, each instant dividing the absolute past from the future, these being the same for all things alike. The instant is a world-wide infinitesimally thin durationless present that can nevertheless accumulate in the past and progress to the future. These are two things wrong with the instant: it is universal, and it is vanishingly brief. Whitehead specifies both of these misconceptions by way of summarizing scientific materialism: "[Materialism] can be summarised as the belief that nature is an aggregation of material and that this material exists in some sense *at* each successive member of a one-dimensional series of extensionless instants of time."[134] Thus, there is only the single one-dimensional succession of instants as instantaneous as the "mathematical flow" of numbers, oblivious to matter; yet the instants themselves are instantaneous planes accumulating the space in which matter endures.

There is only the one succession of instants because each instant is world-wide so that all matter exists in it at once; all matter is present together at the same time. Absolute time means absolute simultaneity: one present time applies to all things alike, regardless of the things and what their perspectives on other things are. This is the reason for its absoluteness: it presumes a singular, privileged perspective from which all things alike can be spatiotemporally defined. And all things at any stage can be so defined at any instant; none are in a state of potential existence.

Albert Einstein, of course, is to be credited with the discovery that absolute simultaneity does not exist. "'Now' loses for the spatially extended world its objective meaning."[135] Milic Capek emphatically repeats Einstein's discovery: "Such instantaneous classical spaces literally do not exist; in less provocative language, they are embedded in the dynamic spatiotemporal continuum out of which they are carved only by artificial operations."[136] And for Whitehead too, there is no such thing as the absolute simultaneous presence of all matter. "There is no such thing as nature at an instant posited by sense-awareness."[137]

Thus, the world-wide instant, abandoned by science, is a conception that by misplaced concreteness may still be mistaken for fact. A. S. Eddington, to whom the expression "world-wide instant" belongs, says that such an instant is an imaginary partition:

> If we believe our world-wide instants or Now lines to be something inherent in the world outside us, we shall quarrel frightfully. . . . World-wide instants are not natural cleavage planes of time; there is nothing equivalent to them in the absolute structure of the world; they are imaginary partitions which we find it convenient to adopt . . . like the lines of latitude and longitude on the earth.[138]

And David Bohm describes absolute simultaneity in the same way, as part of the Newtonian "conceptual map":

> Thus, when Newton proposed the idea of absolute space and time physicists did not say that this is only a kind of conceptual map, which may have a structure that is partly true to that of real physical processes and partly false. Rather, they felt that *what is* is absolute space and time.[139]

And in Whitehead's words, it is a "logical concept":

> Instantaneousness is a complex logical concept of a procedure in thought by which constructed logical entities are produced for the sake of the simple expression in thought of properties of nature. Instantaneousness is the concept of all nature at an instant, where an instant is conceived as deprived of all temporal extension. For example we conceive of the distribution of matter in space at an instant.[140]

Thus, a world-wide instant is a conception useful for classical physics but no actuality in fact. Modern physics has shown it to be a fiction.

The other defect of instants is their vanishingly short duration. Here is the conception of time without any duration; there is nothing temporal about an instant. To Whitehead, the conception of an instant is nonsense.

It is nonsense to conceive of nature as a static fact, even for an instant devoid of duration. There is no nature apart from transition, and there is no transition apart from temporal duration. This is the reason why the notion of an instant of time, conceived as a primary simple fact, is nonsense.[141]

Absolute instants are the idealized points, lines, and planes of geometry, infinitesimally thin. Whitehead remarks that an instant is as durationless as an ideal point: "It needs very little reflection to convince us that a point in time is no direct deliverance of experience. We live in durations, and not in points."[142] There is no time for time in an ideal point, line, plane, or number. There is no time for the progression of time in the accumulation of instantaneous planes. Time has been omitted where an instant is simply an ideal demarcation of events by which to declare a universal present. Whitehead reminds us that there is no time for the passage of nature in an instant: "The passage of nature which is only another name for the creative force of existence has no narrow ledge of definite instantaneous present within which to operate."[143] No Whiteheadian occasion can be reduced to a point, a line, a plane, a number, or any other ideal and contentless configuration. No Whiteheadian epoch is world-wide; no epoch is without duration; no succession of epochs combine into one persisting space, an absolute spacetime container for all things alike. There is nothing instantaneous in the Whiteheadian philosophy; Whitehead believes that nothing of the sort exists. "But we deny this immediately given instantaneous present. There is no such thing to be found in nature."[144]

*Whitehead misinterpreted.* Many confusions about Whiteheadian time stem from replacing epochs or a part thereof with instants. The potentiality of occasions is all too readily precluded and the entire process of concrescence conceived as either instantaneous or as actual and present at each of successive instants; or the satisfaction alone is taken to be instantaneous. In other words, an epoch is too often regarded as either one instant or as a succession of instants. Such a confusion of Whiteheadian time with absolute time shows up, for example, in Rasvihary Das: "We cannot possibly conceive that derivation and integration take place in a world of unreality, and we get all at once to the unified reality."[145] But potentiality is not unreality; on the contrary, it is a sort of being; and unified reality or satisfaction is not instantaneous. It is only our habitual scientific materialistic mentality that obliges us to preclude potentiality from existence and to imagine actuality to be present in an instant, and always present at every instant. Das describes the Whiteheadian epochs as if they were instantaneous planes: "We have, as it were, all at once a stretch of time, and then another, and so on."[146] Thus, stretches of time occur instantaneously, all at once. This contradiction—an instantaneous stretch—comes of accepting both Whiteheadian time and absolute time. The Whiteheadian epoch is a stretch, temporally extensive, but it is not also an instant, occurring instantaneously.

Lewis S. Ford too has imagined satisfactions to be instantaneous: "If the satisfaction subjectively occupies the entire duration of the present, then the concrescence must take no time at all, from which I can only infer that it must be instantaneous."[147] But neither concrescence nor its satisfaction are instantaneous. The Whiteheadian present, the entire process of concrescence including its satisfaction, is intended to replace the instantaneous present of absolute time, not to be reconciled with it.

And William A. Chirstian maintains the same confusion, converting Whiteheadian time to absolute time: "The satisfaction contains, one might say, the whole of the *temporal* duration of the occasion."[148] On the contrary, the temporal duration of an occasion extends from the initiation of its subjective aim through its satisfaction. The satisfaction seems the safest candidate for an instantaneous present because it is the actualization of an occasion and absolute time is only applied to actuality. Christian continues: "It is by producing their satisfactions that actual occasions produce the temporally extended world."[149] Here is the conception of successive instantaneous planes combining into one persisting space—absolute spacetime, not the Whiteheadian creative advance. There is no such thing in Whitehead as *the* temporally extended world, one world all of which occupies the same succession of instantaneous planes. The conception of one world extending throughout one spacetime is Newtonian. So inconceivable is any alternative to absolute time, with its singular, unique, uniform temporal series for all the world, that the temptation is to correct Whiteheadian time so that it is absolute. And in fact, the Whiteheadian epochs are used principally to reinstate absolute time, disguised in the new Whiteheadian vocabulary.

## CONCLUSION

The conception of an absolute time has been with us since time immemorial, so to speak. Clocks, by their mathematical regularity, lend themselves to the reification of time. In fact, the perfect running of a great cosmic clock has been imagined as the veritable cause of absolute time. The idea of a great cosmic clock of clocks, time-keeper of all the universe, was entertained, for example, by Plato, whose master clock actually turns the heavens and the earth:

> . . . The extremities of its fastenings stretched from heaven . . . holding together the entire revolving vault. And from the extremities was stretched the spindle of Necessity, through which all the orbits turned. . . . And the spindle turned on the knees of Necessity. . . . And there were . . . the daughters of Necessity, clad in white vestments with filleted heads. . . . Lachesis singing the things that were, Clotho the things that are, and Atropos the things that are to be.[150]

Plato's cosmic clock has been dismantled only in this century. Relativity physics has shown time to be the sequential relations between causally connected events only; it means that there can be no absolute temporal passage with respect to one event only, and no absolute simultaneity wherein all present events of the universe are actual at the same time. Quantum mechanics followed upon relativity, showing that quanta of energy do not develop or move continuously through a continuous absolute spacetime. Plato's cosmic clock, unsprung by the advances of physics, can no longer be invoked to interpret Whitehead's epochal time. Milic Capek is there to admonish us should we think even for a moment that we rely on absolute spacetime.

> According to Newton, time is independent of concrete motions and changes occurring within it; it is by its own nature homogeneous and flows at a constant rate no matter how different the speeds are of particular motions of physical bodies. It would flow at a constant rate even if the whole material universe should completely disappear; and according to Newton, it flowed so even before the creation of the world. This separation of time from its own content is the basis of its homogeneity. . . . Such a separation cannot be maintained any longer in the light of the relativity theory. . . . Time itself, like space, in virtue of its merging with the heterogeneous and dynamic content, loses its character of homogeneity and uniformity. . . . There is no unique serial temporal series in nature; time does not flow at an even rate.[151]

The Whiteheadian universe is a plenum of actual occasions in all stages of becoming and perishing, and with their ingredient eternal objects becoming realized again in new occasions. There is nothing in this universe that can possibly be instantaneous. Eternal objects are eternal; and actual occasions come into being through the duration of their processes of concrescence. A present duration is extant as long as is a process of concrescence. Therefore, the present necessarily embraces both the potentiality and the actualization of the occasion. The actuality of an occasion does not succeed its potentiality: rather, it satisfies it, it terminates its development. No potentiality can be actualized instantaneously.

An actual occasion has a present of some duration in order to make room for final causation. The subject must decide on the stance it is to take on all its feelings as a whole; it must accommodate all its feelings, and react to their final concrescence together.

> This category can be condensed into the formula, that in each concrescence whatever is determinable is determined, but that there is always a remainder for the decision of the subject-superject of that concrescence. . . . This final decision is the reaction of the unity of the whole to its own internal determination.[152]

A subject is indeterminate and undecided until its final phase of satisfaction when its final decisions come into effect. Then it becomes determinate with respect to all the antecedent occasions whose aspects compose its actual world; but because of its own inherent real potentiality, it is creative of subjects beyond itself. Then it enters, with other objects, into the indeterminate phases of new subjects. The present is indeterminate; this period is needed so that there may be a present and future differing from the past. A subject's relationship to the past is not already completely predetermined by the past, and not even completely predetermined by God, but by some autonomous decisions of the emerging subject. It may objectify its past and react to its objectifications in part as it chooses, so that the past may not be exactly reduplicated.

This is the peculiarity of final causation: its action is in the present and respecting the past and future without either retroactively affecting the past or prematurely effecting the future. The occasion harmonizes and reacts to the past and directs itself toward the future all in the present without passing, without dividing itself into past and future. Final causation, involving as it does an ideal and its attainment, requires an undivided time period in which to function.

For this reason, the potentiality and actuality of an occasion cannot be treated as two different occasions, or two different periods of time. There is no temporal order for one present duration, since temporal order requires two successive occasions. There is not first the occurrence of a potentiality, whether considered temporal or non-temporal, then the occurrence of actuality. An actual occasion, potential and actual, is one occurrence, one temporal duration. It is the duration of a subjective aim. A subject's present extends from the time when it first seeks the realization of the eternal objects of its subjective aim, to the time when their ingression is obtained. This applies to God as well, who is ever present, ever fulfilling his subjective aim which is the intensification of experience. These "time whens" referred to here are relative times, judging the beginning and end of an occasion retrospectively by comparing its spatiotemporal extension to that of other occasions. The subject itself does not pass in time; it does not successively occupy a series of instants. It is not even prehendable; it experiences its own present without prehending it. It has nothing to compare its own present to, while present; so it experiences no passage—there is no before to compare to an after within the present. Before is before the present, after is after it. The present does not pass but becomes an occasion of some spatiotemporal proportion. In other words, temporal duration becomes with the occasion.

The eternal objects of a subjective aim are abruptly realized in an occasion upon its satisfaction; but not even this abrupt realization takes place "in" time, nor signifies time's passing since it is still a part of the present duration. The conception of time as a bare sequence of abrupt realizations or satisfactions, a succession of halts or standstills in time devoid of potentiality, is a revival of absolute time. Satisfactions, while they may be intellectually considered in abstraction from occasions, do not exist in abstraction from occasions. They are the culmination and termination of an extended present, not instantaneous planes. "There is an intellectual theory of time as a moving knife-edge, exhibiting a present fact without temporal duration."[153] It does no justice to Whitehead to supplant his satisfactions with the "moving knife-edge" of successive instantaneous planes.

An occasion comes into being as a new set of eternal objects ingresses in it—the *set* being new, not any particular eternal object. The emerging occasion selects certain of its eternal objects from among those preevaluated for it by God. God selects them for the occasion's subjective aim from among all the general potentiality of the universe on the basis of their relevance to and real possibility for realization in the occasion. It is the eternal objects that characterize an occasion as a definite type of occasion; therefore, an occasion is partially formed by God and partially self-characterized. And there is no uncharacterizable occasion, no occasion that becomes actual without definite formation, its eternal objects. "There is no character belonging to the actual apart from its exclusive determination by selected eternal objects."[154]

A novel set of eternal objects is the formation of a novel occasion, unlike any one predecessor altogether, although like various predecessors in various ways, the different eternal objects being characters in common with different predecessors. It is God's shifting to new sets of eternal objects for subjective aims of occasions that makes for the possibility of novel occasions. And with each new subjective aim is a new epoch to intensify experience.

The birth of a new instance is the passage into novelty. . . . The novelty which enters into the derivate instance is the information of the actual world with a new set of ideal forms. In the most literal sense the lapse of time is the renovation of the world with ideas.[155]

# 4

# Process

*In defending myself I shall have to test the theory of my father Parmenides, and contend forcibly that after a fasion not-being is, and on the other hand, in a sense being is not.*

Plato, *Sophist* 241D

## INTRODUCTION

All things are made up of other things, yet do not wholly contain them; nexūs and societies may converge in one actual occasion, but are not wholly taken up therein. And one time-span is a part of other time-spans without being limited to any one other. Actual occasions include one another without building up and up so that the larger occasions are simply stacks of the smaller occasions. This would result in the universe being only one gigantic occasion constituted of all the smaller occasions each within others of larger size, a static object wholly containing all the lesser objects. Needless to say, this is not the Whiteheadian creative advance.

Occasions and their epochs create and constitute their successors without being wholly and literally contained by them. I attempt to show that this is not a problem that destroys the Whiteheadian cosmology. On the contrary, neither the cosmology nor its epochal time are intelligible without the mutual immanence of occasions and their epochs. No occasions or their epochs exist in isolation but necessarily include, overlap, and are included within others. This chapter addresses the issue of the inclusion of occasions within occasions and attempts to sketch a realistic picture of epochs within epochs consistent with Whitehead's intentions and principles.

There is no absolute measure of the duration of any epoch. Epochal time, being relative, differs in duration from different perspectives. A temporal duration, like a spatial distance, cannot be measured in comparison to itself alone, but only in comparison to others. Time-spans even among occasions of the same type will differ, just as the duration of each day from sunrise to sunset differs, or the duration of percipient experiences when sleepy, drinking, or wide-awake. And the duration of the very same time-span will differ with perspective. A day may be a very lengthy duration for a cloud, a leaf, an egg, or a child, for it spans a greater proportion of their existence; but it may be very brief for a glacier, a clay, a fossil, or a pine tree. There is no privileged perspective from which alone the duration of an epoch is to be defined. Whitehead illustrates the relativity of size and time-span this way:

> In all discussions of nature we must remember the differences of scale, and in particular the differences of time-span. We are apt to take modes of observable functioning of the human body as setting an absolute scale. It is extremely rash to extend conclusions derived from observation far beyond the scale of magnitude to which observation was confined. For example, to exhibit apparent absence of change within a second of time tells nothing as to the change within a thousand years. Also no apparent change within a thousand years tells anything as to a million years; and no apparent change within a million years tells anything about a million million years. We can extend this progression indefinitely. There is no absolute standard of magnitude.[1]

In this chapter I show that misinterpretations of Whiteheadian time, like misinterpretations of the actual occasion, are based upon presuming an "absolute standard of magnitude."

## THE PAST

*The creativity of the past.* There is nothing passive or static about objects, the antecedent occasions which are the data of prehensions. Endowed with creativity, they are in fact very forceful and energetic, aspects of the efficient causation of new subjects. A subject's prehension of objects is no accidental matter, since the subject is itself built of its prehensions of objects, including its own objectifications of them. Objects are not simply the passive recipients of the actions of subjects, but the very activity fueling the subjects. A subject's appropriation of objects is not the appropriation of things which are merely there awaiting prehension, indifferent to their appropriation, since objects are partially creative of these very appropriating subjects. For objects to be there at all is for them to be efficacious, to be constituents in the becoming of subjects. An object is not something that may or may not

be prehended, may or may not be a component in subjects; it must be prehended, either positively or negatively, if it be an object at all. It must
engage relationships with others and thereby enter into the becoming of
subjects, though its role in becoming is determined in part by the subjects.

It is not only subjects that are active, then. While subjects are active with
prehending, which includes evaluating, deciding, adjusting, modifying, and
objectifying, objects are active with creativity, the driving force of process,
the efficient causation that powers their efficacy for all the world beyond
their origination. As we have seen, the term "creativity" has been chosen to
suggest this energy and activity of objects, this power of efficient causation
that is not deterministic. Whitehead points out that "creativity" is his idea of
matter—matter as activity. His own term, "creativity," has the advantage of
getting away from the static, passive connotation of "matter."

'Creativity' is another rendering of the Aristotelian 'matter,' and of
the modern 'neutral stuff.' But it is divested of the notion of passive
receptivity, either of 'form,' or of external relations; it is the pure notion
of the activity conditioned by the objective immortality of the actual
world—a world which is never the same twice though always with the
stable element of divine ordering.[2]

Creativity is conditioned by what the objects are; it is causal activity that is
conditioned by the limitations of their real, finite potentialities.

Thus, it is incorrect to claim that Whiteheadian objects are inactive, that
the past is inert, that the perished are passive. Ivor Leclerc, for example,
would have it so:

It is important to note that in this doctrine the relation is effected
by the prehending entity, by its act of prehending. There is not a mutual
act of prehending; in this relation the prehended entity is not itself active.
Its activity has ceased; it is the 'past' of the prehending entity.[3]

Certainly there is not a mutual act of prehending; objects do not prehend but
are prehended. However, prehension includes the creativity of objects which
are the data of prehension. Prehension may be considered the only activity
that there is provided that the creativity, the efficient causation, of its data
are taken into account. For, as we have seen, prehension includes both the
efficient causation of its data and the final causation of the prehending
subject. A subject's prehending is partially effected by the creativity of the
objects constituting it. The activity of subjects is self-creation; the activity of
objects is other-creation: neither works without the other, outside of the
other, or independently of the other. Again, it is not activity that has ceased

upon perishing, but subjective immediacy, self-functioning. So far from ceasing, the activity of the past is responsible for the present. Whitehead states that his position is the "exact contrary" to that presented by Leclerc:

> But both words ['objects' and 'data'] suffer from the defect of suggesting that an occasion of experiencing arises out of a passive situation which is a mere welter of many data. . . . The exact contrary is the case. The initial situation includes a factor of activity which is the reason for the origin of that occasion of experience. This factor of activity is what I have called 'Creativity'.[4]

Not one iota of Whitehead's cosmic epoch is without activity. Search where you will, there is not a single static, passive particle to be found in all the creative advance: all matter is creative. Whitehead speaks of the activity of objects in different ways: he speaks of objects as driving the world, as intervening in subjects, as provoking the activity of subjects, as fashioning creative actions, and so on.[5] However it be described, the creativity of objects must not be overlooked; it is the same to overlook process, real potentiality, time. The past does not remain past; anything past is presently effecting a present subject, and anything present is in process. Not even satisfaction is a stasis in process, since it is the beginning of perishing and objective immortality. Objects are never simply there waiting for subjects to prehend them, since they are actively creating these very subjects.

*Crude addition simpliciter.* The past that is actively creating the present is in the present. A subject includes within it the real potentialities of antecedent occasions, that is, the objects of which it is constructed. Of course, the subjective immediacy of antecedents is gone; but their objective immortality is here and now. Objects are parts of the subject which concresces into a whole. And once whole, this occasion too becomes a part of many other wholes. "The relation of part to whole has the special reciprocity associated with the notion of organism, in which the part is for the whole. . . ."[6] That is, whole and part are relative designations; a whole depends on its parts to be the particular whole that it is, and parts depend on the whole of which they are the parts to be what they are. "If you abolish the whole, you abolish its parts; and if you abolish any part, then *that* whole is abolished."[7] Destroy a particular whole, and its parts do not remain behind as *its* alone; they become new parts for new wholes with that whole's destruction. Remove a part or add a part to a whole, and you no longer have the same whole. And there is no whole without parts and no parts that do not constitute a whole. "In this way the world is physically felt as a unity, and is felt as divisible into parts which are unities, namely, nexūs."[8] Each nexus is comprised of its member occasions and itself composes each successive member: the antecedent members are parts of their successors. Because every occasion is a whole, a unity, a concrescence, its analysis necessarily yields parts, ingredients, components. The parts are accommodated to fit the particular whole, having been objectified together by the whole so that they form together its unified content. And these parts are subsequently prehended as that whole had objectified them, i.e., as its parts, but they are objectified anew by their prehending successors. So that no object remains a part of one whole only, but becomes a part of every successor to it. This is the way in which objects are objectively immortal, not enduring as the self-same things, but as successive objectifications completely integrated in other occasions. Objects emerge from each objectification as new ingredients to be specially adapted to new occasions. They cannot remain the same since their transition from a cause to an effect in each new occasion alters them as it creates the new occasions.

The immanence of causes in effect, of objects in a subject, of parts in a whole, is not the same thing as the simple inclusion of some things in another thing. An antecedent occasion of a flower is one cause of my subsequently seeing it (by the time it takes light reflected from it to reach my eyes), my friend's touching its petal, a bee collecting its pollen, an air current being diverted, the air carrying its odor, light entering into the chemistry of its leaves, a caterpillar eating its leaves, its sexual cells readying its seed, and so on. The flower occasion had many real potentialities: for reflecting light, attracting bees, for food, for odor, for pollination, for seed manufacture, and so on. And the occasion is objectified in every occasion in which it has effect, every occasion for which it was an antecedent. Its petaled format, color, and pollen are objectified differently in bee, butterfly, bird, bacterium, and herbalist; its sight and odor are objectified differently in me, being allergic to it, and my friend, a horticulturist. The antecedent flower occasion becomes a part of each successor in which it is objectified, including succeeding flower occasions. But its existence in the experience of successors, in bees, insects, seeds, noses, touches, memories, bacteria, the air, the ground, is not the same as its existence as a flower was. What was a whole unto itself becomes a part of many, a different part in a different way for each successor. It contributes to successors without being a simple addition wholly onto any one successor.

Whitehead points out that it is the principle of relativity, in universalizing the efficacy of every occasion so that it becomes a part of every successor to it, that calls for a theory of objectification.

The principle of universal relativity directly traverses Aristotle's dictum, 'A substance is not present in a subject.' On the contrary, according to this principle an actual entity *is* present in other actual entities. In fact if we allow for degrees of relevance, and for negligible relevance, we must say that every actual entity is present in every other actual entity. The philosophy of organism is mainly devoted to the task of making clear the notion of 'being present in another entity.' This phrase is here borrowed from Aristotle: it is not a fortunate phrase, and in subsequent discussion it will be replaced by the term 'objectification.' The Aristotelian phrase suggests the crude notion that one actual entity is added to another *simpliciter*. This is not what is meant.[9]

Thus, the theory of objectification explains that an occasion is included in other occasions without this inclusion being the simple addition of the occasions. It requires that an antecedent occasion not be wholly included in any one subsequent occasion, since it must be included in all occasions subsequent to itself, however negligibly, or negatively prehended. For, any antecedent occasion is objectively immortal by virtue of partially causing and constituting many occasions future relatively to itself. Its effects are scattered throughout the subsequent world rather than being concentrated in any one occasion and one only.

Objects are included in their successors in the way that causes are immanent in their effects; and the cause and effect relationship is not the same as simple containment, one box within another. A person is not a simple addition of cells, a rock is not a simple addition of crystals, a star is not a simple addition of subatomic occasions. Wholes are not made by simply adding the would-be parts. The parts must enter into relationships and concresce together; but each relationship expresses only one aspect of their power. No occasion exhausts the potentiality of any other. Evander Bradley McGilvary says that occasions are not simply and wholly additive in this way: "Everything is actually and actively taken up into everything else. Not the *whole* of everything is thus taken up, but only what the prehending monad can use in effecting its concrescence."[10]

However, it is obvious that there are innumerable occasions within occasions and overlapping occasions, once we allow that an occasion is any concrete existent. Every material body of our acquaintance is not only an occasion at any moment of its existence but a mass of occasions within and overlapping occasions, societies within societies within societies, the occasions in all states of concrescence. Certainly the fact of smaller occasions being within larger occasions affects their relationships. Proportions and positions of occasions relative to one another affect their possible objectifications by the others, that is, their real potentialities for efficacy with the others. But the literal inclusion of the smaller within the larger must not be identified with objectification.

To be within is not necessarily to be objectified, or even to be objectified as within, though whatever is objectified is included within experience. A smaller occasion may be within a larger occasion without even being prehended because it is still a subject, still itself a potentiality. And without being prehended, it cannot be objectified. Without being objectified, it is not a part of the larger occasion, not a component of its constitution. Also, a smaller occasion may prehend and objectify a larger occasion; then an aspect of the larger occasion is included within the smaller occasion. Each antecedent occasion, or object, is both whole in itself and a part of the subsequent occasions it partially effects, whether smaller or larger than itself.

For example, some cell within an animal body may be potentially cancerous, but neither prehended nor objectified as such by any other cell or antibody since it is still a subject, as yet no actuality, *qua* cancer—no cancerous stubborn fact, no cancerous object. Also, a person within a building objectifies it as beautiful, or inviting, or sterile, or gloomy, or anything else; the building is within the person's percipient experience without the whole building being within the person. Some aspects of the building, sights, textures, distances, are within the person's experience where they are objectified with the help of comparisons with remembered buildings; that is, the seen building, the touched building, and the building's felt spatial proportions are a part of the person.

Occasion $A$ does not prehend occasion $B$ *simpliciter*, but $B$ under a limitation which is its objectification. This objectification is provided by the eternal objects whereby $B$ is prehended into $A$ as an example of those objects. Thus $B$ is objectified for $A$, and the eternal objects are the relational elements which effect the objectification.[11]

A flower smaller than I and larger than a bee enters both our experiences without being wholly within either of us. I do not have to eat the flower to prehend and objectify it. It is within my percipient experience without having to be within my mouth and stomach. And even should my blood carry it on to my brain, I do not thereby have a more real or more definite experience, or the only possible experience, of the flower. To see a building or a flower is to objectify it in some way appropriate to visual perception; the seen building or flower are objects in my experience without the actual antecedent occasions being in my eye. This is one way antecedent occasions become a part of their successors: by being seen.

Prehension is relating; prehension and the objectification of its data that comes with it occurs wherever there is a relationship. The flower enters my experience as soon as the flower and I are in relationship, any kind of relationship whatsoever. Efficacy is not limited only to that of the smaller upon the larger that literally includes it. Just as a building is in Rome, a rock in the earth, a tree in a forest, a subatomic occasion in a chair, a person in America, a bird in a flock, so too Rome affects its buildings, the earth its rock, the forest its trees, the chair its subatomic occasions, America its people, a flock its birds, a body its cells, and so on. The flower is in the air, but the air has affected it too. Occasions include their objectifications of antecedent occasions; they may or may not literally include the occasions. But even where smaller occasions are literally included in a larger one, their efficacy is not thereby restricted to it.

*The actual world.* The aspects of antecedent occasions which effect a successor to themselves are the actual world of that successor. An occasion is composed of its actual world. We have seen that the actual world is a nexus: "The nexus of actual entities in the universe correlate to a concrescence is termed 'the actual world' correlate to that concrescence."[12] And the occasion is not something over and above its actual world as if it were an extra part in addition to its parts or another thing crudely added to the things that make it up. A whole, as distinguished from its parts, is not a thing or substance at all; it is rather, an organization or connection among its parts. Only in this way can it be said to be more than its parts: it is its parts as integrated, it is their integration. Therefore, an occasion is composed of a nexus of other occasions, its actual world, its content, without itself being one of these in addition to them, but rather, their connectedness or togetherness. If the occasion were one thing that was simply added on to other things that composed it, then the occasion could be a member of itself.

For example, a building or a person is not a special part over and above the bricks or cells composing them; the building is not a brick on top of all the other bricks composing it; the person is not another cell on top of the other cells composing him or her. Rather, a building is a novel togetherness of bricks, a person a unique connectedness of cells: they are the way that bricks or cells are organized together in one occasion. A building is more than its bricks and a person more than her or his cells only inasmuch as the organization of their parts is more than the parts. And certainly it is more, as long as "more" does not mean an additional part. A building is not part of itself, but of its successors; a person is not a member of himself, but of a nexus that includes him.

An actual world is always a plurality of occasions, always unique, and always relative to the perspective of the occasion it composes. It is necessarily comprised of more than one antecedent occasion, since the occasion it composes necessarily has more than one prehension and more than one datum or cause, being a concrescence of feelings (in the plural). All the data of an occasion combined under one perspective are its actual world. "Thus, by reason of transition, 'the actual world' is always a relative term, and refers to that basis of presupposed actual occasions which is a datum for the novel concrescence."[13] The objective datum is the initial data having been objectified; the initial data are aspects of the plural antecedents, the objective datum is the singular world that is the total content and unified experience of the occasion. Thus, an actual world is both plural and singular; it is many occasions composing the one world of one occasion.

Occasions of an actual world are a nexus with respect to their role in the occasion they compose because they have been bound together therein, prehended by the one occasion. And these same occasions may be amidst many another nexus as well, with respect to both occasions that they have prehended and other occasions that have prehended them. An occasion's actual world is prehended by every successor that prehends the occasion.

We thus arrive at the notion of the actual world of any actual entity, as a nexus whose objectification constitutes the complete unity of objective datum for the physical feeling of that actual entity. This actual entity is the original percipient of that nexus. But any other actual entity which includes in its own actual world that original percipient also includes that previous nexus as a portion of its own actual world. Thus each actual world is a nexus which in this sense is independent of its original percipient. It enjoys an objective immortality in the future beyond itself.[14]

And the occasions forming the actual world are inextricably and irrevocably involved in the occasion they composed so that they are prehended as parts of that occasion. Thus, a nexus is antecedent occasions whose aspects are bound together within an occasion, composing the occasion, comprising its actual world; and the occasion is the togetherness of these antecedent occasions.

The complete objective datum of a flower that has come into being is the actual world of that flower and that flower only. The real potentialities of particular antecedent occasions of elements of the earth, of water, of plant, of air, of light interacting with one another have effected the being of this flower and consequently have become inextricably *it*. For this reason, this very same combination of antecedents is not also the complete actual world of anything else. Just as an actual occasion is unique or novel, its actual world is unique to it. However, the actual world of the flower has efficacy beyond the flower, though now its efficacy is in the way that a flower has, rather than the way of the elements, earth, air, water, and light that were before. The flower is objectively immortal, and so is its actual world, the ingredients that have transformed themselves into a flower.

*Shared worlds.* There is no such thing as *the* actual world, the same for all occasions alike. "No two occasions can have identical actual worlds."[15] Actual worlds are defined by actual occasions, each being the perspective each occasion has upon its antecedents. "Each actual occasion defines its own actual world from which it originates."[16] An actual world, therefore, is relative to, unique to, particular to, one actual occasion and no other. If there were an absolute actual world, that is, if actual worlds could be identical and occasions experienced only the same things and had only the exact same causes, then monism has been resurrected and relativity lost.

Although no two actual worlds are exactly identical, they may differ only in the most insignificant way; one actual world need include or exclude only a few occasions that the other does not. Thus, actual worlds of two occasions may be the same but for one mote, one flake, one molecule, or a few photons, a few perceptions, a few flames.

> . . . no two actual entities originate from an identical universe, though the difference between the two universes only consists in some actual entities, included in one and not in the other, and in the subordinate entities which each actual entity introduces into the world.[17]

Because no two actual worlds are perfectly identical, and every actual world has efficacy beyond the occasion it composes, then some portion of every actual world is shared by other occasions. An actual world is unique *qua* complete objective datum, to one occasion and to no other, but this does not mean it, or some portion thereof, cannot be prehended by other occasions, only that it cannot be the complete actual world of any other occasion. An actual world or some portion of it is in fact prehended by every occasion to succeed it, so that it or some portion of it becomes a part of the actual worlds of every succeeding occasion. Successive occasions may even objectify a predecessor's actual world in the same way (reenacting it, or sympathizing with it) but their own actual worlds must differ from any predecessor's by at least one occasion.

Therefore, the actual world of any occasion is necessarily shared by many successive occasions as they prehend the occasion, though not all need share it in the same proportion. An unshared actual world would be one prehendable only to the one occasion whose world it originally is; it would have no further efficacy, no objective immortality. But no actual world simply drops out of existence when the subjective immediacy of the occasion it constitutes perishes. Nor does it endure forever just as it is. It goes on to create other occasions, but may not be the complete objective datum of any other. Actual worlds are necessarily shared, but none are shared equally such that two occasions have the same actual world. If occasions had the very same actual world, there would be no process from occasion to occasion but only one occasion viewed from differing perspectives. For Whitehead, however, each view is the achievement of a new occasion.

It is inevitable that a succeeding occasion prehend (whether positively or negatively) at least one occasion not prehended by its predecessor: namely, the predecessor itself. For this reason, it is not possible that actual worlds of successive occasions be completely identical: each succeeding occasion takes account of at least one occasion not available to its predecessor, that predecessor itself. A flower prehends its actual world; it does not prehend itself. But a successor prehends the flower. Then each successor necessarily has one predecessor to include or exclude in its actual world that its predecessor did not have.

Successive actual worlds include portions of their predecessors actual worlds only because they include portions of their predecessors; as the complete objective datum of an occasion, an actual world is an inextricable part of the occasion and cannot be prehended as if this occasion did not exist. Historical routes are traced through a succession of occasions; the ancestors of any route cannot be found in their original condition as though successors never existed. We do not today prehend dinosaurs, but bones, tracks, and oil, which show the relationships with other occasions that dinosaurs have entered into since; we do not today prehend ancient Rome, but modern Rome through which we see the historical route that ancient Rome has taken. The ancestor occasions in an historical route are not prehended except through their descendents. Objective immortality is not the endurance of an occasion, but its creation of descendents with which it is bound.

The following passage expresses how the relativity of actual worlds follows from the metaphysics of a pluralism in process.

There is not one completed set of things which are actual occasions. For the fundamental inescapable fact is the creativity in virtue of which there can be no 'many things' which are not subordinated in a concrete unity. Thus a set of all actual occasions is by the nature of things a standpoint for another concrescence which elicits a concrete unity from those many actual occasions. Thus we can never survey the actual world except from the standpoint of an immediate concrescence which is falsifying the presupposed completion.[18]

This passage, with its assertion that "There can be no 'many things' which are not subordinated in a concrete unity" echoes the togetherness passage of Chapter 1 and echoes the creativity passage with which Chapter 2 concluded, with its assertion that any set of occasions is a standpoint for the creation of another occasion.

An occasion surveying the actual world falsifies its completion as all the world, or the only actual world, because it omits itself which is as yet to be completed. Itself can only be included in the actual world by a successor to it. The successor prehends its predecessor as part of its own actual world, but again does not prehend itself, and so on. The very act of prehending many things creates an occasion of them with the prehender. There is no such thing as a "set of all occasions" without taking into account the prehender of this set; and the prehender is only taken account of by a succeeding prehender, and so on. Prehending any set of occasions creates another occasion of the prehension of that set; there is no set otherwise. Thus, there can be no complete set of all actual occasions.

Sets are put together within occasions—all togetherness is togetherness in occasions. All occasions have multifarious real potentialities so that their membership in any one set is the realization of one of their potentialities in an occasion they create. But this creation is a concrete unity and the set that constituted it part of its singular objective datum; the set is unified as the components of one experience and this is why they are a set as opposed to a multiplicity. The set is what it is, a set, because it comprises the actual world of an occasion in which it has togetherness as a set. This actual world, being the complete objective datum of an occasion, is all the world to the occasion, so that the occasion naturally presupposes the completion of the set as those of all the world. But this presumption ignores the creativity of these antecedents which are in process of creating the presuming occasion itself. Perceive a set of occasions as all perceived occasions, and the perceiving occasion will have been omitted. This is the nature of process and it means that "there is not one completed set of things which are actual occasions."

The actual world is what is surveyed from a standpoint, so that a new standpoint surveys a new actual world. No two perceptions are the same, though two perceptions close by, whether they are the successive perceptions of one person or those of two contemporary people, have some part of their actual worlds in common. The actual world of any human experience is immensely complex, though one of the functions of conscious thought is to simplify it. It can never be reduced to one thing or one idea, even though it may be objectified as such. The fact that actual worlds are shared does not in any way mean that they are simple, although they may appear so after undergoing transmutations in complex processes of concrescence.

I do not so much as see a rock but I prehend something of my environment and its environment and of my own bodily history as well. An occasion of visual perception includes more than an image of a rock; it includes every biochemical transaction that conjured the image, and their causes. The state of my eyes and general health contribute to the occasion. Also, the quality of the light, the weather, the place affect the percipient occasion. It is not merely a rock I see, but a damp rock or a rock corroded by air pollution that stings the eyes. And I objectify the rock with attitudes that reflect my own history. Whether the rock be a door stop or a gem, whether I see it on the ground or set in a building, in an instrument, or in jewelry, I objectify it with attitudes toward nature, or architectures, or technology or decoration that come of prehending occasions of my own past experience with similar things. The rock is seen as a certain kind of thing in a certain kind of condition and under certain attitudes in a certain state of health. The actual world of an occasion of visual perception includes far more than an image. "When we register in consciousness our visual perception of a grey stone, something more than bare sight is meant."[19]

A rock image in a brain does not exist in isolation, nor does a brain, nor an eye, nor a body, nor a rock, nor the ground, and so on. There is a vast supporting matrix for any actual occasion, and that part of it actively forming the occasion is its actual world. And this world is shared by any successor. Any occasion of my remembering this perception of a rock includes some portion of the same actual world; and anyone with whom I share my memory prehends my actual world as including a seen rock. In this way my communicated memory is a part of another person's actual world under his or her attitude toward me and rocks.

And my perceptions, memory, and communications may result in my doing something to the rock, or helping someone else to do something. I may dislodge it, throw it, destroy it, grind it, buy it, sell it, study it, wear it, or use it to build a wall or an instrument. My real potentialities to some such effect then become part of subsequent occasions of the rock's existence. The actual worlds even of subsequent occasions of the rock, then, share something of my actual worlds that included antecedent occasions of the rock. Just as the effects of the rock upon me can be traced from occasion to occasion back to my first perception of it, so the effects of my handling of the rock can be traced in the successive rock occasions affected by it. The rock and I are one society among many others, as long as we are in relationship, as long as the rock's historical route and mine intersect. And with each intersection, some portion of an actual world is shared.

However, it is not only successive occasions that share portions of actual worlds. Contemporaries may also prehend one another's actual world, although they cannot prehend one another. Again, their actual worlds cannot be identical, though they may be nearly so. "The differences between the actual worlds of a pair of contemporary entities, which are in a certain sense 'neighbours,' are negligible for most human purposes."[20] In perceiving a rock, it is an antecedent rock that I perceive, although its real potentialities for being seen, for effecting visual perception when interacting with others, are present.

Two contemporaries are in no position for one to cause the other, since causation requires that the causing occasion be the antecedent of the caused. A contemporary cannot be in the past or future with respect to its contemporary. "Actual entities are called 'contemporary' when neither belongs to the 'given' actual world defined by the other."[21] I perceive an antecedent rock surface and project a contemporary rock in that place where I perceive the antecedent, if the rock is resting, and am justified in doing so because I am perceiving the antecedent occasions which are constituting the contemporary rock occasion. Similarly, two people in conversation each perceive antecedent occasions of the other: never is the contemporary person perceived. One perception is antecedent its successor and distant from its contemporary by that amount of time it takes for light and sound from the one person to reach the eyes and ears of the other and to be converted into intelligible sights and meanings. No present occasion is prehendable; yet it is presently under construction by its antecedents which are prehendable. We perceive the antecedents and make a guess as to the present occasion which is arising from them.

The antecedent rock occasions that I perceive are a part of the contemporary rock's actual world. So my percipient occasion and the occasion of the rock that is contemporary with me share a part of the same actual world: the antecedent rock occasions. Similarly, percipient occasions of two people in conversation are contemporaris if neither is in the past of the other. But some part of the actual worlds of the contemporary occasions will be common to both. A sentence spoken by one person is heard by both so that this sentence is a part of both their actual worlds. This shared actual world is antecedent to both contemporary auditors, whose present thoughts are already superseding the sentence they hear. Nevertheless, the listener gauges the position and manner of the contemporary speaker from his antecedent sentence, and the speaker formulates his next sentence on its basis. Two contemporaries in sharing the same actual world know something of what to expect from one another, without knowing one another.

> The further disclosure must be indirect, since contemporary events are exactly those which are neither causing, nor caused by, the percipient actual occasion. Now, although the various causal pasts (i.e., 'actual worlds') of the contemporary actual occasions are not wholly identical with the causal past of the percipient actual occasion, yet, so far as important relevance is concerned, these causal pasts are practically identical.[22]

That is to say, prehending one another's actual worlds is tantamount to prehending one another. To share a part of an actual world, which any successor and every contemporary does, is to have something in common with other occasions. The rock and I have been in the same place; the person and I have been in the same conversation.

*Mutual sensitivity.* These descriptions seem to imply an infinite regress of prehension: prehension of an occasion is prehension of some occasions of its actual world; prehension of these occasions is prehension of some occasions of their actual worlds; and so on. It would seem that a subject prehends an infinitude of occasions to become something finite itself. But of course, since the subject is to be some finite occasion, it has not got the time to prehend every remote antecedent, the ancestors of ancestors of ancestors, and so on.

However, prehension is not only a relating with antecedents, but a terminal of relationships such that a definite perspective is obtained. Antecedents are prehended only insofar as they are relevant to the subject and their relevancy is further refined as the subject transmutes, objectifies, and appropriates aspects of its antecedents for its own internal constitution. Occasions are indeed in relationship to all the universe. "Each fully realized fact has an infinitude of relations in the historic world and in the realm of form; namely, its perspective of the universe."[23] But not all the universe is equally relevant to the occasion.

It is the necessity for objectification, for forming a perspective in accordance with a subjective aim, that limits the prehension of the subject, or, in reverse, limits the efficacy of the antecedent world in the subject. A subject can only feel about its antecedents one way. It takes another occasion to feel another way about antecedents.

It follows that in every consideration of a singe fact there is the suppressed presupposition of the environmental coordination requisite for its existence. This environment, thus coordinated, is the whole universe in its perspective to the fact. But perspective is gradation of relevance; that is to say, it is gradation of importance. Feeling is the agent which reduces the universe to its perspective for fact. Apart from gradations of feeling, the infinitude of detail produces an infinitude of effect in the constitution of each fact. And that is all that is to be said, when we omit feeling. But we feel differently about these effects and thus reduce them to a perspective. 'To be negligible' means 'to be negligible for some coordination of feeling'.[24]

Then an occasion does relate to a virtual infinity of antecedent occasions, if enough antecedents are taken into account. But the relationships are terminated in the occasion by transmuting and objectifying them into one effect, one final feeling of one actual world. "Each entity possesses essentially an individual character, and also is essentially a terminal of relationship, potential or actual."[25] Also, while a subject is immersed in an infinitude of relationships to antecedents, it does not itself establish these relationships one by one. Then it would have no time for itself, as it were, since it would have to prehend each of an inifinity of antecedents itself. Rather, the antecedents determine the initial stage of the subject, and the antecedents' relationships to their antecedents, the more remote ancestors, are already established in what the antecedents themselves are. The occasions to constitute a subject's actual world are given; the subject chooses its perspective upon them but does not choose them. In the immediate antecedents are already objectified the predecessors of these, and in these are already objectified the predecessors of these antecedents, and so on, so that even the remotest of ancestors may be prehended as objectified in some presently efficacious occasion. The subject, therefore, does not have to prehend an infinity of occasions before it can concresce; a virtual infinity of antecedents is already given it, along with God's guidance as to their relevancy for it. "Thus there is no vicious regress in feeling, by reason of the indefinite complexity of what is felt. Kant, in his 'Transcendental Aesthetic,' emphasizes the doctrine that in intuition a complex datum is intuited as one."[26]

The antecedent world, containing within it effects from the whole of history and potentialities for all the future, is not given the present subject in the sense that the subject is already there waiting to accept or reject the past as it will. The antecedent world is the given initiation of the subject, its first phase, coming to be the subject itself making such decisions as to acceptance and rejection. This antecedent world of occasions is already compatible for concrescence into a particular new occasion by virtue of God's provision of an appropriate subjective aim for it. The prehensions of the new subject are compatible at all, adjustable and harmonious to one another as components of the same occasion, because creativity is obligated to create wholes only of compatible parts. "In conformity with this pre-established harmony, 'incompatibility' would have dictated from the beginning that some 'feeling' be replaced by a negative prehension."[27] The harmonizing of prehensions is a matter of eliminating the contradictions and contrasting their compatibilities for the sake of intensifying experience. The categoreal obligations or rules by which feelings concresce, insure that one unique conjunction is realized from all the diverse potentialities of the antecedent world. The prehensions are amenable to one another because the aim they share has been pre-established as compatible for them by God. "There is a mutual sensitivity of feelings in one subject, governed by categoreal conditions. This mutual sensitivity expresses the notion of final causation in the guise of a pre-established harmony."[28]

A newly arising subject is itself nothing other than these prehensions and their mutual aim. The prehensions are the subject's by virtue of this subjective aim they have in common. But they are the causal activity of the antecedents aiming at the subject. They are necessarily compatible to constitute the one subject together because their harmony has been pre-established by God as one possible within the general potentiality of the universe. The subject is not a master prehension above and beyond the prehensions instigated by the antecedent occasions which are their data and efficient causes. The subjective aim is the aim all the prehensions share in common; it is not the aim of another prehension that represents the subject more than the prehensions derived from the antecedent occasions. Prehensions are mutually sensitive so that their subjective forms can be correlated by their mutual subjective aim: their sensitivity and aim is not a separable subject in addition to themselves.

*One and many.* The actual world has been described so far as the relative past of an actual occasion, the causal past that becomes the objective content, the internal constitution, of a new present occasion. Then it would seem that the actual world is both past and present. But it is not past; rather it is the real potentialities of past occasions transformed into a present occasion.

Thus, relatively to any actual entity, there is a 'given' world of settled actual entities and a 'real' potentiality, which is the datum for creativeness beyond that standpoint. This datum, which is the primary phase in the process constituting an actual entity, is nothing else than the actual world itself in its character of a possibility for the process of being felt.[29]

The actual world is not a set of occasions belonging to an absolute past; rather, it becomes the past as immanent in the present. There is not an absolute past transformed into a present occasion at any absolute time, as though time were a fine line or instant through which an occasion passes. Nor does the present concresce at any time conceived as an instant; there is no absolute time in which the present drops into the past. The entire process of concrescence including its satisfaction is present, which is a potentiality for time, actualizing upon satisfaction. With the epoch's actualization begins its transition into new occasions: but this transition is not the unfolding of a series of instants; rather, it is the transformation of past occasions into a present occasion from the present occasion's standpoint.

An actual world is not past with respect to the occasion whose world and constitution it is, because it is the real and present potentialities for becoming the new occasion. The present occasion does not pass through a temporal sequence: nor are its stages temporally ordered, earlier and later. For, time in becoming is as yet a potentiality. The actual world, the occasion's primary phase, is not past but present as is the occasion, though the occasions from which the actual world is derived are past. The past is immanent in the present as real potentiality, not actuality. There are no time divisions in a present occasion.

There is the totality of actual fact; there is the externality of many facts; there is the internality of this experiencing which lies within the totality. These three divisions are on a level. No one in any sense precedes the other.[30]

The internal composition of an occasion cannot precede it even though it is derived from the past relative to itself, retrospectively determined; for, the occasion does not develop in a temporal sequence part by part. The parts must all be together as a whole before there is the whole. That is to say, the actual world relative to an occasion does not come into being, as its complete objectified datum, until that occasion has come into being, until it has achieved satisfaction as that occasion with that objective content. The actual world of an occasion is potentiality just as much as is the occasion until the occasion is an actuality. Occasions cannot prehend one another's actual worlds as their completed content, but they prehend the real potentialities of the occasions belonging to the actual worlds. An occasion's relative past comes into being with the occasion, not before. There can be no past of an occasion not yet in being, only a potential past of a potential occasion. Rome came into being with its buildings, its people, its literature, its government; they were not there before Rome. An occasion of visual perception comes into being with all its bodily and environmental ingredients, the electrochemical interactions that create the perception; these are not there as the actual world of the occasion of perception before the occasion. The occasions whose real potentialities make up an actual world are objectively immortal rather than absolutely past, since their being past depends upon a perspective on them being present. The past is relative to the prehension of it, not absolute regardless of what arises from it. No experience precedes its composition from the external world; nor does any actual world precede the experience of it. Whitehead's statement of the temporal nature of the experience of an occasion in relation to its actual world of other occasions must be repeated and emphasized: "No one *in any sense* precedes the other."

The only way to establish location "in" time and space is by establishing, retrospectively, which occasions have objectified which. An actual world and all the antecedent occasions whose potentialities are immanent in it, while given the actual occasion, is not defined as the occasion's actual world until the occasion has defined itself. The occasion's relative past comes into being with the occasion, not before. There is no past of an occasion not yet in existence, only the potentiality for it. The actual world is given the occasion as potentiality and becomes actual, its definite actual world, only upon the occasion's completion. "In positive prehensions the 'datum' is preserved as part of the final complex object which 'satisfies' the process of self-formation and thereby completes the occasion."[31]

Consequently, an occasion is never many without being one, and never one without being many. It is always both many and one, the one togetherness of many constituents. The constituents are real potentialities of past occasions that become actual aspects or parts of the new occasion. At no time are there the parts of that particular occasion without the whole occasion and at no time is there a whole without parts. There is no one occasion without its actual world of many antecedents and no actual world before the actual occasion whose world it is. The occasion does not succeed its actual world such that it is one without parts; nor does the actual world precede the occasion such that it is many without togetherness as a whole. There is no one occasion without its actual world of many occasions and no actual world before the actual occasion whose world it is. The actual world, derived from antecedent occasions, is always immanent in its occasion and never separable or preceding it.

It can be seen that the same many-one, parts-whole relationship applies to time. There are no temporal parts of an epoch before there is an epoch. And the epoch as a whole does not succeed its own parts such that there is a whole epoch that has no parts, one epoch that is not also a unity of many antecedents. This is the nature of Whiteheadian becoming. It is the creation of an epoch of time, such that the epoch is not a spatiotemporal location involving only one thing, in one absolute place and time. An epoch of human sustenance derived from one drink of water contains the transformations of antecedents from a far-reaching spatiotemporal range. The real potentialities of water for human sustenance when interacting with the real potentialities of cells is immanent in the new occasion of sustenance which is located in many cells spread throughout the body. This new epochal occasion is not more in one cell's nutritive activity than in another among those that it involves; that is, it is not more in one part of itself than in another. It is an activity involving and requiring many things, all of which are essential contributors to its content and spatiotemporal dimensions.

Similarly, the occasion of seeing a building has the spatiotemporal location of many parts of the body and environment, with antecedents derived from distant epochs. This epochal occasion of perception is not located more in the eye balls than in the brain, more in photons than in nerve cells. An epoch is always one spatiotemporal unity encompassing many parts, none of which are more the epoch than the others. The epoch of ancient Rome encompasses all Rome from the initiation of its subjective aim, the aim to be Rome, to its satisfaction as the Rome achieved. The epoch is not in one part of Rome more than another. Also, many other epochs include it, are included in it, and overlap it in the same way that occasions include and overlap one another by virtue of their multiple ingredients. "There are an indefinite number of prehensions, overlapping, subdividing, and supplementary to each other."[32]

Frederic B. Fitch observes:

The prehended occasion is fully present *as an ingredient* in the prehending occasion, but this does not mean that it is present in a spatiotemporal sense. A remembered occasion, for example, is not located at the same time and place as the remembering occasion, but it is present in the remembering occasion as an ingredient in the latter. In other words, the ingredients of an actual occasion do not have to share the spatio-temporal location of the actual occasion.[33]

But if the ingredients of an actual occasion do not share its spatiotemporal location, then nothing shares its spatiotemporal location; then its spatiotemporal location is an isolated, empty, simplistic little container of spacetime all to itself. A Whiteheadian epoch cannot be conceived of as an inaccessible little container of time, the container being a miniature Newtonian universe proceeding in absolute time. A percipient occasion is not located somewhere where nothing else is, though it is a relationship among other occasions that no other occasion is. A percipient occasion is not located more in the brain or in the seen building's proportions than in the daylight or the perceiver's eyes or mood. The coming into being of this particular occasion, which is this particular person seeing this building on this day in this way, involves a wide spatiotemporal location, taking in aspects of the building, the day, photons, brain, eyes, muscle, memories, bodily feelings, and so on, as they contribute to the one perception. This is the percipient occasion, involving all these things, as the person will tell you if she or he describes it. Similarly, a Roman building encompasses the Roman hands, thoughts, lives, technology, and cluture that built it and made it Roman. Its epoch is not ended at some designated atoms on its edge.

## THE FUTURE

*Superjection.* The real potentialities of antecedent occasions are real, particular, finite agents of creativity because their potential for future efficacy was built into them as subjects. An actual occasion is a subject-superject, taking into account its potential future efficacy, its future immanent in its present and transcending its present thereafter. "An actual entity is at once the subject experiencing and the superject of its experiences. It is subject-superject, and neither half of this description can for a moment be lost sight of."[34] The occasion as superject is the occasion as objectively immortal, the potential for which is determined in the construction of the occasion. "An actual entity is to be conceived both as a subject presiding over its own immediacy of becoming, and a superject which is the atomic creature exercising its function of objective immortality."[35] An occasion's subjective aim regulates what the occasion is and therein regulates the range of its possible efficacy upon others. The subject in becoming a particular occasion becomes a superject in that it establishes its creativity beyond itself. Its aim at a certain type of efficacy upon others, the aim at being prehendable as a certain type of object, projects or superjects beyond its own creation and defines the occasion's real potentialities. "The real internal constitution of an actual entity progressively constitutes a decision conditioning the creativity which transcends that actuality."[36]

It is significant that Whitehead does not term the actual occasion a "subject-datum" but rather, "subject-superject." This is indicative of the indeterminacy of causal efficacy, of the indeterminacy of any given occasion as regards its future effects. Under the fallacy of simple occurrence, the actual occasion might as well be termed "subject-datum," conceived as a determinate given entity, the same for all prehending it. But instead the occasion is a subject-superject conceived as a transmitter of creativity rather than a determinate, substantial, permanently the same, absolute, given passive datum.

> The philosophies of substance presuppose a subject which then encounters a datum, and then reacts to the datum. The philosophy of organism presupposes a datum which is met with feelings, and progressively attains the unity of a subject. But with this doctrine, 'superject' would be a better term than 'subject.'[37]

Here Whitehead says that subjects are not already there, before they are created. They are not standing in the future awaiting their data for them to prehend. And a subject having perished subjectively does not then become a datum of an already existing, already completed, actual subject. A datum is met, not with subjects, but with feelings. An occasion always perishes into the becoming of other occasions, not into a void of nothingness between occasions, to be prehended by an already completed subject waiting in an absolute spatiotemporal location for its objects to come near.

If a datum can be met with feelings, then it can be met with a subject in process. The datum joins with other data in process of effecting a subject: all are the real potentialities for the subject. The subject is not closed to additional data in its first phase; rather, the phase is that of the data coming together for the subject, toward the subject. It is the phase wherein the antecedent world (strictly speaking, the antecedent-to-be world) provides the data of the new subject. A datum is met with feelings and becomes one of them if it shares the subject's aim and begins transformation into the subject, if the subject does not negatively prehend it.

There is a discrepancy between superject and datum, and again between datum and objectification. Indeterminacy comes into the picture in these discrepancies. Whiteheadian superjects are immortal in that an occasion's potentiality for effect is immortal, without determining what the actual effect shall be. The superject is what the antecedent, immortal occasion aimed to be prehended as; it is what the subject proposes itself to be and to be prehended. The datum is what is given to activate prehension or to be negated; and the object is what the completed subject actually prehends. Between the object-as-intended, the datum given, and the actual objectification, all of which are the superjected antecedent occasion, there is room for indeterminacy.

The view that a subject is already constituted and waiting to prehend data has eliminated time. A Whiteheadian datum cannot meet an already constituted future subject, since it is this very subject that it creates and constitutes. To say that a datum is met with feelings, then, is to say that a datum is met with causally efficacious activity which engages it in the present, creating with it a present occasion. Thus, Whitehead speaks of a datum as concrescing; a concrescing datum is not future relative to itself, that is, there is no separation in time within a process of concrescence. "A converse way of looking at this truth is that the relevance to other actual entities of its own status in the actual world is the initial datum in the process of its concrescence."[38] The concrescing datum is future relative to the antecedent subject which created the datum; and the next subject is future relative to it; but an occasion is not future with respect to its own data.

A superject may be seen as all the objects that a given occasion becomes upon its own perishing; it is the occasion as objectively immortal. An edible vegetable once was a subject when it was created, but subsequently became a battery of nutrients spread throughout an animal body which it joins in creating a new occasion of bodily health, providing objects for many diverse and scattered cells. All these objects taken together are the vegetable considered as superject. Similarly, ancient Rome was a subject in its creation. But now its efficacy as an object is scattered all over the earth; the singular subject has become many an object, many an objectification, for many subsequent subjects. These objects taken together are ancient Rome considered as a superject, Rome as objectively immortal.

This is why an occasion is always subject-superject. It cannot be considered as something without efficacy or apart from its efficacy. Its efficacy is future relative to its creation as a subject, but it is the present of other subjects. And its future efficacy is conditioned by the present occasion in which it is created. Therefore, the potential future of a subject is immanent in it just as much as is the past (or past-to-be, potential past). An occasion is subject-superject because its potentiality for a future is immanent in it, and transcends it as its objective immortality in others. "In the analysis of a feeling, whatever presents itself as also *ante rem* is a datum, whatever presents itself as exclusively *in re* is subjective form, whatever presents itself *in re* and *post rem* is 'subject-superject.'"[39]

*Future actuality.* Both the potentiality of the past and the potentiality for a future are immanent in the present, then. The past is immanent in the present because the present is essentially the relationships among potentialities of the past. Similarly for the future: "The future is immanent in the present by reason of the fact that the present bears in its own essence the relationships which it will have to the future."[40] The evidence for the immanence of the past is in the perception of causal efficacy. The evidence for the immanence of the future is in anticipation.

But one element in the immediate feelings of the concrescent subject is comprised of the anticipatory feelings of the transcendent future in its relation to immediate fact. This is the feeling of the objective immortality inherent in the nature of actuality.[41]

The actual future, however, is not present. "But no future individual occasion is in existence."[42] What is determinate is antecedent occasions in relation to occasions antecedent to them, that is, the past considered without taking into account its present and future efficacy. What is indeterminate and becoming determinate is a present occasion's relationship to the past. The future is ever indeterminate since it is never actualized. ". . . the completed actualities of that future are undetermined."[43] In any nexus or society of occasions we can speak of the past occasions and the future occasions relative to any given occasion in the sequence; but this is only a manner of speaking, a way of designating which occasions precede and which succeed which. No actual occasion is actually future, actually existing in the future relative to any occasion. All the occasions of a nexus or society are past with respect to a present occasion in which they are prehended together as a nexus. None are actually future. The future is not here or anywhere. Nor is it predetermined in the past or present since it is not an actuality in the past or present; it is only anticipated. What is immanent in the present is not the future but the potentiality for it. "For it is inherent in the constitution of the immediate, present actuality that a future will supersede it."[44] This potential future, the occasion as superject, and the anticipation it engenders, is the only thing that can be meant by "future."

Therefore, anticipation and the occasion's subjective aim to be a certain superject as well as a subject is an anticipation and an aim at no actuality future with respect to the occasion. The aim of feelings at a subject-superject is their aim at a present concrescence and a future prehendability as a particular object, and not any actual future occasion. It is not the actual future which is prehended, nor the actual future at which prehensions aim; it is the reconstructed past. No future occasions nor their eternal objects are data, physical or conceptual, for any actual occasions. This would make future occasions efficient and final causes of present occasions, which is impossible. It is the past, and not the future, that is the efficient cause of the present. "Thus there are no actual occasions in the future to exercise efficient causation in the present."[45] The relativity of time does not upset this rule. "The retroactive action of future events remains impossible as long as we adhere to the requirement of the relativity theory that no causal action can escape from the frontward causal cone of 'absolute future.'"[46]

The anticipation and subjective aim of a present occasion is for eternal objects exhibited in various past occasions, not future occasions. And God, the repository of subjective aims and eternal objects, is neither future nor present nor past with respect to any occasion, but non-temporal. Then the aim and the anticipation inherent in the nature of a present occasion is an aim and anticipation for a reconstructed past. A present occasion is a novel togetherness of elements prehended in diverse antecedents.

*The incompleteness of time.* The past is stubborn fact and real potentiality, causing itself to be prehended, but not determining the occasion of its prehension. This occasion partially determines itself, actualizing for itself real potentialities of the past. There is no past occasion or occasions whose creativity has stopped so that no present occasion or occasions are being created of their real potentialities for effect. A perished occasion is burgeoning into new present occasions. Its completion is now past, but its real potentialities have yet to be realized with the completion of each new present occasion it makes a transition into. "Thus each actual entity, although complete so far as concerns its microscopic process, is yet incomplete by reason of its objective inclusion of the macroscopic process."[47] The macroscopic process is that of the occasion's objective immortality, the occasion *qua* superject. Then there is no place and no time that is not also a present occasion, since creativity is ceaseless.

No occasion or occasions are past without their potentialities being present. This is not to say, of course, that all present time is the same instant, or that all present occasions are the same. It is only to say that wherever there are actual occasions, there is a present occasion burgeoning from them. This is the incompleteness of time. Time is never complete or completely past. The indeterminate, incomplete present actualizes, perishes, and actualizes anew; nowhere are occasions completed with respect to their real potentialities for the future, their creativity. "Time requires incompleteness. . . . Each occasion is temporal because it is incomplete. Nor is there any system of occasions which is complete."[48]

Ancient Rome is determinate and complete only with respect to the antecedents whose potentialities constituted it. But it is no determinate and complete occasion taking into account its existence as superject—which must be taken into account inasmuch as any occasion is subject-superject. The occasion as superject takes into account its entire career, post-satisfaction, of efficacy for others. The full consequences of ancient Rome on the history of human civilization are indeterminate, incomplete. Similarly, even the full consequences of an occasion of visual perception, the memory of it and its integration with subsequent experiences, are incomplete considered as superject. And the age of dinosaurs is not determinate or complete with respect to occasions yet future; its full consequences on later planetary life is not determined until all that later life has itself been completed.

To presume that an occasion can be determinate and complete in all respects is to presume substance and simple location. It is to presume that an occasion requires nothing but itself in order to exist, that it does not require relations to other occasions either for its own existence or for its adequate description. But the Whiteheadian creative advance means that no occasion is ever completely determinate in all respects, nor any nexus. The potentiality of any occasion is infinite, "immortal." A superject is creative of a virtual infinity of occasions. And the occasions that are past with respect to its actual world themselves are superjects effecting a virtual infinity of successors. No occasion is part of a completed nexus of relationships that are determinate in all respects since it is currently engaging further relationships. No occasion and no nexus of occasions is ever complete such that it causes no further relationships, such that it is not part of an incomplete present occasion.

But there is no definite nexus which is the nexus underlying that society, except when the society belongs wholly to the past. For the realized nexus which underlies the society is always adding to itself, with the creative advance into the future. For example, the man adds another day to his life, and the earth adds another millennium to the period of its existence. But until the death of the man and the destruction of the earth, there is no determinate nexus which in an unqualified sense is either the man or the earth.[49]

In other words, a society is not complete until its last occasion has perished. A society is the reproduced likeness of its member occasions from the first reproduction to the last; until that last occasion has perished, reference to *that* society as though it were a complete and finished fact, is hypothetical. And even when the entire society perishes, its member occasions are still objectively immortal; they still effect succeeding occasions, but no longer members of that society.

*Time's transcendence.* This incompleteness of time, the fact that there is always an incomplete present in process of completion, may also be expressed as the immanence of the potential future in the present. This is the reason for the incompleteness of the occasion and of time: it harbors potentiality. This incompleteness of time means that "time . . . extends beyond the spatio-temporal continuum of nature" as Whitehead says in the following passage:

> The event is what it is, by reason of the unification in itself of a multiplicity of relationships. . . .
> But this exhibition of the actual universe as extensive and divisible has left out the distinction between space and time. It has in fact left out the process of realisation, which is the adjustment of the synthetic activities by virtue of which the various events become their realised selves. . . . This adjustment is what introduces temporal process.
> Thus, in some sense, time, in its character of the adjustment of the process of synthetic realisation, extends beyond the spatio-temporal continuum of nature.[50]

The past is creative of a "transcendent world," transcendent beyond itself, beyond its time. "The world is self-creative; and the actual entity as self-creating creature passes into its immortal function of part-creator of the transcendent world."[51] Nature and time do not remain complete, and cannot be past except insofar as they are creative of a present; in creativity the past is transcended. It is in the present that both immanence and transcendence occur. "Immanence and transcendence are the characteristics of an object: as a realized determinant it is immanent; as a capacity for determination it is transcendent; in both roles it is relevant to something not itself."[52] Becoming is that aspect of time that transcends itself. It is the becoming of an occurrence and the becoming of its time that has not yet occurred.

The theme of transcendent creativity and the constant renovation of the world threads through the Whiteheadian philosophy without introducing the future. Creativity is transcendence of antecedent occasions, antecedent epochs, that never completes even the present if completion is the termination of potentiality. Whitehead describes objective immortality as transcending creativity rather than as time progressing evenly into the future and accumulating the past. "There is, in this way, transcendence of the creativity; and this transcendence effects determinate objectifications for the renewal of the process in the concrescence of actualities beyond that satisfied superject."[53]

*The potentiality of time.* It is evident that the macroscopic and microscopic species of process are also two aspects of time.

> . . . there are two kinds of fluency. One kind is the *concrescence* which, in Locke's language, is 'the real internal constitution of a particular existent.' The other kind is the *transition* from particular existent to particular existent. This transition, again in Locke's language, is the 'perpetually perishing' which is one aspect of the notion of time; and in another aspect the transition is the origination of the present in conformity with the 'power' of the past.[54]

The concrescence that Whitehead mentioned first is the other aspect of the notion of time. Then time is both transition and concrescence; both macroscopic transition from occasion to occasion and microscopic process of becoming; both objective immortality and subjective immediacy, both the perishing of the past and the becoming of the present.

Thus, Whitehead does not identify time exclusively with transition, or what he also calls "physical time," as John B. Cobb, Jr. suggests: "Whitehead distinguishes between two types of process. 'Time,' he reserves for physical time, the transition from one actual occasion to another."[55] Transition is only one aspect of time; becoming is the other. And these two aspects of time are not two aspects by virtue of applying to two separate kinds of things, as though there were one kind of thing in transition and another kind of thing becoming or concrescing. They are not aspects of two different, ontologically distinct, kinds of reality. They are two aspects of the one process of concrescence, into which antecedents are in transition.[56]

Transition is the transition of many occasions into the one; becoming is the becoming of the one occasion out of those many. There is no transition that is not a part of the becoming of an occasion; transcending the past creates the present. "The creativity in virtue of which any relative complete actual world is, by the nature of things, the datum for a new concrescence is termed 'transition.'"[57] Considering the many transitions that any one actual occasion makes into occasions succeeding its own creation, then transition is objective immortality.

> The doctrine of objectification is an endeavor to express how what is settled in actuality is repeated under limitations, so as to be 'given' for immediacy. Later, in discussing 'time,' this doctrine will be termed the doctrine of 'objective immortality.'[58]

Then Whiteheadian time is objective immortality: the perpetual actualization of the potentialities of the past as new creations. But the past is not past relative to the new occasion until that occasion has concresced. It is only past retrospectively, rather than before the occasion; for, before the occasion there cannot be a past of that occasion. The present is the process of actualization of objective potentialities of antecedents-to-be; and the future is the same immortality of the past-to-be, but remaining ever potential.

However, it is somewhat misleading to speak of the transitions of occasions "into" other occasions, since the other occasions are as yet becoming, as yet incomplete. Transition is from the actual to the "merely real," not from the actual to the already actual. No actual occasions are standing in the future or the present waiting for the past to be put into transition to them. There is no point in transition between two or more already completed occasions; for then it is not giving rise to a new occasion, and also the present would be instantaneously actual rather than becoming so.

> In truth, from the standpoint of the general relativity theory, the preposition 'into' is misleading since it is tinged by the outdated classical distinction between a container-like space and its physical content.[59]

If transition is physical time, then becoming is not time. It is the potentiality for time, neither temporal nor spatial, but the becoming of a spatiotemporal unit, i.e., an epoch. Until an occasion has become, *it* is not yet there or then. An occurrence is not an occurrence until it has occurred. This is why Whitehead speaks of occasions as transcending time. Their becoming is their becoming temporal; they are not already temporal. The potentiality for time is not time and not temporal, yet neither is it nothing at all, just as the potentiality for a melody is not melodious, neither is it nothing at all, or the potentiality for an explosion is not exploding, yet neither is it nothing at all.

It is no wonder, then, that the process of becoming of an actual occasion is regarded as timeless: it is not time and makes no temporal progression or flow. In the words of Bertrand Russell: "Consequently, from the standpoint of the event itself, if one could imagine a being of whose biography it formed a part, there is no time between the beginning and the end."[60] A. H. Johnson too attests to the timelessness of the microscopic process: "In a sense, temporalization . . . is an atomic succession of actual entities, the inner life of each being timeless."[61] And M. K. Haldar says the same thing: "The potential is non-temporal."[62] But such expressions are not meant to eliminate time. Time has not been eliminated in becoming or concrescence because it is this very potentiality for time that creates time: time is created, not eliminated.

*Perception of time.* The perception of causal efficacy, or perception in the mode of causal efficacy, being the perception of the past causing the present and the anticipation of the future and including perception of the final aims that are a factor in all causal efficacy, is also perception of time. Here Whitehead says that the perception of causal efficacy is perception of derivation—perception that perception is derived from the environment which includes the body:

> For the organic theory, the most primitive perception is 'feeling the body as functioning.' This is a feeling of the world in the past; it is the inheritance of the world as a complex of feeling; namely, it is the feeling of derived feelings.[63]

The perception of inheritance or derivation is perception of time. Thus, time is perceived with every perception of causal efficacy.

> Thus 'perishing' is the assumption of a role in a transcendent future. The not-being of occasions is their 'objective immortality'. A pure physical prehension is how an occasion in its immediacy of being absorbs another occasion which has passed into the objective immortality of its not-being. It is how the past lives in the present. It is causation. It is memory. It is perception of derivation. . . . How the past perishes is how the future becomes.[64]

And perception of time includes the aim at superjection as well, the inherent immortality of potentiality for the future in every occasion.

It is in the mode of causal efficacy that our perceptions themselves are felt as caused, inherited, or derived. And it is from this mode of perception that we abstract time if we wish to consider it separately, though this consideration can only be intellectual. That is, temporal transition, past, present, and future may be considered abstractly as an abstract temporal order without reference to its content. But time and temporal order are not in fact abstract; we perceive time in perceiving the causes, inheritance, and derivation of our experience.

Time is known to us as the succession of our acts of experience, and thence derivatively as the succession of events objectively perceived in those acts. But this succession is not pure succession: it is the derivation of state from state, with the later state exhibiting conformity to the antecedent. Time in the concrete is the conformation of state to state, the later to the earlier; and the pure succession is an abstraction from the irreversible relationship of settled past to derivative present.[65]

It is obvious that, for Whitehead, time is neither an appearance nor an abstraction; nor need it be inferred or deduced from any characteristics of sense perception. It is directly perceived in the mode of causal efficacy. Whitehead identifies perception of time with that of causal efficacy.

Thus perception, in this primary sense, is perception of the settled world in the past as constituted by its feeling-tones, and as efficacious by reason of those feeling-tones. Perception, in this sense of the term, will be called 'perception in the mode of causal efficacy.'[66]

Thus, Whitehead contradicts William W. Hammerschmidt who writes: "We know spatio-temporal nature because we can rigorously infer it from the extensive character of nature in the gross."[67] But spatiotemporality need not be inferred from nature since it is nature: it is open for us all to perceive since we are all actual occasions in and of it. Hammerschmidt's suggestion that the nature of time is known by inference is a throw-back to the Kant-Hume-Newton situation: "The gist of this position is that the evidence for multiple space-time arises in presentational immediacy and logically needs to go no farther."[68] On the contrary, the evidence for multiple spacetimes arises from perception of causal efficacy. Hammerschmidt's inference and evidence are based on traditional, Humian, epistemology of empiricism founded on sense-perception or presentational immediacy alone, rather than on Whiteheadian epistemology founded on the perception of causal efficacy. For Whitehead the evidence for multiple spacetime systems is the objective immortality of antecedent occasions of ourselves, coming from the environment including our bodies, in successive occasions of ourselves.

"Thus physical memory *is* causation, and causation *is* objective immortality."[69] There is more than one objectively immortal actual occasion, more than one sequence of objectively immortal occasions, as our experience inevitably witnesses. For Whitehead, whatever has reality has by its very nature the capability for being perceived in some way, for it contributes to the constitution of the perception of the percipient occasion itself.

### THE ARRESTED EPOCH

*Atomism.* The epochal theory of time in particular has been adopted by Whitehead for cosmology because of its requirement in quantum mechanics. "The epochal theory of time is the foundation of the theory of atomic organisms, and of the modern physical quantum-theory."[70] The Newtonian instantaneous mathematical flow has given way to the discrete epoch of modern physics. For, the epoch is a quantum, or atom, of time. "In respect to time, this atomization takes the special form of the 'epochal theory of time.'"[71] What this atomization amounts to in the case of time is that time comes in indivisible (i.e., arrested) units. "The word 'epoch' is understood in its Greek sense of arrest."[72] Thus an epoch is an atomic unit of time, atomic in the case of time meaning an indivisible arrest: there are no further units of time within this atomic or arrested unit.

Just as a portion of matter was considered to be atomic if it was indivisible, so a portion of time which is indivisible is arrested. An indivisible unit of matter was an atom; an indivisible unit of time is an arrest, an epoch. Then the word "atom" may be misleading if it suggests anything more than indivisibility. It too readily evokes a pictorial, solid, enduring, independent, simple, self-sufficient, complete body at home in the empty spacetime container of classical physics.[73] Thus, new terms, such as "epoch" are being provided to put the modern conception in its own proper perspective.

The term "epoch" is well suited to Whitehead's purposes since it mitigates the influence of scientific materialism. For it does not suggest an empty period of time or one instantaneous but a time standing out for special notice because of its particular content. It suggests temporal evolution and more: something significant happening for which an entity is noted. It also suggests that the event in which a particular entity is noted is one event among others, a temporal event in a context of a surrounding world of other temporal events.

The Whiteheadian occasions and their epochs, then, are atoms not because they are completely simple, or because they are too small, too solid, or too impenetrable to be destroyed. "Whitehead cannot be using the word 'atom' in the original sense, for his atoms are not simple."[74] Occasions and their epochs are not atomic because they are entities simpler than which there are none, or smaller than which there are none, or briefer than which there are none. They are atomic because they are undivided, and undivided because they are units, not because they are impenetrable or otherwise resistent to division. A unit is never actually divided, only new units are created. An occasion can no more be divided than can an intention, a lure, a subjective aim:

> A reference to the complete actuality is required to give the reason why such a prehension is what it is in respect to its subjective form. This subjective form is determined by the subjective aim at further integration, so as to obtain the 'satisfaction' of the completed subject. In other words, final causation and atomism are interconnected philosophical principles.[75]

Occasions and their epochs are always units, then, no matter what their size and complexity happens to be.

> As used here the words 'individual' and 'atom' have the same meaning, that they apply to composite things with an absolute reality which their components lack. . . . The term 'monad' also expresses this essential unity at the decisive moment, which stands between its birth and its perishing.[76]

This point, the fact that Whiteheadian atoms are as complex and sizeable as may be any actual occasion, that is, any actual concrete existent at all, distinguishes Whiteheadian atomism from many traditional atomisms requiring simple atoms. Whitehead makes this point about his own atomism explicitly: "But atomism does not exclude complexity and universal relativity. Each atom is a system of all things."[77]

In fact, Whitehead speaks of actual entities as molecular: "In the first place, the *Timaeus* connects behaviour with the ultimate molecular characters of the actual entities."[78] Then Whitehead's atomism is actually a molecular theory of actuality. This may seem confusing; and indeed there are many terminological confusions in the philosophy. In this case, it must be kept in mind that Whitehead's atoms are molecules, if the term "atom" is to be retained in referring to the undivided character of actual occasions. Whiteheadian atomism is not that of Capek's conception:

We have to remember that the concept 'atom of time' is basically self-contradictory because (a) it implies a surreptitious return to the concept of mathematical instant, and (b) because it seems to imply that the temporal process is *made up* of parts which themselves are devoid of temporality.[79]

However, there are no actual temporal parts of an epoch or atom of time since it is the unit of time. Only a retrospective perspective can find the epoch divisible into temporal parts. Also, while it may be said that the temporal process is void of temporality, it nevertheless is in process of realizing a temporal potentiality.

*The chronon theory of time.* A chronon is the briefest possible duration of time, by the light of present knowledge, 4.5 x $10^{-24}$ seconds.[80] Chronons were proposed for science in order to replace the Newtonian instant by a real duration of time when the Newtonian instant was undermined by quantum theory.[81] Since instantaneous space or instantaneous planes were inadmissible to modern physics, chronons were proposed to allow for a short, but non-instantaneous, interval which could not be divided; atoms of time, where "atoms" does mean completely simple and briefer than which there is none. But chronon theory failed in that it did not really offer an alternative to the spatialized time of classical physics.

The theory of chronons, though outwardly denying the existence of instants, really assumes their existence. What does the alleged existence of chronons mean if not the assertion that two successive *instants* are separated by an interval of the order of $10^{-24}$ second? . . . . The concept of chronon seems to imply its own boundaries; and as these boundaries are instantaneous in nature, the concept of instant is surreptitiously introduced by the very theory which purports to eliminate it. A similar consideration can be applied to the atomization of space.[82]

The hope of the scientific materialist approach to Whiteheadian time has been to assert that all periods of time are the briefest possible, so that no real possibility of divisibility can be seriously entertained: the brief atoms of time happen too fast to be divided. The hope of scientific materialism is that the Whiteheadian epoch is simple by virtue of its brevity as the unit of time that composes all larger quantities of time, quantities which are compounds of the simple and briefest units. The scientific materialist hope is, then, that the Whiteheadian epoch is a chronon.

The epoch is interpreted as a chronon when it is interpreted as an interval between instants, regardless of the duration of the interval. For, it is the chronon that borders on instants, not the epoch. For example, Harold N. Lee interprets the Whiteheadian epoch as, "a period of time bounded by limits": "An epoch is an arrest. The epoch needed by the historian is a period of time bounded by limits, and a limit in time is an arrest."[83] But the conception of the epoch as an interval between limits is the chronon theory of time, not the epochal theory. It is the conception of time as occasional instants.

The epoch is neither a chronon nor any other single, privileged, absolute, simple, predetermined interval or measure of time which supposedly all add up, simpliciter, to all the other longer times, or appearances of longer times. The translation of the Whiteheadian epoch into a chronon is simply another way of imposing scientific materialism on the Whiteheadian cosmology, obliging Whiteheadian time to be Newtonian. But the epochal theory of time neither requires nor allows any chronon or instant. An atom of Whiteheadian time is a complex molecule, not a chronon.

*Time quanta.* An epoch is a quantum of time and conceptually adequate for modern physics, then, without being only a duration of the briefest possible extent. For, the epoch has the temporal duration of the actual occasion, whatever be the occasion. Whitehead calls the epochs of occasions time-quanta, again concerned to say that they are not of equal duration. "I do not say that all the time-quanta involved in supersession are equal. But some time-quantum is always involved."[84] Whitehead's epochal theory of time is the theory that all occasions whatsoever are undivided units, atoms, or quanta of time. "The actual entity is the enjoyment of a certain quantum of physical time."[85]

Epochs or time quanta come into being and perish as do the occasions of which they are the epochs. The epoch of ancient Rome is no longer extant today; the epoch of my writing the preceding sentence is gone; the epoch of gasoline automobiles will also perish. Time perishes with its occasion. There is no continuously existing, actual time, absolute, reified, substantialized. William P. D. Wightman ignores epochal time and reintroduces absolute time into the philosophy by removing it from the actual occasions: "It is not *time* that perishes but the actual entities."[86]

In becoming and perishing time exhibits the same discontinuity observed of spacetime in quantum physics. "The scientific events in which scientific objects are ingredient yield chunks of time, rather than the continuously flowing entity of Newtonian physics."[87] Whitehead's metaphysics requires that epochal time apply equally to all things, not only "scientific events," so that the epochs of all occasions must be regarded as discontinuous quanta, not only those of electromagnetic occasions. "An investigation of quantum physical time must not be limited to the microcosmos."[88]

Rem B. Edwards objects:

> If real temporal change at the microscopic level of quantum phenomena does occur discontinuously, does it follow inevitably that real temporal change at *every* level of existence is also atomic in its structure? Whitehead generalized, perhaps over-hastily, that all temporal change within the created world has this structure, including changes within the stream of human experience.[89]

Certainly it does not follow inevitably that the longer epochs have anything in common with the epochs of the briefest quanta known to physicists. But Whitehead is concerned to construct a cosmology wherein the knowledge acquired from all experience, that of common life as well as that of science, is coherent and consistent and also adequate for interpreting everything from the quanta of physics to the occasions of human knowledge and percipience themselves. Whitehead's generalization, applying undivided quanta of time to every actual concrete existence instead of only to the microphysical, must be judged along with the entire philosophy and its applicability; it does not follow as an immediate conclusion from quantum mechanics alone. If Whitehead's generalization has been over-hasty, then it behooves us to provide a better theory that can coherently and consistently and adequately account for the evidence from both modern physics and ordinary human life and thought.

*Transition.* Final causation and atomism are interconnected because an occasion is one and whole by virtue of its subjective aim and its epoch actualized only upon the attainment of satisfaction of this final cause. It is for the same reason that an epoch or quantum of time is undivided: there are no subdivisions of a subjective aim, no parts of an ideal. Whitehead explains that not even the phases in the process of concrescence (the genetic process) amount to temporal divisions; in fact, to the contrary, the phases are relative to the whole epoch:

> But the genetic process is not the temporal succession: such a view is exactly what is denied by the epochal theory of time. Each phase in the genetic process presupposes the entire quantum, and so does each feeling in each phase. The subjective unity dominating the process forbids the division of that extensive quantum which

originates with the primary phase of the subjective aim. The problem dominating the concrescence is the actualization of the quantum *in solido.*[90]

Just as there can be no speaking of before and after except retrospectively of relations between occasions already actualized, or hypothetically assuming their actualization, so there can be no speaking of earlier and later temporal divisions or phases during a process of concrescence until there has been a complete concrescence. There are no temporal subdivisions of an epochal occasion before there has been a whole occasion. The completed epoch is the unit of time, which cannot come before itself. It is always units that come into being, although they come into being divisible into parts. But they do not come into being part by part; for, the real organic togetherness aimed at cannot be effected by the simple addition of parts.

The first phase of the occasion is the first phase of the subjective aim, which is not in time but initiates a potential epoch. The first phase generates the particular spatiotemporal quantum without being the quantum or a spatiotemporal part of one itself. The first phase determines the extension of the quantum, rather, its extension-to-be; the last phase of satisfaction produces it. This is not the retroactive action of the future on the past, since there is no future in actuality; it is the development and completion of present potentialities.

Then the process of concrescence or microscopic process is not itself in transition. Transition is the macroscopic process which provides the data for the initial phase of an occasion. "The creativity in virtue of which any relative complete actual world is, by the nature of things, the datum for a new concrescence is termed 'transition.'"[91] Macroscopic process is the assemblage of the real potentialities of antecedents capable of sharing one aim together. This process, transition, is that of the efficient causation bringing about the new occasion. Then transition, which is "into" the first phase of the new occasion and initiating the occasion, is physical time retrospectively speaking. Transition is not in physical time except retrospectively since antecedents-to-be and the first phase of the new occasion are not temporal, but as yet potentialities for time.

*Physical time.* Neither the phases of concrescence nor transition, then, are in physical time except retrospectively speaking. That is, neither the transition of antecedents into a new concrescence nor the process of concrescence itself unfold in time or are divisible into any temporal parts, before and after one another, until the occasion has perished. In the following passage, Whitehead states that physical time is only to be found in the retrospective analysis of the completed occasion:

> This genetic passage from phase to phase is not in physical time: the exactly converse point of view expresses the relationship of concrescence to physical time. It can be put shortly by saying, that physical time expresses some features of the growth, but *not* the growth of the features. . . .
> Physical time makes its appearance in the 'coordinate' analysis of the 'satisfaction.'[92]

This passage is very important in any consideration of Whiteheadian time, since it denies the temporal succession of phases of concrescence and also denies that transition is physical time since physical time only appears retrospectively. The passage asserts that physical time does not even appear until there has been an analysis of the satisfaction. The occasion has to have attained satisfaction and perished before there can be physical time. This remarkable fact, that physical time is found only by retrospective analysis of a completed occasion, is a consequence of the relativity of time. The duration of an epoch is determined retrospectively, when it is completed, by comparing it to other epochs; and the transition initiating it and the phases developing it are determined retrospectively. For, there are no actual temporal transitions or phases in process; these are only ways of analyzing an epoch *ex post facto*.

In fact, no aspect, factor, or ingredient of an occasion is prehendable before the whole occasion is prehendable. Of course, the whole occasion is only prehendable in some aspect of it; nevertheless the whole occasion must be an actuality before any aspect of it can be prehended. The question as to the prehendability of the ingredients of an occasion before its perishing was actually put to Whitehead by A. H. Johnson:

> Your usual statement of the doctrine of objectification is to the effect that an actual entity does not provide data for a new actual entity until it (the first actual entity) has 'died.' 'Data' are available only after the internal existence of the actual entity 'has evaporated, worn out and satisfied.' The superject is not of the *substance* of the subject. When you say:—An actual entity 'at any stage . . . is subject-*superject*' you *don't* mean to say that *at any stage* in the development of an actual entity data are available, do you? Whitehead answered: 'No.'[93]

Thus, an occasion cannot be both subject and superject "at once"; it cannot both come into being and be an object for other occasions at once. The actual occasion as subject-superject is not the occasion as both subject and object, objectively immortal, both present and future, at once. The occasion as subject-superject is the occasion as present with the potentiality for a future. It is only the superject that can be coordinately analyzed, only the satisfaction of the occasion, not the subject. Only the superject as an object in the experience of subsequent occasions is prehended. Of course, while a subject may not be prehended, the occasions that are making up its actual world may be prehended.

The unprehendability of an occasion or any ingredient, phase, or cause of it until that occasion has perished and been objectified is not because it is invisibly sealed against observation or otherwise mysteriously closed to examination, impenetrable, elusive. It is because *its* particular togetherness of things has not yet arrived to be distinguished from all the other things. The occasion does not come into being in nothing, when and where nothing was before. Its coming into being is beyond the spatiotemporality of other occasions, not because there is nothing beyond them, but because *it* was not there before.

All analysis is from a retrospective perspective because the occasion only becomes available for prehension and analysis if it is an antecedent. The phases of a concrescence do not distinguish actual temporal divisions since the occasion does not arise by the addition of temporal parts; but retrospectively the occasion, once prehended, may be analyzed as divisible in temporal parts. This retrospective divisibility of an epoch is physical time, not the epoch's becoming. Physical time is the superimposition of the occasion as superject back onto the occasion as subject. It is the content of the satisfaction, retrospectively discerned, as if it had occurred in a temporal order.

*Passage and arrest.* An epoch is temporally arrested, because it is an undivided atom or unit of time. Its process of becoming is the process of the actualization of a potentiality for a spatiotemporal quantum. This process involves no temporal order or temporal passage except retrospectively. An illustration of the potentiality of time in an epoch's process of becoming may be taken from one of Whitehead's examples of the perception of causal efficacy. This example is not intended to illustrate the potentiality of time in the process of becoming, that is, epochal arrest, but it can be used just the same to illustrate this inasmuch as any example of an actual occasion coming into being can be used.

Whitehead calls the perception of causal efficacy in this case, for this example, "non-sensuous" perception to distinguish it from the sense-perception of traditional empiricism founded upon sense-perception alone. If traditional empiricism is based upon sense-perception, then Whiteheadian empiricism may be said to be based upon non-sensuous perception, such as the perception of causal efficacy in memory. An example of non-sensuous perception that Whitehead gives uses the enunciation of the phrases "United States" and "United Fruit Company."[94] He is concerned here to show the genuine perception of causation, in contradistinction to Hume for whom there can be no perception of causation.

While we are enunciating the word "United" we are anticipating the word "States." And while we are enunciating the word "States," we are remembering the word "United" with it so that the words together form a meaningful phrase. Whitehead makes the point that the anticipation and the memory are non-sensuous, that is, that they are felt without the accompaniment of the actual sounds of the words. For the (sensuous) sound of the word "States" is not present when it is anticipated, and the (sensuous) sound of the word "United" is not present when it is remembered. Consequently, there is non-sensuous perception of the causal efficacy of a phrase. "This is an instance of direct intuitive observation which is incapable of reduction to the sensationalist formula."[95] Both words of the phrase, "United" and "States," are held together conjointly in the one phrase; they "live" together. ". . . the speaker is carried from 'United' to 'States', and the two conjointly live in the present, by the energizing of the past occasion as it claims its self-identical existence as a living issue in the present."[96] This felt energizing of the past, as well as the anticipation of the future, is, of course, the perception of causal efficacy. And it is not really the actual words that live together in the present phrase occasion, but their potentiality for one phrase. Together they create a new occasion, the phrase.

It is not the sounds that unite this phrase, "United States," but intention, the subjective aim of the speaker for the phrase. "Also, insofar as there was consciousness, there was direct observation of the past with its intention finding its completion in the present fact."[97] But the phrase is not a whole and completed phrase, an actual phrase occasion, until the subjective aim, the intention that this whole phrase be enunciated, is met. The efficacy of the causes, both the past sounds and the past and present intention regarding them, is experienced as the phrase is being completed. And the completion of the phrase is not experienced as something separate from the phrase, as though one thing were the phrase and its completion were another thing altogether. The completion of the phrase means that one whole experience, of a phrase, its completed epoch, has come into being. It is the epoch of this particular utterance of the phrase, United States. Its spatiotemporal extension is obviously intermixed with many many other occasions, overlapping some, including others, included in others. It has no simple location because it cannot be fully described spatiotemporally without its relationships to other occasions.

The temporality of the phrase in process is a potentiality, just as is the phrase until its completion. In its "living" present, there is the intention, the potentiality for the phrase-time epoch, but no passage or temporal order. While anticipating and remembering and uttering the various syllables involved in saying "United States," utterances which themselves constituted many another occasion, the phrase-time is not actually passing. The phrase does not pass in its own midst. It is not in transition to becoming another occasion in its own midst. The phrase itself is not yet; *it* cannot be in transition when it is not even there.

Certainly various occasions involved in the making of the syllables of the words are passing as they perish within the duration of the phrase epoch. But phrase-time cannot pass before it is created. The phrase is completed and perishing when "States" has been completely enunciated and remembered and understood as a phrase together with "United." But while uttering the syllable "-ted" or while remembering "Uni-" and anticipating "States," the total phrase-time is a potentiality. While the syllables pass, their potentiality for a whole phrase does not. The phrase is, and is experienced as, temporally potential, until it perishes. And the syllables are and are experienced as, occasions themselves which pass within the duration of the phrase. And the relationships of the consonant and vowel sounds of the syllables to the syllables, as parts to whole, is the same as that of the syllables to the phrase.

David A. Sipfle illustrates the epochal arrest of a whole phrase in process of becoming showing that there is also a passage of potentially component words within it, potentially component because they do not belong to that phrase until that phrase is an actuality.

We do experience a present which has duration but which also has a before and an after which are present in it. When I hear the word 'Bergson,' I do hear the whole word—indeed a whole phrase of which it is a part—within a single experience (if I did not it would be unintelligible), but I also hear the 'Berg'- before, and temporally before, I hear the -'son.' If our conceptual apparatus cannot simultaneously reproduce both features of this experience—the 'all-at-oneness' *and* the temporal succession—then so much the worse for our conceptual categories.[98]

Thus, the phrase epoch does not actually pass with the sound of each syllable or word; it is ever present, the "living" present of potentiality, until it is completed. But surely the various syllables, sounds, and words may be considered parts of the phrase; then surely parts of the phrase are passing before the phrase is completed. But syllables are only parts of a phrase if and when the phrase has actually occurred, verifying that it had that potentiality for a division into such parts. Syllables can only be interpreted as parts of a particular phrase retrospectively, given the phrase. The syllables and words pass as such, actual occasions in their own right; but as parts of a phrase, and as temporal parts of a phrase epoch, they are but a potentiality with respect to it. There can be no part of the epoch without that epoch's being there. Syllables *become* the parts of a word; words *become* the parts of a phrase.

If the speaker chokes and does not finish his phrase, his ability to make sounds has been energized to make a choke and not a phrase in this instance, the choke being another of the potentialities of the past.

For instance, if the speaker had been interrupted after the words 'United Fruit', he might have resumed his speech with the words 'I meant to add the word Company'. Thus during the interruption, the past was energizing in his experience as carrying in itself an unfulfilled intention.[99]

If the subjective aim of the phrase had not been met, there would be no phrase, and no parts *of* a phrase.

The same situation is to be found in actual occasions of a much different scale. There were innumerable transitions of occasions within the duration of the epoch that was ancient Rome, for example. Innumerable occasions and societies came into being and perished while Rome was a potentiality and still a living present. Rome did not pass, Rome was not in transition to other occasions, with the perishing and transition of any epoch within it. And had there been a volcano, flood, or earthquake instead of a completed ancient Rome, then Rome too would have been an unfulfilled intention and potentiality.

The importance of the subjective aim as accounting for the wholeness of an epochal occasion can be seen in these examples. The syllables involved in a phrase are affected by the subjective aim of the whole phrase to be what they are in relation to the phrase. Syllables are pronounced differently depending on the word and phrase they become a part of: their pronunciation is affected by the intention to utter a particular phrase. Similarly, the intention of the creation of ancient Rome had effect on everything that became objectified as a component of it. The subjective aim of Rome had real effect on the building of each building and statue, the rearing of each child, the writing of each poem and essay, the rule of each emporer: all became Roman, both artifacts and people, by sharing the subjective aim of Rome.

## TIME SPANS

*Inexactitude.* Coming into being is coming into being a particular, definite concrete existent distinct from other and antecedent existences. But becoming definite is not becoming exact.

Now the question is— Has he observed exactly, or, Has he had exact notions elicited in his conceptual experience? In what sense did he observe exactly one chair? He observed a vague differentiation of the general context of his visual experience. But suppose we pin him down to one billionth of an inch. Where does the chair end and the rest of things begin? Which atom belongs to the chair, and which atom belongs to surrounding space? The chair is perpetually gaining and losing atoms. It is not exactly differentiated from its surroundings, nor is it exactly self-identical as time slips by.[100]

Then actualities are definite, the chair being a definite chair, but not exact, the chair having no exact borders and not remaining the same. An actuality does not have an exact boundary between it and other actualities; there is no exact spatiotemporal location. Borders are ambiguous in that they are shared with other occasions. Exact spatiotemporal locations are only possible when and where they are bordering on nothing. But there is no nothing to border on. There is no exactness in actuality since an actuality is not simply an eternal object and is not surrounded by nothing.

And what Whitehead says of the chair, he says also of the human body and of any other body at all. None are exact, none have exact spatiotemporal boundaries.

Also, if we are fussily exact, we cannot define where a body begins and where external nature ends.

Consider one definite molecule. It is a part of nature. It has moved about for millions of years. Perhaps it started from a distant nebula. It enters the body; it may be as a factor in some edible vegetable; or it passes into the lungs as part of the air. At what exact point as it enters the mouth or as it is absorbed through the skin, is it part of the body? At what exact moment, later on, does it cease to be part of the body? Exactness is out of the question. It can only be obtained by some trivial convention.[101]

We have seen that there are no exact instants and no chronons with exact boundaries; now we see that there are no exact epochs either. Whatever an occasion is, its actual world is not unshared with others; it becomes itself shared by others; it is not actually separable from the environment of others.

Whitehead is a philosopher for whom vagueness is a reality, as his category of transmutation witnesses. This may seem strange coming from the philosopher who has necessitated one ultimate category, eight categories of existence, twenty-seven categories of explanation, and nine categoreal obligations. Nevertheless, these categories are designed to accommodate (among other things) the real potentiality, the real indeterminacy, the real incompleteness, the real inherent creativity, the real relativity, the real inexactitude, the real and vague perception of causal efficacy, the real inextricable togetherness of antecedents that are involved in any actual occasion. "The problem is to discriminate exactly what we know vaguely."[102] Thus, it is Whitehead who says: "My point is that the final outlook of philosophic thought cannot be based upon the exact statements which form the basis of special sciences. The exactness is a fake."[103] Then Whitehead's own exactness and precision in formulating his philosophical system is, in part, exactness about how actuality is inexact and indeterminate and precision in stating how actualities are imprecise and vague. It is Whitehead who reminds us that: "It follows that philosophy is not a science."[104]

In sum, Whiteheadian reality including Whiteheadian time is inexact since real concrete existences are inexact experiences. Actualities have not the exactitude of ideas.

There is a conventional view of experience, never admitted when explicitly challenged, but persistently lurking in the tacit presuppositions. This view conceives conscious experience as a clear-cut knowledge of clear-cut items with clear-cut connections with each other. This is the conception of a trim, tidy, finite experience uniformly illuminated. No notion could be further from the truth.[105]

This includes the spatiotemporal quanta. There are no clear-cut epochal occasions with clear-cut connections with each other. The epoch is inexact.

*The specious present.* The measure of the time-spans of the coming into being of a human percipient occasion, especially vision, is the duration of its "specious present" by the clock. The human percipient occasion, such as an act of seeing, is not there, not yet in existence, in a shorter interval than that of its specious present. Every movie camera is geared to run just enough faster than the specious present of human vision so that the film is not perceived as a series of stills.

However, for Whitehead, every actual occasion might be said to have a specious present inasmuch as every occasion has a time-span very much shorter or longer than which the occasion does not come to be. The durations of specious presents or time-spans are nothing exact in actuality, though they may be estimated with enough accuracy necessary to predict them. The duration of a specious present of an occasion depends upon what the occasion is. The specious present of the coming into being of an ant communication is not that of the coming into being of an ice age; the specious present of a flap of a hummingbird wing is not that of a forest fire; the specious present of the sprouting of a grass seed not that of the creation of a mountain range. "The "specious" present is obviously misnamed:

The fact that the mathematical instant is never experienced did not shake the belief in its existence in any way. This explains why the psychological present which is the only present, the only 'moment' which we can experience and which is always of non-zero duration, was called 'specious present.' The choice of this term is significant: it was coined to suggest that the only *true* present, the only true instant is without duration, a mere temporal point; in contrast to this true mathematical present our psychological present, which we experience as 'minimum sensibile,' is necessarily only 'specious.'[106]

Averages of the specious presents of various actualities may be taken. But every individual will not measure up to the exact average. There is variation from individual to individual. Whitehead notes that even the specious presents of human perceptions vary from perceiver to perceiver. That is, the time-spans of two human percipient occasions by the clock are not necessarily the same. He also remarks that no specious present of a percipient occasion is *the* present, is *the* universal and uniform present for all perceptions alike. He is denying that percipient occasions are *the only time,* that they are the only present that there can be. In this way, he is denying absolute time, the time that is the same for all things alike, and regardless of the perspective. Time for Whitehead is not the "unique factor in nature" that it is for Newton since it is not universally and uniformly in nature but rather is in systems of actual occasions.

> . . . the temporal breadths of the immediate durations of sense-awareness are very indeterminate and dependent on the individual percipient. Accordingly there is no unique factor in nature which for every percipient is preeminently and necessarily the present.[107]

The average specious present for a certain type of occasion may be taken, then, but an individual of that type will not necessarily accord with the average. The specious presents of human percipient occasions, both of sight and sound, may differ somewhat in different human beings, as well as in different occasions of the same human being. And similarly for all occasions: the time-spans of any type may be averaged, but this average is no exact standard that they all have to meet. The duration of time-spans is that of the subjective aims of the occasions, which aims are not realized instantaneously or contained within exact boundaries like a chronon or which inevitably must attain satisfaction in the exact same period. Subjective aims are realized as concrete occasions, which are acts and experiences, come into being.

*The presence of the past.* The variety of types of occasions that Whitehead recognizes has been emphasized throughout this book, and I stress it again now so that their differing time-spans may be appreciated. Here we find Whitehead listing varieties of occasions:

> In order to discover some of the major categories under which we can classify the infinitely various components of experience, we must appeal to evidence relating to every variety of occasion. Nothing can be omitted, experience drunk and experience sober, experience sleeping and experience waking, experience drowsy and experience wide-awake, experience self-conscious and experience self-forgetful, experience intellectual and experience physical, experience religious and experience sceptical, experience anxious and experience care-free, experience anticipatory and experience retrospective, experience happy and experience grieving, experience dominated by emotion and experience under self-restraint, experience in the light and experience in the dark, experience normal and experience abnormal.[108]

It is obvious that an experience of grief and an experience of sleep do not occur in the same time-span as a visual perception; and a drunken experience and a drowsy experience require a different time-span than does a religious experience and an intellecutal experience. Whitehead speaks also of "judging entities": "The same proposition can constitute the content of diverse judgments by diverse judging entities respectively. The possibility of diverse judgments by diverse actual entities. . . ."[109] Then judgments may be added as another type of experience on the part of actual judging occasions. Judgments cannot take only the fraction of a second that visual perceptions take; and all judgments cannot be of equal duration. It is obvious that there are innumerable types of human experiences that are not necessarily brief. Solving a problem, whether mechanical, medical, musical, or mathematical may be an occasion requiring a time-span of a year, a month, a morning, or a minute: its duration cannot be dictated beforehand.

An occasion, being the effect of many antecedent causes, reveals them in its construction. It only comes into being the occasion that it is when the causes have accomplished their effect. Its time-span is initiated with the sharing of the subjective aim for that effect among the potentialities that can accomplish it together, potentialities to become the actual world of the occasion, and it is completed as the occasion becomes a prehendable object to other occasions. The time-span is the duration of the present of the occasion. When it is past with respect to a successor, *it* has no duration; its present duration perishes with the occasion. As past, it is in transition to a present, it is creative potentiality for new occasions for which it is divisible into any number of spatiotemporal parts.

A meteor crashes to earth and burns to a cinder. Nothing is left of the meteor, but a burned crater and cinder. An inspection of the crater, when its present moment of subjective immediacy has perished, and it is antecedent to some human perceptions of it, reveals no actual meteor. And the crater's actual duration in becoming is gone. Henceforth its divisible spatiotemporal dimensions are new relations with successors prehending it and in which its potentialities have efficacy. And effect reveals its causes without the causes being present themselves; the present reveals the durations of its antecedents without the antecedent durations being present themselves. Causes cannot be present inasmuch as they are transformed into effect. The crater reveals even a stream of causes, an historic route of predecessors that contributed to it, without these being present themselves. This is the society of antecedent occasions that together formed the present crater occasion, without them or their time-spans being present as wholes and subjects themselves. The time-span of an antecedent occasion does not continue into its successor; the successor is made anew from the potentialities inherent in its relationships with it.

The crater is composed of its feelings of antecedents. They reveal what is felt as objectified by the crater, that is, from the crater's perspective. The crater's size, shape, and quality are all effects testifying to a past meteor of a certain size, mass, and speed moving in air at a certain angle with respect to earth, burning, and impacting in ground of a certain consistency and content. The crater's feelings of these antecedent causes *are* the crater. Its depth and shape, the width and height of its rims, its burns and residues, are feelings on the part of ground of specific consistency of the impact of an object of certain dimensions traveling at a certain speed and burning both in air and on the ground. The air, fire, smoke, the meteor and its consistency and the ground and its consistency are all real potentialities for making the crater what it is once these potentialities engage one another in relationship upon impact. This is the common sense of Whitehead's causal efficacy: the present is created and constituted by the real potentials inherent in the past. But the actual past is gone. An occasion's relationships to its antecedents are revealed within it as its feelings of them, and its relations to successors are in process.

There is a passage wherein Whitehead says that the "endurance of a block of marble" is an event and spatiotemporal happening:

> I give the name 'event' to a spatio-temporal happening. An event does not in any way imply rapid change; the endurance of a block of marble is an event. Nature presents itself to us as essentially a becoming, and any limited portion of nature which preserves most completely such concreteness as attaches to nature itself is also a becoming and is what I call an event.[110]

If an event is a society, the spatiotemporal happening is that of the society as a spacetime system. There is no spacetime but that there is succession; each occasion is spatiotemporal only if there is a potential past and future with respect to it and inherent in it. The life-time of a block of marble, its endurance as an enduring object, is a spatiotemporal event; but the relationships of this event are absorbed in each succeeding member occasion. The block as an enduring object is comprised of successive marble occasions, each one of which has a time-span significantly longer than, for example, the electromagnetic occasions within it. And each of the member occasions incorporates aspects of the past members which have perished so that the entire society, the enduring marble block, is not present at one time, except insofar as it is the composition of a present time-span coming into being. The antecedent society only exists in its formation of a present member. Like the meteor in relation to the crater, the antecedent marble occasions are causes and potentialities, no longer the whole occasions that they were. The succession of member occasions of a society do not occur all at one time so that all may be surveyed at once. The antecedents are only revealed in their successors.

Whitehead speaks of the soul in the very same way as the block of marble. The soul is a life-time of occasions of experience. This linear succession of occasions of experiences is that personal society whereby a human being is an enduring personality or soul. Each member occasion incorporates those preceding it, thereby embodying the entire antecedent society, although not simply additively. The antecedents are retained only in their divisible, objectifiable relationships as these affect occasions prehending aspects of them. Like the crater and the marble, each occasion of experience reveals the effects of an historical route of antecedent occasions of experience in its own constitution. The time-span of an occasion of experience cannot be especially brief, nor is the succession of these occasions very fast since it is that of a human life-time. In the case of marble, the succession of marble occasions is not rapid either because the marble occasions themselves do not come into being in a brief time-span. Neither the endurance of a block of marble nor that of a soul "imply rapid change."

> The soul is nothing else than the succession of my occasions of experience, extending from birth to the present moment. Now, at this instant, I am the complete person embodying all these occasions. They are mine. On the other hand it is equally true that my immediate occasion of experience, at the present moment, is only one among the stream of occasions which constitutes my soul.[111]

Thus, there is a straightforward comparison between the block of marble and the soul. Each marble occasion and soul occasion is one among many and also embodies the many that preceded it, although not in their original state.

A Whiteheadian epoch has always this depth of becoming, such that it embodies the antecedent society from which it arises. The epoch is always both one and many, the one epoch with its many parts derived from its divisible antecedents. It is composed of the antecedent members of this society or spacetime system without being the crude addition of them *simpliciter*. The antecedent members have perished and been objectified in the present epoch, as the present epoch. And the epoch is one member of this same spacetime system the antecedent members of which created it.

*Gaps and voids.* In the following passage, Whitehead tells us that the "realization of personal identity," which is one sequence of actual occasions, "varies with the temporal span." He points out that the reason that we do not notice our own percipient occasions being realized one after another in sequence, is that it is such an obvious and common experience, so "overwhelming" that we take it for granted without recognizing it.

A whole sequence of actual occasions, each with its own present immediacy, is such that each occasion embodies in its own being the antecedent members of that sequence with an emphatic experience of the self-identity of the past in the immediacy of the present. This is the realization of personal identity. This varies with the temporal span. For short periods it is so overwhelming that we hardly recognize it. For example, take a many-syllabled word, such as 'overwhelming' which was employed in the previous sentence: of course the person who said 'over' was identical with the person who said 'ing.' But there was a fraction of a second between the two occasions. And yet the speaker enjoyed his self-identity during the pronunciation of the word, and the listeners never doubted the self-identity of the speaker.[112]

In this instance Whitehead is speaking of two percipient occasions of a person, the percipient occasions being those of hearing syllables uttered. But he is speaking particularly of the gap between these two occasions, a gap of a fraction of a second. This fraction of a second is that between the uttering and hearing of "over" and the uttering and hearing of "ing," these being two distinguishable occasions of human percipience. This fraction of a second is in no way a measure of the interval between any two occasions whatever or even between any two human percipient occasions, but simply the interval between "over" and "ing" in this particular case.

Also, this interval between the two percipient occasions of hearing these two particular syllables is not a void of nothingness. Many other occasions of all types become and perish, some within the interval, some including it, and some overlapping it. Many an electromagnetic and electrochemical occasion as well as other percipient occasions are created and perish within the interval; and many an occasion of thought, judgment, and experience overlap the interval; and other physiological occasions and occasions of consciousness and personality include the interval. All are occasions of experiences of the same person, same with respect to his or her ability to reproduce him or her self in important respects.

Just as the time-spans of different types of occasions differ, so do the intervals or gaps between them. The gap between two drunken experiences is vast compared to that between utterances of two syllables in a word; the gap between two successive occasions of sleep is vast compared to that between two successive anticipations; the gap between two successive memories is short compared to that between two successive occasions of religious experience, and so on.

However, epochs are too often treated as uniform, brief, isolated, fixed durations with nothing in between them, as though they were inaccessible spatiotemporal holes themselves bordering on nothing. For example, Francis Seaman says, "However, in the cosmology of *PR* . . . events do not overlap but succeed one another."[113] But if no occasions overlap, then there is nothing in between them: the gaps between epochs are voids of nothingness. Rem B. Edwards, supposing that Whitehead holds that there are voids of nothing between occasions, finds the view intolerable:

> The brand new, atomically existing, subjects or selves appearing every tenth of a second or so with which the orthodox Whiteheadians confront us are the empty abstractions from the continuous flow of human experience and activity. *They* are the ones who commit the 'fallacy of misplaced concreteness.' Some of them come very close to conceding that concrete human experience fails to confirm the theory that we flash in and out of existence every fraction of a second.[114]

Edwards has imputed to Whiteheadians and Whitehead the view that all occasions of human existence are necessarily very brief; that all are as brief as those of human percipience, the specious presents of sight and sound. This restricts all of human existence to that of perceptions—not a very likely account of the Whiteheadian philosophy. Edwards evidently thinks that Whitehead or Whiteheadians identify human experience so much with brief experiences, such as perceptions, that it is not only these that become and perish rapidly, but "we." And Rasvihary Das consents: "I am, at the moment of perception, nothing but the occasion of perceptual experience, and my actual being is defined by what is given in my perception. . . ."[115] However, a person is not "nothing but" his perception. It is only the percipient occasion that is defined by what is given in the perception, not the person's entire being. There are many diverse human experiences, physiological and psychological, concurrent with and overlapping those of perception.

Averages of different rates of becoming and of succession may be taken, but none of these is a standard for all the others. Whitehead, so far from identifying the human being with percipience, regards a human being such as himself primarily as a unity of emotions. A person is primarily a sequence of emotional experiences, characterized by her or his own individuality. A lifetime is primarily a society of such occasions of personality. Such occasions and the gaps between them are not at all of uniform duration but vary considerably. Whitehead uses such occasions as paradigm actual entities; nevertheless, they are not the only actual entities and their durations are not a spatiotemporal standard which all actual entities necessarily conform to. The reduction of human experiences or human beings or human personalities to occasions of perception and the time-spans of these has no foundation in the philosophy. Whitehead counts the "visual feelings" as only one type of occasion among others: "Philosophers have disdained the information about the universe obtained through their visceral feelings, and have concentrated on visual feelings."[116]

The view that all occasions are necessarily brief, that human existence is necessarily a sequence only of the briefest percipient experiences, is a revised edition of absolute time, revised to accommodate the Whiteheadian vocabulary and conception of a plurality of occasions instead of a single universe. For, the succession of brief epochs, uniform and unique such that no other temporal succession is intermixed with it, is either a succession of periodic renewals of absolute time with voids of nothingness in between its members, or it is a succession of holes, empty containers, in an absolute time flowing outside the members. That is, absolute time is either renewed at the beginning of each brief epoch and ended with the epoch's completion, or else the epochs are themselves timeless holes against a background of the supposedly real time, the absolute time flowing independently of them. A succession of brief epochs is regularly imagined to be either "in" absolute time, or "in" nothingness. These conceptions are closer to the chronon theory of time than the epochal theory.

In either case, the epochs are treated as miniature Newtonian universes. If regarded as empty themselves they have been spatialized as the timeless, spatial containers of things, just as Newtonian time was spatialized so that the entire universe was regarded as one enduring space. If the epochs are treated as passing in time themselves but residing in nothingness, then they are miniature Newtonian universes with absolute time flowing in them however briefly. Whether absolute time is considered to be running in the cosmic container of all epochs, or whether it is considered to run only within epochs, Whiteheadian epochal time has not even entered the picture.

One confusion resulting from retaining absolute time is expressed by

Martin Jordan: "Time is the measured interval between things happening."[117] The gaps between occasions can only be treated as temporal if absolute time is presumed to be filling in the gap. If the gaps between occasions were nothingness, pure voids, they could hardly be a measure of time: there is no duration of nothingness. If the gaps between occasions are temporal, then they are so in the sense of absolute time, since only occasions become temporal in the Whiteheadian philosophy. Jordan's measure of time as that of gaps between occasions presumes that there is an absolute time continuous between occasions.

Confusions stemming from reintroducing absolute time into Whiteheadian cosmology can also be seen in this statement of Edward's:

> The dilemma is, either there is *a gap between* occasions, or there is not. If there is a gap between occasions, if occasions are 'divided from each other,' then it would appear that *a completely perished* occasion could not function causally to present data to its successor. On the other hand, if there are no gaps between occasions, if occasions do partly overlap, then the atomic theory of time has been abandoned. There are no *discrete* events. Time is a continuous flow. . . . Whiteheadians have never addressed themselves to the question of *how long the gap is between occasions.* . . . How long *between* occasions are we *not* in existence? And how do we *test* the answer which we give to this question?[118]

The continuous flow is Newtonian mathematical time. And here is the conception of a duration of a void; a gap of nothingness which is yet a measure of time. This is the conception of absolute time flowing outside and independently of the occasions. Here also is the conception of an absolute succession of occasions which are necessarily all of a size and uniform such that they always leave the exact same gap between them. Edwards asks how long is the gap between occasions, just as other interpreters of Whitehead ask or suppose a certain fixed size or range of sizes for all actual occasions. It is the same as to ask how long is the gap between all concretely existing things. It is not different gaps between different types of occasions whose measure is inquired here, but *the* gap between *the* occasions, as though all were of one type and duration and as though all were in one unique sequence such that there could be empty gaps between them.

It must be repeated that the gaps between epochs are neither continuous spacetime in the sense of the Newtonian mathematical flow, nor are they nothing. What is a gap between two epochs is the becoming of many another epoch. The gap between two successive perceptions may be filled with an epoch of happiness; the gap between two wars may be filled with an epoch of imperialism; the gap between two rain falls may be filled with an epoch of draught.

In response to Edward's dilemma, it may be said first of all that occasions do not vanish. They perish subjectively, but are immortal objectively. It is just these objectively immortal occasions that do "function causally." Secondly, Whiteheadian epochs are not atomic and discrete in the sense of bordering on nothing, being included in nothing, or including nothing themselves. They are discrete and atomic in the sense of being a distinguishable entity in the relationships among other things. Whitehead's atomism is not a simply located atomism of clearly isolated simply located atoms in the midst of nothing. The atomic actual occasions overlap many another potential atomic occasion and actual atomic occasion. All are included in others and include others: none are simply located.

Thirdly, there can be no measure of the spacetimes between spacetimes that is not also a measure of the spacetimes of other occasions. There is no measure of nothing or of a length of nothingness, or of a different type of spacetime between the spacetimes of actual occasions. Every gap between any occasions is a gap relative to the duration of other occasions. For example, it might be said that we are not in existence relative to our conscious states when we are asleep. But it is only our conscious states that are asleep; the gap is only a gap between conscious states and may be compared in duration to that of the night.

And fourth, we can test how long a gap between specific occasions is by using a clock. If we slept eight hours by the clock, then we have measured the gap between two conscious states to be eight hours by the clock. There was no complete gap in existence, wherein there was nothing. There was only a gap in between conscious states. And if there were a complete gap in existence, there would be no question of how to measure it: there is no measure of nothing. A state of consciousness becomes and perishes at a different rate than occasions of perception and many other physiological occasions. Just as a state of consciousness has a longer time-span than that of many successive syllables and many successive perceptions, so the gaps between states of consciousness are also longer than those between successive syllables and perceptions. The gap between states of consciousness is sleep.

Yet when we examine this notion of the soul, it discloses itself as even vaguer than our definition of the body. First, the continuity of the soul—so far as concerns consciousness—has to leap gaps in time. We sleep or we are stunned. . . . Again there is a curious variation in the vividness of the successive occasions of the soul's existence . . . we doze; we dream; we sleep with a total lapse of the stream of consciousness.[119]

And the gaps between states of consciousness, that is, unconsciousness, are overlapped by and included in many another occasion. For example, childhood overlaps and includes many a gap in the consciousness of a child. And vacations too are actual occasions with many effects on subsequent planetary and human life, just as are children. While there are gaps in a person's consciousness, she or he may still be a child or on vacation.

*Intersecting paths.* There is no gap wherein no actual occasion lies because there is no space or time where or when there is not an occasion whose space and time it is in relation to that of other occasions. The fraction of a second between two percipient occasions is not a gap of nothingness, nor is it a measure of the gap between any two actual occasions. A person does not only visually and aurally perceive, but fires nerves, thinks, breathes, moves, circulates blood, digests, secretes, feels moods, and operates in millions of ways. The discontinuity between any two occasions of one temporal sequence is continuity with many other occasions. Thus, in the following passage we find Whitehead saying that although a human being is a serial succession of dominant occasions of a human personality, he is many other things as well, which things intersect with the dominant occasions of human personhood.

But this analogy of physical nature to human experience is limited by the fact of the linear seriality of human occasions within any one personality and of the many-dimensional seriality of the occasions in physical Space-Time.

In order to prove that this discrepancy is only superficial, it now remains for discussion whether the human experience of direct inheritance provides any analogy to this many-dimensional character of space. If human occasions of experience essentially inherit in one-dimensional personal order, there is a gap between human occasions and the physical occasions of nature.

The peculiar status of the human body at once presents itself as negating this notion of strict personal order for human inheritance. Our dominant inheritance from our immediately past occasion is broken into by innumerable inheritances through other avenues. Sensitive nerves, the functionings of our viscera, disturbances in the composition of our blood, break in upon the dominant line of inheritance. . . . So intimately obvious is this bodily inheritance that common speech does not discriminate the human body from the human person.[120]

Thus, a human life is not only an enduring personality, it shares in many other enduring objects and many other types of societies as well. Member occasions of many of these, intersecting with the dominant occasion, are therein prehended so that aspects of them form a part of the constitution of the dominant occasion. Several important points brought out in this book can be seen in this passage. For example, Whitehead speaks of "human occasions" referring to those human experiences which characterize people as individual personalities, rather than only to occasions of visual perception. And this society, the enduring personality which is a human life-time, is one spatiotemporal system amidst multitudes of others including it, included in it, and overlapping it. It is not an isolated system surrounded by nothing with voids between its occasions, but interrelates with the societies comprising its environment, which environment includes the body and the external world of which it is an extension. And this society of human occasions, human experiences, is a paradigm of all enduring objects of nature: each of its member occasions is enriched by virtue of members of many other societies intersecting with it. The occasions inherit not only from the antecedent members of their own society, but from those of many others; all levels of nature interact and interrelate, thereby enjoying novel experiences and creating novel occasions while maintaining and promoting the activity of the same level.

Nor is this an isolated passage in Whitehead. Its message recurs again and again. Here it is succinctly stated in the simplest terms: "There is not one simple line of transition from occasion to occasion, though there may be a dominant line. The whole world conspires to produce a new creation."[121] And here it is stated again, perhaps even more clearly:

> Our perception of this geometrical order of the Universe brings with it the denial of the restriction of inheritance to mere personal order. For personal order means one-dimensional serial order. And space is many-dimensional. Spatiality involves separation by reason of the diversity of intermediate occasions, and also it involves connection by reason of the immanence involved in the derivation of present from past. There is thus an analogy between the transference of energy from particular occasion to particular occasion in physical nature and the transference of affective tone, with its emotional energy, from one occasion to another in any human personality.[122]

Then it is clear that the very fact of the spatiotemporal discontinuity between some occasions is what leaves room for other occasions between them. But the discontinuity does not preclude the objectification of an antecedent by a successor. It is only occasions as actual that are discontinuous; but as actual they have perished and their real potentialities immortally remaining take on the new spatiotemporal dimensions of the new epochs they create. This is why each member of a society embodies the antecedent members; this is the only way antecedents are retained since they cannot be present themselves in their original state.

The intermixture of societies from those of the lowest grade occasions to those of human beings, is again expressed here, emphasizing that it is their intersection that strengthens the societies:

> In a short lecture a discussion of social systems must be omitted. The topic stretches from the physical Laws of Nature to the tribes and nations of Human Beings. But one remark must be made—namely, that the more effective social systems involve a large infusion of various sorts of personalities as subordinate elements in their make-up—for example, an animal body, or a society of animals, such as human beings.[123]

Whitehead regards a human society, such as any tribe or nation, as a society of occasions just as is an animal body such as a human being, then. Therefore, a human society is a spatiotemporal system just as is every society, and intersects many other social systems both smaller and shorter and larger and longer. A human society is interdependent with all the ecological systems of the land. And the more diverse other societies one society includes, varieties of personalities in the case of the human society and varieties of biological systems in the case of the personalities—the inclusion being a consequence of the intersection of members of the diverse societies—the richer the heritage for them all. This cosmic epoch is a plenum of intersecting societies, not static, but in creative advance producing more complex systems.

*Whitehead misinterpreted.* The preceding passages from Whitehead fit naturally in with the present interpretation of Whitehead that does not restrict actual occasions only to those of microphysical scale and human visual perceptions. This interpretation attempts to restore the power and scope of the Whiteheadian philosophy which is too often stripped of significance by scientific materialist oriented interpreters who would have the philosophy be merely a revision of ancient atomisms. Milic Capek summarizes the view: "The atomists of all ages lodged matter *in* space while leaving the interstices of the void between its parts."[124] Capek speaks of space but his assertion is equally valid for spacetime. For atomist interpreters, actuality is fundamentally the briefest of existences, conceived as occurring in a void or in absolute spacetime which blinks either on or off as the occasions occur.

The typical interpretation of actual occasions as necessarily following each other in rapid succession is expressed in this passage of John B. Cobb: "These momentary occasions succeed each other with a rapidity beyond any clear grasp of conscious attention. The direct analysis of a single occasion of experience is impossible."[125] Direct analysis of an occasion cannot be impossible if it is an occasion of the soul, a conscious human experience. It is only a difficulty if it is conceived as the smaller, simpler, more intangible of microphysical entities. We have seen that occasions on a larger scale, such as those comprising a block of marble and a human soul, are not in rapid succession. Donald W. Sherburne expresses the same view that actual occasions are brief, because they are microphysical occurrences, very clearly: "Actual entities are *micro*cosmic entities, not only spatially, but temporally, for each actual entity is but a flash of existence whose becoming is yet its perishing also."[126]

But actual occasions are also regarded as brief even if they are not regarded as only vibrations of subatomic scale. A. H. Johnson writes: "Ordinary actual entities . . . are droplets of experience, creatures of short duration."[127] But storms and stars and stones and seas are also ordinary actual occasions, without being of short duration. The time-spans of occasions are widely regarded as brief because Whitehead's language of becoming and perishing, of occasions as moments, of the abruptness of satisfaction, of the rush of feelings, seems to imply speediness if care is not taken to interpret such expressions in the light of the entire philosophy. For example, Robison B. James says, "The rush of the cosmic process is such that the being itself cannot hold on to its fullness once attained."[128] However, rush is as relative as process; not all processes are equally rushed. The rush of feelings for a city or a glacier has not the time-span of the rush of feelings for a perception or a sunset.

Such presumptions of a brief time-span for all actual occasions are scientific materialist in their covert adoption of an absolute time. Time-spans are necessarily brief and uniform because they are regarded as equal, predetermined, already actual slices marked out in the mathematical march of absolute time. But there is no absolute rate of time or absolute range of speeds of the passage of occasions in succession, providing that it is not faster than light. In fact, occasions are commonly so tied to conceptions of absolute time that it is not surprising to find them defined by brevity. For example, Reiner Wiehl writes: "In view of their momentary character, instances of becoming can also be spoken of as events, yet not as events which take place *in* time, but rather self-happening events."[129] Thus, events are events because they are momentary, or brief. Wiehl shows that he has interpreted "momentary" to mean brief: "The short moment of interior fulfillment is extinguished only to flash out anew, in endless succession, in the exterior world of becoming."[130] Defining an occasion as necessarily that which is brief is to take an absolute, privileged spatiotemporal standard by which to posit existence. This, in spite of Whitehead's own definition of conrete existence as that which is causally efficacious. William W. Hammerschmidt holds the same opinion, that an occasion may be defined by brevity: "The essence of becoming and transition requires a minimum of time for its expression."[131] The very essence of Whiteheadian time is invariably short. Certainly there are minimum durations, the time-spans of vibrations of photons, but these are not the essence of all occasions, all process.

The time-spans of actual occasions are subject to many a curious calculation. They have not been left merely as brief without attempting to establish exactly how brief. For example, Lewis S. Ford has produced a diagram which, among other things: ". . . standardizes the temporal length of an occasion, which may be presumed to vary considerably, perhaps between 20 milliseconds for a human occasion and $20^{-24}$ seconds for subatomic occasions."[132] However, time-spans are not limited to this range of duration since all actual occasions are not found only within this range. Certainly the average time-spans of many types of occasions may be taken and certainly these averages may have practical and scientific value, but it is of little consequence in a discussion of Whiteheadian occasions.

There is even debate as to the exact specious present, the exact duration of the time-span of God—whom Whitehead regards as the non-temporal actual entity. Apparently God is to become and perish faster than any earthly actual occasion:

> Hartshorne and Cobb have argued that the divine specious present must be *much shorter* than ours, if God is to be present at the beginning of each worldly occasion to present it with a subjective aim and at the end of each worldly occasion to receive it as objectively immortal into himself. The problem is, how short? (Also, how long are the intervals between divine occasions?)[133]

If there could be intervals between divine occasions, then there would be a succession or society of God occasions, some members of which would be antecedent relative to their successors. However, as has been seen, Whitehead's God has no past and no temporality. God has no problem being timelessly eternal since God, like the eternal objects, is non-temporal.

The insistence on establishing the exact duration of the time-spans of certain selected types of occasions is an attempt to fix them in the absolute spacetime framework. The epoch is readily exchanged for a chronon and world-wide instants because epochal time is not often recognized as even a distinctive theory of time. It is not often recognized even as a theory of relative time. V. C. Chappell, for example, shows no sign of distinguishing epochal time from absolute time: ". . . the existence of each [becoming] begins at one definite time, ceases at a later time, and extends through all the times between."[134] The "times between" can only be Newtonian instants just as are the beginning and ending times conceived as exact limits, since these times are independent of the becoming and serve only as a grid against which to measure the becoming retrospectively. Chappell *et alia* propose to measure, calculate, and standardize the exact time-spans of Whiteheadian occasions as if they were chronons or other intervals, instantaneously and ever actual, requiring the instantaneous planes of absolute spacetime for them to occupy. In short, many an interpreter of Whitehead does not even consider any alternative to absolute time.

Once an epoch becomes, its time-span can be measured retrospectively by comparison against that of other epochs, such as the movement of a clock or the decay of a radioactive element. Longer epochs may be better compared against other long epochs such as earth years or light years. The time-span of an epoch still in process of becoming cannot be measured but can be guessed and anticipated, predicted. But Whitehead's philosophy is not the least clarified or improved by knowing the expected time-spans of certain types of occasions. As Victor Lowe points out: "Whitehead does not say what the time-span of an actual occasion is, even in the cosmic epoch in which we live. The theory of actual occasions is a *general way* of thinking about the pluralistic process of the universe. . . ."[135]

Whitehead's conception of the actual occasion need not even be introduced into such discussions of average time-spans of certain brief occurrences, or in discussions of exact beginnings and ends of things by the clock, or in discussions of the passage of the becomings of occasions through absolute time. For no reason is given why these occurrences, such as the decay of subatomic particles or the specious present of visual perceptions, are to be considered as Whiteheadian actual occasions at all, rather than as the well-known occurrences that they are, namely, particle decay and human perception of light. Exact calculations of time-spans contribute nothing to an understanding of these specific occurrences as Whitehead's actual occasions.

It may seem scientifically respectable to limit the time-span of the actual occasion to that of the average time-spans of specious presents of human visual perception and vibrations of subatomic scale: but it is not. For, the view of science that would have lent such a view respectability is now obsolete. Scientific materialism, including the view that all occurrences are exactly circumscribed and bordering on nothing or occupying an absolute spacetime, having exact simple locations both in space and in time in terms of instants without any necessary relation to any other occurrences, has been superseded by modern science. Attempts to arbitrarily limit all time-spans to a very brief selection, and attempts to establish the correct, the exact, the precise and the only measure of *the* time-span of *the* actual occasion, are misguided attempts to retain scientific materialism. *The* actual occasion is a conception and as such, has no time-span to measure. And measuring all the time-spans of all the actual concrete existences to which the conception refers has no relevance to Whitehead's philosophy. Those calculating exact measures of time-spans need only be reminded of the thought of the metaphysician who wrote: "The exactness is a fake."

## CONCLUSION

Whitehead's writings are certainly ambiguous on many important points. There is no way to conclusively prove a particular interpretation of the philosophy, since it contains enough ambiguous statements to satisfy opposing theories. Without being able to confirm my proposals decisively, I have attempted in this chapter to show how epochs of every dimension are intermingled. This chapter has seen many ways in which Whiteheadian time differs from absolute time: how the duration of epochs is relative to the standard of comparison; how they are a potentiality until their completion; how they are within one another and overlapping; how they are open such that they have no exact borders; how the gaps between some includes and overlaps others.

The difficulty of interpreting Whiteheadian time, due to the ambiguity of Whitehead's statement, is noted by Stephen C. Pepper:

So right at the beginning we meet with a serious difficulty. If a purposive act in its full integrity from its initial aim to its terminal satisfaction is intended as the concrete observable model for the description of an actual occasion, then the duration of the occasion must be quite long. On the other hand . . . if the occasion must be limited by the duration of a specious present, then again it must be rather short. . . . Could the discrepancy be harmonized by recognizing occasions of quite different durations—very short ones and long ones? Whitehead sometimes seems to sanction this solution. . . . Can lesser occasions be included in larger ones? There are passages that would seem to support this solution too.[136]

This solution that Whitehead seems to sanction and support, that there are occasions both short and long, and that aspects of smaller occasions are included in larger ones—as well as aspects of larger ones being included in smaller ones—is the solution argued here at length.

The variation in the proportion and time-span of actual occasions causes difficulties only in scientific materialist oriented interpretations of Whiteheadian time wherein a strict atomism is insisted upon. Scientific materialist atomism is based upon simplicity and indivisibility; but Whiteheadian atomism, while also based upon indivisibility, is primarily based upon final causation, the unity that a single but complex purpose brings to an action engaged in by many parties. There is no such thing as an utterly simple occasion and epoch, one empty or isolated or unrelated to others, one so small that it has no actual world, so brief that it is not composite, so simple that it reveals no antecedents in its make-up. And regulating the time-spans of actual occasions so that the Whiteheadian metaphysics might seem more scientific is unbelievable.

Nathaniel Lawrence recognizes the variation in time-spans according to what an occasion is to become, that is, according to the subjective aim that is to be met.

Some values will require a comparatively great extent of time, in order to ingress. Other values will mature in a briefer span. Since the actual occasion is definable in terms of the values it apprehends, I infer that it is greater or smaller owing to its type.[137]

Consequently, Lawrence is sensitive to the differences in proportion and time-scale warranted by different grades of occasions. He bases major gradations in time-scale on major grades of occasions, but recognizes variations of size and time-scale within the same grade as well.

The living body is liable to a variety of types of analysis. (1) There are the least physical particles, electrons, protons, neutrons, and the like. In the endurance of each of these particles each actual occasion is a pulse measured in microseconds. The pulses are of greater extent as we move up to atoms, molecules, cells, etc. (2) A major size jump occurs when we think of the living body as a perceptual being. Whitehead speculates on the minimal unit's being somewhere between half and a tenth of a second. . . . (3) When we make another jump from perception to the more active aspects of consciousness which involve memory, attitude, disposition, foresight, planning, prediction, etc., the scale of the occasions becomes vastly enlarged again.[138]

The crucial difference between absolute time and Whiteheadian time is potentiality. Absolute time, spatialized, reified, is ever actual, already and instantaneously actual without any necessity for becoming actual. But the unexpected and paradoxical features of Whiteheadian time revolve around the potentiality of the epochs in process and in transition to other epochs. Epochs are only potentials until their completion, and only real potentials can create them, can make the transition into them. For, they have no actual and determinate past until they have become actualities themselves. The ideas of this chapter on epochal time's potentiality are succinctly expressed by David A. Sipfle:

> The act of becoming, however, is neither abstract nor instantaneous. . . . The process does not take any time to occur only because time is created by its occurring. Before its occurring there is no time within which it can be instantaneous. There is no temporal extension—only the potentiality of temporal extension. It is either this potentiality or a retrospective judgment which gives meaning to the word 'before' in the preceding sentence. This potentiality is actualized by the occasion and the process or act of becoming by which it is actualized is an indivisible epoch.
>
> What has become is extensive; it has not taken time to become, but it has created time by becoming.[139]

Epochal spacetime becomes and perishes with the becoming and perishing of epochal occasions.

# 5

# Becoming and Perishing

*Time, then, came into existence along with the heaven, to the end that having been generated together they might also be dissolved together, if ever a dissolution of them should take place; and it was made after the pattern of the eternal nature, to the end that it might be as like thereto as possible.*

Plato, Timaeus 38B

## INTRODUCTION

This chapter delineates three important quantum characteristics of actual occasions: their discontinuity, indeterminacy, and indivisibility. That the actual occasion should have these salient characteristics in common with the quanta under research with modern physics is the more remarkable since Whitehead wrote *Process and Reality* even before quantum theory, as it is in its present form, was developed. Abner Shimony says:

> The philosophy of organism was presented in a preliminary form in the Lowell Lectures of 1925 and . . . published as *PR* in 1929. It was during the years 1924-1928 that DeBroglie, Schrodinger, Heisenberg, Born, Jordan, Bohr, Dirac, and others formulated the 'new' quantum theory. . . . Whitehead never refers to the new quantum theory. . . . The theory which he has in mind is the 'old' quantum theory, consisting of the hypothesis of Planck and of Einstein . . . together with Bohr's model of the atom.[1]

However, Milic Capek conjectures that Whitehead was not unaware of the new developments of quantum theory underway at the time of his writing.[2] But further, Capek points out that, whether or not Whitehead was directly influenced by contemporary developments in quantum mechanics, his philosophical perspective anticipated them. "The whole trend in quantum physics pointed in this direction."[3] Capek refers to the fact that Whitehead's theory of time is the theory required by Heisenberg's principle even though Whitehead conceived his theory before Heisenberg published. "Whitehead's comment is even the more remarkable since it appeared prior to Heisenberg's famous article, although *after* the first theoretical investigations of Louis de Broglie."[4] Certainly Whitehead's denial of simple location and his conception of an actual occasion rather than substance is supported by Heisenberg's principle; and that is the important point—that Whitehead's cosmology and theory of time should be adequate for interpreting modern physics, consonant with its important principles, whether or not his conceptions were in fact derived therefrom. It is again Victor Lowe who puts the matter in the right light: "It is natural to include the quantum theory among influences on Whitehead; I think, however, that in fact this was to him a supporting illustration rather than a formative influence in the creation of his atomic pluralism."[5]

Whitehead certainly says very little about the quantum physics being developed in his life-time. For this reason, very little is known of what and how much quantum theory Whitehead actually used for his philosophical reconstruction of cosmology. Whitehead certainly should have made it easier for those who study him by speaking more about the relationship of quantum theory to his philosophy. As Robert M. Palter says,

> In view of the great intrinsic philosophical interest of the new quantum mechanics, Whitehead's utter silence on the subject is both astonishing and disappointing—especially disappointing since there does seem to be some general consonance between the broader implications of this theory and the categories of the philosophy of organism.[6]

This chapter discusses a number of such general agreements between Whitehead's cosmology and quantum theory, such as becoming and perishing whole, actualizing discontinuously, and entering an indeterminable future. The resemblance between Whitehead's idea of an actual occasion and David Bohm's interpretation of a microphysical event is especially remarkable since Bohm in his writings seems unaware of Whitehead's philosophy.[7] This chapter, then, attempts to make the relationship between Whitehead's philosophy and quantum theory clearer with the aid of Milic Capek, David Bohm, and other physicists, insofar as interpretations of quantum theory are clear. This aspect of Whitehead's philosophy is not more obscure than any other; it has already been seen that Whitehead's entire philosophy is so obscure as to lose many readers.

It is the quantum characteristics of epochs that exempt them from paradoxes of infinite regress. Whatever are the logical conundrums and paradoxes to which epochs are susceptible, those of Zeno can be avoided. This chapter shows that the very adequacy of epochal time to quantum requirements of modern physics argues against the alleged unintelligibility of the theory. Phases of concrescence, unique to Whitehead's philosophy, are not intelligible in the context of absolute spacetime, but in Whiteheadian epochal time.

## THE QUANTUM CHARACTERISTICS OF OCCASIONS

*(A) Discontinuity.* Actual occasions are discontinuous with respect to one another as wholes. Each occasion becomes and perishes whole, a unique togetherness of antecedents that no other occasion is, once and once only. In this respect all actualities are discontinuous. "The ancient doctrine that 'no one crosses the same river twice' is extended. No thinker thinks twice; and, to put the matter more generally, no subject experiences twice."[8] In other words, actuality, *qua* actuality, jumps from occasion to occasion. But it must be remembered that the discontinuity between successive occasions is the displacement and supersession of preceding occasions by their successors, although the predecessors are immanent in them. The actual predecessor is no longer there in the way that it was; it has been superseded. Also, the discontinuity between any occasions is the continuity of other occasions that include them. And so, the spatiotemporal discontinuity of Whitehead's actualities is not the same thing as simple location which allows that only one thing occupy one place at one time. The individuality and wholeness of an occasion lies in its peculiar togetherness of aspects of antecedents, not in any alleged simplicity or simple location. Whitehead credits the individuality of an occasion to its particular satisfaction, not to any absolute or simple spatiotemporal location. "'Satisfaction' provides the individual element in the composition of the actual entity. . . ."[9]

*The quantum jump.* This discontinuity of actual occasions as wholes is the way in which they "obey quantum conditions":

Mathematical physics translates the saying of Heraclitus, "All things flow,' into its own language. It then becomes, All things are vectors. Mathematical physics also accepts the atomistic doctrine of Democritus. It translates it into the phrase, All flow of energy obeys 'quantum' conditions.[10]

A quantum is simply a discrete unit; in physics it is an emission of energy as a discrete unit, not gradually or continuously. "Planck supposed that radiation was emitted according to certain small atomic quantities which he called quanta, and this work of his is the first form of the quantum theory of modern physics."[11] But this character of energy emission, that it occurs in discrete quanta, is the character of all subatomic or microphysical events. The subatomic particles too become and perish in discrete units and wholes, without gradual and continuous increment. A subatomic particle, like a quantum, is created or destroyed whole, not part by part. This is its quantum characteristic. "Thus the phenomena of materialization and dematerialization of 'particles' are not basically different from the emission and absorption of quanta."[12] This is the feature of quantum physics that Whitehead culled and adapted to all concrete material existences, all actual entities. His study of physics convinced him of the truth of the quantum mechanical postulates and he sought to generalize them so that philosophy could be founded on what he believed to be true of physical existence as long as it is in keeping with what we already know of our own existence.

The quantum characteristics of microphysical events are remarkable, even incredible: applied to Whitehead's actual occasions, they may seem preposterous. All actualities, chairs, perceptions, empires, occur only as discrete wholes, and not as the gradual and continuous addition of parts or as a gradually and continuously increased quantity. Actuality jumps from whole to whole with no continuous transition in actuality between. All concrete things whatsoever, on whatever scale of size, complexity, quality, intensity, palpability, or duration that they are have quantum characteristics in common, if Whitehead's description and definition of an actual occasion, and his intentions and principles regarding it, are to be consistently applied, as he intended, to all things.

Then the conception of actual occasions that become and perish whole, never the same twice, and never less than whole, is consistent with quantum physics, without actual occasions all being microphysical quanta. The quantum jump originally referred to electrons jumping from one orbit around an atom to another as they emitted or absorbed energy, without so much as existing in between orbits.

At present physics is troubled by the quantum theory. . . . But the point is that one of the most hopeful lines of explanation is to assume that an electron does not continuously traverse its path in space. The alternative notion as to its mode of existence is that it appears at a series of discrete positions in space which it occupies for successive durations of time.[13]

The appearance of the electron jumps from occasion to occasion; rather, it is not the same electron that disappears and reappears, but one electron perishes and another comes into being. Similarly, all occasions come into being, or appear, without gradually appearing part by part. There is not half or three quarters of an electron before there is an electron, nor half or three quarters of a snow flake, a person, an orange, a city, a stone, before that being, that flake, person, orange, city, or stone has become an actuality. Whitehead remarks on the oddity of this notion that quantum theory presents:

> The point of interest in this theory is that, according to it, some effects which appear essentially capable of gradual increase or gradual diminution are in reality to be increased or decreased only by certain definite jumps. It is as though you could walk at three miles per hour or at four miles per hour, but not at three and a half miles per hour.[14]

*Particles.* It is well to emphasize that the discontinuous existence of subatomic occasions must not be interpreted as a discontinuity of all existence. This might be to presuppose the existence of absolute space and time, absolute spaces and times being occupants between the discontinuous actualities. For example, Rem B. Edwards writes:

> Microscopic pulsations of energy which constitute the subject matter of quantum physics do seem to exist discontinuously, but to say this is to acknowledge that between any two successive occasions at this microscopic level *there is a gap during which nothing exists.* The occasions do not touch or overlap.[15]

But nothing does not exist, nor empty time and space. There is certainly no time "during which" there is no time; and certainly the discontinuities between some actualities does not mean that others may not touch or overlap. Two electronic occasions within a chair are discontinuous, but the chair has been continuous between them. Or two cellular occasions of an animal body are discontinuous, but the animal has been continuous between them. Two perceptions are discontinuous, but consciousness has been continuous between them. And the continuity of things is nothing else than their divisibility into discontinuous portions.

David Bohm, in saying that microphysical events act both like waves and like particles, is reluctant even to use the term "particle," probably because of its implicit scientific materialist connotations, including substantial endurance and simple location.

> . . . the field acts as a wave, and yet (because of non-linear terms in the equations) shows a tendency to produce discrete and particle-like concentrations of energy, charge, momentum, mass, etc. Thus, we are led to a point of view . . . that the particle-like concentrations are always forming and dissolving. Of course, if a particle in a certain place dissolves, it is very likely to re-form nearby. Thus, on the large-scale level, the particle-like manifestation remains in a small region of space, following a fairly well-defined track, etc. On the other hand, at a lower level, the particle does not move as a permanently existing entity, but is formed in a random way by suitable concentrations of the field energy.[16]

Bohm's particle-like concentrations of energy form, dissolve, and re-form; Whitehead's actual occasions become, perish, and become. The nature of microphysical reality suggested by quantum physics and adopted in principle by Whitehead refuses the conceptions of enduring substance, simple location, and simple occurrence. Whitehead undoubtedly owes his conception of a becoming and perishing occasion to quantum physics; but he equally undoubtedly owes his conception of becoming and perishing as a process to Bergson. Bergson is really the pioneer for Whitehead's conception of reality as a process of becoming the very nature of which is the prehension of its origination.[17]   For process philosophy, no quantum, no particle, no material body, no instance of actual concrete existence whatsoever is a permanently enduring body in absolute spacetime, simply located such that it is describable without reference to anything else, or any time or place else.

Capek labors again and again to combat the materialist vestiges of the particles of physics. "Like simultaneity and instantaneous space, particles and motions simply *do not exist*, and we should use more adequate terms to describe the individuality of microphysical events."[18] The position and motion of particles is established by a coordination of absolute instants with their occupation of successive absolute places. But absolute particles occupying absolute places at absolute instants do not exist. "We cannot visualize simultaneously a particle having a definite momentum and position. Quantum theory has shown that it is unnecessary to try, because such particles do not exist."[19] This is the verdict of quantum physicists.

By Capek's account, not only particles are inadmissable because of the materialist implications in the conception of particles, but their creation and annihilation as well. For, the language of creation and annihilation is equally as materialist as particles. Then even the "quantum jump" has materialist connotations, if it suggests that it is an enduring, simply locatable particle that has jumped, that is, that has been destroyed and recreated. Therefore, it is better that occasions become and perish than that particles are annihilated and created.

> To speak on the microphysical level of the precise values of energy is as meaningless as to speak of well-defined positions and velocities of alleged particles. . . . In other words: to speak of a definite quantity of energy within a single subatomic occurrence is as little meaningful as to speak of the definite temperature of a single molecule of gas. . . . the idea of *creation* or *destruction* of energy *is as illegitimate as its constancy* for the simple reason that the very concept of . . . *quantity of any kind* loses its adequacy on the subatomic level.[20]

The subatomic particles of physics, then, are not the clearly definable, in principle isolatable, simply located, self-sufficient, independent, enduring substances, explicable without reference to their contexts and environment, that they are in our materialist imaginations. Bohm observes:

> Thus, the word 'electron' as used in quantum theory refers to something whose properties are much less fixed and independent of the environment than those contemplated in the classical concept of an electron. . . . The idea that the basic properties of matter do not, in general, exist in a precisely defined form constitutes a far-reaching change in the kinds of concepts used for the expression of physical theories.[21]

If a subatomic particle of physics cannot be regarded as a Newtonian body or as a common sense substance, Whitehead suggests that it be regarded as an actual occasion. This means that it cannot be completely simple or simply-located, that it must have an internal structure which is a compound of aspects of antecedent occasions. It means that it came into being whole, culminated upon the satisfaction of its subjective aim (to be a certain subatomic particle) and perished whole. The subatomic particles perish only to become aspects of other occasions, including other subatomic particles. Their destruction does not result in actual parts of themselves, but in the creation of other whole particles.

There is no ejection of the pre-existing particles from the atoms or its nucleus. Nor is there any persistence of the particles in the atoms or in the nucleus which they invade. The traditional term 'particle' clearly designates nothing but temporary modification of the spatio-temporal medium from which various 'corpuscles' arise and into which they return. To ignore this fundamental link between 'particles' and their surrounding was the basic fallacy of atomism—'the fallacy of simple location' as Whitehead called it.[22]

The subatomic particles become out of and perish into one another, the way of all Whiteheadian actual occasions.

Just as the destruction of a subatomic particle does not result in parts of that particle remaining behind, so the destruction of any occasion does not result in actual parts of *that* occasion being left behind. Destroying a chair, a rock, a vegetable, or an animal does not result in actual parts of that same chair, rock, vegetable, or animal, but in whole new creations having come to be out of the real potentialities of the destroyed occasions. A broken chair is a new creation; a broken rock becomes new stones; a digested vegetable becomes new bodily plasma; a dead animal is another entity entirely from the live.

*Matter.* In the following passage, Whitehead says that the discovery of the quantum jump, or "discontinuous existence" prompted him to "revise all our notions of the ultimate character of material existence." This strong statement shows his intentions in writing *Process and Reality,* that it be a new cosmology to replace scientific materialism with its conception of material existence as enduring substance. He is citing quantum theory as the inspiration for his own philosophy. The revision of the ultimate character of material existence that he proposed has taken the form of the actual occasion, a system which is wave-like in concrescing, particle-like in objectification.

This discontinuous existence in space, thus assigned to electrons, is very unlike the continuous existence of material entities which we habitually assume as obvious. . . . Accordingly if this explanation is allowed, we have to revise all our notions of the ultimate character of material existence. For when we penetrate to these final entities, this startling discontinuity of spatial existence discloses itself.

There is no difficulty in explaining the paradox, if we consent to apply to the apparently steady undifferentiated endurance of matter the same principles as those now accepted for sound and light. A steadily sounding note is explained as the outcome of vibrations in the air: a steady colour is explained as the outcome of vibrations in ether. If we explain the steady endurance of matter on the same principle, we shall conceive each primordial element as a vibratory ebb and flow of an underlying energy, or activity. Suppose we keep to the physical idea of energy: then each primordial element will be an organised system of vibratory streaming of energy. Accordingly there will be a definite period associated with each element; and within that period the stream-system will sway from one stationary maximum to another stationary maximum—or, taking a metaphor from the ocean tides, the system will sway from one high tide to another high tide. This system, forming the primordial element, is nothing at any instant. It requires its whole period in which to manifest itself. In an analogous way, a note of music is nothing at an instant, but it also requires its whole period in which to manifest itself.[23]

This important passage not only foreshadows Whitehead's grand cosmology, but anticipates Heisenberg's principle of indeterminacy. "This passage, in particular the last sentence, is a precise and rarely encountered formulation of the philosophical significance of the second form of the Heisenberg principle."[24] It is in this passage that Whitehead shows his conviction that the ultimate character of nature is the process character, having been opened to scientific investigation on the microphysical level with the emergence of quantum physics. It takes a certain time-span, a process of becoming, for matter, any material body at all, to come into being; no concrete existent comes into being instantaneously but requires a whole process in which to become. Nor is the whole process compressed into any instant or even bounded by instants. "Heisenberg's principle. . . . in its second formulation . . . ruins the possibility of a sharp *localization in time*."[25]

Because matter is in process, and process engenders epochal time, matter and time are inextricable for the Whiteheadian philosophy. But for materialism they are essentially unrelated. Whitehead describes how matter is unrelated to time in the materialist conception of nature:

First, as regards time, if material has existed during any period, it has equally been in existence during any portion of that period. In other words, dividing the time does not divide the material. Secondly, in respect to space, dividing the volume does divide the material. . . .

Furthermore, this fact that the material is indifferent to the division of time leads to the conclusion that the lapse of time is an accident, rather than of the essence, of the material. The material is fully itself in any sub-period however short. Thus the transition of time has nothing to do with the character of the material. The material is equally itself at any instant of time.[26]

Absolute time, being independent of matter, passes it by without any essential relation to it. Such relationship as there is is accidental, external to the matter, a coincidence. Matter is equally itself at an instant where time is absolute spacetime and matter is enduring substantial existence that is ever actual. Whitehead's description of absolute time and its superficial relationship to matter is matched by Louis de Broglie's description of the time of classical physics: "The variable $T$ of classical mechanics, which serves to mark the instants of the passage of the moving object at the diverse points of its trajectory, may be conceived as unrolling infinitely fast without anything being changed in the previsioned coincidences."[27] Here are the instantaneous spaces of classical physics providing for infinitely fast causation: the progression of instants that is of no consequence to the matter.

In discussing the general principle that epochal time, in contrast to absolute time, is of the essence of material, Whitehead speaks of an electron: "Accordingly, in asking where the primordial element is, we must settle on its average position at the centre of each period. If we divide time into smaller elements, the vibratory system as one electronic entity has no existence."[28] But he in fact applies this principle to all material bodies on whatever scale they exist. Process is of the essence of material, all matter, living and non-living. For this reason Whiteheadian bits of matter are called "organisms"; Whitehead replaces the Newtonian bits of matter colliding in absolute spacetime with organic processes interacting in epochal time.

The essence of an organism is that it is one thing which functions and is spread through space. Now functioning takes time. Thus a biological organism is a unity with a spatiotemporal extension which is of the essence of its being. This biological conception is obviously incompatible with the traditional ideas. This argument does not in any way depend on the assumption that biological phenomena belong to a different category to other physical phenomena. . . . This is no special peculiarity of life. It is equally true of a molecule of iron or of a musical phrase. Thus there is no such thing as life 'at one instant'; life is too obstinately concrete to be located in an extensive element of an instantaneous space.[29]

All concrete existence, all matter, comes in quanta. This is the actual occasion in its atomic character. A chair, cloud, vegetable, organ, tree, city, conversation, season, rock, sound, war, storm, building, whatever there is does not exist as itself in much less or much more than the time-span in which it has come into being. A perception does not come into being at the speed of light or at the speed of ocean tides. A conversation does not come into being at the speed of two syllables or at the speed of an ice age. A vegetable does not exist in $10^{-24}$ seconds or at the speed of a millennium. Half the period required for a perception does not yield half a perception, but something else, a glimmer. Similarly, half the time-span required for a chair, vegetable, rock, elephant, or thought to come into being does not yield half these things but something else: a stool, a withered flower, a lump of clay, a fetus, or an inkling. These things, all things, are nothing at any instant, and not themselves at half-time.

The quantum characteristics of sound, of music, are perhaps the most striking. A single note requires a certain time-span to be a note; in much less time it is not a note at all, just as an electron is not an electron in less than the time-span of its electronic occasion. As Norbert Wiener says,

> If you take a note oscillating at a rate of sixteen times a second, and continue it only for one twentieth of a second . . . it will not sound to the ear like a note but rather like a blow on the eardrum. . . . A fast jig on the lowest register of the organ is, in fact, not so much bad music as no music at all.[30]

Similarly, neither a melody nor a concerto come into being in two notes or two strokes of a bow or in the time-span required for the formation of stalactites or pine forests. The quantum physical reality is that of all actual existing things. Capek says it shortly: "Every musical structure is by its own nature unfolding and incomplete; so is cosmic becoming, the time-span of modern physics. . . . Their existential minimum cannot be shortened without being destroyed."[31]

Thus for Whitehead, the quantum theory of physics speaks for all matter, all actualities, not only quanta.

> The physical theory of the structural flow of energy has to do with the transmission of simple physical feelings from individual actuality to individual actuality. Thus some sort of quantum theory in physics, relevant to the existing type of cosmic order, is to be expected.[32]

The flow of energy is "structural" in that it is informed with eternal objects and informs successive occasions. It is obvious here that Whitehead is speaking of actual occasions, not only of quanta or other subatomic scale vibratory events. If he were referring to a transmission of simple physical feelings from quantum to quantum, from electromagnetic occasion to electromagnetic occasion, from subatomic vibration to vibration only, he would have said as much. But his statement is not confined to the microphysical domain; he explicitly says that the flow of energy is from actuality to actuality, that is, actual occasion to actual occasion. Thus, not only the quanta of physics are quanta of energy, but all actual occasions are. Energy in Whiteheadian terminology is activity, and activity is not a privilege of the microphysical events alone.

*(B) Indeterminacy.* In Mary Hesse's description of the quantum jump, quanta or photons and electrons are annihilated and created. But the pictorial orbit of an electron around a nucleus has become an "energy state" in Hesse's description.

> The 'quantum jump' of an electron from one energy level to another with emission and absorption of radiation now appears as a successive occupation of energy states, with corresponding creation or annihilation of photons. There is no causal action of one state on the other in the sense that an individual transition can be predicted, and there is no necessary continuity even of the electron itself. . . . One can envisage the process, not as a transition of one existing entity, but as annihilation of one electron in the first energy state and creation of another in the second state.[33]

Hesse says that there is no causal action of the one state on the other in the sense of materialist causality of predeterminable external forces. In Einstein's words, "The great results of classical mechanics suggest . . . that all phenomena can be explained by the action of forces representing either attraction or repulsion, depending only upon distance and acting between unchangeable particles."[34] It is at the microphysical level that the materialist and determinist causality failed. It has been replaced by statistical probability in physics and causal efficacy in Whiteheadian cosmology. The behavior of the microphysical events is altogether unlike that of the Newtonian bodies propelled through absolute spacetime.

*Determinism.* Indeterminacy and determinism, then, refer to causality; determinism (or predeterminism) is the causality of materialism wherein the future state of a body is completely predetermined by its past. Indeterminacy of causality arose as the result of the failure of determinism in quantum physics. Max Born speaks of the difference in the two conceptions of causality:

> . . . quantum theory altered our attitude to the concept of causality. Classical theory uses differential equations which are of a deterministic character, since they allow us to predict the future from present observation in a rigorous way. The laws of quantum theory are of a statistical character and allow us only to predict probabilities for future events.[35]

Whitehead describes the causality of materialism as that of accidental relations and he derives its unintelligibility from its presumption of simple location and substance. But the alleged intelligibility of materialist causality lay in its determinism. The power of prediction seemed unlimited, leading to the conviction that strictly efficient causes predetermine all effects. No causation was to be admitted except that of efficient causation. Max Born's exposition is exceptionally clear:

> Newtonian mechanics is deterministic in the following sense. If the initial state (positions and velocities of all particles) of a system is accurately given, the state at any other time (earlier or later) may be calculated from the laws of mechanics. . . . Mechanical determinism gradually became an article of faith—the universe as a machine, an automaton.[36]

With "mechanical determinism" the past was the efficient cause of the future, and there was no recourse for the future. The future was completely predetermined by the past. If it seemed to differ from predictions based on knowledge of the past, this was a matter of inadequate observation of the past, human error. The future in fact supposedly contained nothing new, nothing that was not dictated by necessity, the efficient causation of the past. Capek remarks on the similarity between the determinism formalized in classical physics and ancient atomism:

> Twenty-two centuries before Laplace, Democritus unambiguously stated that 'by necessity are foreordained all things that were, are, and will be.' The only difference between Greek atomism and nineteenth-century physics was that the latter had incomparably more efficient technical and conceptual tools at its disposal than Democritus and Leucippus; the vague necessity of Greek atomism has been replaced by the precise conservation laws of modern dynamics.[37]

And Capek shows that determinism eliminated time; that is, it eliminated any real distinction between past and future, since the future is only another set of relationships among enduring particles of the past. The past as efficient cause of the future makes of the future a tautological implication of the past. There is no such thing in determinism as an autonomous decision having any (unpredictable) effect on the future.

The accidental and superficial character of time in the mechanistic scheme can be demonstrated in another way. Causes imply their effects; but conversely as well, from effects causes can be derived. The causal relation is not only a logical implication but also a tautologous implication (equivalence). From any particular state of the universe, not only any of its future states but also any past state is derivable. In virtue of the law of causality not only is it possible to anticipate the future in all its details, but even the past can be reconstructed completely, provided all the features of the present state are fully known.[38]

Capek's analysis of the unintelligibility of determinism, then, is along the same lines as Whitehead's. Capek considers deterministic causality to be purely conceptual, belonging only to the world of ideas, just as does Whitehead. Whitehead shows the non-empirical, the purely conceptual, nature of materialist causality, for example, in demonstrating that it renders induction unintelligible. Whitehead, like Capek, insists that nature, and the knowledge of nature, cannot be wholly derived from logical implication. Only eternal objects imply one another; past actualities reveal future possibilities without dictating future actualities. Whitehead states his empiricism this way: "There is no valid inference from mere possibility to matter of fact, or, in other words, from mere mathematics to concrete nature."[39] If there is to be empiricism and induction, then the future cannot be logically calculated or otherwise conceptually derived from knowledge of the past.

*Unintelligible causality.* What especially characterizes Western thought is a belief in the total bifurcation of nature between mind and body, reason and sense, spirit and sensuality, rationality and emotion, final cause and efficient cause, the a priori and the synthetic, the necessary and the contingent, theory and observation, deduction and induction, logic and intuition, and so on. Materialism is the belief in one half of this bifurcation in regard to one half of a bifurcated nature.

But when materialism is applied to oneself, it is often rudely denied and replaced by the other scheme of ideas. We explicitly as well as implicitly view ourselves as the final cause of our actions, as acting on aims and purposes, and as influencing the actions of others, even though we are material bodies and others are also material beings. We view ourselves as guided or misguided by our minds, reason, rationality, logic, thought, and spirit even though our mere material bodies supposedly cannot be guided at all but are supposed to act in ignorance of any purpose, aim, reason, logic, mind, or spirit. Our merely material body is at the disposal of purely accidental and external forces acting upon it, determining its future. And we even view ourselves as thinking and coming to logical conclusions even though our merely material bodies cannot conclude anything and are not supposed to be affected by thought. Materialism is to suffice for nature, but not for man, not for human nature: this puts man outside of nature.

> At present the scientific world is suffering from a bad attack of muddle-headed positivism, which arbitrarily applies its doctrine and arbitrarily escapes from it. The whole doctrine of life in nature has suffered from this positivist taint. We are told that there is the routine described in physical and chemical formulae, and that in the process of nature there is nothing else.
> The origin of this persuasion is the dualism which gradually developed in European thought in respect to mind and nature.[40]

Western man has found it convenient to think about nature within the materialist scheme of ideas and sometimes to exempt himself from it. To Whitehead, the bifurcation of nature into two realities, one for man and another for all the rest, is the very proof of the inadequacy of materialism. His philosophy recognizes man as part of nature so that man cannot make himself an exception to everything he believes about nature. Materialism is not supposed to be applied to men: and no wonder, for it cannot be. Applied to men, it is patently false.

> We shall of course be told that the doctrine is not meant to apply to the conduct of men. Yet the bodily motions are physiological operations. If these latter be blind, so are the motions. Also men are animals. . . . The conduct of human affairs is entirely dominated by our recognition of foresight determining purpose, and purpose issuing conduct. Almost every sentence we utter and every judgment we form, presuppose our unfailing experience of this element in life. The evidence is so overwhelming, the belief so unquestioning, the evidence of language

so decisive, that it is difficult to know where to begin in demonstrating it. . . . Scientists animated by the purpose of proving that they are purposeless constitute an interesting subject for study.[41]

The valuelessness, purposelessness, and lifelessness—to wit, the lack of final aims—in the mechanistic world view of materialism vitiated its rationality to Whitehead and consequently its credibility to him. ". . . the absence of Value destroys any possibility of reason."[42] If men reason in order to come to some conclusion, but purposes are to be excluded as natural causes, then there can be no reasoning. "The movement to exclude final causation has thus ended by making the doctrine of efficient causation equally inexplicable. . . . Reason is inexplicable if purpose be ineffective."[43] Materialism has shown itself inadequate to explain an evolutionary nature, the evolution of living matter from lifeless matter, and the evolution of a reasoning and purposeful creature from living matter. The absence of final aims in materialism is more than a mere flaw: it destroys it. This is Whitehead's view.

Therefore, the absence of final aims in materialism is no insurance as to its greater empirical reliability. On the contrary: "In the animal body there is, as we have already seen, clear evidence of activities directed by purpose."[44] And the absence of final aims in materialism is no guarantee of its greater rational and explanatory power. On the contrary, its capacity for explanation is contradicted in the very utterance of its exclusion of final aims. For, there can be no rationality or explanation where there is no reason and purpose. "All ultimate reasons are in terms of aim at value."[45] Materialism, cultivated in the dualism of Western thought, has made man a stranger to nature.

In the following passage Whitehead derives the unintelligibility of materialist causality from the conception of simple location that it uses. The fallacy of simple location is expressed in the statement that "one of them is comprehensible without reference to the other." Whitehead's criticism again focuses on the absence of final aims and immanence (the two features that most importantly characterize Whiteheadian causal efficacy) from the materialist, and common sense, conception of causality. He concludes that the consequences of materialist causality are that conditioning and influence are unintelligible and that effort is foolish:

Consider our notion of 'causation'. How can one event be the cause of another? In the first place, no event can be wholly and solely the cause of another event. . . . But some one occasion in an important way conditions the formation of a successor. How can we understand this process of conditioning?

The mere notion of transferring a quality is entirely unintelligible. Suppose that two occurrences may be in fact detached so that one of them is comprehensible without reference to the other. Then all notion of causation between them, or of conditioning, becomes unintelligible. There is—with this supposition—no reason why the possession of any quality by one of them should in any way influence the possession of that quality, or of any other quality, by the other. . . . Science is then without any importance. Also effort is foolish, because it determines nothing. The only intelligible doctrine of causation is founded on the doctrine of immanence. Each occasion presupposes the antecedent world as active in its own nature.[46]

The causality of materialism is called unintelligible by Whitehead because it presupposes the already self-sufficient, enduring existence of substances in simple locations. Their substantial existence and simple location means that they are fully comprehensible, and in principle isolatable, without reference to any other substantial existence in any other simple location. That is to say, they are already comprehensible without causation. Any causal connection between already self-sufficient, already constituted substances is irrelevant to them, meaningless: they are already sufficient unto themselves. And Whitehead points out that it is a contradiction to suppose that influence is impossible and effort is foolish when the evidence is that no one acts or speaks or reasons even for a moment as if this were true. Materialism has a grip on Western minds because of the weight of its long heritage. But modern physics destroyed its credibility for natual science. David Bohm reminds us that: "The underlying structure of matter, however, is not mechanical. . . . This means that the term 'quantum mechanics' is very much of a misnomer."[47] And process philosophy has begun to destroy its credibility for philosophy and common sense.

*The principle of indeterminacy.* The indeterminacy of the causality found appropriate for the microphysical world of quantum mechanics has its formulation in Heisenberg's principle of uncertainty or indeterminacy. As Capek explains:

According to Heisenberg's principle, which is also called the principle of indeterminacy, it is impossible to determine simultaneously the velocity and the position of an electron or any other microphysical particle; the more accurate the determination of its velocity (or momentum) is, the hazier its position becomes and vice versa.[48]

This indeterminacy means that there is an absolute limit of accuracy of measurement, and consequently a limit to the accuracy of the prediction of future states. The future is not predetermined by the past, but a probability of it.

The haziness in our knowledge of a present state inevitably entails a limitation of our knowledge of future states. Because the present state of any particle is given by the correlation of the precise values of its position and momentum, it is obvious that its future positions and velocities can be predicted only with a certain probability. . . .[49]

The inaccuracy of observation at the quantum level, and the consequent haziness of our knowledge of subatomic occasions, is not due to faulty equipment or any other remediable type of human error. Rather, the subatomic occasions do not have both position and velocity at the same time. This is why the inaccuracy of observation at the quantum level is built into quantum theory itself. Max Born tells us: "The discovery of the existence of an absolute limit of accuracy is, however, of great importance to the logical structure of the theory."[50]

And Whitehead's theory of causal efficacy and of epochal time concurs with Heisenberg's principle:

Whitehead emphasized equally strongly that no successive relation is possible in each instantaneous space; from this he inferred that the concept of 'instantaneous velocity,' useful as it may be as a methodological device, is, philosophically speaking, devoid of meaning.[51]

Newtonian instantaneous space provided for instantaneous causation. For, if all bits of matter can become present with respect to one another instantaneously, then they have come into relationship infinitely fast. That is, if something is there now which was not there before, yet its being there now has happened instantaneously, then it has arrived infinitely fast. The presence of all matter at the same time, its instantaneous mutual juxtaposition, is absolute simultaneity.

The advent of relativity physics destroyed this notion. It was found, for example, that no causal relationship occurred faster than the speed of light. Therefore, there could be no evidence of instantaneous spaces. In the words of Einstein: "Simultaneity led for a long time to no contradiction due to the high propagational velocity of light."[52] The speed of light had been known, but it was not known to be the maximum possible speed of causal interaction, as Capek explains:

Infinite velocity means instantaneous interaction. No upper limit was imposed on the range of possible velocities, that is, on the speed of causal interactions. It is true that classical physics knew since Roemer's discovery in 1675 the finite velocity of electromagnetic waves; but it remained completely unaware of the limiting character of this velocity.[53]

Instantaneous velocity, wherein both position and momentum can be theoretically established at the same time, was shown to be baseless by modern physics, and with its deposition went absolute time and materialist, deterministic causality.

For Whitehead, as for quantum physics, the efficient causes adequate for materialism have only a probable effect. The objective probability of quantum mechanics is translated into real potentiality in Whiteheadian terms. In Whitehead's cosmology, as in quantum theory, a cause does not dictate or predetermine an effect; it acts as an influence rather than an efficient cause in the deterministic sense. For both Whiteheadian causal efficacy and the probabalistic causality of quantum physics, the past is not the complete and entire source of the present. In the case of quantum theory, David Bohm says directly: "With the advent of quantum theory, the idea of complete determinism was shown to be wrong and was replaced by the idea that causes determine only a statistical trend, so that a given cause must be thought of as producing only a tendency toward an effect."[54]

This "trend" or "tendency toward an effect" is realized in the philosophy of organism as real potentiality. Whiteheadian causal efficacy is indeterminate causality, providing for a series of transformations from subject to superject to datum to object to subject such that no one operation determines a final satisfaction. Indeterminate causality is the verdict of quantum theory. In the words of Capek, "The applicability of probability laws to microphysical events clearly indicates that the concept of causality should be broadened rather than given up; what is to be eliminated is only its obsolete static necessitarian form."[55] Causal efficacy is just such a broadened conception of causality. Broadened with the introduction of final aims and immanence into the workings of efficient causality, it meets the requirements of modern physics in a way that determinism cannot. The causality of materialism did not admit of only "determining influences" but required predetermination.

In other words, for both Whitehead and quantum theory, the efficient causation of the past is indeterminative rather than determinative. The real potentiality of the antecedent entities is creative and causal, but not sufficient to account for all the factors of a new entity, since the new entity is partially self-creative. The new entity is partially effected by its own selection among relevant alternative potentialities, both real and pure. Louis de Broglie makes this remark referring to Bergson, but it also shows how much the Whiteheadian philosophy takes after quantum theory: "If Bergson could have studied quantum theory in detail, he would doubtless have observed with joy that in the image of the evolution of the physical world which it offers us, at each instant nature is described as if hesitating between a multiplicity of possibilities."[56]

David Bohm points out the common sense equivalent of Heisenberg's principle:

> . . . our naive pictures and quantum theory are alike in that they both have the following property: It is possible to give a continuous picture of the motion only if the position is blurred or made indefinite, and it is possible to give a picture of a particle in a definite position only if we forego the possibility of picturing it in a continuous motion.[57]

Whitehead remarks that: "The new situation in the thought of today arises from the fact that scientific theory is outrunning common sense."[58] But the common sense that is being outrun is that of scientific materialism. The conceptions of quantum physics and the Whiteheadian cosmology are just as amenable to ordinary experience and thought if we look out for them.

*Indeterminate observation.* The state of affairs reported by many quantum physicists now is that observations and measurement at the quantum level are necessarily inaccurate not because of a lack of adequate techniques of observation but because the subatomic entities observed are not determinable in all respects—at "the same time." It is impossible to observe and calculate the definite position and momentum of a particle at the same time because such particles (enduring substances) and such "same times" (absolute simultaneities) do not exist. Knowledge and accurate observation have an indeterminate element because the objects of knowledge and observations are indeterminate as regards their origin in antecedents and their effects in the future.

Milic Capek gives the reason why the indeterminacy of microphysical events applies to their observation as well: "For the influence of the physical apparatus on the observed phenomenon is only a *special instance of physical interaction in general.* . . ."[59] David Bohm gives the same reason: ". . . changes in the definition of various properties take place not only in interaction with a measuring apparatus but, more generally, in interaction with all matter."[60] And Whitehead carries the same principle through his cosmology: "Thus the data upon which the subject passes judgment are themselves components conditioning the character of the judging subject."[61] The observation is itself an actual occasion that includes objectifications derived from the antecedent data observed. Just as the microphysical entities are occasions engaged in relations with other occasions, so are the observations with their objects. Bohm describes the observing apparatus and its objects as an "indivisible system" which is an "indivisible entity":

> For it must be remembered that the observing apparatus is also subject to the laws of the quantum theory. . . . Bohr pointed out that in the usual interpretation of the quantum theory one must regard the measuring apparatus and observed object as a *single indivisible system,* because they are united by an indivisible quantum which connects them during the process of interaction. . . . This is possible only if the combined system consisting of the observing apparatus and the observed system is, in some sense, a single indivisible entity which cannot correctly be analysed (even conceptually) into more elementary parts.[62]

What is completely determinate is a completed occasion's relationship with antecedents which are, as its objectified actual world, its constitution. But this occasion as well as the antecedent occasions have a real potentiality for a future yet. And this fact, which is creativity, is of the very essence of the nature of actual occasions such that to ignore it is to fail to understand any occasion and causation as well. This is the import of quantum theory, as interpreted by Whiteheadian cosmology.

*(C) Indivisibility.* Another important quantum characteristic of actual occasions is their indivisibility. It is indivisibility that makes each epochal occasion a unitary, atomic quantum with respect to time, an epoch. "Thus time is atomic (i.e., epochal), though what is temporalised is divisible."[63] Then time is not only indivisible (atomic) but it is also divisible. But since these are contradictory, it is better to say that time is both divisible and undivided, rather than both divisible and indivisible.

This is to say that an epochal occasion is undivided in actuality but potentially divisible. Its process of becoming is undivided since there is no way to divide the final end which directs the concrescing antecedents. But the completed epochal occasion is divisible in potentiality: it has diverse real potentialities acting in diverse subsequent occasions. That is, the epochal occasion is divisible considering its separable consequences in diverse occasions hence. But the completed epochal occasion is not in fact actually divided; it perished whole. It is not it, in actuality, that is divisible into innumerable effects hence in its objectively immortal career, but its potentialities. The occasion is potentially divisible because its subsequent effects, scattered about the world, would add up to the occasion, although the actual occasion itself perished an undivided whole. Thus an epochal occasion is always undivided (or indivisible) whether in process of becoming or whether already completed, even though it is potentially divisible.

Another way of seeing the basic indivisibility of occasions is to say that there are occasions to be divided, but that any act of dividing them is in indivisible transition with them so that no occasion is actually divided. No occasion is actually divided either from itself or from any other in which it has effect—from itself because it is united by one final end and from any successor because it is in indivisible transition with it and becomes an inextricable or indivisible part of it. Becoming is undivided and what becomes is divisible but in fact undivided. Prehended occasions are thus divisible in being capable of diverse effects upon successors, and these effects may be taken as divisions of them, but they are in fact undivided in themselves since a final end can never be divided. Division is always potential, never actual.

In dividing the region we are ignoring the subjective unity which is inconsistent with such division. But the region is, after all, divisible, although in the genetic growth it is undivided.

So this divisible character of the undivided region is reflected into the character of the satisfaction. When we divide the satisfaction coordinately, we do not find feelings which *are* separate, but feelings which *might be* separate. In the same way, the divisions of the region are not divisions which *are*; they are divisions which *might be*.[64]

In what sense *might* feelings and regions be separate if in fact they *never* are separate? They might be separate in the sense that they embody diverse real potentialities of diverse antecedent occasions, though none of these are actually divided within the occasion objectifying them. The feelings of an occasion are inextricable, although each feeling is the causally efficacious transition of antecedents into the feeling occasion. These antecedents and the feelings of them are separably distinguishable, being the causes and effects composing an occasion, but in no way are they actually separated from one another since they are inextricable parts of the occasion. The occasion of hearing a tune involves feelings that include diverse sounds of diverse instruments and voices, moods, memories, and the environment of music, people, thought, politics, even climate. These are all separably distinguishable features of the one occasion, but they are not in fact divided from one another. Similarly, the crystals, minerals, mixtures, layers, shape, compactness, and other conditions of an occasion of a rock are its feelings of antecedents which partially effected these conditions, feelings which while undivided from one another in fact are nevertheless separably distinguishable.

*Indivisible transition.* The indivisibility of microphysical quanta of energy is one of the most remarkable discoveries of quantum physics. Bohm speaks of the consequences of this discovery, namely, that the quanta cannot usefully be regarded as objects, but rather, they are indicators of interacting processes.

> We are led . . . to a new point of view, based on the idea that the quanta connecting object and environment constitute irreducible links that belong, at all times, as much to one part as to the other . . . these quanta do not constitute separate objects, but are only a way of talking about indivisible transitions of the objects already in existence.[65]

Thus, the indivisibility of events unearthed in quantum physics is not that of a single, in principle isolatable, simply located substance, but it is the indivisibility of occasions in relationship with one another. Bohm's indivisible transitions are Whiteheadian processes. Bohm says the same thing about microphysical entities as Whitehead says of actual occasions: "Thus, at the quantum level of accuracy, an object does not have any 'intrinsic' properties belonging to itself alone; instead, it shares all its properties mutually and indivisibly with the systems with which it interacts."[66] This is to say that the microphysical object, like the Whiteheadian occasion, is not a substance qualified by essential or accidental properties explicable without reference to any other substances.

The inadequacy of the materialist conception of substantial bits of matter enduring permanently is evident from Bohm's descriptions of nature at the quantum level. Bohm offers an example of a single indivisible transition:

> Consider, for example, a hydrogen atom in the ground state interacting with an electromagnetic field carrying some energy. The atom can absorb a quantum but, during the process of transition, it is not in a definite energy state. Instead, it covers an indefinite range of energy states. The energy of the electromagnetic field is equally indefinite.

During the process of transition, both systems are coupled because they are exchanging an indivisible quantum of energy belonging as much to the electron as to the electromagnetic field. It is, therefore, impossible to ascribe the future behavior of the system in a unique way, as can be done classically, to the state of each 'part' (i.e., electron and electromagnetic fields), because the state of each part is indefinite and yet inextricably linked with that of the other part.[67]

Bohm's process of transition is indeterminate until its completion, that is, its outcome is not certain in advance, just as is a Whiteheadian process of concrescence. Bohm's microphysical events are systems, the parts of which are inextricable and indefinite considered as entities in themselves, the same being true of Whiteheadian occasions.

It is obviously quantum physics that is destroying the last vestiges of scientific materialism, at least as far as its claim to any scientific validity goes. And it is obvious that Whitehead has taken important principles from quantum theory and applied them to all concrete existents whatsoever, such that all concrete existents are to be considered as indivisible processes, indeterminate activities the outcome of which cannot be predetermined. The electrons, quanta, atoms, and other microphysical entities have no independent existence. They are aspects of indivisible processes of becoming, just as are all things. A human percipient occasion, for example, is a process of becoming that is an inextricable transition with the objects of perception, as Bohm declares: "Nevertheless, what happens in scientific research is, in regard to the problem under discussion, not *fundamentally* different from what happens in immediate perception. . . . the main significance of scientific *knowledge* is (as happens in immediate perception) that it is an adjunct to this process."[68] Bohm, like Whitehead, is willing to extend salient principles of quantum physics to the visible and familiar world of human life, that is, to perception, to knowledge.

*The common sense of indivisibility.* An actual occasion, then, is actually undivided, but potentially divisible. An actual division cannot be effected upon *it*; it is past and gone and there is no retroactive efficacy of the future on the past. But the occasion's potential divisibility is revealed subsequently in the way that it is differently objectified in different successors. A chair may be broken up into fire wood or left to decay in an attic. In neither case is it the very same enduring chair that burns or decays. The whole chair is past and gone but the burning or decaying chair reveals the potential divisibility of the whole chair of the past, its divisibility into pieces of fire wood, and into combustible elements, or its divisibility into shreds and dust. Similarly, an eaten vegetable perishes without being actually divided. Yet its subsequent processing in diverse animal cells reveals the bygone vegetable's potential divisibility into diverse nutrients and non-nutritive components.

If a thing were an enduring substance, then it would be the same thing that was actually divided again and again. Its divided portions would exist through the same absolute spacetime. Dividing the thing would not create new things, future with respect to the thing, but would be irrelevant to its substantial endurance. Division would amount to relocation rather than recreation; the divided portions of the thing would be coincident with successive instantaneous planes which cannot create actual temporal distinctions, rather than being new epochal occasions spawned by the bygone thing.

In fine, actual indivisibility does not preclude potential divisibility. All that actually exist are undivided wholes and their potentialities. Parts of an occasion are the potentialities of antecedent occasions within it. The state of affairs of Whiteheadian divisibility and Whiteheadian time, whereby an undivided occasion is divisible, prehended and appropriated, although the occasion itself has passed, is well put by Evander Bradley McGilvary:

> Whitehead's 'concrescent occasion' has therefore the good fortune of being able as it were both to eat its cake and have it. The actual occasion ingests all its cakes into its own 'inner constitution' and also leaves them out where they were before.[69]

An edible vegetable is an actual occasion. Its real potentialities include attractability to animals, edibility, nutritive value for animals, stimulation of plant growth, reproduction of vegetables, soil enrichment for plants, as well as choppability, bruisability, chewability, cookability, dryability, spoilability, dissolvability, rottability, and so on. These capabilities become efficacious in the future with respect to this vegetable occasion, when these potentialities combine with those of other occasions. The vegetable's subsequent effects amount to a revelation of its (former) potentialities and potential divisibility. But this vegetable occasion, being past, is past being affected, that is, actually divided.

This individual vegetable occasion's future is not predeterminable in specifics, although the future of masses of vegetables may be determined as a probability. But none of these future activities can in fact change or divide the original vegetable occasion, as though the future could act upon the past. And each prehension of an aspect of the whole antecedent vegetable occasion is a prehension on the part of a whole successor of that whole antecedent vegetable as in that prehended part, so that there are never actually separated, divided parts of that antecedent vegetable. That is to say, the vegetable's real potentialities in subsequent occasions are potentialities of *it*, the one antecedent vegetable, and not entities or parts in themselves, unrelated to it. The potential divisions of the vegetable are ways that *it* is prehended by others, the ways that *it* partially effects others. The whole vegetable is active in each of its parts, each of its potentialities, since its singular subjective aim is active in each of its own prehensions.

The vegetable is divisible into pieces of vegetable, into vegetable fibers and seeds, or into vegetable cells or organic molecules, or further into atoms or into vibrations of subatomic scale. All of these parts share the whole vegetable so that prehending any part is prehending the whole vegetable as in that part. And the whole vegetable occasion is itself part of other occasions such as a plant, a garden, a bin of vegetables, a meal, such that prehending it is prehending the plant or garden or bin or meal as in that part. The vegetable parts are retrospectively determined potentialities of the vegetable occasion in combination with the potentialities of other occasions, for creating new occasions succeeding the original vegetable. The vegetable may be ingested to become aspects of the metabolisms of diverse bodily cells. Both its potentialities and that of the animal cells become together new occasions of cell life, for which they have the potentiality together. The breakdown of the vegetable on the chopping block or in animal metabolism reveals its potential divisions into diverse parts, nutrients, cellulose, molecules organic and inorganic, and so on.

It remains to be explained how the original vegetable is not actually divided while it is nevertheless chopped or digested. The original vegetable, a knife, a hand's grip on the knife, the intention to chop, and so on are all partial causes among many others of the creation of the chopped vegetable. The new occasion of chopped vegetable expresses some real potentialities of the original vegetable, its easy choppability for example. To claim that the original vegetable and the chopped vegetable are the very same, that is, to claim that it is the same original vegetable that is chopped, is to eliminate time and reinstate substantial endurance. Rather, the chopped vegetable is a new occasion created from the potentialities of the old.

Therefore, a piece of vegetable is not an actually separated part of a whole vegetable, but exists as a new epochal occasion temporally distinct from the original whole vegetable. The act of chopping the vegetable and the chopped portions postdate it. The whole vegetable occasion, once having been completed and perished, joins with potentialities of certain other occasions, such as the metallic edges of a knife, air, a board, exertions of a hand, and so on, creating together a new chopped vegetable occasion by dint of the intention to do so. The pieces of chopped vegetable as they are cut are new occasions in their own right but are not temporally prior to the occasion of the entire chopped vegetable until the vegetable is entirely chopped, just as the syllables of a phrase are not its syllables until the phrase has been accomplished. The chopped vegetable occasion is a potentiality until the vegetable is entirely chopped and does not occur actual piece by piece. The past is compulsively creative, but what it creates cannot be predetermined. The knife, hand, and vegetable might end in a cut finger and discarded vegetable instead of a chopped vegetable. Therefore, there is no time in which a whole vegetable has been half-chopped, but rather, there is a time in which a half vegetable has been created, a quarter vegetable, and an entirely chopped vegetable.

Chopping a vegetable severs certain of its cells and molecules from certain others, introduces more air in between them, shapes them a bit in conformity with the knife's blade, introduces a trace of metal into them, and so on. How much air in between vegetable cells is to count as a division of the vegetable? At what point in the knife's descent into it is it a division of the vegetable to be declared? At what cell is there a division rather than a cut or scar? How many pieces of vegetable are to count as a chopped vegetable? All such potential divisions depend upon the actuality of the completed chopped portion or chopped vegetable or whatever actuality accrues.

The same, rather labored, vegetable occasion will also serve to illustrate how occasions are also temporally undivided. Certainly a line can be drawn or imagined anywhere, dividing anything. But neither the completed vegetable occasion nor its process of becoming that occasion are actually divided: it is an indivisible epoch. There is no line actually dividing its past, present, and future, nor is its present squeezed into an instantaneous plane. A line, whether drawn or imaginary, rather than marking an actual division, introduces new actual occasions, a line occasion or lined occasions or new occasions of the imagination, the old ones ever undivided.

There is no actual dividing line where and when an actual vegetable ends and a perception or digestion of it begins, and likewise there is no actual division where the vegetable ends and its own attractiveness or nourishment for us begins. Its attractiveness or nourishment is its relationships to human perception or metabolism that create new occasions of perception or health with it. It is only from a retrospective standpoint that a potential division of the vegetable into elements attractive, perceived, or digested can be discerned. The vegetable's real potentialities that contribute to making an occasion of perception or nutrition are not divided out in advance of these occasions. No fine line actually divides causes from their effect; causes do not end and *then* their effect begin; causes are not there and their effect here. Causes and effect are united in an undivided transition, or process of becoming, wherein both potentialities of past and future are immanent and present. However, their potential divisibility, cause there, effect here, cause before, effect after, may be separably discerned retrospectively just as the original vegetable may be distinguished as a cause of subsequent nutrition. Temporal distinctions come into being only if and when the results of causal efficacy are in. "In the first place, the separation of the potential extensive scheme into past and future lies with the mode of causal efficacy and not with that of presentational immediacy."[70]

The scientific materialist hope for a spatiotemporal unit that is undivided because it is absolutely simple is not founded in any actuality. Indivisibility is not a fact about an alleged completely simple entity. Epochal occasions are undivided whether they are those of photons, perceptions, memories, understanding, meals, rocks, mountains, lichens, cities, wars, inflations, buildings, melodies, seasons, conversations, or chairs. Non-division does not lie in absolute simplicity, impenetrability, or inaccessibility. It lies in the fact that a togetherness has efficacy because of what it was as a togetherness so that there is no dividing *what* it was. However, potential subdivisions of a togetherness, once obtained, can be retrospectively entertained and compared, inasmuch as it has spatiotemporal extension. However brief an epoch be, it is nevertheless a period of some (short) duration and potentially divisible. All epochs, or time-quanta, of any duration whatever are potentially divisible without being actually divided into parts of time.

But we could not even discuss the relative sizes of time-quanta unless these quanta were also divisible, and were also comparable in respect to their parts, thus elicited. For if time-quantum $T_1$ be greater than time-quantum $T_2$, it must mean that $T_2$ is comparable to some part of $T_1$ in respect to equality. Thus there is also a continuity in time, arising from indefinite divisibility. This continuity is an instance of the potentiality which is an essential element in the actual world.[71]

*Motion and change.* The indivisible transitions of actual occasions has replaced absolute motion and change for process philosophy. Causal efficacy, succession, transition, becoming, perishing—these must not be construed as in any way motion or change through an absolute spacetime. This is one consequence of an occasion's indivisible transition into other occasions: it precludes the motion or change of the same occasion as if through an absolute spacetime. Louis de Broglie mentions that there is no possible course of motion for microphysical entities: "But with the ideas of quantum physics, when one regards things on a small enough scale there is no trajectory assignable to the moving object. . . ."[72] And Whitehead holds that there can be no motion for any actual occasion: "In the 'organic' doctrine, motion is not attributable to an actual occasion."[73]

There is no motion at the quantum level or any other level since there is no absolute spacetime through which a quantum or anything else might move. Nor is any quantum an enduring thing such that it is the same quantum traveling from absolute place to absolute place. And the same is true for all things; just as microphysical entities are immobile and unalterable, so are all actual occasions: "Thus an actual entity never moves; it is where it is and what it is. . . . Actual entities perish, but do not change; they are what they are."[74]

Newton, who postulated absolute motion along with absolute spacetime, decidedly rejected relative motion as out of the question: "Relative motions . . . like other relations, are altogether destitute of any real effect."[75] And indeed, motion of an enduring substance through absolute spacetime has no real effect inasmuch as there is no motion, no substances, and no absolute spacetime at all. Relativity physics, by supplanting absolute motion with relative motion, essentially eliminated motion in the familiar sense. Relative motion is not motion of one enduring thing with respect to another through an absolute spacetime. Milic Capek explains that relative motion amounts to motionlessness depending on the definition of the spatiotemporal reference to be taken as absolute:

> Every moving particle can by an appropriate change of the frame of reference be converted into a motionless one, and no frame of reference has a privileged character: this is the meaning of the relativistic denial of the motionless Newtonian space.[76]

The ever-actual substantial Newtonian absolute times and places accommodated the ever-actual, already constituted, enduring and substantial Newtonian bits of matter. Capek points out that absolute motion is only compatible with absolute substance: "We know that the classical definition of motion as a displacement of matter in space was introduced in order to preserve the principle of constancy of substance; for the only kind of change which does not threaten this principle is *change of position*."[77] Substances no longer need to be accommodated and no longer can be, given the advances of modern physics. Absolute motion is not compatible with actual occasions conceived as processes of becoming and perishing.

Becoming and perishing on the one hand, and motion and change on the other, cannot suffer the same universe. Motion requires already constituted bodies and an already actual spacetime in which to move. Becoming, however, requires a creative advance wherein the projected future spacetime of an occasion is not predeterminable, not yet actual in advance of the occasion. As an occasion becomes, so does its spatiotemporal quantum. Ancient Rome came into being and perished; it did not move. An occasion of perception becomes and perishes; it does not move. And the epoch of ancient Rome has perished unaltered, as has yesterday's perception of a chair.

The conception of an actual occasion, as opposed to a substance, treats every activity as a unit. It is the entire unitary activity that is immobile and unalterable, rather than a substantial bit of matter considered as a static object. It is only the latter that are immobile and unaltered if they are not propelled through absolute space and changed through absolute time. For Whiteheadian cosmology, however, no chair and no rock are utterly inactive even if they are not propelled by external forces. Their very structure and content at each moment (occasion) of their existence depends on how their relationships with their environment have been established. There is no such thing as an utterly static existence, devoid of activity. Yet each quantum of activity is immobile. Concrete existences are not static, in the sense of inactive, even while they are immobile in the sense of not traveling through absolute space and unaltered in the sense of changing in absolute time. A rock is an activity whether it be under ground or flying through the air. The flying rock, just as the rock under any other condition, is one actual occasion that neither moves nor changes. The occasion of flying rock enjoys one immobile epoch that perishes, rather than moving to another place and changing through times coincident with itself. Similarly, the occasion of a forest fire is one immobile epoch without changing places or changing to another epoch.

In Whiteheadian terms, motion is the difference between the spacetime quanta of successive occasions. Occasions of a nexus or society all create their own spacetime quanta as they come into being. Motion is the differences between these quanta, not moving across an absolute and pre-existing space.

Now the motion of the molecule is nothing else than the differences between the successive occasions of its life-history in respect to the extensive quanta from which they arise; and the changes in the molecule are the consequential differences in the actual occasions.[78]

Then change is the difference between the occasions themselves, rather than that of their spatiotemporal quanta. ". . . 'change' means the diversities among the actual entities which belong to some one society of a definite type."[79] Again, change is the comparison between the occasions of a society, and motion is the difference between their epochs. There is no enduring but moving and changing thing. Occasions create new epochs; they do not move to them or change within themselves. Whitehead insists that: "If time be taken seriously, no concrete entity can change. It can only be superseded."[80]

Since motion is the difference between immobile spatiotemporal quanta, the quanta themselves can be regarded as absolute places:

> . . . we must identify the atomized quantum of extension correlative to an actual entity with Newton's absolute place and absolute duration. Newton's proof that motion does not apply to absolute place, which in its nature is immovable, also holds.[81]

This is not to say that the immobile quantum of spacetime is a simple location or that it does not perish but remains ever actual and permanently the same. Whitehead is willing to equate his spatiotemporal quanta with Newtonian absolute places just as he is willing to equate his enduring objects (which are societies of occasions) with common sense material bodies, and his actual occasions with atoms, monads, and substances of previous philosophies. They are not the same things, but they are comparable in some respects. Although the equation is not perfect, then, it may be said in general that each quantum of Whiteheadian spacetime corresponds to a Newtonian absolute place.

> According to Newton, a portion of space cannot move. We have to ask how this truth, obvious from Newton's point of view, takes shape in the organic theory. Instead of a region of space, we should consider a bit of the physical field. This bit, expressing one way in which the actual world involves the potentiality for a new creation, acquires the unity of an actual entity. The physical field is, in this way, atomized with definite divisions: it becomes a 'nexus' of actualities. Such a quantum (i.e., each actual division) of the extensive continuum is the primary phase of a creature. This quantum is constituted by its totality of relationships and cannot move. Also the creature cannot have any external adventures, but only the internal adventure of becoming. Its birth is its end.[82]

Each epochal occasion is an absolute perspective for comparing other occasions and the extent of their epochs. Each is an absolute determination of certain relationships among others pertaining to itself; each is an absolutely immobile and unaltered epoch with respect to itself. But multitudes of epochal occasions become and perish everywhere, including one another and included in one another. While none move or change relative to themselves or to any absolute spacetime framework, all are standpoints for comparing other occasions, including their rates of supersession. The plurality of absolute standpoints or perspective upon others is relativity.

Just as change is explained as the differences between successive occasions of a society, so permanence is explained as the likenesses between these occasions. Both relative motion and rest and relative change and permanence are a consequence of the fact that there are societies, that is, successions of occasions alike in some respects and different in others. There can be no comparison of any occasions but that they are alike in some ways and different in others. Comparison requires a causally efficacious sequence of occasions to compare, a sequence which perforce affects the comparing occasion since it cannot compare what it cannot prehend. Thus, change is the diversity among like occasions, and permanence or endurance is the sameness among diverse occasions, as compared by a successor to them.

> In the world there is nothing static. But there is reproduction; and hence the permanence which is the result of order, and the cause of it. And yet there is always change; for time is cumulative as well as reproductive, and the cumulation of the many is not their reproduction as many.[83]

## THE PHASES OF CONCRESCENCE

*The paradox of phases.* In the following passage Whitehead speaks of an initial stage of feelings and subsequent phases of feelings, implying that an occasion is actually divided into temporal parts or phases. In fact, he states unequivocally that a process of concrescence has a succession of phases.

> The process of concrescence is divisible into an initial stage of many feelings, and a succession of subsequent phases of more complex feelings integrating the earlier simpler feelings, up to the satisfaction which is one complex unity of feeling. This is the 'genetic' analysis of the satisfaction.[84]

Such passages undermine what has gone before in this book if they are left uninterpreted. I have attempted to establish that occasions are never divided, that there are no actual parts of occasions or of their epochs occurring at different times, that an occasion's epochal time does not pass within it, that the only succession is succession of occasions. Now it remains to interpret the phases of concrescence, even the succession of phases, consistently with theses such as these that have been presented here. If the divisibility of undivided occasions is paradoxical, the difficulty of non-temporal phases of concrescence is even more so since these phases, peculiar to Whitehead's philosophy, are less amenable to translation and analogy.

Whitehead most often divides an occasion into three basic phases or stages, as in the preceding passage. The second of these phases he subdivides into further phases, depending on the complexity of the occasion. He adds a fourth phase when taking into account the primordial nature of God.[85] Then a process of concrescence is divisible into at least two phases, two "temporal halves," physical and mental; but it is usually considered divisible into three phases, an initial phase of physical prehensions, a subsequent phase of conceptual prehensions integrating with the physical, and a final phase of satisfaction; and it may be considered divisible into four phases, God's primordial nature being also a phase. This divisibility into phases appears under genetic analysis of an occasion.

The problem is, what kind of "genetic" analysis can this be that discloses the "temporal" phases of an admittedly non-temporal process of concrescence. The very real question is, what kind of time is this that at once has phases and yet is only actual as a phaseless whole? I shall let Reiner Wiehl's understatement suffice to represent the proliferation of doubts among interpreters of Whitehead: "The abstract scheme of the logic of becoming does not lack a paradoxical structure."[86]

We have seen that a process of concrescence is ever-present without passing itself, the potentiality for time rather than temporal transition. Yet Whitehead does not hesitate to refer to the phases of concrescence as temporal; the terminology describing phases all has temporal significance. For example, the terms "succession," "antecedent," "subsequent," "initial," "final," "earlier," "later," "phase," "process," "becoming," and "genetic" all connote temporal order. It is certainly disconcerting that Whitehead has not qualified his many references to earlier and later, first and second, antecedent and subsequent phases or stages, and to a succession of phases.[87]

Thus, there is paradox in Whitehead's own exposition of epochal time. His epochal theory is therefore open to the charge of unintelligibility and blatant contradiction. Vere C. Chappell, for example, claims that Whitehead's epochal theory "ends in a contradiction," that consequently it is "an odd notion at best," in fact, "senseless," and in sum "unintelligible."[88] Because epochal time is that appropriate to Whitehead's epochal occasions, the intelligibility of the entire cosmology is at stake. David A. Sipfle points out: ". . . if Chappell's arguments are allowed to stand . . . they render the whole Whiteheadian cosmology unintelligible."[89] Incoherency in Whitehead's epochal theory of time would weaken his claim to a coherent metaphysics. In response to Chappell, Sipfle argues that Chappell finds Whiteheadian time unintelligible precisely because Chappell's standard for time is Newtonian. "We must conclude, rather, that the attempt to reduce an epoch to an instant fails. . . . Once Chappell's arguments are restated in terms appropriate to the theory under consideration, the contradictions disappear."[90] These extremes of interpretation show how ambiguously Whitehead expressed himself. In those instances where Whitehead has chosen to expound his view most paradoxically, the intention and import of the entire philosophy must be brought to bear to interpret them fairly and consistently.

I support Sipfle's thesis that Whitehead's epochal theory is necessary to the metaphysics and intelligible: "If our arguments are sound, the epochal theory of time is both necessary . . . and tenable . . . it is therefore worthy of serious consideration."[91] And I shall attempt to further defend Sipfle's position, elaborating many points brought out in his arguments against Chappell, in order to argue against even more misinterpretations of epochal time. It is my hope to render the timeless phases obvious common sense rather than baffling paradox.

*Physical and mental poles.* In the following passage Whitehead speaks paradoxically of occasions indivisible by virtue of their subjective aims that are nevertheless divisible into temporal halves.

> The *res vera*, in its character of concrete satisfaction, is divisible into prehensions which concern its first temporal half and into prehensions which concern its second temporal half. . . . A prehension, however, acquires subjective form, and this subjective form is only rendered fully determinate by integration with conceptual prehensions belonging to the mental pole of the *res vera*. . . . Thus the subjective aim does not share in this divisibility. If we confine attention to prehensions concerned with the earlier half, their subjective forms have arisen from nothing. For the subjective aim which belongs to the whole is now excluded. Thus the evolution of subjective form could not be referred to any actuality. The ontological principle has been violated. Something has floated into the world from nowhere.
>
> The summary statement of this discussion is, that the mental pole determines the subjective forms and that this pole is inseparable from the total *res vera*.[92]

Here an occasion is considered divisible into two basic phases or temporal halves, earlier and later. But the earlier half is a half only if the occasion's subjective aim is excluded from consideration. But in reality a subjective aim is not separable from any of its occasion's prehensions; in reality a subjective aim does not come later than physical prehensions. The mental pole is the seat of an occasion's conceptual prehension, including its subjective aim. "Conceptual prehensions, positive or negative, constitute the primary operations among those belonging to the mental pole of an actual entity."[93] Like the poles of a magnet, at no time is an occasion possessed of one pole without the other.

We have seen that conceptual prehension is an aspect of every feeling. Every physical feeling acquires subjective form, form which has been selected from among those conceptually prehended. And the physical feeling acquires forms because it shares with other prehensions the subjective aim for one occasion. It aims to participate in those eternal objects pre-established for it by God. Conceptual prehension of eternal objects on the part of every occasion is witness to a mentality on the part of every occasion. "The basic operations of mentality are 'conceptual prehensions.'"[94] Then every occasion, no matter how lowly on the scale of complexity, possesses mentality, no matter how insignificantly, inasmuch as it conceptually prehends. For, every occasion prehends certain forms of definiteness of other occasions and itself exhibits certain forms that it shares with them. An occasion of a virus, an amino acid, an oxygen atom, an electron, and a photon all have mentality, although to a lesser degree than mammals. There would be no chemical bonding but that the molecular, atomic, and subatomic occasions had mentality enough to "recognize," conceptually prehend, and select forms of definiteness of occasions to which they attach themselves. Similarly, there would be no nuclear bonding but that subatomic occasions pair with other subatomic occasions the forms of which they prehend. The fact that all occasions prehend both physically and conceptually endows them with a physical and mental pole.

Thus, every occasion is dipolar. There is no such thing as an actuality devoid of a mental pole, devoid of mentality. "But matter of fact essentially involves a mental pole."[95] Similarly, there is no such thing as an actuality devoid of a physical pole, devoid of physical nature. For this reason there is no uningressed eternal object such that it exists on its own without an occasion, as though there could be blueness or triangularity without anything blue or triangular. Similarly, there is no actuality existing on its own without eternal objects as though there could be an occasion without any shape or characteristics. There is no occasion and no eternal object that has reality by itself without the other. Whitehead's philosophy is distinguished by this thesis that all actualities of every grade and type are dipolar, such that they both prehend and demonstrate a physical and a conceptual nature, although the mental pole of many an actuality is negligible indeed.

The most complete concrete fact is dipolar, physical and mental. But, for some specific purpose, the proportion of importance, as shared between the two poles, may vary from negligibility to dominance of either pole.[96]

*Genetic analysis.* The actual non-division but potential divisibility of an occasion applies whether the occasion be analyzed coordinately or genetically. No occasion is actually divided. Therefore, in speaking of division, Whitehead refers to a retrospective and intellectual analysis of an occasion, not any actually segmented occasion. "Division" for Whitehead is a term for analysis. Analysis reveals prehensions and prehensions, as we have seen, are inextricable or undivided from one another and the occasion they compose together.

. . . the first analysis of an actual entity, into its most concrete elements, discloses it to be a concrescence of prehensions, which have originated in its process of becoming. All further analysis is an analysis of prehensions. Analysis in terms of prehensions is termed 'division.'[97]

Coordinate analysis is division of a satisfaction into regions and genetic analysis is division of a satisfaction into concrescent phases. "There are two distinct ways of 'dividing' the satisfaction of an actual entity into component feelings, genetically and coordinately. Genetic division is division of the concrescence; coordinate division is division of the concrete."[98] It should be noted that genetic division is not division of a concrescence during the process of concrescence, but is division of a satisfaction so as to disclose concrescence retrospectively. That is, genetic division does not segment or even describe an actually segmented process of concrescence but is a way of analyzing it after its completion. It is only and always a satisfaction that is analyzed, whether coordinately to distinguish regions, or genetically to distinguish phases, as Whitehead indicates.

Genetic analysis, then, is analysis of a satisfaction for the phases of concrescence. And the phases are the physical and conceptual prehensions and their integrations and the satisfaction. "The analysis of the formal constitution of an actual entity has given three stages in the process of feeling: (i) the responsive phase, (ii) the supplemental stage, and (iii) the satisfaction."[99] Thus, Whitehead speaks of "phases of feeling," that is, physical and conceptual feeling, in discussing concrescence. "Conceptual feelings and simple causal feelings constitute the two main species of 'primary' feelings. All other feelings of whatever complexity arise out of a process of integration which starts with a phase of these primary feelings."[100] The phases of concrescence are phases of feeling culminating in the satisfaction considered as a final phase.

The first phase of concrescence is naturally that of the physical prehensions of the data that, by virtue of this prehension, become the actual world of the prehending occasion. The second phase is the conceptual prehensions of eternal objects that are delegated to objectify the data and inform the feeling of it. The operations of this phase are conducted by decisions originating with the occasion's mental pole, decisions implementing and modifying the occasion's subjective aim.

> The first phase is the phase of pure reception of the actual world in its guise of objective datum for aesthetic synthesis. . . . The second stage is governed by the private ideal, gradually shaped in the process itself. . . .
>
> In this second stage the feelings assume an emotional character by reason of this influx of conceptual feelings.[101]

All prehensions of an occasion, physical and conceptual, are inextricable, inseparable, undivided. Just so, the two poles of an occasion, expressing its dual physical and mental functions, are inextricable. "The mental pole originates as the conceptual counterpart of operations in the physical pole. The two poles are inseparable in their origination."[102] One pole does not precede the other in time; physical feelings do not actually precede conceptual feelings in time because the conceptual feelings are a development of the physical feelings themselves. A reaction, emotional and mental and decisive, does not occur in a different time period than the physical action to which it responds. The mental reaction acts on the physical action, qualifying it and infusing it with subjective uses, which would be impossible in a different time period after the physical action had already passed away. A conceptual prehension is not a future entity acting retroactively on a past physical prehension; it is an extension of the physical prehension itself. "The mental pole starts with the conceptual registration of the physical pole."[103]

There can be no succession of feelings since concrescence is not temporal but only potentially temporal. Temporal order does not refer to phases of concrescence but to causally efficacious sequences of occasions. Whitehead writes, "Every actual entity is 'in time' so far as its physical pole is concerned, and is 'out of time' so far as its mental pole is concerned."[104] If the mental pole is "out of time" it cannot be said to succeed the physical pole. The phases of concrescence, or phases of feelings, are phases of the operations of the physical and mental poles, poles and operations which are not complete in themselves such that they make whole occasions, whole epochs.

To claim that the phases of concrescence follow in temporal sequence is to treat them as actual occasions in themselves. But there is no actual occasion which is the physical pole of an actual occasion, and no actual occasion which is the mental pole. The poles are counterparts of feeling, not independent occasions; and feelings are causal activities, not separable actualities. The poles are like the poles of a magnet, complementary, or like a face and its expression, a person and her or his attitude, a poem and its meaning, a reflection and its color, a rock and its shape: undivided and inseparable but distinguishable. It cannot be said too emphatically that the Whiteheadian cosmology does not allow for the bifurcation of nature into a separable physical and mental substance, matter and mind as independent and as independently acting actualities. "The theory of 'prehensions' embodies a protest against the 'bifurcation' of nature. It embodies even more than that: its protest is against the bifurcation of actualities."[105] Whitehead postulates physical and mental prehensions, not substances or actualities. It is just prehension that refuses a dualism of substances. The physical and the conceptual factors of nature are both prehended and both counterpart operations of every actuality.

Thus, an actual occasion is not itself a unity of physical and mental actual occasions. Its basic phases are not three kinds of actualities, matter, mind, and the link between them. Insofar as physical nature and mentality and a link between them are conceived as substantial and separable entities in themselves, Whitehead's philosophy has not been heeded. Edward G. Ballard, for example, writes:

> It becomes more and more difficult to see that Whitehead has in any sense solved or avoided the problem inherent in any effort to discover an intelligible linkage between the physical and the mental. Whitehead holds that his doctrine avoids the Cartesian dualism; nevertheless, he seems rather to have generalized than to have avoided it, for every entity turns out to possess both a physical and a mental pole.[106]

Prehension, however, is Whitehead's "intelligible linkage between the physical and the mental." Ballard's language is dualistic. Whitehead speaks of physical and mental poles, of physical and mental prehensions, factors, and operations of dipolar occasions. Ballard, however, speaks of "the physical" and "the mental" as requiring "linkage." Of course there can be no way of avoiding Cartesian dualism if the dualism is to be assumed. The physical pole is not one actuality or one type of substance, the mental pole another, and the link between them a third. Rather, the phase of physical prehension is what in the world an occasion feels, the phase of conceptual feeling is how it feels, and the phase of satisfaction is the attainment of its purpose in feeling, a certain degree of intensity of experience.

There is no division of time in genetic division, but division of genesis, division of origination. Genetic division is not another term for temporal division. The process of concrescence is a genesis or origination of an epochal occasion with spatiotemporal extension. Certainly antecedent occasions are in transition to a present occasion in process, but their transitions are not the phases of concrescence of the present occasion. The phases are not in transition to their successors; they are stages of indeterminate feeling on the way toward a unified, satisfied feeling. The phases are no more actually separated than are a dream and its emotional tone or a chair and its appeal; they are no more actually removed in time, before and after, than hearing a sound comes before enjoying it or gripping a stone comes before feeling its coldness.

Of course, Whitehead brought confusion onto himself with his unfortunate temporal terminology, referring to "earlier" and "later," "antecedent" and "subsequent," "successive" and "supervening" phases, when he explicitly insists that the process of concrescence, a unity by virtue of its subjective aim, forbids divisions. A concrescence is only divisible into "temporal" parts if its subjective aim is excluded. These temporal designations applied to phases, then, cannot refer to an actual temporal order of phases; rather, they are Whitehead's way of deferring to our ordinary habits of thought. We usually think in terms of a physical action and a mental reaction, as though they occurred consecutively. Whitehead's usage of temporal phases is a concession to this preference in our thinking. For Whitehead, there is no physical prehension where and when no conceptual prehension accompanies it. But we ordinarily separate physical event from mental and emotional response as though they could have happened at different times.

Whitehead's term "enduring object" is just such a concession to our ordinary habits of thought as is this. "Enduring object" is his name for a society of occasions and is no enduring object at all. Such a name only confuses a philosophy which protests enduring substances. And designating phases of concrescence "earlier" and "later" only confuses a theory of time wherein concrescence does not proceed in time at all. "Enduring object" is a concession to substantialism; "successive phases" is a concession to dualism. Such concessions are unfortunate since our ordinary habits of thought are substantialist and dualist. But they are few and far between in Whitehead's philosophy.

*Intellectual analysis.* Whitehead naturally comes under attack for dividing indivisible occasions into prehensions and phases. Donald W. Sherburne points out the difficulty:

> Whitehead's point is that the analysis into phases of concrescence is 'only intellectual' and that there is 'some arbitrariness' in distinguishing individual prehensions. The reader is encouraged to ask himself whether Whitehead puts such weight on the separation and sequence of prehensions that it will not do to say that the genetic analysis is 'only intellectual.'[107]

The passages that Sherburne is referring to in this instance are as follows. First, Whitehead says there is "some arbitrariness" in distinguishing one prehension from the entire physical and conceptual content of an occasion:

> Thus a prehension, considered genetically, can never free itself from the incurable atomicity of the actual entity to which it belongs. The selection of a subordinate prehension from the satisfaction . . . involves a hypothetical, propositional point of view. The fact is the satisfaction as one. There is some arbitrariness in taking a component from the datum with a component from the subjective form, and in considering them, on the ground of congruity, as forming a subordinate prehension. The justification is that the genetic process can be thereby analysed.[108]

And in the following passage Whitehead says that analysis of occasions is "only intellectual":

> The analysis of an actual entity is only intellectual, or, to speak with a wider scope, only objective. Each actual entity is a cell with atomic unity. But in analysis it can only be understood as a process; it can only be felt as a process, that is to say, as in passage. The actual entity is divisible; but is in fact undivided. The divisibility can thus only refer to its objectifications in which it transcends itself. But such transcendence is self-revelation.[109]

This passage summarily states much that I have been at pains to say heretofore. An occasion is in fact undivided; but it subsequently reveals its potential divisibility in the way that it has effect in many diverse descendents.

Both of these passages show clearly that an occasion's physical and conceptual content, its objective, inherited, experienced elements and its subjective, emotional, elective elements, are in fact inseparable but retrospectively distinguishable. Distinguishing one prehension from an occasion is picking one of the multitudes of causes of the occasion and a part of its emotional, experiential make-up that is appropriate to that cause. But cause and effect, creative action and creative response, do not occur as separate events or acts at different times, on different occasions, but are the efficacy of the past at work for the one occasion. Nor does one cause of an occasion have effect at one time and another at another time from the standpoint of the occasion which is in a state of potentiality. All potential effects become determinate and effective only upon satisfaction. These passages show that intellectual analysis creates no actual divisions in occasions but only discriminates possible ways of dividing them. "But the full subjective form cannot be abstracted from the pattern of the objective datum. The intellectual disjunction is not a real separation."[110] But there is no way to recover particular cause and effect transitions except by intellectual analysis of an occasion; there is no way to distinguish the given elements of an occasion from those that are chosen except by intellectual analysis. The partial effects contributing to an occasion, its prehensions, are not separable but they are differentiable.

Whitehead's theory of prehensions, for all the reasons submitted in this book, makes more sense than his paradoxical language would lead one to suppose. Neither his prehensions, nor his phases of concrescence, or his intellectual analysis need be regarded as spurious because actual occasions are wholes and become as wholes. The theory of prehensions and their phases can be preserved by adhering to his strictures regarding epochal time and consistently refusing to give significance to the temporal language applied to becoming that contradicts the epochal theory. It is well to be reminded of the epochal theory: "But the genetic process is not the temporal succession: such a view is exactly what is denied by the epochal theory of time."[111]

Whitehead may regard his genetic analysis as somewhat arbitrary; yet he does not at all regard his metaphysics as in the least arbitrary. In fact, he regards his theory of reality, that nature is a plurality of successions of creative and interrelated occasions such as he describes, as a good attempt at truth. He takes his conception of the actual occasion to be a unifying conception capable of interpreting every experience and thereby absolute or "necessary" in this respect.

Thus the philosophic scheme should be 'necessary,' in the sense of bearing in itself its own warrant of universality throughout all experience, provided that we confine ourselves to that which communicates with immediate matter of fact. But what does not so communicate is unknowable, and the unknowable is unknown; and so this universality defined by 'communication' can suffice.[112]

No doubt this discrepancy, the "necessary" metaphysics supplied with analyses that are "only intellectual" casts serious doubts on Whitehead's accomplishment. Analyses that "involve some arbitrariness" would certainly seem to vitiate any claim to a coherent metaphysics adequate for interpreting all experience. Some discussion of this discrepancy is in order; it may not be as insoluble as it seems.

First of all it must be remembered that prehensions do not occur singly, isolated, independently. They develop out of real potentialities of many antecedent occasions for a new creation by sharing the aim to be that creation. In process they are creative potentials, indeterminate causally efficacious transitions, indefinite partial occasions. Every occasion is a complex of prehensions mutually sensitive, mutually adjusted, intimately and inextricably together. No occasion is "composed" of only one prehension. Each is a creation and composition of "the whole of history": ". . . each creature including in itself the whole of history and exemplifying the self-identity of things and their mutual diversities."[113] This being the case, it is only natural that the discrimination of particular prehensions will be somewhat arbitrary, somewhat hypothetical.

Secondly, it must be recognized that intellectual analysis is itself a process. Perceptions, consciousness, knowledge, reason, imagination, thought, *et alia* name various types of complex prehensions which are constitutive of various kinds of complex occasions. None are exempt from causal efficacy. Whitehead makes a case for perceptive feelings, imaginative feelings, propositional feelings, indicative feelings, predicative feelings, physical recognition or recollection as a feeling, comparative feelings, and intellectual feelings.[114] For Whitehead, "Understanding is a special form of feeling."[115] And so too is thought: "Thought is one form of emphasis."[116] And mentality is also a mode of feeling (being conceptual feeling): "Mental activity is one of the modes of feeling belonging to all actual entities in some degree, but only amounting to conscious intellectuality in some actual entities."[117] And neither judgment nor belief are beyond the scope of feeling: ". . . we substitute the broad notion of 'feeling' for the narrower notions of 'judgment' and 'belief.'"[118] And knowledge and consciousness too are the outcome of complex prehensions which are prehensions of simpler prehensions, originating with the integration of the simpler prehensions. "But all forms of consciousness arise from ways of integration of propositional feelings with other feelings, either physical feelings or conceptual feelings."[119] All the important attributes of man are feelings according to the philosophy of organism. "The philosophy of organism aspires to construct a critique of pure feeling, in the philosophical position in which Kant put his *Critique of Pure Reason.*"[120]

An intellectual analysis, therefore, is an actual occasion that comes into being and attains satisfaction on the same principles as any other occasion. The intellectual discrimination of prehensions and phases of an antecedent occasion is an activity on the part of an analyzing occasion succeeding it.

The conception of knowledge as passive contemplation is too inadequate to meet the facts. Nature is ever originating its own development, and the sense of action is the direct knowledge of the percipient event as having its very being in the formation of its natural relations. Knowledge issues from this reciprocal insistence between this event and the rest of nature, namely, relations are perceived in the making and because of the making.[121]

Analysis is prehending too, aiming to achieve an occasion of objective assessment of other occasions. The data of an occasion of analysis are the potentials of antecedent occasions in transition to itself, just as are the data of any other occasion. Its subjective form reflects its own interests and purposes in how it prehends its data, just as does that of any occasion. And it objectifies its data by means of eternal objects selected from among those ingredient in the data, as do all occasions. Intellectual analysis of antecedent occasions, then, has only the validity and objectivity that attaches to objectification, which is to say, none but what has been subjectively interpreted. There is no simple occurrence, the objectivity of which is the same for all prehending it. The objectifications are the data as felt under a perspective. An analyzing occasion is no more objective than its perspective, which is unavoidable.

However, it must also be recognized, thirdly, that intellectual analyses ignore the fact of their own perspective. Intellectual analysis supposes that it is not itself a perspective, that the objects of analysis are not in process with it. But in fact, the data as objectified are the actual world, the very content of the occasion of analysis. Intellectual analysis presumes itself free of effect from the data which are the felt constitution of its own world.

Perspective cannot be omitted. It can, however, be ignored. But this very ignorance is a perspective also. Then ignorance is another trait of intellectual analysis. Analysis is always from this perspective, of the constitution of that antecedent perspective. Its conclusions can only be hypothetical inasmuch as the perspective under analysis cannot be its own. It is the hypothetical reconstruction of an antecedent occasion with its antecedent perspective. But analyzing necessarily ignores the subjective unity of the occasions analyzed, whether coordinately or genetically.[122] And ignorance of its own subjective unity with its objects may be a part of its own subjective unity as well.

And fourth, the Whiteheadian metaphysics does not depend for its validity upon intellectual analyses alone, but upon experiences of all kinds, including intellectual analyses. The tenets of the metaphysics do not presuppose the accuracy of the intellectual analyses; on the contrary, the possibility of the intellectual analyses presuppose the truth of the metaphysics. The assumptions of intellectual analysis and the meaningfulness of its conclusions presuppose the validity of the metaphysics; they presuppose that what there is for analysis are actual occasions, that these are divisible into prehensions, and so on. Intellectual analysis cannot be used as an exclusive test of the merits of a metaphysical system which justifies it. Whitehead's theory of prehension cannot be judged alone by intellectual analyses, but by the light of all kinds of experiences. These are some of the reasons why intellectual analysis may be somewhat arbitrary and "only objective" without the metaphysics necessarily being the same.

*Retrospective satisfaction.* It is not only intellectual analysis that requires a retrospective standpoint but satisfaction itself. Both coordinate and genetic analyses are analyses of satisfactions. But even satisfaction is not felt or experienced or known as such in process; it is only determined retrospectively by a successor. Of course, it can be known rather quickly by immediate successors to brief occasions. The satisfaction is what a successor prehends, objectifies, analyzes. It is the antecedent occasion as superject. "But the 'satisfaction' is the 'superject' rather than the 'substance' or the 'subject.'"[123] This means that satisfactions are only determinable by the succeeding occasions in which aspects of them are objectified. Satisfactions are only recognized as such in their effect upon subsequent occasions.

> In respect to the entity in question the satisfaction can only be considered as a creative determination, by which the objectifications of the entity beyond itself are settled. In other words, the 'satisfaction' of an entity can only be discussed in terms of the usefulness of that entity. It is a qualification of creativity.[124]

The satisfaction of an occasion is the occasion as a complete togetherness so that whatever aspect of the occasion is prehended or analyzed it is the whole together occasion as in that aspect. For, it is only satisfactions that are divisible, prehendable, and partial causes or creators of successors.

This abstractive 'objectification' is rendered possible by reason of the 'divisible' character of the satisfactions of actual entities. By reason of this 'divisible' character causation is the transfer of a feeling, and not of a total satisfaction.[125]

Satisfaction is the final phase of concrescence. But since it is not something experienced separately by the subject, being prehended only after the fact, then there is no "time when" it settles the occasion. The same is true of all phases of concrescence. There is no "time when" their indeterminate activity phases in and out and no time "when" the whole process becomes determinate relative to itself alone. Satisfaction is not a separate occurrence added to the end of a process; it is not itself an occasion within an occasion. "[Satisfaction] cannot be construed as a component contributing to its own concrescence; it is the ultimate fact, individual to the entity."[126] The satisfaction is not a separable part of an occasion that can be experienced individually as a separate phase or prehended in separation from its occasion.

If the phases of concrescence actually divided an occasion temporally, then it would be two or more spatiotemporal units rather than one. Neither the satisfaction nor any other phase of concrescence is temporal. The phases can no more be actually divided from one another than the universe can be divided from a perspective upon it; than the occasions that constitute a self can be divided from the self. Referring to temporal order, referring to when occasions occurred is referring to a comparison of their spatiotemporal extensions. There is no more referring to "when" an occasion became satisfied than "when" an occasion felt like itself or "when" an occasion transforms from potentiality to actuality.

Whitehead describes a process of concrescence as an occasion's realizing a certain maximum value:

> The categoreal conditions which govern the 'subjective aim' . . . consist generally in satisfying some condition of a maximum, to be obtained by the transmission of inherited types of order. This is the foundation of the 'stationary' conditions in terms of which the ultimate formulations of physical science can be mathematically expressed.[127]

This is the satisfaction of the occasion; satisfying a maximum value is satisfying a process of concrescence. The maximum that an occasion obtains is simply that which it in fact obtains, not the maximum most possibly attainable, just as the satisfaction is the complete unity that an occasion actually obtains rather than the greatest unity it might obtain. This maximum in fact attained is ascertainable only retrospectively. "Thus the primate is realised atomically in a succession of durations, each duration to be measured from one maximum to another."[128] The maximums are only measurable by other occasions prehending them. Only from the vantage point of a subsequent occasion can the attainment of a former occasion be assessed, as an attainment. For the former occasion itself, its attainment was an integral part of its living present and indistinguishable as a separate condition of the process. The occasion experiences itself as a process of becoming out of antecedents, but it does not experience the fact that it has reached a maximum since for all it knows the maximum is yet to be reached. Awareness of the fact that a maximum was attained can only come in the next occasions when a comparison of the facts is possible.

A present occasion is not in the position to feel its own satisfaction. With satisfaction, an occasion's self-functioning ceases. This loss of self-functioning cannot be felt in the present since it requires self-functioning to feel it. It is only in a self-functioning successor that the fact of an antecedent's cessation can be detected. The antecedent itself, upon loss of self-functioning, no longer experienced itself, and no longer felt that it did not experience itself since it no longer felt. The fact that the satisfaction can only be recognized retrospectively, being the superject rather than the subject, means that, "No actual entity can be conscious of its own satisfaction; for such knowledge would be a component in the process, and would thereby alter the satisfaction."[129]

Such a statement does not mean that there is no consciousness or that there is no conscious actual occasion. It means to say that an occasion cannot be conscious over and above its own present conscious state. That is, it cannot be conscious of its satisfaction on top of its own consciousness without becoming another occasion that is conscious that the previous occasion was conscious. A conscious occasion cannot be conscious of its own consciousness without slipping into another occasion, one prehending that previous occasion as conscious. As soon as an occasion is conscious of its being conscious, the *it* of which it is conscious has become past. To be conscious of being conscious is really to be conscious of having been conscious; to be aware of a satisfaction is really to be aware of a previous satisfaction. The fact that an occasion cannot be conscious of its own satisfaction does not prevent its being conscious of satisfactions just past.

*Retrospective phases.* The phases of concrescence are modes of feeling, physical and mental, distinguishable but not in fact, i.e., spatiotemporally, separated, like height and weight or sound and hearing. They are independently prehendable but not in fact independent. The mental phases are reactions or responses to the physical phases.

Each actuality is essentially bipolar, physical and mental, and the physical inheritance is essentially accompanied by a conceptual reaction partly conformed to it, and partly introductory of a relevant novel contrast, but always introducing emphasis, valuation, and purpose.[130]

Conceptual prehension, therefore, accompanies physical prehension rather than succeeding it in time. The conceptual reaction or response to the physical prehension is not a spatiotemporal occurrence in itself. We have seen Whitehead's remark that the mental pole is not temporal, that it is "out of time." He remarks likewise that it is not spatial: "So though mentality is non-spatial, mentality is always a reaction from, and integration with, physical experience which is spatial."[131] Mentality, conceptual prehension, is not spatiotemporal, then, and cannot be said to occur as a spatiotemporal entity all its own, to be added to a separable physical entity. Therefore, the phase of conceptual feeling cannot possibly be a temporal or spatiotemporal phase.

A physical feeling acquires forms, but forms shared by and compatible with those acquired by other physical feelings so that the acquirement of forms waits upon the whole determinate occasion. Each feeling is one potentiality for a whole occasion and dependent upon all the other feelings to be what it is as finalized. The forms or eternal objects themselves and the decisions regarding them, being non-spatiotemporal in themselves, take no special temporal interval to appear; the physical feelings acquire spatiotemporal extension with the ingression of the forms belonging to their subjective aim. Conceptual feeling, which is the way that physical feeling is felt based on a decision about how it should be characterized, and the attainment of the aim to feel that way, is a part of the act of physically feeling itself. The becoming of a new occasion is the becoming of its united prehension of, its determinate relationships with, its antecedents, the very antecedents in process of creating it. Before this complete concrescence, the antecedents are not determinately prehended, nor are they actually antecedents, first before the prehending subject is completely created. A prehension, with its physical and mental ends, requires the entire occasion for it to be a completed act of cause and effect transition, a partial creator of the new occasion.

Whitehead distinguishes between phases of what is in fact a whole in process, only potentially divisible, because he wants to distinguish retrospectively between what belongs uniquely to a new occasion and what is the contribution of each of its antecedents. An occasion is its own composition of aspects of other occasions; its particular togetherness, involving its own decisions as to the forms of its antecedents it takes upon itself, is unique. This distinction is that between the efficient and final factors of an occasion. Efficient and final factors have differential effects but are not themselves two different actualities occurring on two different occasions. Robert Neville points out that the distinction between phases is an abstraction:

> The point of the appeal to phases in an epoch is to explain the subjective form of prehensions divided out of the satisfied actual entity. . . . To speak of an occasion's satisfaction as itself a phase, the last in the genetic process, is only an abstraction derivative from the intention to give a genetic analysis.[132]

Prehensions, potentialities in themselves, belong to the construction of an occurrence which is the actual occasion. The antecedent occasions which are the data for the new occasion are in passage to it as they are prehended and objectified. Once all the data are in, the occasion can conclude its first phase. There is no specific time when each datum meets with feelings of the new ongoing occasion since these are as yet potentialities for the occasion and not yet spatiotemporal. But the prehension of all the data which compose the occasion's actual world constitutes its initial phase. The passage of antecedent occasions, their real potentialities, is into this first phase as they are assimilated as data for the new occasion. But the further transformation of the data into the new subject is not the passage of actual occasions but process, their process of concrescence into one occasion. There is no passage of the next phases of concrescence as though these were occasions; there is no passage from physical feelings, to decisions, to ingressions, to intentions, to achievements. There is not first in time the physical feeling of an actual world, then a decision regarding that feeling, then the ingression of selected eternal objects characterizing that feeling, then the intention that there be a togetherness of certain feelings, decisions, and characterizations for the sake of an actual occasion. The interior development of an occasion, its phases, involves no passage, no temporal order.

For example, there is not first a feeling of the texture of a stone, then a feeling of its shape, then a feeling of some disposition with respect to the stone, whether it is felt with liking or dislike, curiosity or aversion, indifference or resistance. There is not first a feeling of smoothness or roughness, warmth or coldness, heaviness or lightness, roundness or squareness; then afterwards a feeling of liking or dislike, pleasure or displeasure; then after that a feeling of the hand as shaped in some way around the stone so as to account for the shape of the stone in some way as to hold it; then after that a feeling of an aim to hold a stone in the hand having been fulfilled.

For that matter, there is not first the movements of the eye balls that detected the stone on the ground; then afterwards the firing of the nerves in the body and brain that engineer the initiation of the attempt to hold the stone; then after that the movements of the body, its bones, blood, nerves, muscles, legs, arms, and hands that conclude in the holding of the stone; then afterwards the feeling of holding a stone. There is not even first a stone and a hand then afterwards a stone-holding occasion. For, the stone and hand, and all their attendant interaction are the actual occasion of holding the stone in the hand. Stone and hand may be intellectually separated from the stone-holding occasion retrospectively, and retrospectively may be considered first, antecedents of the stone-holding occasion. But in fact they were not first before the occasion without the occasion being there. There is no first until there has been a second; no before until there has been an after. Stone and hand would not be antecedents of the stone-holding occasion if the stone were never held. John Dewey set down the same idea long ago:

> We do not have first a sound and then activity of attention, unless sound is taken as mere nervous shock or physical event, not as conscious value. The conscious sensation of sound depends upon the motor response having already taken place.[133]

And another example may be taken from Whitehead: "For example, 'thirst' is an immediate physical feeling integrated with the conceptual prehension of its quenching."[134] There is not first a feeling of thirst and then a feeling of the desire to quench it, though we commonly consider the latter to be later in time. It is latter and later only as a way of speaking, as though conceptual reaction were separable from physical feeling. Whitehead distinguishes mentality from physical nature without requiring a duality of actualities.

The stone and the hand are no more actual parts of the stone-holding occasion before that occasion is an actuality than is the pleasure or displeasure of holding the stone before the stone-holding occasion is there. The stone and hand no more come before the stone-holding occasion than its experienced shape and color. And the felt texture and temperature and weight of the stone are distinguishable but not separable from the stone and hand. It is the end of an act of becoming that determines its beginnings. The act of becoming is itself indeterminate. There is no first within it and no before it except that there is an after from the standpoint of which a before and a first can be decided. Antecedents are only potentially antecedent until their consequences have been realized.

*Whitehead's account of Zeno's Paradoxes.* If the phases of concrescence are treated as actual occasions in themselves, then a process of concrescence is subject to infinite regress. For, if the phases are occasions, then the phases of these occasions are occasions, and their phases too are occasions, and so on *ad infinitum.* An actual occasion can never come into being if an infinite succession of phases which are themselves actual occasions must come into being beforehand. Treating the phases of concrescence as actual occasions, therefore, makes a paradox of Whiteheadian time. Paradoxes of infinite regress may be credited to Zeno; infinite regresses of time, of motion, and of division are renowned as Zeno's Paradoxes. It is not only quantum physics that requires an epochal theory of time, but "the consideration of Zeno's arguments."[135]

Whitehead's resolution of Zeno's Paradox "Achilles and the Tortoise" in particular will be left aside here, since it depends upon a mathematical treatment of Zeno's argument. "Zeno produces an invalid argument depending on ignorance of the theory of infinite convergent numerical series."[136] However, Zeno's Paradox of "The Flying Arrow" will be discussed here since Whitehead's treatment of it is relevant to the broader concerns of this book. Zeno's Paradox of "The Flying Arrow" is as follows:

Anything which occupies a space just its own size is stationary. But in each moment of its flight an arrow can only occupy a space just its own size. Hence at each moment of its flight the arrow is not moving but stationary. But what is true of the arrow at each moment of a period is true of it throughout the period. Hence during the whole time of its flight the arrow is not moving but stationary.[137]

This Paradox applies to actual occasions and their phases if the whole period of the arrow's flight is understood as an actual occasion, and "each moment of the period" is taken as a phase of concrescence on the supposition that a phase is itself an actual occasion. The Paradox is meant as a proof against motion but it is equally a proof against time. Whitehead leaves aside the reference to motion in the Paradox and takes up its reference to time. "But the introduction of motion brings in irrelevant details. The true difficulty is to understand how the arrow survives the lapse of time."[138] Given the Paradox, the arrow cannot pass from moment to moment since it must first pass an infinite series of portions of the moments, e.g., half-moments.

Whitehead then translates the Paradox into terms applicable to actual occasions this way:

The argument, so far as it is valid, elicits a contradiction from the two premises: (i) that in a becoming something (*res vera*) becomes, and (ii) that every act of becoming is divisible into earlier and later sections which are themselves acts of becoming.[139]

Thus, the flight of Zeno's arrow, the flight that never was, has turned into an act of becoming that never became. For, nothing can become, such as Zeno's flight or Whitehead's actual occasion, if its becoming awaits an infinity of prior acts of becoming. "Therefore there is nothing which becomes, so as to effect a transition into the second in question."[140] This "second" represents the whole period of time, the epoch, required for an occasion to come into being. An act of becoming requiring a second is divisible into earlier and later acts of becoming each requiring one-half second; these are each divisible into earlier and later acts of becoming each requiring one-quarter second, and so on. An infinite progression of such acts infinitely forestalls the possibility of the whole one second act of becoming. This is how Zeno's paradox of motion is converted into a paradox of time. The contradiction inherent in the paradox lies in the fact that something is said to become which cannot possibly become.

Whitehead denies the second premise of Zeno's argument, the premise that, "every act of becoming is divisible into earlier and later sections which are themselves acts of becoming." This eliminates the contradiction and paradox; the actual occasion is not stymied in infinite regress. Whitehead's consideration of Zeno's Paradox concludes with his formulation of the epochal theory of time.

The conclusion is that in every act of becoming there is the becoming of something with temporal extension; but that the act itself is not extensive, in the sense that it is divisible into earlier and later acts of becoming which correspond to the extensive divisibility of what has become.[141]

Here, then, is Whitehead's denial of Zeno's second premise, "the act itself is not . . . divisible into earlier and later acts of becoming. . . ." Interpreters of Whitehead who wish to claim that phases of concrescence are themselves acts of becoming, earlier and later, must contend with this statement. But more than this, they must reckon with Zeno since each phase, regarded as an act of becoming, is divisible into earlier and later phases, *ad infinitum*.

Whitehead's conclusion, requiring epochal time whereby spatiotemporal extendedness becomes but its becoming is not extended must be repeated: an act of becoming is not divisible into earlier and later acts of becoming. A process of concrescence is not divisible into earlier and later processes of concrescence; actual occasions are not actually divided into temporal sections that are earlier and later actual occasions. In short, an act of becoming is not spatiotemporal, although it becomes something spatiotemporal, an actual occasion. Lesser and lesser periods of time do not add up to a greater period, just as the crude addition *simpliciter* of antecedents is not a process of concrescence creating a new occasion. A period of time comes into being, but not *after* any lesser part of it has come into being—except retrospectively it may be considered divisible into such lesser parts. An epochal occasion does not become part by epochal part, but becomes as a whole which is then divisible. "The epochal duration is not realised *via* its *successive* divisible parts, but is given *with* its parts."[142] Any temporal parts of an epochal occasion are parts only once the occasion is given; the parts are not themselves whole occasions with respect to the occasion of which they are the parts. Any part is an incomplete aspect of a whole occasion already given, not a complete whole itself. In fine, Whitehead's conclusion, against Zeno, is that a process of concrescence is not actually divided into temporal parts, before and after, at all. "Thirdly, in the epochal theory Zeno's difficulty is met by conceiving temporalisation as the realisation of a complete organism."[143]

Infinite temporal divisibility cannot apply to an act of becoming inasmuch as the act is a potentiality and not yet a spatiotemporally extended occasion to be temporally divided. A process of concrescence is not the same thing as a succession of occasions, even though such a succession is within an occasion and becomes its data. The succession of epochal occasions is time: "Time is sheer succession of epochal durations."[144] —not parts of epochal durations. Succession is time; but the process of concrescence is becoming without being temporal. The temporal transitions of some occasions is into others, but this is not the same thing as becoming. Becoming and time are the two sides of process, microscopic and macroscopic, alive in every act of becoming. Even though they work inextricably together creating actual occasions, they are not the same thing and must not be confused with one another. "Supersession is not a continuous process of becoming. If we try to combine the notions of supersession and continuity we are at once entangled in a vicious infinite regress."[145] Successions of antecedent occasions supply a process of concrescence with its data; but the process itself is no succession. An occasion cannot succeed itself in its own midst. The occasions in supersession are not the same as the occasion they create, which occasion cannot supersede itself in process of being created itself.

*Parts of time.* Zeno's Paradox of "The Flying Arrow" may be read as another materialist or substantialist mystification. "What is true of the arrow at each moment of a period is true of it throughout the period." But throughout the period there has been an arrow's flight whereas it has been stationary at any instantaneous moment. The arrow occupies an absolute Newtonian place at each absolute instant of the flight. "In each moment of its flight an arrow can only occupy a space just its own size." An absolute instantaneous space independent of the arrow is already actual as its prearranged container.

Here is a veritable substantial arrow residing in an absolute spacetime essentially irrelevant to its material endurance. The passage of time is merely coincidental with its material subsistence. What is true of a moment of the flight is true of it throughout the whole period since the whole period is but a collection of stationary absolute instantaneous spaces. The arrow has not moved since it is exactly contained by material spaces outside of it which are immobile. Such are the perplexities of materialism: a period of time the passing of which is external and accidental to material actions such as an arrow's flight; material action which occurs in a series of coincidental absolute instantaneous spaces which do not themselves refer to, require, depend upon, or participate in the whole spatiotemporal period of the action.

For Whitehead, however, the entire flight of the arrow is one actual occasion and epoch, immobile and arrested. It is the whole flight that is an absolute Newtonian place and stationary; neither the flight nor any part of it travels through an absolute spacetime. If the whole period of flight is divided into lesser temporal parts retrospectively, one does not find the arrow occupying an absolute space in such a part. For the flight's absolute spacetime has yet to be. And each part depends for what it is upon the whole flight. No portion is a portion of that flight until that flight has actually occurred. Whitehead's rejection of materialism can be seen in his example of Zeno's flying arrow. The substantial enduring arrow is not his actual entity; rather, the arrow's whole flight is; it is the flight of the occasional arrow or the arrow-activity on this occasion. The whole flight does not "occupy a space just its own size" during any incomplete part of itself. Nor does it ever occupy an independent space, but exhibits its spatiotemporal extension on its completion.

Thus, Whitehead disagrees with Zeno's assertion that what is true of the arrow at each moment during its period of flight is true of it throughout the period. For, the arrow at any moment during the flight has not completed the flight, which is not true of the whole period of flight. In any portion of its flight, the arrow is a potential part of an incomplete flight that comes into being as a whole. Portions of the flight are potentialities with respect to the whole flight. The Whiteheadian epoch is not a simple additon of lesser epochs. Any parts of it are always incomplete with respect to the whole of which they are parts. In respect to this Whitehead quotes a passage of Kant to show his own agreement with its statement that there are no parts of time but only whole times:

> 'This peculiar property of quantities that no part of them is the smallest possible part (no part indivisible) is called continuity. Time and space are quanta continua, because there is no part of them that is not enclosed between limits (points and moments), *no part that is not itself again a space or a time. Space consists of spaces only, time of times. . . .* Mere places or parts that might be given before space or time, could never be compounded into space or time.'[146]

A scientific materialist interpretation of Whitehead might read this passage thus: "Larger spaces consist of smaller spaces only, longer times of shorter times. There is no part of a space or a time that is not itself a whole space or a whole time." This interpretation exposes Whiteheadian time to Zeno's attack: "For Zeno would object that a vicious infinite regress is involved."[147] Therefore, the passage ought rather to be read, in line with Whitehead's intentions for his metaphysics, thus: "Space itself consists of whole spaces only, time itself of whole times. There is no part of space itself or of time itself that is not a whole space or whole time." It is this reading of the passage from Kant that enables Whitehead to agree with it. "I am in complete agreement with the second extract if 'time and space' is the extensive continuum. . . ."[148]

Thus, any epoch of any spatiotemporal extension whatsoever is divisible into spatiotemporal parts retrospectively; but none is actually divided. It is the very nature of spatiotemporal extension that it is divisible into parts.

> By extension I mean that quality in virtue of which one event may be part of another or two events may have a common part. Nature is a continuum of events so that any two events are both parts of some larger event.[149]

Then extension is the ability to have a part and be a part. But the parts are not themselves whole epochal occasions, though they are aspects of antecedent occasions. Extension comes into being continuous and hence divisible into parts but does not come into being continuously or part by part, since it is the ability to have a part and be a part. Qualities and abilities do not come into being part by part although the occasions in which they inhere are divisible into parts and become parts. The fact that epochal occasions with their epochal time do not come into being part by part is well expressed in concrete terms this way: "No one thinks that part of a stone is at one time and another part of the stone is at another time."[150]

Because for Whitehead all times are whole times, the ability to have a part and be a part comes of the relationships among wholes. A whole epoch comes into being; it is succeeded by another whole epoch which comes into being prehending it in some part. The prehended and objectified part of the former epoch is now part of the latter, revealing the former's potential divisibility into parts. The ability to have a part and be a part is the ability to have a part and be a part of other wholes; only wholes become parts of one another. But the parts that antecedent wholes become are not realized until the succeeding whole is an actuality; then the antecedent wholes, each in part, are the constituents and actual world of their successor.

*Whitehead misinterpreted.* If the foregoing sections have validity, then it can be said unequivocally that the phases of concrescence are not themselves successive actual occasions, acts of becoming occurring in temporal order one after another. It may also be said unequivocally that Whitehead intends the division into phases of concrescence, genetic division, to be an intellectual analysis of occasions; not thereby pointless and spurious, but a way of ascertaining the different factors of causal efficacy that brought particular occasions into being. The merit of Whitehead's analysis in particular is that it discriminates effects of final causation as well as those of efficient causes. Whitehead takes pains to show how even occasions on the subatomic scale, where his theory of bipolar occasions is least likely to be applicable, can be interpreted by means of his analysis as entertaining conceptual feelings and showing signs of final causation. Whitehead's analysis, as laid out in his Theory of Prehensions, applies to occasions of any degree of complexity and not only to occasions of human life. No occasion is so brief or so witless that it has no phases of concrescence and no final causation.

However, there are interpretations of Whiteheadian time that treat the phases of concrescence as actual occasions and epochs in themselves. Then an actual occasion is itself an infinite succession of actual occasions; an epoch is an infinite succession of epochs. The phases are occasions and epochs which in turn necessarily have phases which are occasions which in turn have phases which are occasions, and so on. This circular reasoning has been suggested, for example, by John W. Lango:

But I contend that the succession of actual entities and the succession of phases of prehensions are both successions of becomings. . . . In short, both prehensions and finite actual entities (as completed unities of feeling) are 'atomic' acts of becoming. . . . The succession of phases of prehensions in the concrescence of an actual entity is such that each phase in the succession is either 'earlier' or 'later' than each other phase.[151]

Then Lango is saying that the phases of concrescence are earlier and later acts of becoming corresponding to the earlier and later actual occasions which became. But we have seen that Whitehead says that there is no such correspondence, that earlier and later phases are not earlier and later in the same sense (in the sense of time) as actual occasions are earlier and later. Whitehead says unequivocally that the phases of concrescence are not spatiotemporally extended as are the actual occasions.

And Lewis S. Ford expresses the same opinion as Lango: "My position is that genetic phases are earlier and later than one another in exactly the same sense that successive occasions are earlier and later."[152] The phases of concrescence are regularly interpreted as literally earlier and later just as Ford has done. This is the same as to treat them as actual occasions in themselves since it is only actual occasions that are in temporal sequences. And in so doing, becoming is eliminated. No occasion can become since it is stymied by an infinity of becomings preceding it.

Reiner Wiehl also divides an occasion into actual temporal halves: "Insofar as its differentiation from its own actual world first *arises* in the course of its becoming, its coming to be 'itself' as distinct from the other is obviously later than its being and becoming in the other and out of the other."[153] However, we have seen that for Whitehead the actual world does not precede the actual occasion, but becomes the occasion's world as the occasion becomes. There are not even antecedents of an occasion that has not yet become; and how antecedents-to-be will constitute a subject in process is no actuality before the subject. For Wiehl, the actual world becomes, then the self becomes. Thus, the self becomes after its own content. The self becomes something other than and later than the very actual world constituting it. Then there are two becomings, the actual world and the self are successive actual occasions. In this case, the actual world does not become a self by virtue of its togetherness, and the self does not become anything by virtue of the togetherness of its component actual world: they are two different things, each a becoming by itself. Whitehead's actual occasion which is one act of becoming has been eliminated. We have seen Whitehead deny that an act of becoming is divisible into component acts of becoming. Whitehead has this to say about the status of a phase of concrescence:

> If we recur therefore to the several kinds of 'proper' entities, and ask how to classify an incomplete phase, we find that it has the unity of a proposition. In abstraction from the creative urge by which each such phase is merely an incident in a process, this phase is merely a proposition about its component feelings and their ultimate superject.[154]

Thus, a phase has the unity of a proposition, not the unity of an actual occasion or act of becoming. And a phase is described as incomplete with respect to an occasion, not a complete occasion in itself.

Such interpretations of Whiteheadian time as these show no attempt to explain why Whitehead could have thought to introduce phases of concrescence into his philosophy at all. If the phases are indeed acts of becoming, then why have they been added as an additional conception, and why called "phases of concrescence" rather than actual occasions? Such interpretations make of phases an unnecessary appendage to an already overburdened vocabulary. There is no way, given such interpretations, to justify the need for phases at all; which leaves Whitehead's genetic analysis spurious and meaningless.

Any interpretation of phases of concrescence as corresponding to or equivalent to, successive actual occasions is far afield from Whitehead's intention. Whitehead criticizes the view that becoming is only a sequence or addition of occasions or acts of becoming not only as infinite regress but also as crude addition *simpliciter,* against which his theories of prehension, of causal efficacy, of objectification, and of time are directed. Objections to such interpretations have already been put forward; a few are repeated at this juncture because of the obscurity of this entire issue, owing to Whitehead's paradoxical language when referring to (successive) phases of concrescence. The following points summarize the main objections raised in this book.

First, an interpretation of phases as temporally successive may be seen as an influence of scientific materialism. It shows the tendency to reintroduce absolute time into the Whiteheadian cosmology by treating the actual occasion as a miniature Newtonian universe wherein time necessarily passes, time is always flowing uniformly as a unique succession of instants. The phases, being occasions with phases within them *ad infinitum,* are thereby taken for the infinitely fast succession of Newtonian instants. The occasion unfolds in time by way of a succession of phases just as the Newtonian universe advances through a succession of instantaneous spaces. Nor can we pretend that the phases are acts of becoming that do not themselves have phases since Whiteheadian acts of becoming are genetically analyzable into concrescent phases. Conceiving an occasion as a sequence of phases within phases within phases, then, is an attempt to preserve the instantaneously unfolding spacetime of materialism.

Secondly, such interpretations abolish the process of concrescence altogether. For, if an occasion's phases are themselves occasions, then an occasion is a linear succession of occasions, i.e., an enduring object which is a society. And if occasions are only societies and not also occasions in themselves, they are not processes of concrescence; they neither prehend nor become in a time-span that is not itself in transition. The process of concrescence and its phases, the actual occasion as an act of becoming for the duration of a non-temporal epoch, is then meaningless, mere words. The conception of the actual occasion is then identical with that of a society; then the distinction between occasion and society breaks down and all of Whitehead's work on the interior development of an occasion is pointless. If occasions are no more than societies, then the process of concrescence has been eliminated and with its elimination societies also have been eliminated since there can be no society of occasions if no occasion has come into being. Abolish the process of concrescence by treating its phases as occasions, therefore, and abolish the entire metaphysics.

Thirdly, such interpretations reify the physical and mental poles of occasions. The physical and conceptual prehensions are treated as independent substances which succeed each other as do actual occasions. The physical phase is treated as physical actuality and substance, independently existing, temporally preceding the conceptual phase, another independently existing actuality and substance. In spite of Whitehead's efforts to portray an integral bipolar occasion, a dualism of matter and mind is the reality for interpretations for which phases are actual occasions. For the basic phases are those of physical prehension, conceptual prehension, and satisfaction: if these are occasions, then Whitehead's theory of prehensions and their concrescence into bipolar occasions—being a protest against the bifurcation of nature required by dualism—has been to no avail.

Such interpretations, fourthly, belong to the materialist insistence on the explusion of potentiality from reality. They require that even the phases of concrescence be actualities so that the actual occasions are always and completely actual. For materialism, all that exists must be already actual and transpiring in ever-actual absolute time, or nothing at all; potentiality has no real existence; there is only actuality and nothing. This expulsion of potentiality from reality eliminates the process of concrescence which is the process of real potentialities of antecedents becoming an actuality. With the expulsion of potentiality, epochal time is also eliminated since an epoch in process is a potentiality for time; and prehension is eliminated too since prehensions in themselves are not actualities but potentialities for the actualities. Becoming and process have no place in scientific materialism.

And in the fifth place, such interpretations make a paradox of Whiteheadian time. The phases of concrescence are treated as occasions which must in turn have phases, *ad infinitum*. An occasion can never come into being since an infinite number of occasions must come into being beforehand. The phases of concrescence are Whitehead's way of analyzing an act of becoming. But if the phases are themselves acts of becoming, acts of becoming are impossible: each act is but other acts and each depends upon the conclusion of the others before it can begin. Therefore no act can begin, and Whitehead's act of becoming has been eliminated by infinite regress.

Sixth, interpretations which virtually eliminate phases of concrescence and supplant them with successive occasions, infinitely regressive or otherwise, cannot justify Whitehead's usages, "phases of concrescence," "epochal theory of time," "process of becoming," "atomic unity," "indivisible extensive quantum," and so on. Going by such interpretations, Whitehead's epochal occasions are quite inexplicable. The Whiteheadian vocabulary and its intentions are steadfastly ignored in the interests of interpreting Whitehead in the scientific materialist mold. Such accounts of Whitehead naturally insist that the intellectual analysis is unintelligible, and, by implication, the entire metaphysics that uses it. At the same time, no alternative cosmology that takes account of final causation, real potentiality, process, relativity, immanence, and becoming and perishing quanta is offered. Whitehead's conceptions are generally interpreted as either materialist or unintelligible. And no wonder no alternative cosmology is offered; efficient causation, instantaneous actuality, motion, and absolute spacetime are not considered to need any alternative since they are generally considered to be the matter of fact. Scientific materialism does not call for any alternative to itself.

Whitehead's theory of time is obscure and difficult as it is without the interference of materialism and the substitution of absolute time. But such are the impositions Whitehead is heir to. His epochal time is regularly eliminated not only by infinite regress, crude addition *simpliciter,* its substitution by absolute time, but by sheer confusion. The phases of concrescence are taken to be both successive and co-present. William W. Hammerschmidt writes: "For if time is created in lumps, then different sections of a lump are both (a) simultaneous and (b) before and after each other."[155] Meaningfulness as well as time are eliminated with earlier and later simultaneous sections with respect to the same occasion. But we have seen that there are no parts of Whiteheadian time. Whiteheadian time seems to engender only confusion in its students.

For William A. Christian, earlier and later phases are essentially inexplicable. His claim is that Whitehead has resorted to an unexplained notion of priority:

> The internal process of concrescence is a succession of 'phases. . . .'
> Here we encounter a notion that is not easy to understand or explain. One phase must be in some way prior to another. What sort of priority is this? Negatively, this genetic priority must be distinguished from other sorts of priority. (i) We are not to think of it as priority in physical time. . . . (ii) Since the concrescence is a creative process in which decision occurs, it would seem that genetic priority is not the logical priority of a premise to a conclusion. (iii) For a similar reason the relation of one phase to another cannot be construed as a whole-part relation. . . . (iv) . . . It seems risky to construe concrescence as a dialectical process in Hegel's sense. . . .
> So it seems that though genetic priority may have analogies with other sorts of priority we must accept it as something of its own kind.[156]

Christian has taken the succession of phases at face value, as a literal succession wherein phases are literally past and future with respect to one another. But he is reluctant to call this succession time, transition, or temporal order because Whitehead forbids it: "We are not to think of it as priority in physical time." Whitehead denies that the passage from phase to phase is temporal. So naturally Christian says that it is something else, a priority "of its own kind." He says this while accepting that there is in fact a literal succession of phases. Then there is a succession of phases that is not temporal: a succession that we are not to believe is a succession. Then there is a succession that may not be called a succession; phases that are literally earlier and later are nevertheless not temporal. Whiteheadian time has been eliminated in confusion.

If anyone has misjudged Whiteheadian time it is Vere C. Chappell. His allegation following is utterly unfounded:

> If my claims are just, the epochal theory of time or becoming is both untenable and unnecessary; there is no sense to the doctrine that the process of concrescence or act of becoming that constitutes an actual occasion is temporally nonextensive, and no reason to hold such a

doctrine. But this result, far from striking at the heart of Whitehead's philosophical position, only cuts off a minor appendage, an appendage which has no function other than that of protecting Whitehead's system from the—supposed—upshot of Zeno's argument, and which has no ground in or connection with any other element in the system.[157]

This passage demonstrates that Chappell is not only unacquainted with the actual entity but with the rudiments of modern physics. Epochal time is required by quantum physics as well as an out from Zeno's Paradox. Chappell says that Whitehead has no reason to hold such a theory of time, but Whitehead, and obviously not Chappell, made a study of modern physics. And Chappell's saying that epochal time does not "strike at the heart of Whitehead's philosophical position" shows that Chappell is unaware of Whitehead's philosophical position and what its heart might be. Such are the abuses of Whiteheadian time.

I have been urging that the phases of concrescence are not successive; that there can be no causal and temporal relationship between phases since they are not themselves occasions or actualities but are the distinguishable physical and mental factors of prehensions and their integrations; they are the physical and conceptual features involved in the interplay of prehensions. The data of physical prehension is no cause but for its counterpart from conceptual prehension; a subject is no effect but for the transformation of causes. Cause and effect, physical action and mental reaction are not independent occurrences, separate entities occurring one earlier and one later. I urge, therefore, that the temporal designations of phases are misnomers. Whitehead calls the phases "successive" just as he calls prehension "feeling." "Successive" suggests time, the time that is to become, just as "feeling" suggests experienced self-functioning. Not all occasions literally feel, literally experience as human beings do; similarly, phases are not literally successive.


CONCLUSION

Three important principles of quantum theory have been adopted by Whitehead and applied universally to all actualities: discontinuity, indeterminacy, and indivisibility. David Bohm states that it is just these three principle conceptions that distinguish quantum theory from classical physical theory:

(1) Replacement of the notion of continuous trajectory by that of indivisible transitions. (2) Replacement of the concept of complete determinism by that of causality as a statistical trend. (3) Replacement

of the assumption that the world can be analyzed correctly into distinct parts, each having a fixed 'intrinsic' nature (for instance, wave or particle), by the idea that the world is an indivisible whole in which parts appear as abstractions or approximations, valid only in the classical limit.[158]

The salient ideas of quantum theory are not scientific materialist. No microphysical entity, whether a quantum, electromagnetic occasion, or pion is a substantial Newtonian bit of matter enduring numerically one. Gerald Feinberg, discussing particle physics, speaks of the difference between the modern and the ancient conceptions of elementary particles in the following passage. His idea that particles are transitory while energy is constant is a direct equation with Whitehead's perishing occasions and constant creativity.

> Physicists, however, can provide some help to philosophy by explaining what these particles are not. It is clear from what I have said that they are not the immutable atoms of Democritus, since neither their number nor kind remains fixed with time. The only things that do remain constant in the transformations that the particles undergo are certain quantitative properties that the particles carry, such as charge, energy, and momentum. It is as if these properties were the reality, while the particles are just transitory manifestations of them.[159]

This chapter has been the attempt to show that Whitehead's actual occasion is indeed indebted to quantum theory, as Whitehead has himself indicated. I intended to show that the actual occasion has important quantum characteristics without itself having to be exclusively a quantum or photon. Although all occasions are not microphysical in scale, all share important characteristics of the quanta: they become and perish whole; none are whole at any instant; they require a process of becoming to manifest themselves; they are potentially continuous and actually discontinuous; they are potentially divisible and actually indivisible, disclosing no actual parts existing separately; their efficacy present and future is indeterminate; they become determinate by realizing a maximum value of some kind; they are a process of becoming that is not a mere addition of other whole entities; their indeterminacy in process is because of their creativity.

It is the quantum characteristics of occasions that make of them an alternative to the substances of classical philosophies and physics. Where substances endure numerically one through absolute time, propelled by external forces through absolute space, actual occasions become an actuality and spatiotemporal epoch by way of an indeterminate and indivisible creative process and perish many potentialities for other processes. Scientific materialism, with its basis in substantialism and dualism, has not survived quantum physics although it lingers on in common sense. Modern physics has changed our basic conception of material existence. Organism, incorporating the quantum characteristics of matter, is equipped to replace materialism with its substantialist conception of matter. Organism applies to all concrete existence just as did substantialism. Materialism or substantialism is now a myth, as Victor Lowe says: "Independent existence is a myth, whether you ascribe it to God or to a particle of matter in Newtonian physics, to persons, to nations, to things, or to meanings."[160] Quantum physics put away independent substances and posited interdependent processes instead. The two are mutually exclusive. There is not both enduring, ever-actual substance and potential, perishable process of becoming. Similarly, there is not both an enduring absolute time and a plurality of epochal processes. In the words of G. J. Whitrow, "*Time is not itself a process in time.*"[161] Epochal time is not in absolute time. "In one sentence: *Concrete physical processes do not need any static container.*"[162]

Discontinuity, as found in quantum theory and interpreted in Whitehead's cosmology, means that actualities become and perish, their spatiotemporal extension with them, rather than moving through an absolute spacetime. Actuality jumps from occasion to occasion, neither instantaneously nor necessarily briefly. The discontinuity of actualities applies to all, of any size, time-span, quality, degree of complexity and intensity whatsoever. Two perceptions are discontinuous as are two quanta; two sleeps are discontinuous as are two lightning strokes. Actuality jumps from satisfaction to satisfaction, the process of concrescence being a state of potentiality. There is a jump because time, being relative, is defined by the two different occasions. There is no time where there is no perspective of an occasion. Time is the succession of occasions; until an occasion has succeeded it is not in succession. Temporal and causal order is the succession of occasions, and depends upon completed occasions, completely caused, participating in the succession. Time is not continuous but jumps from occasion to occasion in succession. "Hence supersession cannot be regarded as the continuous unfolding of a continuum."[163] For quantum theory and for Whitehead, matter does not endure, continuously actual; actuality is discontinuous. "Nothing in realized matter-of-fact retains complete identity with its antecedent self."[164]

The indeterminacy basic to quantum physics, formulated as Heisenberg's principle of uncertainty, is nothing that can be credited to human ineptitude.

In all probability, the indeterminacy of microphysical events is a fact about them and the human observations of them as well. Abner Shimony states the view widely accepted among quantum physicists:

> It follows that the uncertainty principle of Heisenberg, which limits the simultaneous determination of complementary quantities such as position and momentum, refers to the objective properties of the particle and not simply to human knowledge about these properties.[165]

Just as for quantum physics the physical apparatūs employed for observing microphysical events joins with them in indivisible processes, so also is the human body in conjunction with the data of its prehensions. For Whitehead, human organs of perception are similarly physical apparatūs, and like those of quantum physicists, part of the external world that has to be taken account of on the same principles as the objects under observation. ". . . the animal body is nothing more than the most intimately relevant part of the antecedent settled world."[166] Human observations, while having special features of their own due to the complex environment of human bodies, are in principle objectifications of bodily occasions. The animal body, being part of the actual world of percipient occasions, contributes to them and is partially creative of them, being among their antecedents, just as the physical apparatūs of quantum physicists is partially creative of the observed microphysical phenomena. There can be no observation of an entity that has not interacted with the apparatūs or with organs of observation.

The theory of prehensions is not meant to be a description of definite acts on the part of complete actualities in a series of definite actions culminating in a final act. Prehensions are the construction of an act of becoming, an act of causal efficacy, not acts themselves. The process of becoming takes the prehensions from indeterminate potentiality for an occasion to a determinate concrescence. "The process is the elimination of indeterminateness of feeling from the unity of one subjective experience."[167] The process of concrescence may also be viewed as "solving" the indeterminacy of potentialities. "Thus all indeterminations respecting the potentialities of the universe are definitely solved so far as concerns the satisfaction of the subject in question."[168] It is the one subject occasion that is a unity and act and not any prehension. The relationships of a subject in process to actualities of the past are as yet potentials until the subject has concresced; this is the reason actualities of the past are real potentialities with respect to a subject. Prehensions, and the data of prehensions, both physical and conceptual, are "potentialities of the universe," not actualities, occasions, or acts.

All aspects of a process of becoming are indeterminate until satisfaction, then, including the data. There is no absolute data; there is no simple occurrence just as there is no simple location. That is to say, there are no data that are not transformed by prehension, no data that are not objectified in a specific way by an individual subject. There is no simple occurrence that does not depend for what it is upon other occurrences such that it refers in itself to others, just as there is no simple location that does not refer to other locations. Until the process of their transformation is completed, data are indeterminate potentialities with respect to the subject prehending them. "Neither the indeterminate phases, nor the datum which is the primary phase of all, determine the final phase of determinate individuation."[169] The relationships among the data are likewise indeterminate with respect to the subject prehending them until its satisfaction: "In any of its antecedent stages the concrescence exhibits sheer indetermination as to the nexus between its many components."[170] All phases and factors of prehensions are through and through indeterminate because they are potential until their concrescence into one act.

Final causation is responsible for the indivisibility of actual occasions. The subjective aim shared by prehensions makes of them one occasion when the aim is attained. The occasion is a whole so that no part of it is prehendable except as an aspect of the whole. And the occasion comes into being as a whole and not part by part since its parts are aspects of the occasion as a whole and therefore presuppose the whole. Rasvihary Das states the Whiteheadian case well:

> These durations are extended and so have parts. But these parts are never realized independently. A whole duration does not become real as a result of its parts becoming real one after another. This would mean that the whole presupposed the parts. But here in fact the parts presuppose the whole. As in the case of an actual entity, constituted by several feelings, a constituent feeling is determined by the whole it is going, along with others, to constitute, so in the case of an epochal duration, its parts are what they are only as elements in that whole and are not separately and independently real.[171]

In this respect, all parts, aspects, factors, prehensions, poles, and phases of an occasion are equal and indistinguishable: all share the very same subjective aim. "Thus 'together' presupposes the notions 'creativity,' 'many,' 'one,' 'identity' and 'diversity.'"[172] Prehensions and their phases are diverse and distinguishable in some respects, as are physical nature and mentality, but they are identical in respect of sharing the one subjective aim and consequently the one actual occasion.

Actual nutritional value is an aim of a process of digestion and assimilation of food. In process, the potentiality for nutritional value is indeterminate and undivided. Only as a completed occasion is it determinate as an actual occasion of nutrition potentially divisible into nutritional parts, so much here and so much there. An edible vegetable, determinate only with respect to its own past and actual world is indeterminate in process of being digested with respect to just how much nutrition and in conjunction with which particular bodily cells it has effect. The causal efficacy of the vegetable and the cells together, which particular cells will use which particular vegetable molecules, is not accurately predeterminable. The vegetable and cells together have real potentiality for providing a body with some nutrition, depending on the state of the vegetable and that of the cells. But whether it will and how much and in what cells over what area and time period cannot be completely predetermined before the fact, though these things can be estimated. The process of digestion and assimilation has to be completed before the maximum nutritional value of the vegetable in specific cells is determinate and measurable. This example also illustrates that there is no exact beginning of an occasion and no precise end: an occasion has no exact boundaries as though it bordered on nothing. "There are always entities beyond entities, because nonentity is no boundary."[173]

The tendency to interpret Whitehead in the tradition of scientific materialism obscures his considerable contribution to cosmology. It obscures even the fact that his work is cosmology. Materialism obscures even modern physics, interpreting it in terms of absolute spacetime and substance. This chapter has attempted to show how erroneous is Dorothy Emmet's remark: "It is clear from this chapter that Whitehead's particular view of actual occasions is in no way bound up with the Quantum Theory, which is, of course, still highly speculative and uncertain."[174]

Certainly the best interpretation of quantum theory has yet to be conceived. Nevertheless, such interpretations as can be proposed will presumably have to take account of outstanding principles of quantum theory such as have been discussed here. These principles are central to quantum mechanics; without them quantum mechanics would not be quantum mechanics. The Whiteheadian cosmology is intended to be adequate for interpreting quantum theory as it is, even the problematical quantum theory that we have at present in its general outlines. "But the general principles of physics are exactly what we should expect as a specific exemplification of the metaphysics required by the philosophy of organism."[175] Should quantum theory turn out one day to be as limited as classical physics now seems in the light of quantum physics, then Whitehead's cosmology would turn out to be just as limited as quantum theory in the light of the new physics and cosmology. A mortal wound to the physics is a mortal wound to the cosmology. "Heaven knows what seeming nonsense may not tomorrow be demonstrated truth."[176]

This chapter has attempted to show that the Whiteheadian cosmology is indeed bound up with quantum theory as far as quantum theory is known and understood by Whitehead and many a physicist. Whitehead has taken great care to see to it that his cosmology be consistent with principle tenets of quantum theory. ". . . the cosmological outlook, which is here adopted, is perfectly consistent with the demands for discontinuity which have been urged from the side of physics."[177] This is the reason Whitehead considers that he has written "An Essay in Cosmology" and not a fantasy or a poem. To claim that the cosmology is not bound up with quantum theory is simply another way of denying that Whitehead wrote cosmology at all. What is the Whiteheadian cosmology if it is not a clarification and interpretation of the foundations of modern physics, including quantum theory? The tendency among interpreters of Whitehead is to retain scientific materialism as the only possible cosmology.

The quantum characteristics of occasions make them ineligible for paradoxes of infinite regress. Neither an actual time nor an actual space nor an actual entity endure ever-actual so that they can remain the same substantial actualities while subdivided into actual divisions. This chapter has attempted to show that the phases of concrescence cannot be confused with epochs; that the process of concrescence is not a simple addition of occasions. There are no spatiotemporal parts of occasions in process. In the words of J. M. Burgers, "The term 'process' must be understood as an ultimate unit: there are no fractional processes."[178]Phases of concrescence neither are nor correspond to actual occasions, whole acts of becoming, in themselves because they depend for what they are upon the whole and completed occasion whose phases they are. Thus, we find Whitehead speaking of phases as "incomplete" with respect to the whole occasion whose phases they are. "The subject completes itself during the process of concrescence by a self-criticism of its own incomplete phases."[179] The treatment of phases as whole epochal occasions in themselves has been shown to lend itself to dualism, infinite regress, absolute time, Whiteheadian time elimination, and meaninglessness. It is to obliterate Whitehead's distinctions between epochs and phases, actuality and potentiality, becoming and succession, occasion and society. Robert Neville summarizes the views I argue for: "The early phases of concrescence are only the becoming of the concrete fact; therefore they are not anything yet, only the becoming of something. They are not real earlier than the satisfactions because they are not by themselves real."[180]

However, Whitehead and quantum physics can both agree with Zeno that there is no motion. There is the becoming of diverse epochs but no motion through them. The epochs or spatiotemporal quanta correspond to Newtonian absolute places which do not move. Spatiotemporal extension becomes with the occasion whose extension it is. There are no already actual spatiotemporal quanta which an occasion moves into. Spacetime is a potentiality that is actualized by the same creative advance that unifies the real potentialities of antecedents into whole occasions. "It is necessary to understand that space-time is nothing else than a system of pulling together assemblages into unities."[181]

Readers of Whitehead naturally suspect that they are being dealt Whiteheadian paradox with his process of concrescence. Whitehead seems to have resolved Zeno's Paradoxes by creating others of his own. Contradictions abound, as Jerome Ashmore observes:

> In Whitehead's own terms, philosophic discourse should produce self-evidence. . . . However, there are opaque spots. Some of these occur in the case of the actual entity where there is an assertion of: the unity of creativity and creature; the concurrence of divisibility and indivisibility; the pervasion of atomicity by nonatomicity; and the conversion of something indeterminate into something determinate.[182]

However, there is not the same enduring occasion that goes from one set of characteristics to a contradictory set. There is not an enduring and wholly actual occasion that is first parts, then whole; first potential, then actual; first divisible, then indivisible; first continuous, then discontinuous; first indeterminate, then determinate; first objects, then subject; first many, then one; and so on. For, in spite of our linguistic habits, there is no before until there has been an after; there is no time before time; no past until it has been succeeded. This is a consequence of the epochal theory of time. Temporal divisions of occasions can only be a retrospective judgment as to their potential divisibility.

Contradictions must apply to the same thing at the same time. The epochal nature of processes means that contradictory characteristics attributed to actual occasions can apply neither to the same occasion at the same time nor to the same occasion at different times. The contradictions apply to potentialities as opposed to actualities. They cannot apply to the same occasion at the same time since there is no such "time when" an occasion is a potentiality, for its time is but a potentiality as well. There is no such "time when" an occasion is indeterminate, for its time is indeterminate as well. The potentiality for nutrition has no actual time since the actual nutritional occasion might not become fulfilled. Epochal time means that the potentiality for an occasion and the actual occasion created cannot be compared at the same time as though both were actualities occupying the same instantaneous space. Epochal process means that occasions can come into being from one contradictory set of attributes to another, without changing. For, it is not the same enduring occasion that changes, but one that comes into being. "Now process is the way by which the universe escapes from the exclusions of inconsistency."[183]

# 6

# The Extensive Continuum of Occasions

*Wherefore, let us not speak of her that is the mother and receptacle of this generated world, which is perceptible by sight and all the senses, by the name of earth or air or fire or water, or any aggregates or constituents thereof; rather, if we describe her as a kind invisible and unshaped, all receptive, and in some most perplexing and most baffling way partaking of the intelligible, we shall describe her truly.*

Plato, *Timaeus* 51A

## INTRODUCTION

Whitehead's extensive continuum is his rendition of the spacetime, or better, timespace of relativity physics. Time for relativity physics is united with space as timespace. "The new relativity associates space and time with an intimacy not hitherto contemplated. . . ."[1] There is no time independent of space, no spatial extension that is not also temporal. Milic Capek tells us: "For we know today that there are no purely spatial distances; every concrete physical distance is *spatio-temporal*, that is, it stretches through time."[2] Terms such as "spacetime" tend to eliminate time by spatializing it when what is needed is a term such as "timespace" that temporalizes space. Space is temporal just as time is spatial: an epochal occasion is a quantum of spatiotemporal extension. Capek refers to the modern union of space and time as the "dynamization of space" as well as "timespace" to call attention to the temporality of spacetime.[3]

By Whitehead's account, the timespace of modern physics can even be traced back to Plato. Whitehead likens timespace, his extensive continuum which he calls here the "community of the world, which is the matrix of all begetting," to Plato's Receptacle (the Receptacle of the *Timaeus*). Plato's Receptacle, Whitehead's extensive continuum, and the timespace of relativity are all alike in being potentialities in process rather than concrete actualities.

> There is the one all-embracing fact which is the advancing history of the one Universe. This community of the world, which is the matrix for all begetting, and whose essence is process with retention of connectedness,—this community is what Plato terms The Receptacle. . . . The Receptacle imposes a common relationship on all that happens, but does not impose what that relationship shall be. . . . I have directed attention to Plato's doctrine of The Receptacle because, at the present moment, physical science is nearer to it than at any period since Plato's death. The space-time of modern mathematical physics, conceived in abstraction from the particular mathematical formulae which applies to the happenings in it, is almost exactly Plato's Receptacle.[4]

It can be seen that "receptacle" is not used to mean "container" in this case, though the words are ordinarily synonymous. Modern timespace is no substance and no actual occasion in itself, nor is it a container of actual occasions. The absolute spacetime of Newton was completely actual, an independent substance, an actual occasion. "Descartes, with Newton, assumes that the extensive continuum is actual in the full sense of being an actual entity."[5] But modern timespace is neither an actuality of any kind nor an actual container of actualities. ". . . space-time cannot in reality be considered as a self-subsistent entity."[6] Rather, it is potentiality. "Newton in his description of space and time has confused what is 'real' potentiality with what is actual fact."[7] Nor can it be conceived as an eternal object or eternal objects; timespace is devoid of all forms: "Thus, as Plato declares, space-time in itself is bare of all forms."[8]

Timespace is represented in Whitehead's metaphysics as the extensive continuum, then, no entity and no eternal object in itself but the spatio-temporal potentiality of all entities. Physics itself does not provide its own interpretation. As G. J. Whitrow observes, "The theory of relativity does not provide a complete account of the role of time, even in physics."[9] Whitehead is concerned to elaborate the meaning of timespace and not merely echo its use in theoretical physics.

> Time and Space are among the fundamental physical facts yielded by our knowledge of the external world. We cannot rest content with any theory of them which simply takes mathematical equations involving four variables and interprets three as space and one as a measure of

time, merely on the ground that some physical law is thereby expressed. This is not an interpretation of what we *mean* by space and time.[10]

This chapter, through a discussion of the extensive continuum, attempts to explain what Whitehead means by timespace and in what it is relativistic such that it is adequate for interpreting the timespace of relativity physics. According to Robert M. Palter, "The continuum of events is so vague that nothing very definite can be said about it."[11] This chapter is an attempt to do some justice to Whitehead's timespace—a subject on which Whitehead had original ideas, as Victor Lowe notes:

> Each concrescence is an indivisible creative act; and so the temporal advance of the universe is not continuous, but discrete. But in retrospect and as a potentiality for the future, the physical side (though not the mental) of each atom of process is infinitely divisible. The theory of this divisibility is the theory of space-time—a subject on which Whitehead was expert, original, and involved.[12]

This chapter proposes some explication of Whiteheadian timespace consistent with other Whiteheadian principles and intentions already advanced in this book.

## CONTINUITY

*The physical field.* An electronic occasion is one paradigm actual occasion. In the following passage Whitehead speaks of the relationship between the electron and the electromagnetic field.

> But energy is merely the name for the quantitative aspect of a structure of happenings; in short, it depends on the notion of the functioning of an organism. . . . Accordingly, in the language of physics, the aspects of a primate are merely its contributions to the electromagnetic field. This is in fact exactly what we know of electrons and protons. An electron for us is merely the pattern of its aspects in its environment, so far as those aspects are relevant to the electromagnetic field.[13]

Here Whitehead does not refer to electrons and protons as "subatomic particles." Instead he calls them "primates," probably to avoid the particle-wave duality that appears at the subatomic level. Subatomic occasions behave as particles or as waves and Whitehead probably wanted to avoid suggesting that they could only be particles. "In physics, such transmission can be conceived as corpuscular or undulatory, according to the special importance or particular features in the instance considered."[14] As a "primate" the subatomic event is neither intrinsically a particle nor a wave in itself but a potentiality for either. The term "primate" is particularly well-suited to suggest organism and actual occasion rather than a particle, avoiding both the substantialism of "particle" and the particle-wave ambiguity.

The relationship of the electron to the electromagnetic field is an example of the relationship of any occasion to "the physical field." Whitehead has generalized the conceptions of particular fields of force so as to conceive of one field, "the physical field" of all occasions. This is the extensive continuum. The continuum is the timespace continuum because it has no other potentialities than those of extensive spatiotemporal connection.

> According to the philosophy of organism, the extensive space-time continuum is the fundamental aspect of the limitation laid upon abstract potentiality by the actual world. A more complete rendering of this limited, 'real' potentiality is the 'physical field.'[15]

The same relationship is explored in terms of matter and its environment:

> Matter has been identified with energy, and energy is sheer activity. . . . But in the modern concept the group of agitations which we term matter is fused into its environment. There is no possibility of a detached, self-contained local existence. The environment enters into the nature of each thing. Some elements in the nature of a complete set of agitations may remain stable as those agitations are propelled through a changing environment. But such stability is only the case in a general, average way. . . . The fundamental fact, according to the physics of the present day, is that the environment with its peculiarities seeps into the group-agitations which we term matter, and the group-agitations extend their character to the environment.[16]

Matter and energy are alike in principle, that is, in point of being describable in terms of organic relationships among actual occasions. The relationship between an electron and the electromagnetic field is the same as that between matter and its environment; and this relationship is most generally expressed as that between any actual occasion and the physical field or extensive timespace continuum.

And every environment, as it overlaps other environments, ultimately extends to all the universe, or "all that there is" as Whitehead says here:

> Accordingly, a theory of science which discards materialism must answer the question as to the character of these primary entities. There

can be only one answer on this basis. We must start with the event as the ultimate unit of natural occurrence. An event has to do with all that there is, and in particular with all other events.[17]

Then even the subatomic occasions "have to do with all that there is." Such an occasion with such an influence cannot be simple or elementary or simply-located such that it can be understood independently of other occasions. The agitations of subatomic occasions ultimately extend to all the universe. And the same is true for any actual occasion.

> For an actual entity cannot be a member of a 'common world,' except in the sense that the 'common world' is a constituent of its own constitution. It follows that every item of the universe, including all the other actual entities, is a constituent in the constitution of any one actual entity.[18]

This applies to every actual occasion, of all sizes, durations, intensities, and degrees of complexity whatsoever. Converting the same idea into terms more obviously relevant to timespace, we have: "This organism is an event holding in its essence its spatio-temporal relationships (both within itself, and beyond itself) throughout the spatio-temporal continuum."[19] What is meant by an occasion having a relationship to a timespace continuum is that it potentially has extensive connection with all other occasions. Potentially, an occasion can become a part of any other occasion.

*Simple location.* The possibility of simple location is denied by the fact of an occasion holding in its essence relationships throughout the continuum. Just as the conception of a becoming and perishing occasion replaces that of an enduring substance, so also the conception of focal regions of the timespace continuum replaces that of simple location. Whitehead defines simple location this way:

> Newtonian physics is based upon the independent individuality of each bit of matter. Each stone is conceived as fully describable apart from any reference to any other portion of matter. It might be alone in the Universe, the sole occupant of uniform space. But it would still be that stone which it is. Also the stone could be adequately described without any reference to past or future. It is to be conceived fully and adequately as wholly constituted within the present moment.
>
> This is the full Newtonian concept, which bit by bit was given away, or dissolved, by the advance of modern physics. It is the thorough-going doctrine of 'simple location' and of 'external relations'.[20]

The simply-located stone is one essentially unaffected and inefficacious, neither necessarily prehending nor prehended, a stone complete, adequate, self-subsisting, and understandable by itself. This is the crucial characteristic of simple location: something being essentially fully describable and understandable without reference to anything else, any place else, any time else. "This occupation of space is the final real fact, without reference to any other instant, or to any other piece of matter, or to any other region of space."[21]

The Whiteheadian stone, however, is one stone occasion in a society of stone occasions, the antecedent members of which contribute to (by causing) the given stone occasion, the nature of which also causes subsequent occasions, whether stoney or otherwise. The given stone occasion is not fully describable without considering its antecedents and its efficacy. For, the features of its own constitution, its structure, its mineral content, its layers, and streaks and crystals, its markings and fossils, its hardness, surface, and texture, are present effects of the past. They essentially refer to the stone's history, the route of occasions both of stone and of many other elements and compounds that have culminated as the present stone. And the stone is not fully describable without taking account of its real potentiality for effecting other occasions, not only other occasions of stone, but also occasions of perception, occasions of soil enrichment, occasions of certain uses to animals and plants, and so on. The present stone essentially refers to both antecedent and subsequent occasions, both stone and other sorts, which have acted upon it and upon which acts and which are consequently a part of its nature. A present stone that has no past and no future, no membership in a lengthy society of stone occasions that has been affected by water and air and living things is not understandable as a stone: we understand by a stone an instance of an apparently interminable enduring object, weather-beaten or earth-worn or animal-trodden or otherwise used. And a present stone that has not the real potentialities to be seen and felt—a stone without efficacy upon subsequent occasions of human perception—is not understandable as a stone. The stone's internal constitution and its real potentialities essentially refer not only to other occasions, past and future, of its more or less immediate environment, but to the remote environment as well. The entire stoney society may date back to the sedimentation of muds on the bottom of an early ocean and the antecedents of the mud go back to the origins of the planet the historical route of which extends back to the birth of the universe. And the present stone occasion will have effects on occasion after occasion extending to the end of the cosmic epoch. "Thus the physical fact at each region of space-time is a composition of what the physical entities throughout the Universe mean for that region."[22]

Simple location is an instance of the fallacy of misplaced concreteness.[23] It is an abstraction from matter and timespace that is taken to be actuality. A bit of matter, a stone, which is essentially related to all the universe such that without the universe it would not be the stone which it is, is conceived abstractly as an independent thing the past and future of which is basically irrelevant to its present existence. Whitehead tells how far removed from actual experience and observation this conception of simple location is, even though it is taken for granted that it is a direct deliverance of experience. For Whitehead, simple location, simple occurrence, absolute spacetime, and other conceptions making up the scientific materialist cosmology do not reflect experience at all, but the "world of ideas":

> I insist on the radically untidy, ill-adjusted character of the fields of actual experience from which science starts. To grasp this fundamental truth is the first step in wisdom when constructing a philosophy of science. This fact is concealed by the influence of language, molded by science, which foists on us exact concepts as though they represented the immediate deliverances of experience. The result is that we imagine that we have immediate experience of a world of perfectly defined objects implicated in perfectly defined events which, as known to us by the direct deliverance of our senses, happen at exact instants of time, in a space formed by exact points, without parts and without magnitude: the neat, trim, tidy, exact world which is the goal of scientific thought.[24]

This substitution of the world of ideas for that of actualities is reification or the fallacy of misplaced concreteness. Whitehead was not the first to recognize simple location as an instance of this fallacy. Milic Capek reminds us: "Well before Whitehead, Bergson put us on guard against the 'fallacy of simple location.'"[25]

For simply-located enduring substances, no past and no future essentially relates to them since substances endure in an absolute spacetime that is independent of them. Absolute time has only an accidental, coincidental, and external relationship to them. Whitehead objects:

> The usual opinion, or at any rate the more usual mode of expression, is that space and time are relations between the material objects implicated in events. It is difficult to understand how time can be a relation between two permanent objects.[26]

A bit of matter is essentially unrelated to its own past and future; time has nothing to do with *it* particularly. The matter itself is essentially unaffected and inefficacious since its own past and its own future are irrelevant to its nature. Whiteheadian causal efficacy, in contradistinction to the causality of scientific materialism, requires the immanence of both the past and potential future in the present occasion. Here Whitehead says that it is the conception of immanence that is absent from the doctrine of simple location and external relations:

> It must be remembered that just as the relations modify the natures of the relata, so the relata modify the nature of the relation. The relationship is not a universal. It is a concrete fact with the same concreteness as the relata. The notion of the immanence of the cause in the effect illustrates this truth.[27]

Relations among substances are superficial, accessory, and external because the substances are already enduring and self-sufficient by themselves.

For John W. Blyth, Whitehead's doctrine of internal relations is "disastrous":

> The result is disastrous. There is then a scheme of relations between relata which themselves are nothing but relations. There are plenty of relations, but there is nothing for them to relate.[28]

Indeed, there are no relata which are enduring substances between which there are relations. And there is no need in any case to relate already ever-actual substances since they are sufficient unto themselves. But Whiteheadian relata are not "nothing but relations"; they are organizations and evaluations of relations, relations mutually adjusted and fused so as to be reduced to one determinate perspective. They become a single fact by virtue of the single aim bringing them together and making with them a united decision regarding the perspective on their own derivations and on the potential future. The relations that combine as a stone have not the same perspective and consequence as those of a poem or a string bean. For Whitehead, relata are more than relations; they are "entities in themselves":

> The notion of a pattern emphasizes the relativity of existence, namely, how things are connected. But the things thus connected are entities in themselves. . . . The crux of philosophy is to retain the balance between the individuality of existence and the relativity of existence.[29]

*Focal regions.* Whitehead replaces the conceptions of simple location and external relations with that of focal regions within the extensive continuum and the internal relations of the regions. For both modern physics and Whiteheadian cosmology, "the thing itself is what it does" and what it does is act on and become a part of diverse other occasions. It becomes a creation of its environment and creates an environment for others in turn.

Modern physics has abandoned the doctrine of Simple Location. The physical things which we term stars, planets, lumps of matter, molecules, electrons, protons, quanta of energy, are each to be conceived as modifications of conditions within space-time, extending throughout its whole range. There is a focal region, which in common speech is where the thing is. But its influence streams away from it with finite velocity throughout the utmost recesses of space and time. . . . For physics, the thing itself is what it does, and what it does is this divergent stream of influence. Again the focal region cannot be separated from the external stream. It obstinately refuses to be conceived as an instantaneous fact. It is a state of agitation, only differing from the so-called external stream by its superior dominance within the focal region.[30]

Translating this statement into the terms of the metaphysics, it is to say that an occasion is both subject-superject and cannot be adequately described as only one or the other. The thing itself, the subject, cannot be adequately understood without taking into account its objective career as superject, its immortal efficacy upon a virtual infinity of others. Therefore, there cannot be a perfectly complete understanding, description, or explanation of an occasion at all, for its efficacy is immortal. Each description or understanding of an antecedent occasion is from one perspective, a perspective which the antecedent itself helped to engender thereby realizing certain of its own real potentials. And each perspective is on the part of one occasion succeeding the antecedent. There is no way to take into account absolutely all actual and possible perspectives on an antecedent occasion any more than absolutely all occasions actually or possibly to be affected by it can be taken account of. There can be no utterly complete description of an occasion that takes in all perspectives. An occasion's real potentialities are virtually infinite since the occasion has virtually an infinitude of effect beyond itself.

[The new physics] has thus swept away space and matter and has substituted the study of the internal relations within a complex state of activity. This complex state is in one sense a unity. There is the whole universe of physical action extending to the remotest star-cluster. In another sense it is divisible into parts. We can trace inter-relations within a selected group of activities, and ignore all other activities. By such an abstraction, we shall fail to explain those internal activities which are affected by changes in the external system which has been ignored. Also, in any fundamental sense, we shall fail to understand the retained activities. For these activities will depend upon a comparatively unchanging systematic environment.[31]

Here Whitehead is saying much the same thing as in the previous passage, but more abstractly. Focal regions within the timespace continuum have become internal relations within a complex state of activity. This state of activity, the continuum, is "in one sense a unity" since it is the system of all relations internal and external. For this reason, any occasion of it cannot be adequately understood without taking it all into account. The occasion depends for what it is upon its interrelationships to others, even potential others since it will contribute to their creation, relationships which in turn include others as environments extend into other environments until all the continuum of occasions relates to any one occasion. Any definition, description, understanding, or explanation necessarily selects some features and omits others so that a complete comprehension of all relationships and virtually infinite potential relationships is impossible.

Timespace and matter are different aspects of the realization of the continuum or physical field. For physics, space is regarded as having the physical properties of a field and matter is regarded as being a condensation of this field. In other words, matter does not occupy a field as it might be supposed to occupy empty space but it is a concentration of the field itself.

Modern physics sides with Descartes. It has introduced the notion of the 'physical field.' Also the latest speculations tend to remove the sharp distinction between the 'occupied' portions of the field and the 'unoccupied' portion.[32]

Thus, timespace, energy, and matter are all ways in which the physical field or continuum manifests itself. Timespace is the spatiotemporalization of the continuum and matter is its materialization. But these only exist together. The continuum temporalizes only as it materializes. "The atomization of the extensive continuum is also its temporalization; that is to say, it is the process of the becoming of actuality into what in itself is merely potential."[33] There is nothing simple about this atomization. There is nothing simple about a focal region. Each focal region is the spatial way of designating an occasion and an occasion is a system of aspects of other occasions which it has objectified—its actual world. There is no such thing as one occasion occupying one space at one time. Rather, any region whatsoever is a spatiotemporal location of multitudes. "Again, with the denial of simple location we must admit that within any region of space-time the innumerable multitude of these physical things are in a sense superposed."[34]

*Extension.* Timespace is unbounded and infinitely divisible. "The notion of a 'continuum' involves both the property of indefinite divisibility and the property of unbounded extension."[35] This is because the continuum in itself is potentiality; it does not determine any limitations of timespace, the actual occasions do that. But even the occasions may not be actually divided, they are only potentially divisible. "These possibilities of division constitute the external world a continuum."[36] Then extensive continuity is nothing other than potential divisibility. And an occasion is not divisible potentially until it is there in actuality, having come into being.

Extension is the most general requirement that real potentialities of occasions have for others. The creation of occasions divides the extensive continuum; but since the continuum is potentiality, this division is not an actual division of an actual thing. That the continuum should be divided simply means that an occasion has come to be here rather than there, when it had the potentiality to come into being either "place."

> Extension is the most general scheme of real potentiality, providing the background for all other organic relations. The potential scheme does not determine its own atomization by actual entities. It is divisible; but its real division by actual entities depends upon more particular characteristics of the actual entities constituting the antecedent environment.[37]

Whitehead remarks that the actual entity is named "actual occasion" after its extensiveness, at the same time saying that the continuum's divisibility is not actual but potential.

> In this sense, actual entities are extensive, since they arise out of a potentiality for division, which in actual fact is not divided. . . . It is for this reason, as stated above, that the phrase 'actual occasion' is used in the place of 'actual entity.'[38]

The continuum remains continuous, then, even though it is atomized by actual occasions, since these very occasions are the real potentialities for other atomic occasions. ". . . the plenum is continuous in respect to the potentiality from which it arises, but each actual entity is atomic."[39] The entire plenum of actual atomic occasions is continuous by virtue of the infinite divisibility of the antecedent occasions whose real potentialities compose the present discontinuous occasions. The extension of an occasion gives it a capacity for division into parts, although it is not actually in parts nor can it be. These potential parts are aspects of other whole occasions. An occasion's continuity with itself means that there is no space or time in between its parts where and when the occasion is not; there is no border when one part ends and another begins because this would be a break in the occasion, a fractional process. The discontinuity of a whole occasion with respect to another whole occasion means that there is something else, and not itself, between itself and the other whole occasion. But discontinuous occasions are subsequently united in the continuity of a successor to them. The extensive continuum is the fact that all actual occasions have the potentiality for being together one continuous occasion; all have the potentiality for being parts of one extended spatiotemporal occasion. Although all occasions are not in fact together as parts of one occasion at one place and time, they have the potentiality to be.

Extension is the fact that subjects inevitably are composed of objects as their parts and themselves become objects in other subjects. "Extension, apart from its spatialization and temporalization, is that general scheme of relationships providing the capacity that many objects can be welded into the real unity of one experience."[40] The relationships among objects providing this capacity for their unity are very general: "An extensive continuum is a complex of entities united by the various allied relationships of whole to part, and of overlapping so as to possess common parts, and of contact, and of other relationships derived from these primary relationships."[41] Then the extensive continuum is the general requirement made by all real potentials of all occasions that occasions to come shall be divisible into parts and contact and overlap one another. This is extension apart from its spatiotemporal realization, since the continuum in itself is potentiality. Quanta or epochs of timespace are realized with the realization of extended epochal occasions. "The extensiveness of space is really the spatialization of extension; and the extensiveness of time is really the temporalization of extension."[42]

The timespace continuum, then, is not broken by the discontinuous occasions. Rather, these actualize the spatiotemporality that is the potentiality of the continuum. Timespace everywhere and everywhen on every scale is potentially continuous although in fact it is a plenum of discrete epochs. The actual timespace of all photons is discrete; so also is that of all stone occasions. The timespace of all atoms is discontinuous; so also is that of all cabbages. All ice ages, all bones, all states of consciousness, all meals, all sounds, all hands, all cities are discontinuous just as are the microphysical quanta. Yet all are potentially continuous. Any two occasions have a potentiality such that together they can create a new occasion of some sort, however trivial, relevant to their mutual aim and real potentiality with respect to one another. The pre-established harmony provides that all occasions have such a capacity for togetherness with all others. The discontinuous actualities are nothing static but join together to make other actualities, superseding and superposing the old. In this way, the discontinuity of epochs and the continuity of the timespace continuum need not be viewed as contradictory.

*No continuity of becoming.* The spatiotemporalization of the extensive continuum as atomic occasions, then, is not realized continuously. For it is not like the continuously unfolding instantaneous space of classical physics. Spatiotemporal extension and continuity, that is, the capacity for division into regions and periods, does not come into being continuously or part by part and period by period, but is realized with the occasions which come into being divisible into parts and periods.

> But if we admit that 'something becomes,' it is easy, by employing Zeno's method, to prove that there is no continuity of becoming. There is a becoming of continuity, but no continuity of becoming. The actual occasions are the creatures which become, and they constitute a continuously extensive world. In other words, extensiveness becomes, but 'becoming' is not itself extensive.[43]

Epochal occasions come into being neither piece by piece, region by region, nor period by period. Their internal relations are an intimate togetherness of potentials evaluated for participation in one occasion, not simply a stack of unrelated parts. Nor is there any such thing as the timespace of any one occasion and one only; such a conception is a return to simple location. Timespace systems are successions of occasions. Whiteheadian timespace may be conceived of as a continuum of shifting focal regions superseding one another, each one of which relates essentially to all the others of the continuum. "Thus realisation proceeds *via* a succession of epochal durations; and the continuous transition, i.e., the organic deformation, is within the duration which is already given."[44] The becoming of an occasion is only potentially spatiotemporal; with its satisfaction the potential of its relationships with other occasions becomes a definite fact which is expressed in part by its extensive connection with other occasions, in part by the eternal objects it exhibits.

The point is, since becoming is not in time, the physical time of Whiteheadian philosophy makes its appearance with retrospective analysis. This does not mean physical time is an illusion any more than divisibility, however potential, however retrospective, is illusory. Spatiotemporal extension characterizes only occasions that have been actualized so that there is no possibility of physical time before actualization. "Physical time expresses the reflection of genetic divisibility into coordinate divisibility."[45] Genetic analysis reveals phases of concrescence, but coordinate analysis reveals physical time. And analysis of an occasion is not possible until the occasion has become an actuality to be analyzed.

The following passage may help to make this conception more understandable. It explains the retrospective appearance of physical time as "potential supersession" that comes of the divisibility that the completed occasion affords.

> The epochs in the past are what they have been. But if we abstract from the realized self-enjoyment which is the individual residuum of each epochal occasion, that occasion, considered with the abstractions of physics, might have been sub-divided into epochal occasions which together complete that one occasion. This is the potential supersession internal to each actual occasion. Thus there is no continuity of becoming, but there is a becoming of continuity.[46]

Thus the conception of continuous time, the continuous unfolding of a continuum, is an abstraction from the completed occasions' divisibility into innumerable lesser temporal durations. The Whiteheadian transition of occasions is not physical time nor is it in physical time in the sense of being or being in a continuous becoming. Whiteheadian time is the transitions of antecedents into the becoming of their potential successors. Transition is from actuality to potentiality; becoming is from potentiality to actuality. Neither are instantaneous or continuous: they are not even temporal if time is to be conceived as absolute time or if only one occasion is considered. Transition is not the same thing as physical time, just as a succession of occasions is not the same thing as the phases of concrescence. Physical time is the temporal continuity that a completed occasion has from the retrospective perspective of another occasion succeeding it. Transition is the perishing of an occasion into real potentialities for other occasions, potentialities which as yet have no actual temporal significance until occasions in process have concresced by means of them.

Successions of some occasions will be within others, but they should not be identified with phases of concrescence. Nor is a succession physical time which is the indefinite temporal divisibility that an occasion is capable of presenting on analysis. The Whiteheadian account is, then, that we do not experience physical time, but transition and becoming. Our experience is of a transition of other occasions effecting our present being, a present which reveals upon examination the other occasions to be supersessions of antecedents, that is, it reveals the other occasions to be our past. Transition or passage is not experienced in temporal order or as continuous time but as present becoming: it is retrospection that sees the efficacious occasions as past and that discriminates the temporal order of successions of past occasions.

*Undivided actualization.* Whiteheadian time requires a plurality of occasions becoming and perishing in succession. This is the case for relativistic time as opposed to absolute time. J. M. Burgers points out that: "The notions of a 'definite instant of time' and of an 'interval of time' lack real content when one deals only with a single event. They cannot even be made precise when one deals with a few events."[47] This means that there is no "time when" a single occasion actualizes. The process of concrescence is from the potentialities for an occasion through its actualization. The process is a becoming rather than a changing. "This is a theory of monads; but it differs from Leibniz's in that his monads change. In the organic theory, they merely *become*."[48] Then there is no change from potentiality to actuality; actualization does not change the occasion. This is because actuality is not added on to the occasion or another process occurring in the midst of the occasion's process as a potentiality. The process of concrescence actualizes the occasion; this actualization is not something to be distinguished from the process, from the potential occasion in process.

There is no instantaneous plane, no fine line, no digit on the cosmic clock through which an occasion passes as it concresces. The occasion is both potential and actualizing. Concrescing, it is a potential actual occasion. Concrete, it is an actual occasion with real potentiality for future efficacy. It does not cross from present to past "in time" but jumps to its objectification in others. There is no time at which one occasion and one only is potential or actual since there is no time at all if only one occasion is considered, only the potentiality for time. Distinguishing potentiality from actuality within one occasion is again to divide it into two occasions, treating potentiality as one time period and actuality as another. An effort to make separate epochs of potentiality and actuality so that time can be considered to pass from one to the other shows that time is indeed relative and a comparison of occasions is required for there to be time. An attempt to make of potentiality and actuality a succession of two so that one occasion might be regarded as in temporal order only goes to show that more than one occasion must be considered before any temporal passage can be determined. But one occasion does not in fact make a temporal order or succession. An occasion does not pass from potentiality to actuality in time as though these were two different states or two occasions.

Nevertheless, the creation of one occasion may depend upon multitudes of others; many antecedents may be required to comprise the actual world of a given occasion. Therefore, many antecedent successions must have taken place for the given occasion to have any potentiality. Of course, the given occasion is not achieved by a mere compilation of antecedents; nevertheless, the antecedents' potentialities are required to compose the given occasion. For example, an occasion of seeing a stone depends upon multitudes upon multitudes of microphysical occasions, as well as innumerable occasions more obvious to the senses.

> Unless the physical and physiological sciences are fables, the qualitative experiences which are the sensations, such as sight, hearing, etc., are involved in an intricate flux of reactions within and without the animal body. . . . But consciousness is concentrated on the quality blue in that position. Nothing can be more simple or more abstract. And yet unless the physicist and physiologist are talking nonsense, there is a terrific tale of complex activity omitted in the abstraction.[49]

Many societies of many types of occasions of the human body and of the stone and of both their environments converge in the one occasion of seeing the stone. The antecedent occasions have perished and their real potentialities relevant to the creation of the occasion of seeing the stone "remain an element" for contribution to it. They are the field of potentiality from which the occasion may or may not be realized. Other aspects of their real potentialities may have been creative of many other occasions in the meantime; but those aspects relevant to the occasion of seeing the stone are still available as its data. In other words, the assembling of the real potentials for the creation of different occasions requires different timespace quanta depending on the occasions. That is, the potential spatiotemporal base from which an occasion is derived differs from occasion to occasion. But the assembling of potentials is part of the process of concrescence of the occasion-to-be; it is the first phase of the process. While the process is not in time, yet once the occasion has come into being its timespace quantum compares to others as shorter and longer, the duration depending in part on what antecedents were required for its creation. I am attempting to express the idea that David Bohm sets out in this passage:

. . . we do not perceive momentary sensations, to any appreciable extent. Rather, we perceive an over-all structure that is abstracted from these, a structure evidently built up over some period of time. . . . It evidently makes no sense to say that this new structure is based only on the very last clue to be received. Rather it is based on the whole set of clues. This means that a given stimulus to our perceptions is not restricted to the smallest time interval that can be discriminated. Rather, it may be said that some stimuli take place over much longer intervals. . . . In a similar way, the structure of our perceptual process may also not be essentially related to some hypothetical series of instants, but may be based on entirely different kinds of principles involving (like the television signal) the integrations of what is received over suitable intervals of time, extending far beyond the period of the 'specious present.'[50]

*Solidarity.* Actual occasions atomize and thereby also spatiotemporalize the extensive timespace continuum, the continuum of all occasions, potential and actual, through their prehensions of one another. "Thus in itself, the extensive continuum is a scheme of real potentiality which must find exemplification in the mutual prehension of all actual entities."[51] While a completed actuality has ceased prehending, it is a field of real potentials entering into the prehensions of others. Occasions, once actualized, are again engaged in process of recreation so that discontinuous actualities are nevertheless continuous as potentialities. Herein lies the unity and solidarity of the continuum; it is the fact that all discontinuous occasions are nevertheless united in prehension of one another. It is the fact that the internal relations of occasions bind together the external world. "The extensive continuum is that general relational element in experience whereby the actual entities experienced, and that unit experience itself, are united in the solidarity of one common world."[52]

Whitehead credits the extensive continuum with the solidarity of the world even though it is but a system of potentials and no actuality itself. The world is not one solid body nor is the world's solidarity the fact that it is one actual entity. Nor is the world a disconnected collection of discontinuous wholes with an absolute spacetime subsisting between them. Actual occasions are atomizations of the continuum and as such do not thereby leave it: they are the continuum, actualized. Their atomic discontinuity does not border on nothingness, nor occupy absolute instantaneous spaces: they include, are included by, and overlap one another. And by virtue of their creativity they are again activities, real potentials, causes, actively creating further occasions. The continuum is not "a fact prior to the world," then, since it is not a fact at all in the sense of an actuality, but a fact about the relatedness and potential relatedness of all occasions. The relatedness of occasions is not prior to the world but is the world; the past does not remain past but is ever evolving into the present.

This extensive continuum expresses the solidarity of all possible standpoints throughout the whole process of the world. It is not a fact prior to the world; it is the first determination of order—that is, of real potentiality—arising out of the general character of the world.[53]

Antecedent occasions are the physical field of potentiality out of which present occasions become. This potentiality is not itself spatiotemporal but potentially so. As real potentiality, it requires that new occasions be of some spatiotemporal extension, without requiring any particular extensiveness. Henry Pierce Stapp points out the nature of a continuum: "However, the possible position of any event, before it is actualized, ranges over a continuum. Thus as regards potentiality spacetime is continuous."[54] Thus, the antecedents of new occasions in process are not even antecedent until the new occasions are a completed fact. The antecedent occasions are spatiotemporally ordered among themselves, that is, with respect to their antecedents, but with respect to new occasions in process they do not yet have determinate relationships since they are potentialities with respect to them. The becoming of new occasions transcends the actual antecedents, but not their potentialities. The extensive continuum is the field of "potential objectifications"; the objectifications of antecedent occasions have already been determined, but these too were potentialities of their antecedents.

(ii) The second metaphysical assumption is that the real potentialities relative to all standpoints are coordinated as diverse determinations of one extensive continuum. This extensive continuum is one relational complex in which all potential objectifications find their niche. It underlies the whole world, past, present, and future.[55]

This underlying the whole world, therefore, is not meant to be taken as an actual substance or substratum. The continuum is neither an actuality nor prior to the world. The world in any case is a creative advance, an evolving assemblage of occasions. "The notion of nature as an organic extensive community omits the equally essential point of view that nature is never complete. It is always passing beyond itself. This is the creative advance of nature."[56] Here again Whitehead alludes to the fact that becoming is not in time, not itself temporally extensive but transcends prior extension in potentiality (prior retrospectively speaking). A new epoch transcends the old in that it never existed before; then on being transcended itself it becomes part of the old. Creativity and the extensive continuum are not antithetical. Creativity refers to the nature of occasions that they unceasingly create new occasions; the continuum refers to the nature of occasions that they become extensive and perish with the potentiality for extensions of others.

Another way of expressing the solidarity that the continuum means for the world is to compare it with an absolute spacetime. The continuum means that there is no break in reality "where" and "when" nothing is, and no empty and absolute spacetime which real things occupy. We do not lift up a book and find nothing in its place; we do not throw a stone and leave nothing in its wake; we do not sit in a chair and thereby occupy an empty space. Each new occasion assembles aspects of others from its antecedent environment so that there is a rearrangement of the plenum without voids of nothingness. What was behind or before another has created something else; there are no holes in the timespace continuum. The conception of absolute spacetime provided that there could be empty spaces that may or may not be occupied by bodies. This is the reification of space: the spaces themselves could be of certain sizes. There could be spaces which were not the right size for certain bodies to occupy and therefore could prevent their occurrence there. Empty space was conceived as having the actuality of an object.

But the potentiality of Whitehead's continuum means, however, that anything *could* be anywhere anytime. Timespace does not prevent it. Something becomes in fact "in" one spatiotemporal region; but it could have become in any. Solidarity is not that of an inelastic container, but that of potentiality "everywhere" and "always" (though it is not itself spatial or temporal). Every occasion is potentially everywhere and anywhere—it is a potential for every becoming—since it has the real potentiality to relate to any other occasion whatsoever. There is no occasion which it is impossible to prehend, no two occasions which cannot relate in some way to one another, no occasion which is utterly inaccessible to others, unaffectable and inefficacious. An occasion in fact relates only to certain other occasions, which in turn relate to others. But potentially it relates to all.

This is the meaning of the unboundedness and indefinite divisibility of the continuum. It has no actual boundary and no actual division in it that prevents something from being "there." Objects can prevent objects from interfering with them in certain ways since they must be mutually adjusted in subjects, but not space. The objects that interfere with one another create new occasions which become new objects, realizing real potentialities in relation to one another; space had not prevented it. The continuum means that there is no time and no place where and when there is not or cannot be any occurrence. And conversely, it means that any occasion *could* be anywhere or at any time. This is the import of the timespace of modern physics as interpreted by Whiteheadian cosmology.

All occasions are connected with one another through prehensions of prehensions of prehensions and become connected with those that are to be. This connection is the extensive continuum; it is actual wherein the extension of an occasion is spatiotemporalized and potential in that it may be spatiotemporal anew anywhere anytime with a new occasion. If I do not see or smell a particular flower, someone else may. If a stone does not land in a lake, it may land on the shore. If a person does not understand now, he or she may later. The actual flower has the real potentiality to be seen and smelt and to contribute to the creation of such occasions of perception, whether mine or another's. There is no timespace in which the flower is not seen or smelt; there is no hole in the continuum of the flower and the rest of nature, no end of potentiality "where" or "when" there is not a seen or smelt flower. Nor is there an actual place where the rock did not land. And a person's present lack of understanding is not a void in timespace and not a break or end to her or his potentiality for understanding. Such non-occasions are not empty places and times at all; that is the difference between epochal time and absolute time.

*Internal and external relations.* Whitehead expresses himself on the extensive continuum, as on the phases of concrescence, paradoxically, saying that every occasion is both in one place and everywhere in the continuum, and that all the continuum is in every occasion:

> In the mere continuum there are contrary potentialities; in the actual world there are definite atomic actualities determining one coherent system of real divisions throughout the region of actuality. Every actual entity in its relationship to other actual entities is in this sense somewhere in the continuum, and arises out of the data provided by this standpoint. But in another sense it is everywhere throughout the continuum; for its constitution includes the objectifications of the actual world and thereby includes the continuum; also the potential objectifications of itself contribute to the real potentialities whose solidarity the continuum expresses. Thus the continuum is present in each actual entity, and each actual entity pervades the continuum.[57]

An occasion is everywhere in the continuum considering the entire historical route of occasions that contribute to its present state and considering its entire immortal career as a superject effecting others. It is everywhere considering that it is a finite effect of a virtual infinity of occasions preceding it, occasions which are also the products of innumerable other occasions effecting them, and considering that it becomes a cause of a virtually infinite number of successors which are also effected by innumerable other occasions. Speaking accumulatively, all effect all. If all occasions remotely, indirectly, and even negatively prehended are considered, the entire continuum of all occasions is considered. "Any local agitation shakes the whole universe. The distant effects are minute, but they are there."[58]

It is again potentiality that answers to how every occasion pervades the continuum and how the continuum is present in every occasion. An occasion in fact positively prehends only a selection of antecedent occasions and only a limited succession of occasions prehend it—although these may be nearly infinite in number over the course of the cosmic epoch. But a perished occasion is potentially prehendable by any subsequent occasion, at any time and anywhere the successor occasion be. And succeeding occasions do not exhaust the potentiality of an antecedent, for it is objectively immortal. This inexhaustible potentiality means that an occasion is prehendable to each and every occasion that becomes, at any time and place that it becomes; it is not exhausted even with virtually infinite acts of creativity. If I do not see or smell a particular flower, yet it has effect on some occasion or occasions of my existence in some other way because it is there and its real potentials and mine will create something together. Perhaps there is more pollen or hummingbirds in my environment because of the flower; perhaps it gives joy or allergy to someone I know. Similarly, if neither a stone nor a tree prehend occasions of one another in this century, yet they may in another century when both are part of one soil. A subatomic particle, atom, or molecule may be millions upon millions of years old, passing from countless subatomic, atomic, or molecular occasion to occasion in the one enduring object. Each occasion depends upon all the others for its present existence. It is not possible that there can be an isolated occasion anywhere or that there could be only one occasion in existence. Thus, every occasion affects others and depends upon others; it is for this reason that the entire continuum and every occasion permeate one another. All occasions effect all others: but not all at the same time.

In the meantime, there is no time "when" some potentialities are not realized, no place "where" an occasion has no efficacy: these are potential times and places that other actual occasions are potentially divided into. And the plenum of occasions are all interconnected so that there is no empty times or places, no voids. Also, the occasions do not make for isolated times and places such that they break the continuum. An occasion's prehensions of its actual world become the external data for subsequent occasions. The internal constitution of an occasion is a connection between external occasions. In this way, all occasions are connected. Therefore, there is nothing that remains perpetually internal or external; there is no intrinsic and permanent internality as opposed to an externality. "All origination is private. But what has been thus originated, publicly pervades the world."[59]

The conception of an independent and isolated occasion, the internal relations of which were not derived from the external world and which never became available for prehension by the external world, would indeed amount to a gap in timespace, hole in reality, break in the extensive continuum. For there would be an unknowable, inaccessible, unprehendable occasion that did not communicate to others, its timespace not extending to others. For Whiteheadian reality, however, aspects of external occasions are bound together as the internal relations of another occasion. External occasions are internalized and the internal components of an occasion are externally prehended.

[Prehensions] are also bound together beyond the limits of their peculiar subjects by the way in which the prehension in one subject becomes the objective datum for the prehension in a later subject, thus objectifying the earlier subject for the later subject. The two types of interconnection of prehensions are themselves bound together in one common scheme, the relationship of extension.

It is by means of 'extension' that the bonds between prehensions take on the dual aspect of internal relations, which are yet in a sense external relations. It is evident that if the solidarity of the physical world is to be relevant to the description of its individual actualities, it can only be by reason of the fundamental internality of the relationships in question. On the other hand, if the individual discreteness of the actualities is to have its weight, there must be an aspect in these relationships from which they can be conceived as external, that is, as bonds between divided things. The extensive scheme serves this double purpose.[60]

This "dual aspect" of the continuum brings up another point of Whiteheadian obscurity: how to distinguish internal and external relations. John W. Lango illustrates the problem: he has found it necessary to obliterate Whitehead's distinction between macroscopic and microscopic process for the sake of his understanding of Whitehead and of logic. Lango holds that the microscopic process *is* a (smaller) macroscopic process: "We may understand the relations of prehensions to one another in an actual entity on analogy with the relations of actual entities to one another in the universe."[61] And indeed Whitehead says the same thing himself: "Secondly, each actual entity is itself only describable as an organic process. It repeats in microcosm what the universe is in macrocosm."[62] It is such expressions as these that readily lead to Lango's position.

However, it must not be forgotten that an occasion is more than the aspects of antecedent occasions composing it. It is a togetherness of them, it is what makes of them a composition and whole. In fact, it is by virtue of their mutual relations together as parts of one occasion that the antecedents are a nexus. They would not be connected together as a nexus but that they are bound together within occasions. Since all relationships between occasions are made within them, what is external becomes internal and what is internal becomes external—through time, that is, through a succession of occasions. The internal relationship of one occasion to the antecedent occasions composing it becomes external as it is prehended; the external relationships between antecedent occasions become internal with respect to the occasion prehending them. Then there is no absolute difference between internal and external relations except that of perspective and time. The internal relations are "yet in a sense" external relations; it is the same internal relations that "can be conceived" as external. All occasions are not externally or internally related to the same occasion at the same time; they are potentially, but not actually. Internal and external relations are not the same thing, just as microscopic and macroscopic processes are not the same thing but two sides of process. Internal and external relations are not the same but they exchange roles so that they become the same at another time for another occasion.

There is no permanent and absolute difference between internal and external relations just as there is no ontological difference to be made between subject and object. Subjects become objects and objects subjects. A subject becomes an object alongside the very objects that compose it. Occasions internally related to one occasion are externally related when they and it are prehended as data by another occasion.

> The theory of prehension is founded upon the doctrine that there are no concrete facts which are merely public, or merely private. The distinction between publicity and privacy is a distinction of reason, and is not a distinction between mutually exclusive concrete facts.[63]

The dual aspect of the continuum, then, is no dualism of relations whereby the mutual relations of some entities are permanently and absolutely external and those of other entities are permanently and absolutely internal. Whitehead's reformation of the subjectivist principle insures against such a bifurcation of nature in his philosophy; there is no permanent collection of objects or bits of matter ontologically distinguished from subjects. The subjective experience is certain internal relations among the objects of experience and the occasion they create together. And an object is a subject having perished and been objectified by another subject. Thus, everything is subjective experience and subjectively experienced, but not at the same time or by the same occasion. Whitehead speaks of how he has reformed the subjectivist principle:

> The Cartesian subjectivism in its application to physical science became Newton's assumption of individually existent physical bodies, with merely external relationships. We diverge from Descartes by holding that what he has described as primary *attributes* of physical bodies are really the forms of internal relationships *between* actual occasions, and *within* actual occasions. Such a change of thought is the shift from materialism to organism, as the basic idea of physical science.[64]

Herein is the difference between subjectivity and relativity. Whitehead's reformation of the subjectivist principle is the principle of relativity. There is neither absolute dualism nor absolute perspectives that endure beyond the context of their origination. There is always another possible perspective. The principle of relativity means that an occasion is always a potential datum for another perspective.

With regard to an occasion of holding a stone, both stone and hand are occasions in its actual world, as well as subatomic occasions, atoms, molecules, grains, blood cells, tissue cells, bones, nerve and all the other occasions composing the stone and hand. Of course, there are many other occasions involved going beyond stone and hand as well, such as those in the brain and the rest of the human body. "For example, in touch there is a reference to the stone in contact with the hand, and a reference to the hand; but in normal, healthy, bodily operations the chain of occasions along the arm sinks into the background, almost into complete oblivion."[65] Both stone and hand and all the other antecedent occasions relevant to this occasion of holding the stone relate internally with respect to it as components of the one occasion, but externally with respect to one another. This occasion can be prehended by a successor in any way in which it is potentially divisible: as two occasions, a stone and hand, or as billions of electromagnetic or biochemical occasions. Both stone and hand are members of different enduring objects which now intersect in the one stone-holding occasion which is composed of aspects of both societies. This occasion would not be what it is but for the efficacy of both these societies. And subsequently, upon perishing, the stone-holding occasion is itself prehended as another member of these societies, another occasion of the stone's existence such that it was affected by a hand, and another occasion of the hand's existence such that it was affected by a stone. Stone and hand relate internally in the stone-holding occasion, but externally with respect to all the antecedent and subsequent occasions of their societies, occasions which are not present in actuality, being past or future, but which are very much present in potency. Then an occasion becomes externally related to those very occasions whose aspects it has internalized; it becomes a discrete entity to be prehended alongside its own antecedents. The stone-holding occasion is an additional occasion prehendable alongside the stone and hand composing it. An occasion internalizes aspects of its antecedents and is subsequently added as another member of their societies once it is also internalized by successors. Its internal relations are also external: they make a nexus of occasions.

*The categories of existence.* The extensive continuum is not listed in Whitehead's Categories of Existence. For that matter, the actual world, superjects, subjective aims, physical and mental poles, phases of concrescence, extension, epochal becoming, and God are not listed there either. The absence of the continuum from this list is not because it is potential rather than actual, for potential existences are listed there too: eternal objects and propositions. Nor does its absence mean that it does not exist or that it is ontologically inferior to those things listed. It may be that the continuum is not listed because it is an aspect of those existences already listed. For example, it may be included in the categories of Actual Entities and Prehensions.

In any case, Whitehead could have easily added the extensive continuum and other phenomena important to his philosophy to his list of existences. A. H. Johnson reports that, "In the course of discussion Whitehead was willing to acknowledge several omissions from his list of categories, namely: Continuity, Emergence, God's Primordial Nature."[66] Whitehead's Categories, and his Categories of Existence, then, are not as final and exhaustive as might be supposed. In considering that "Continuity" be added to his Categories, Whitehead may have been thinking of the extensive continuum. Nevertheless, the extensive continuum is a part of Whiteheadian theory whether or not it be listed among his Categories.

Therefore, the extensive continuum cannot be taken as baseless or spurious on the ground that it is nowhere listed in or among Whitehead's

Categories. Similarly, it cannot be "ruled out" of existence on the ground that it is not itself an actual entity, in the way that William A. Christian has "ruled out" creativity in this parenthetical remark: "(Incidentally, the [ontological] principle clearly rules out creativity as an ontological ground. It calls for actual entities, and creativity is not an actual entity, nor indeed an entity of any other systematic kind.)"[67] Christian is speaking of creativity, but the same reasoning would "rule out" the extensive continuum, prehensions, eternal objects, subjective aims, subjective forms, and so on, if the reader of Whitehead does not take care to investigate what an actual entity is or what the ontological principle says. Everett W. Hall claims that the ontological principle rules out eternal objects: "The 'ontological principle,' at least in one of its meanings, is an unequivocal expression of the view that eternal objects, taken by themselves, are nothing."[68] In the same way that the ontological principle apparently rules out creativity and eternal objects, it could apparently rule out the extensive continuum.

However, the ontological principle does not say that everything is an actual entity; it says that everything that there is has its cause (or reason) in actual entities. If the ontological principle did say that everything that exists is an actual entity then eternal objects too would be actual entities and Whitehead would have committed his own fallacy of misplaced concreteness only too obviously. Certainly actual entities are the only concrete actual existences that there are. But their relationships exist too, and their creativity, and their characteristics or eternal objects, and their real potentiality, and their epochal becoming. The ontological principle says that all such factors of existence have their causes and reasons in the actual entities or concrete existences. The ontological principle only says that everything about an actual entity, its existing relations, powers, characters, decisions, has its cause in actual entities, either in antecedent actual entities or in itself as its own final cause. The continuum is not ruled out of existence by the ontological principle or by its absence from the Categories of Existence.


## RELATIVITY

*Subjectivity.* It is important that relativity not be misconstrued as subjectivity. "There has been a tendency to give an extreme subjectivist interpretation to this new doctrine."[69] Whiteheadian relativity subsumes both subjectivity and objectivity. How an occasion has objectified its actual world is what that occasion is subjectively; and how its actual world appears to it subjectively is one of the real potentialities of that actual world objectively. For, an occasion objectifies its world according to its own lights, making its own decisions; at the same time, it makes decisions among alternatives that are objectively there in reality. It selects among the eternal objects that are objectively exhibited in antecedent occasions those by which it subjectively feels the antecedents. Just as Whitehead's pluralistic realism is designed to be incompatible with monism, his epistemology based on the perception of causal efficacy is designed to be incompatible with subjectivity and solipsism.[70] Whiteheadian relativity is the denial of any ontological distinction between knowing subjects and objects of knowledge so that there is no basis for an ontological distinction between subjectivity and objectivity, although this is not a denial of truth, of all distinctions, or even of a distinction between subject and object.

Whiteheadian relativity and epistemology denies the Kant-Hume-Newton situation wherein time is subjective. I include Kant in the Hume-Newton situation because of his importance for time. He accepted Newtonian physics and Hume's empiricism by sense-perception alone. Given the Hume-Newton situation, Kant showed that time had been eliminated, as Capek suggests: "Kant, who was so profoundly imbued by the spirit of classical physics, did not fail to notice this timelessness of classical space."[71] Then the total Kant-Hume-Newton situation is unintelligible to Whitehead, who accepts instead the principles of modern physics and empiricism by the perception of causal efficacy.

> [Kant] adopted a subjectivist position, so that the temporal world was merely experienced. But according to his form of the subjectivist doctrine, in the *Critique of Pure Reason,* no element in the temporal world could itself be an experient. His temporal world, as in that *Critique,* was in its essence dead, phantasmal, phenomenal. Kant was a mathematical physicist, and his cosmological solution was sufficient for the abstractions to which mathematical physics is confined.[72]

That "no element in the temporal world could itself be an experient" means that our experience is not in a temporal world. The absolute time of Newton and materialism is not time but an appearance or illusion of time. ". . . orthodox philosophy can only introduce us to solitary substances, each enjoying an illusory experience."[73]

Nathaniel Lawrence's interpretation of Whiteheadian time is at one point unwittingly subjectivist because he had not attempted to reconcile the continuity and atomicity of actual occasions. Lawrence writes: "The presented atomicity of perceptual time should not be confused with the conceived atomicity of scientific time, especially since the latter also lends itself to being conceived as continuous."[74] Lawrence's unintentional subjectivity here is in his statement that time is both atomic and continuous because it can be conceived as both. Both conceptions of time are used in science: "The wave theory of the propagation of certain kinds of energy requires continuous time; quantum phenomena demand time quanta, discrete chunks of time."[75] Then by Lawrence's account time is both continuous and atomic because we can conceive it so and because we need to conceive it as both if our conceptions are to agree with scientific theory. But surely consistent interpretations that can reconcile apparent contradictions are the more adequate for science and for thought.

But Lawrence holds that time is both atomic and continuous also because it can be experienced either way. Some experiences are of an atomic time, some of continuous time. For example, Lawrence finds that perceptions are given atomically: "If we confine ourselves to the perceived, an excellent case can be made for this atomicity. . . . Perceptual time is given atomically."[76] But Lawrence finds that mental states are continuous:

> Again, suppose I endure a series of horrible experiences without mitigation; each one piles up on the other. The horror of each occasion may be rooted in relatively distinct but contiguous states of affairs, yet I surely will regard my mental condition as one of continuous horror. . . .[77]

Then time is either atomic or continuous depending on whether we are considering perceptions or mental conditions, or depending on whether we are considering quanta or waves: "Conceptual time is atomic or continuous, depending on what you abstract from."[78]

Lawrence's conception of continuous time, however, may be Newtonian. For, the Whiteheadian continuity of time is its retrospective potential divisibility. Whitehead does not admit of an actual continuous flow of time even for the shortest of durations, even for the shortest of waves. The continuity of a wave and of the time that wave theory requires is again a potentiality. To consider a wave and its time as ever-actual is to consider the wave complete at every point: the whole wave would be actualized at every point on the wave. But a wave is a changing periodic magnitude, with minimum, maximum, and zero magnitude points. Its very nature is that it is incomplete and potential at any one point, and only actualized given the full set of points. Mario Bunge tells us: "We find it handy to call psi a *wave* function and to draw pictures of wave fronts—only to point out that the 'wave' is a complex function and that its main duty is to inform us where the *particle* is likely to be found."[79] Neither a wave nor the time in which it is propagated are continuous in the sense of coinciding with a continuous absolute time or in the sense of being actual as a whole at every point, i.e., the continuous unfolding of the whole wave and whole period of time.

*The stream of experience.* However, Lawrence's example of continuous horror is exactly Whitehead's example of an angry man. While Lawrence's example is meant to illustrate a continuous, ever-actual time at least for the duration of the horror, yet the same example should be interpretable in Whiteheadian terms to illustrate Whiteheadian time, since Whitehead uses just the same kind of example himself.

> Suppose that for some period of time some circumstance of his life has aroused anger in a man. . . . The anger is continuous throughout the successive occasions of experience. This continuity of subjective form is the initial sympathy of B for A. It is the primary ground for the continuity of nature.[80]

The anger has been transferred from occasion to occasion as the subjective forms of the prehensions of successors repeat the anger of their predecessors. The successive occasions of angry experiences and Lawrence's series of horrible experiences are each a society, just as Whitehead's example of a man's knowledge of Greek was an example of a society, the succession of occasions of a man's knowing Greek. The anger or horror reenacted in the successive occasions is continuous inasmuch as the antecedent occasions, in point of their anger, are immanent in their successors. Each successor is potentially divisible into a succession of angry occasions, although the actual antecedents are gone and do not remain as actualities in the present successor. The successive occasions are continuous with respect to anger because all the angry antecedents are united in each successor in point of their real potentiality for anger.

We have seen that there is no nexus or society the antecedent members of which have not been bound together as the actual world of an actual occasion. And this is so without necessitating that each successive occasion of the society be larger than the last. For, it is only aspects of the predecessors that are bound together in the successors, not the whole predecessors (though each aspect is affected by the whole), and it is only in respect of these aspects that the predecessors are in this particular nexus. Each angry successor has incorporated the angry aspects of its predecessors; there is a stream of anger through the occasions because it is within each successive occasion. This is continuous anger. The successive angry occasions occur "in" different places and times depending on where and when the person is angered by the same general circumstance. In this way, the succession may be treated as one wave, one actual occasion spread over a spatiotemporal period and region. Whitehead speaks of the succession of angry occasions as one "period of time" just as Lawrence treats the succession of horrors as one "mental condition" of the man suffering horrible experiences. The angry society or horrible society of occasions can be prehended and transmuted as one occasion of continuous anger or horror. Similarly, an entire life-time may be treated as either a succession of occasions or one occasion. In any case, each successive occasion incorporates the entire antecedent society in potentiality, those aspects of the antecedents important to the society. The stream of experience of all the occasions of the society is within each successive occasion; yet the occasions are discontinuous and there is no continuous time or continuously streaming experience in any one occasion. Lawrence's continuous horror may be reconciled with Whitehead's epochal time; continuous horror or anger does not require us to substitute absolute time for epochal time and does not imply that time is subjective.

*Irreversible world lines.* The relativity of time does not mean that time is subjective, that time is illusory, or that causal order can be any way we like. In the words of A. S. Eddington, "The common impression that relativity turns past and future altogether topsy-turvy is quite false."[81] Again, the relativity of time does not mean that causal and temporal sequences are reversible. Milic Capek says it this way: "The succession of causally related events is preserved in *all* frames of reference."[82]

The Whiteheadian societies or historical routes of actual occasions are what are called "world lines" in physics. Such world lines or historical routes are irreversible, in spite of the relativity of time. Capek tells us: "*all causal lines* are irreversible in every system of reference. Every world line of material 'particle' is really an isotopic casual line or what Whitehead called a 'route of occasions.'"[83]

Thus, the loss of absolute simultaneity and absolute time in no way amounts to a loss of irreversible succession, or causal and temporal order. Causal sequences, world lines of particles or historical routes of occasions, are absolute passages from one occasion to another, irreversible and unalterable. "This passage of the cause into the effect is the cumulative character of time. The irreversibility of time depends on this character."[84] The absolute passages or sequences are not absolute in the sense of being predeterminable; they are absolute in the sense of being forever after irrevocable. Once an effect has taken place, it is irrevocable; and its real potentialities for future efficacy are fixed forever, for its immortal career. Potentiality is only "real" inasmuch as it is limited in a particular way. What the occasion has become and the limitations of its potential are irrevocably determined upon satisfaction. Similarly, a sequence of occasions cannot be reversed or obliterated as though it had never existed. Temporal order is causal order; therefore, a causal sequence can no more be reversed than the future can retroactively affect the past. In Capek's phraseology, "In no system of reference can an effect precede its cause. . . . The constancy of the velocity of light in all systems of reference is the reason for this impossibility."[85] The future does not precede the past anywhere.

The relativity of simultaneity cannot be interpreted as the reversal of causal sequences or the retroactive effect of the future upon the past or the interchangeability of future and past. Capek explains that the relativity of simultaneity does not interfere in the absolute, irreversible direction of the causal sequences. Relative time has this absolute feature.

> In this sense my 'now' remains absolute. It is not absolute in the classical Newtonian sense since it is confined to 'here' and does not spread instantaneously over the whole universe. Yet, it remains absolute in the sense that it is *anterior* to its own causal future in *any* frame of reference. . . . No event of my causal future can ever be contained in the causal past of any conceivably real observer. . . . In a more ordinary language, *no event which has not yet happened in my present 'here-now' system could possibly have happened in any other system.* . . . Thus the virtualities of our future history which our earthly 'now' separates from our causal past *remain potentialities to all contemporary observers in the universe.* Something which did not yet happen to us could not have happened 'elsewhere' in the universe.[86]

This is to say, if I have not yet picked up a stone, the occasion of my holding the stone is not future, or past, or present in relation to any occasion. It simply is not (yet) there at all. Similarly, if a vegetable has not yet been eaten, the hypothetical future occasion of its being eaten does not precede any occasion whatsoever. What is not there is not relative either. Only its potentiality in the present is there; *it* is not. Future occasions of my life have not happened somewhere else before they have become occasions of my life. There is no perspective and no frame of reference from which my future or any future occurs before any past and present. Future occasions are not virtualities, in Capek's terms, or actualities in Whitehead's terms. They are not past, present, or anywhere.

*Contemporaneity*. Whitehead's principle of relativity, which insures the succession of occasions in that each occasion is a potential for every becoming occasion, is taken from Einsteinian relativity which calls for the causal independence of contemporaries. ". . . contemporary events happen in *causal* independence of each other. This principle lies on the surface of the fundamental Einsteinian formula for the physical continuum."[87] This is another way of saying that relative simultaneity has replaced absolute simultaneity.

Contemporaneity is the absence of causal and temporal relationship altogether. Milic Capek tells us emphatically, "The term 'independent contemporary' is relatively the best expression we can find in our limited language for characterizing in an abbreviated fashion the relation, or rather, a *lack of relation*, between the world lines *not yet interacting*."[88] As Capek expresses it, contemporaneity is neither absolute simultaneity nor "co-instantaneity," and must not be confused with these. "The word 'contemporary,' unlike the word *co-present*, suggests less the outdated idea of classical simultaneity or *co-instantaneity*."[89] There is no absolute simultaneity across occasions of all the diverse successions in the universe. Temporal order is defined in terms of causal order; what is before and what after (retrospectively determined) is defined by what is cause and and what is effect. Contemporaneity, therefore, which is the absence of temporal order, is defined as the absence of causal order, or causal independence.

It is the definition of contemporary events that they happen in causal independence of each other. Thus two contemporary occasions are such that neither belongs to the past of the other. The two occasions are not in any direct relation to efficient causation.[90]

Thus, an occasion is never contemporary with respect to any occasion that it prehends or that prehends it. Contemporaries do not prehend and are not prehended by one another; however, they prehend occasions of the actual world of each other and both are prehended by a successor to them both. Contemporaries indirectly take account of each other through their prehension of one another's antecedents and they become related through their potentialities effecting the same succeeding occasion together so that eventually all occasions become connected to all.

The [contemporary] occasions originate from a common past and their objective immortality operates within a common future. Thus indirectly, *via* the immanence of the past and the immanence of the future, the occasions are connected. But the immediate activity of self-creation is separate and private, so far as contemporaries are concerned.

There is thus a certain indirect immanence of contemporary occasions in each other.[91]

All occasions are not related to one another at the same time but become related through succession and the intersecting of occasions of diverse successions. Contemporary occasions are those of different successions, successions which intersect at occasions after the contemporaries. It is such an occasion subsequent to the contemporaries that prehends them both as contemporary occasions.

Also, two occasions that are both contemporaries of a third occasion need not be contemporaries of one another. This is a consequence of relativity theory.

Again, according to the notions of time recently developed in modern physics, if A and B are contemporaries and P is contemporary with A, then it is not necessarily true that P is contemporary with B. It is possible that P may be earlier than B, or that it may be later than B.[92]

P and B are contemporaries of A, but not of one another. For example, two contemporary bell towers ring simultaneously at noon. These two events are contemporaries because they are both simultaneous and without any direct causal relationship to one another. A bird flying toward one tower and away from the other hears the sound of the former bells first. The bird on this occasion of hearing the former bells and not the latter is in causal relationship with the former but not the latter: the bird hearing and the former bells are contemporaries of the latter bells but not of one another. Similarly, the earth is traveling toward one star and away from another. The light from the former star has reached the earth but has not reached the other star. The two stars on this occasion are contemporaries and the earth is a contemporary of one star but not the other. For another example, ancient Troy and ancient Rome are in causal relationship. But both are contemporaries of an ancient California redwood tree spanning that thousand year period. They are contemporaries of the tree but not of one another.

*Simultaneity.* Whitehead does not speak often of simultaneity; he speaks rather of the present. The vast differences in the scale of different processes, and the vast differences in the time-spans required for their becoming makes for vast differences in what counts as simultaneous to the different perspectives. Light signals from ancient Troy and modern England are simultaneous in their effect on some distant planet because of the constancy of the speed of light; the light from England catches up with that from Troy. But the relativity of simultaneity applies to all things and not only light. Successive occasions of anger are all simultaneous with respect to the occasion that is that maddening circumstance of life. A person feeling a stone in late afternoon simultaneously feels the effects of all the occasions of the stone warming up throughout the day; successive occasions of heating stone, and cooling stone when shadows cross it, are simultaneously felt as an average heat at the end of the day.

Occasions mutually external with respect to one another are contemporary; occasions internal with respect to another occasion are simultaneous. Then occasions contemporary with respect to one another are also simultaneous with respect to an occasion prehending them both and whose internal constitution aspects of the contemporaries compose. This means that veritable simultaneity only applies to an occasion in relation to its own constituents: it applies only to an occasion in relation to itself alone. As Capek says: ". . . for each event is simultaneous with itself and only with itself."[93] The occasions contributing to a present occasion in process are past (once the occasion has been completed and succeeded), whether those past occasions are themselves contemporaries or whether some preceded others. The contributors from different lines of succession are contemporaries, but contributors from one line of succession, wherein preceding occasions compose the actual worlds of their successors, are in causal order with respect to one another. No matter the causal order or lack of it among the antecedent occasions that together constitute a present occasion: their contribution to the present occasion is simultaneously present.

The syllables of a phrase are in succession with respect to one another. But all are present together and simultaneous in the phrase, as the phrase. With respect to the phrase, neither its first syllable nor its last nor any syllable between are earlier and later parts of the phrase. No epochal occasion comes into being part by part, but is given with its parts. The parts are all simultaneous as one whole. With respect to a phrase, there is no past and future syllables that are its parts. Similarly, Troy, Rome, and England are in succession with respect to one another, but simultaneous aspects of Western civilization. It is only in point of their contributions to the internal constitution of Western civilization that Troy, Rome, and England, past and future with respect to one another, are simultaneous since the epoch of

Western civilization spans them all, ever-present along with all of its constituents.

If occasions preceding and succeeding one another are simultaneous with respect to an occasion prehending them, then how are they known to be successive at all? The succession of antecedents contributing to an occasion can be discovered by analyzing the occasion. The occasion is potentially divisible into parts contributed by the aspects of antecedents that compose it. Also, succession can be inferred by way of other occasions observing an earlier occasion in the succession. The stone that one person sees in afternoon may have been visited by a snake in morning reviving in its heat, seen and marked by another person. The fact that Troy preceded Athens was told Athenians by recitors of Homer who may have observed Troy. Survivors of World War II may tell of the succession of events and themselves and their accounts double-checked by comparison with one another. And succession can be discovered in oneself, recalling that one's life is a succession of occasions of experience, and that one day follows another.

The relativity of simultaneity is a consequence of the fact that there is more than one epochal occasion and epochs mature at different rates. It is a consequence of the fact that the potential efficacy of one occasion reaches others at different times (and places) depending on where and when the other occasions are. It must be remembered that the efficacy of an occasion in others *is* the occasion too, it is the occasion as superject. Different occasions are spatiotemporally discontinuous, spatially and temporally separate. Therefore, the same antecedent occasion will effect different subsequent occasions at different times and places—different times because different occasions concresce at different rates. There must always be a third occasion from which the simultaneity of any two occasions is determined relative to itself. Two occasions can never be simultaneous in themselves, that is, absolutely. In Capek's words, "Classical simultaneity of spatially separated events is gone and is replaced by their causal independence."[94] This is because there is no simultaneity except that occasions are present to the perspective of another occasion. Henri Bergson puts it simply:

> If one grasps simultaneity in this oblique way—and this is what relativity theory does—it is clear that simultaneity contains nothing absolute and that the same events are simultaneous or successive according to the point of view from which they are considered.[95]

*Whitehead misinterpreted.* Misinterpretations of Whiteheadian time include those presuming that Whiteheadian relativity and Whiteheadian time are entirely subjective. Martin Jordan informs us that "*truth* has no effect, in Whitehead's view, on the concrescence of an occasion."[96] Jordan's consideration of Whiteheadian time has convinced him that: "The point emerges that, apart from clocks, time is subjective."[97] On a less naive level, F. S. C. Northrop writes:

> Time as immediately sensed would seem to be capable of relating states separated only by a relatively short specious present, since by its very nature sense awareness can only disclose what is given in the present. . . . Yet time as it enters into physics relates the state of a physical system in the present to states of that system in the distant past and future so far away in time that by no stretching of the imagination can the scientific knowledge of these past and future states be said to be given by sense awareness.[98]

First of all, the presumption that "the" present is necessarily short, as short as the specious present of human visual perception for example, is incorrect. But the confusion in this view comes from the subjectivist premise which is (mistakenly) attributed to Whitehead. Northrop states the premise, agreeing that it is an error: "The error follows also from Whitehead's thesis that nature is nothing but what is disclosed in sense awareness."[99] And Northrop naturally concludes: "On Whitehead's theory there is no meaning for public time."[100] But this is not quite Whitehead's thesis and Northrop's conclusion not quite accurate. Whiteheadian nature is not quite "nothing but what is disclosed in sense awareness," without qualification.

It must be recognized that "sense-awareness" for Whitehead is primarily the perception of causal efficacy and not sense-perception (or presentational immediacy) alone. With this recognition, then nature may be regarded as "nothing but what is disclosed in the perception of causal efficacy." But even this is not quite accurate without qualification, if perception is to be taken as exclusively the privilege of human beings or the effect of sense organs. The perception of causal efficacy for Whitehead is not limited to human beings or even to animals; memory is not the only example of it.

> But animals, and even vegetables, in low forms of organism exhibit modes of behaviour directed towards self-preservation. There is every indication of a vague feeling of causal relationship with the external world, of some intensity, vaguely defined as to quality, and with some vague definition as to locality. A jellyfish advances and withdraws, and in so doing exhibits some perception of causal relationship with the

world beyond itself; a plant grows downwards to the damp earth, and upwards towards the light.[101]

If Northrop's statement be read, "Nature is nothing but what is disclosed in the experience of every creature, animate and inanimate, of causal efficacy," then perhaps it does more justice to Whitehead. Nature is that which is prehended. Read in this way the statement simply repeats Whitehead's ontological principle, interpreted as his definition of actuality: that which is causally efficacious has actuality. Neither Whiteheadian nature nor Whiteheadian time can be subjective in the sense of being limited to conscious human experience or to what perceiving human beings are aware of.

However, past and future states, their remoteness notwithstanding, may indeed be said to be given by sense-awareness inasmuch as their potentialities are immanent in the present. The actual remote past is certainly gone; but its immortal effects transmitted and transformed through generation after generation of past occasions continue with us, *as* us, as the present state of the universe including ourselves. Analyze the present state of the universe and the efficacy of the remote past will be discovered. We and the present state of the universe *are* the consequences of the past, remote, intermediate, and recent. The present condition of a star, for example, is a consequence of its past, remote and near; present starlight and sunlight are given by sense awareness without stretching the imagination. Similarly, the potential future is discoverable in our present as well. Our every anticipation, built into our bodily shape and our every action, tells of the potential future. Each step we take anticipates the earth beneath us; we do not have seeing eyes without anticipating sights in three dimensions. More remotely, people have not built civilizations without anticipating that the sun will shine tomorrow.

A subjectivist interpretation of Whitehead ignores his primary thesis of causal efficacy, that a subject is a creation of the objective world which were subjects before. Thus, the examination of subjective experience discloses an objective world that has been subjectively formed for the occasion, by the occasion. A human being *is* a creation and composition of such things as sunlight, planets, oceans, oxygen, living organisms, many generations of plants and animals, human cultures, and so on *ad infinitum*. A human being is an embodiment of all the world, remote and recent, as is every creation.

The relativity of simultaneity is easily taken to mean that past, present, and future are not only relative, but reversible or interchangeable. William W. Hammerschmidt for one has turned relative past and future topsy turvy in declaring that an occasion can be past and present and future relative to one and the same occasion: "Since an event is in all of these space-times at once, there are events at once present, past, and future to a given event."[102] Then past and future are interchangeable. But an occasion cannot be "at once" in every temporal relation with respect to the very same occasion. Rather, it is past with respect to one occasion, present with respect to another, and future with respect to another, just as Rome is past relative to England, present relative to Western civilization, and future relative to Troy.

However, no occasion is actually future relative to any occasion since no future occasion is actually in existence; what does not exist is not relative either. To speak of a future occasion is only to indicate its status as a successor to a given occasion in a succession of occasions—which means that even this future occasion has successors or occasions future relative even to it. "Futur" refers to a position among occasions already actualized, and therefore past in relation to some occasion; or else it refers to an occasion not yet in existence, a hypothetical occasion, in which case there is no relative position in any succession.


## CONCLUSION

The Whiteheadian cosmology asks that we imagine an extensive continuum that is both really existing and not actual; both the solidarity of the world and only a potentiality; both underlying the whole world and incomplete taking into account the creative advance; both everywhere and somewhere; both the continuity of prehensions and the discontinuity of atomic occasions; both potential divisibility and actual indivisibility; both the extension of occasions bound together in one occasion and the non-extension of an occasion and the real potentialities for it in process; both the external relations among discontinuous occasions prehending one another and the internal relations between an occasion and those it prehends; both the capacity for spatialization and temporalization and no requirement for any specific spatiotemporal dimension. This chapter has been the attempt to clarify this perplexing continuum in terms amenable to the metaphysics and to ordinary experience.

Modern physics, relativity theory and quantum theory, might seem to have provided philosophers with an understanding of nature as sheer chaos alleviated only by solipsism. However, this chapter and that before have attempted to show that relativity and quantum theory call for a conception of becoming and perishing occasions the causal efficacy of which, while indeterminate in process, affords a more intelligible account of causation. So far from chaos and subjectivity, the Whiteheadian cosmology envisions an evolution of more and more complex actualities, made possible by virtue of the fact that their creative processes produce both order and novelty, orderly societies of occasions identical in some respects but unique in others.

Real indeterminacy and real potentiality are not synonymous with irrationality or with physical causelessness: the creation and destruction out of nothing and into nothing. On the contrary, J. M. Burgers reports: "A consequence of this doctrine is that there is no irrationality in the universe, meaning that nowhere are there things which cannot in some way be compared, and that nowhere is there an absolute freedom or lawlessness."[103] Neither indeterminacy nor relativity oblige philosophers to adopt a purely skeptical or purely subjectivist position. Indeterminacy cannot fairly be equated with irrationality, and relativity cannot justly be identified with subjectivity. Rather, they may be more reasonably equated with creativity and potentiality. Certainly many outstanding physicists do not equate relativity and subjectivity; David Bohm for one: "Just because of the very breadth of its implications, however, the theory of relativity has tended to lead to a certain kind of confusion in which truth is identified with nothing more than that which is convenient and useful."[104] And Milic Capek devotes much of his resources to the defense of indeterminacy against the charge of irrationality: "The resistance to indeterminism of any kind is especially strengthened by the wrong assumption that *any* departure from classical determinism, no matter how slight, means the end of the possibility of *any* rational description of the world and, consequently, a suicide of reason."[105]

In fact, relativity in physics is in part a consequence of the discovery of the absolute maximum speed of light. The speed of light at its maximum is the fastest possible causal action, as Capek says: "The fastest causal action is the velocity of electromagnetic radiation."[106] This discovery that the maximum speed of light is also the maximum rate of causation meant that absolute simultaneity is impossible, that no temporal relationship exists between occasions that are not causally connected. Absolute simultaneity meant that occasions not otherwise related could nevertheless be related in time; they could concur in the same world-wide instant though they have no other relation to one another. A temporal relationship between causally unrelated occasions cannot be determined because it does not exist. Contemporaries are not themselves causally or temporally related even though they belong to timespace systems wherein they are causally and temporally related to occasions not their contemporaries. This discovery of relative simultaneity marked the end of classical physics and the beginning of modern physics wherein time has a real value. As Einstein exclaims, the classical conception of absolute simultaneity providing instantaneous causation had eliminated time:

> . . . the speed of the actions along the lines of force must be assumed as infinitely great! The force between two bodies, according to Newton's law, depends only on distance; time does not enter the picture. The force has to pass from one body to another in no time![107]

Relativity, the principle that every occasion is a potential for every becoming, requires a potentially extensive timespace continuum whereby potentialities are realizable and every occasion, once perished, is potentially prehendable everywhere and anywhere, at every rate and any rate, although it is in fact prehended some places and at some rate. Its immortal career contributes to the creation of historical routes of occasions; but historical routes could have been otherwise. An occasion is prehendable in an infinity of ways, being potentially infinitely divisible by a virtual infinity of occasions succeeding it. But because a potentially antecedent occasion is prehended and assimilated at different rates by different occasions succeeding it, "when" it becomes in fact antecedent will differ with different occasions. In the words of Elizabeth M. Kraus:

> What is at issue here is the relativity of time and of position in time, of space and of position in space, a relativity stemming from the fact that the rate of transmission of vector feeling-tone from past to present is not necessarily uniform for all types of feeling-tone, and that the 'speed' of transmission has an upper limit in our cosmic epoch (the speed of light). Every entity in a very real sense 'decides' its own time and space, is not bound to a universal scheme, decides what will be past for it—i.e., operative in its constitution.[108]

This is relativity: what is definitely antecedent with respect to one occasion is a contemporary of another and yet-to-be antecedent with respect to another. And occasions which are in succession with respect to one another are simultaneously present in another occasion. An occasion yet-to-be antecedent is not actually future with respect to any occasion, but is a real potentiality for other creations. The sun that has set on New York has yet to set on San Francisco. That antecedent sun with respect to New York is not the actual future sunset of San Francisco; but the potential for another such occasion of sun there is inherent in its nature. One person on various occasions observes snow flakes to fall in succession throughout the night;

but by morning another person observes a simultaneous mass of snow on the ground.

There is no occasion and no timespace of any occasion that is not prehendable to others and not potentially extensively connected to others. This fact is the continuum of all occasions and it means that there are no holes or gaps in reality. The continuum is the matrix of all occasions by way of their potentialities for one another with regard to occasions in process and by way of their determinate prehensions of one another with regard to concrete occasions. This chapter's thoughts on the extensive continuum are well expressed and fully developed by Elizabeth M. Kraus:

> Therefore, despite the fact that an actual occasion realizes an *extended* temporal duration, that quantum of time is indivisible. . . . The concrescence presupposes the region in the same way as any perspective on a spatial region presupposes the interlocked geometric relations of the perspective. But the region does not elicit the concrescence, which is to say that, in any given spatial extensity, not all possible perspectives must be realized. . . . To speak of *atomic* regions seems to imply, however, regions which are external and unrelated to each other, like an assemblage of monads. It is precisely this misinterpretation of Whitehead's notion of atomic which must be overcome if the logic of extensive connection is to be comprehensible. Each region *is* the totality of space-time realized for the perspective. It must be continually borne in mind that an actual entity and its actual world cannot be torn apart as subject and object. From one perspective, the actual entity *is* its actual world as having grown together. From the alternative perspective, an actual world is the spatio-temporal totum which superjects the actual entity.[109]

A concretely existing thing *is* how it has been effected by its past, and how succeeding occasions have been effected by it. It *is* both a being and experience in itself and an immortal multitude of potentialities not all realized at any one time. This is the threefold character of the actual occasion, no one feature of which adequately describes it: it is an effect of the past or efficient causes, an effect of itself in the present or final causes, and efficient causes of the future. An occasion cannot be adequately described or understood without taking into account all three of these features of its threefold character. For example, we do not know a person at all, much less adequately, without knowing something of his or her past, her or his ideals and commitments guiding her or his present action, and without knowing his or her effect on oneself and even others. Similarly, the sun is not described adequately without reference to its past and future in the sky: it is not understood as a singular occurrence of one day without a history and without effect. This is why the extensive continuum is in every occasion and why every occasion pervades the continuum.

Every occasion communicates its potentiality to all others in process, contributing to their perspectives on itself. But the perspectives nevertheless differ with each occasion since each is unique in some way as well as caused to conform to its antecedents. An antecedent occasion "remains an element" in all the successors it helps to create, and inasmuch as there is a virtual infinity of successive occasions, the antecedent occasion is immortal. The perishing of an occasion is the signification of its existence to succeeding occasions of which it is the part-creator. All the new creations are transformations of the old; present process depends upon perishing antecedents. I would like to end this book with Whitehead's own statement of what his work is all about: a perishing that is converted into immortality:

Almost all of *Process and Reality* can be read as an attempt to analyze perishing on the same level as Aristotle's analysis of becoming. The notion of the prehension of the past means that the past is an element which perishes and thereby remains an element in the state beyond, and thus is objectified. That is the whole notion. If you get a general notion of what is meant by perishing, you will have accomplished an apprehension of what you mean by memory and causality, what you mean when you feel that what we are is of infinite importance, because as we perish we are immortal. This is the one key thought around which the whole development of *Process and Reality* is woven. . . .[110]

*. . . in these matters one must speak rashly if one is to speak at all.*
A. N. Whitehead

# Notes

## INTRODUCTION

1. *IS* 240-247.
2. *MT* 61. Cf. *PR* 3: "'Coherence,' as here employed, means that the fundamental ideas, in terms of which the scheme is developed, presuppose each other so that in isolation they are meaningless."
3. Milic Capek, *PICP* 398.
4. Henri Bergson, "Remarks Concerning Relativity Theory," in *Bergson and the Evolution of Physics,* ed. by P. A. Y Gunter, p. 128.
5. *CN* 72.
6. *CN* 71. Cf. *PR* 51, 70, and 96.
7. *CN* 70.
8. *CN* 54.
9. *SMW* 93.
10. *PR* xi.
11. *SMW* 55.
12. *MT* 177.
13. *SMW* 24 and 25. Cf. *SMW* 157: "The doctrine thus cries aloud for a conception of organism as fundamental for nature." And cf. *Prel* in *WhA* 341: "I think that no one can study the evidence in its detail without becoming convinced that we are in the presence of one of the most profound reorganisations of scientific and philosophic thought."
14. *SMW* 219. Cf. *SMW* 218-219: ". . . a philosophy of nature as organic must start at the opposite end to that requisite for a materialistic philosophy." And cf. *SMW* 25, *PR* 77 and 78, and *MT* 204.
15. *SMW* 74.
16. *SMW* 25.
17. *PR* 11.
18. *PR* 13.
19. *PR* 13 and 12.

## THE ACTUAL ENTITY

1. *PR* 18.
2. *PR* 74-75. Cf. *PR* 128 and 137.
3. *PR* 22. Cf. *PR* 68-70, 166, and 167.
4. *PR* 18. Interpreters of Whitehead who regard the actual entity as necessarily and

absolutely singular and simple need to account for this puff of existence exemplifying the actual entity. A puff is evidently a bit of a plurality.

5.   *PR* 110. Cf. *PR* 7, 19, and 110 (see note 68). And cf. *PR* 77: "In the 'organic' theory, (i) there is only one type of temporal actual entity. . . ." The one genus of actual entities includes God, *PR* 75: "In the philosophy of organism, as here developed, God's existence is not generically different from that of other actual entities, except that he is 'primordial' in a sense to be gradually explained."

6.   Ivor Leclerc, *The Nature of Physical Existence*, p. 286. Cf. Robison B. James, "Is Whitehead's 'actual entity' a Contradiction in Terms?" *PS* Vol. 2, No. 2 (1972), p. 113: "Every proper entity, in order to continue to exist at all, must be suspended in onto-logically more basic droplets of still uncongealed becoming."

7.   *PR* 52 and 53.

8.   *PR* 53, 146 and 242. Cf. *PR* 113.

9.   *PR* 51. Cf. *PR* xi: "The writer who most fully anticipated the main positions of the philosophy of organism is John Locke in his *Essay,* especially in its later books." And cf. *PR* 54, 55, and 113.

10.   *PR* 52. Cf. *PR* 55 and 242.

11.   *PR* 52. Cf. 149 and 219.

12.   *PR* 56. Cf. 55 and 242.

13.   *PR* 76.

14.   *PR* 72. Whitehead agrees with common sense, or Newton's "the vulgar" on this point, *PR* 72: "The philosophy of organism is an attempt, with the minimum of critical adjustment, to return to the conceptions of 'the vulgar.'" Cf. *PR* 50 and 73. And cf. Rasvihary Das, *The Philosophy of Whitehead*, p. 81.

15.   *PR* 211. Whitehead calls the actual entity a "particular existent," *PR* 117, 160, and 210.

16.   *MT* 206. Whitehead calls actual entities "things": *PR* xiv, 18, 21, 40, 41, 43, 52, 59, 71, 225, 231, and *MT* 133, 134, 135, 205, and *AI* 132, 133, 154, 157, 158, 177, 230, 233, 274.

17.   *PR* 45-46. Whitehead calls actual entities "actual things," *PR* 214: "The community of actual things is an organism; but it is not a static organism." And *PR* 56-57: "To be actual must mean that all actual things are alike objects, enjoying objective immortality in fashioning creative actions; and that all actual things are subjects, each prehending the universe from which it arises." Cf. *PR* 40 and 46, *AI* 274, and *S* 26. Whitehead calls the actual entity "something," *PR* 68 and 136.

18.   *PR* 257 and 258. Cf. *PR* 261: "The logical subjects of the proposition are the actual entities in the nexus." And cf. *PR* 24, 43, 186, 193, and 271.

19.   *PR* 261. Cf. Elizabeth M. Kraus, *The Metaphysics of Experience*, pp. 92-93.

20.   *PR* 188. Cf. *PR* 193.

21.   *PR* 265. Cf. *PR* 11, 185, 192, 194, and 258.

22.   *PR* 264.

23.   *PR* 265.

24.   *PR* 265.

25.   *PR* 259. Cf. *PR* 193.

26.   *PT* 258. Cf. *PR* 147: "Every proposition is entertained in the constitution of some one actual entity, or severally in the constitutions of many actual entities." Cf. *PR* 193, 200, and 260. However, entertaining a proposition is not the same thing as judging it, *PR* 187: "The conception of propositions as merely material for judgments is fatal to any understanding of their role in the universe." Cf. *PR* 11, 25, 184, 185, 186, 258, 259, and 260.

27. *PR* 192. Cf. *PR* 11, 12, 13, 193, and 264. Whitehead defines a proposition this way, *PR* 187: "A proposition is an element in the objective lure *proposed for feeling*, and when admitted into feeling it constitutes *what is felt*." Cf. *PR* 27, 186, 188, and 259.
28. *PR* 259.
29. *PR* 91. Cf. *PR* 79. There are also electromagnetic occasions, *PR* 98: "The members of this nexus are the electromagnetic occasions."
30. *PR* 91.
31. *PR* 91.
32. *PR* 64-65.
33. *PR* 118. Cf. *PR* 62-63, 75, 119, and 173.
34. *PR* 43. Cf. *PR* 121: "[A stone] is one of the elements in the actual world which has got to be referred to as an actual reason and not as an abstract potentiality." The actual reasons are the actual entities; Whitehead is saying that a stone is not to be regarded as an eternal object. And cf. *S* 45: "When we hate, it is a man that we hate and not a collection of sense-data—a causal, efficacious man." It is actual occasions that are causally efficacious; Whitehead is saying that a man is not to be regarded as a collection of eternal objects. These passages indicate that both a stone and a man may be regarded as actual occasions.
35. *PR* 229.
36. *MT* 122.
37. *MT* 135, 133, and 134.
38. *IS* 248-249. Whitehead calls actual entities "entities," *PR* 66 and *AI* 178.
39. *PR* 188-189.
40. *MT* 206 and 160.
41. *PR* 119. Cf. *PR* 89: "For example, the life of a man is a historic route of actual occasions which in a marked degree . . . inherit from each other." Cf. *PR* 90, 109 and *MT* 222.
42. *PR* 234.
43. *PR* 221.
44. *PR* 119.
45. *PR* 120.
46. *PR* 120.
47. *MT* 161.
48. *PR* 169. Cf. *PR* 126.
49. *PR* 75.
50. *PR* 141. Cf. *PR* 109 and *AI* 215.
51. *PR* 89-90.
52. *PR* 161. There are actual occasions of varieties of realized knowledge, *PR* 161: "We—as enduring objects with personal order—objectify the occasions of our own past with peculiar completeness in our immediate present. We find in those occasions, as known from our present standpoint, a surprising variation in the range and intensity of our realized knowledge."
53. *PR* 112. Cf. *PR* 143: ". . . the way is thereby opened for a rational scheme of cosmology in which a final reality is identified with acts of experience." Cf. *PR* 47, 126 and *IS* 262.
54. *PR* 119. Cf. *IS* 262.
55. *SMW* 107. Cf. *FR* 15: "Mankind has gradually developed from the lowliest forms of life, and must therefore be explained in terms applicable to all such forms. But why construe the later forms by analogy to the earlier forms, Why not reverse the process? It would seem to be more sensible, more truly empirical, to allow each living species to make its own contribution to the demonstration of factors inherent in living things." Cf. *PR* 47.

56.  *SMW* 219.
57.  *CN* 30. Cf. *MT* 205: "The doctrine that I am maintaining is that neither physical nature nor life can be understood unless we fuse them together as essential factors in the composition of 'really real' things whose inter-connections and individual characters constitute the universe."
58.  *AI* 184 and 185. Cf. Victor Lowe, *Understanding Whitehead*, p. 56.
59.  Compare William J. Garland, "Critical Studies: John W. Lango, *Whitehead's Ontology*," *PS* Vol. 3, No. 1 (1973), p. 51: "My experience *as I live through it at the present moment* is Whitehead's *paradigm case* of an actual entity."; with Craig R. Eisendrath, *The Unifying Moment*, p. 141: "There seems little doubt that Whitehead's argument for an organic duration is based on an analogy from particle physics." And compare Richard H. Overman, *Evolution and the Christian Doctrine of Creation*, p. 173: "Whitehead proposed that each occasion may be analyzed in terms of categories discoverable somewhere in human experience."; with Edward Pols, *Whitehead's Metaphysics: A Critical Examination of Process and Reality*, p. vi: "There is another tendency in Whitehead . . . to find his model for actual entities (other than God) in what he calls electro-magnetic occasions."
60.  *PR* 93. Cf. *PR* 71.
61.  *SMW* 74. Cf. Lowe, *Understanding Whitehead*, p. 159.
62.  *PR* xiv.
63.  *AI* 146. Cf. *PR* 116: "Science should investigate particular species, and metaphysics should investigate the generic notions under which those specific principles should fall."
64.  *PR* 3. Cf. *PR* 3: "Here 'applicable' means that some items of experience are thus interpretable, and 'adequate' means that there are no items incapable of such interpretation." And cf. *PR* 13: "Whatever is found in 'practice' must lie within the scope of the metaphysical description."
65.  *PR* xii. Cf. *PR* xi: "In the second part, an endeavor is made to exhibit this scheme as adequate for the interpretation of the ideas and problems which form the complex texture of civilized thought." And cf. *MT* 2: "Philosophy can exclude nothing." And cf. *PR* xiv.
66.  *RM* 86-87. Cf. *PR* xiv: "One test of success is adequacy in the comprehension of the variety of experience within the limits of one scheme of ideas." And cf. *PR* 5: "The partially successful philosophic generalization will, if derived from physics, find applications in fields of experience beyond physics." And cf. *AI* 237.
67.  *PR* 90.
68.  *PR* 110.
69.  *PR* 151. Cf. *PR* 13, 50, and 96.
70.  William A. Christian, "Some Uses of Reason," *RW* 76. Cf. Garland, "Critical Studies: John W. Lango, *Whitehead's Ontology*," *PS* Vol. 3, No. 1 (1973), p. 51: "Actual entities cannot be laid out on a table, as it were, to be 'examined.'" What cannot be "laid out on a table" is the concept of the actual entity.
71.  *PR* 177. Cf. *PR* 246: "When the datum is an actual entity of a highly complex grade, the physical feeling by which it is objectified as a datum may be of a highly complex character. . . . we have—in the case of the more complex actual entities—an example of the origination and direction of energy in the physical world." And cf. *PR* 15, 18, 19, 101, 102, 108, 168, 178, 222, 254, 315, 317, and *AI* 208, 225, and 314.
72.  *PR* 115. Cf. *PR* 112.
73.  *PR* 119. Cf. *PR* 179: "In a sense, the difference between a living organism and the inorganic environment is only a question of degree; but it is a difference of degree which

makes all the difference—in effect, it is a difference of quality." And cf. *PR* 102 and 120.

74. *PR* 102.

75. *PR* 102. Cf. *AI* 207: "Life may characterize a set of occasions diffused throughout a society, though not necessarily including all, or even a majority of, the occasions of that society."

76. *PR* 103.

77. *PR* 104.

78. *PR* 110. Cf. "Unpublished Letter from Whitehead to Kemp Smith," *SJP* 340: "But what you have rightly insisted on is that I conceive the world to be infinitely fuller and richer in different types of entities (not merely in different entities) and types of relations among entities than (as it appears to me) current philosophy allows." And cf. *PR* 232: "There are an indefinite number of types of feeling according to the complexity of the initial data which the feeling integrates, and according to the complexity of the objective datum which it finally feels." And cf. *PR* 109, 111, 148, 340, and *MT* 215, and *AI* 210. There is an instance of Whitehead using the term "grade" to mean what he elsewhere refers to as "genus" in saying that there is only one genus of actual entities, *PR* 7.

79. *MT* 214.

80. *MT* 215-216. Cf. *PR* 108-109: "The living body is a coordination of high-grade actual occasions; but in a living body of a low type the occasions are much nearer to a democracy. In a living body of a high type there are grades of occasions so coordinated by their paths of inheritance through the body, that a peculiar richness of inheritance is enjoyed by various occasions in some parts of the body."

81. Edward Pols, *Whitehead's Metaphysics: A Critical Examination of Process and Reality*, p. 6. In the index of the Corrected Edition of *Process and Reality*, a student of Whitehead will find only two entries under the heading, "actual entities: examples of." These two entries direct us to pages 19 and 91 wherein God and electronic and protonic actual entities are mentioned. It is interesting that the concerted efforts of Whiteheadian scholarship have been able to come up with just these examples of actual entities and no more, the only examples that might be supposed to lend themselves to a scientific materialist interpretation of Whitehead while claiming him for theology at the same time. This could easily give the impression that Whitehead is being used simply to justify two well entrenched traditions, scientific materialism and Christian theology.

82. *PR* 77. For the synonymousness of "actual entity" and "actual occasion," cf. *PR* 18, 22, 73, 77, 141, and 211.

83. *PR* 88.

84. *PR* 7, 13, 31, 32, 46, 65, 87, 93, 345, and *RM* 91.

85. Pols, *Whitehead's Metaphysics*, p. 5. Cf. John B. Cobb, *A Christian Natural Theology*, p. 40: "The individual occasions are only detectable either by intense introspection or by scientific instruments. None of the entities of which we are conscious in common experience are individual occasions and only rarely do these appear even in the sciences."

85a. Robert M. Palter, *Whitehead's Philosophy of Science*, p. 217. Cf. Frederic B. Fitch, "Sketch of a Philosophy," *RW* 95: "I follow Whitehead in regarding space-time as filled with small indivisible events which Whitehead would call actual occasions."

86. Abner Shimony, "Quantum Physics and the Philosophy of Whitehead" in *Boston Studies in the Philosophy of Science*, Vol. 2 (1965), p. 321. Cf. William W. Hammerschmidt, *Whitehead's Philosophy of Time*, p. 39: "The basic facts are microscopic actual occasions."

86a. Richard Rorty, "Matter and Event" in *The Concept of Matter*, p. 520. Cf. Ann L.

Plamondon, *Whitehead's Organic Philosophy of Science,* p. 24: "The actual world is a macroscopic process, and its process is constituted by the microscopic processes of actual entities."

87. Dorothy Emmet, *Whitehead's Philosophy of Organism,* pp. 183-184. Cf. Christian, "Some Uses of Reason," *RW* 76: "We do not have sufficient powers of discrimination to isolate, perceptually, any one of the multiplicity of actual occasions of which, on Whitehead's theory, our experience of seeing the table is composed."

88. Martin Jordan, *New Shapes of Reality,* p. 54. See Chapter 2, note 191.

89. *PR* 5.

90. *PR* 227. Cf. *PR* 211.

91. *PR* 133.

92. *PR* 147.

93. *MT* 162. Cf. *PR* 58 and *MT* 163.

94. *FR* 31. Cf. *PR* 235.

95. *PR* 51. Cf. *PR* 53, 58, and *MT* 163.

96. *PR* 147. For examples of organizations and compositions, Whitehead uses drops of water, throbs of pulsation, molecules, stones, plants, animals, and men, *MT* 117 and 124. Then here are more examples of actual entities.

97. Lucretius, *De Rerum Natura,* pp. 51-53.

98. Leclerc, *The Nature of Physical Existence,* p. 324.

99. *SMW* 150.

100. *SMW* 157. Cf. Burgers, *E* 76. And cf. R. A. Aronov, "On the Foundations of the Hypothesis of Discrete Character of Space and Time," in *Time in Science and Philosophy,* ed. Jiri Zeman, pp. 265-266.

101. *SMW* 115-116. Cf. *PR* 99-100: "It must be remembered that each individual occasion within a special form of society includes features which do not occur in analogous occasions in the external environment. . . . An obvious instance of such distinction of behaviour is afforded by the notion of the deformation of the shape of an electron according to variations in its physical situation." And cf. *SMW* 116: "In this theory, the molecules may blindly run in accordance with the general laws, but the molecules differ in their intrinsic characters according to the general organic plans of the situations in which they find themselves." And cf. *SMW* 108. And cf. Bohm, *R* 94. And cf. Joseph Needham, "A Biologist's View of Whitehead's Philosophy," *LLP-W* 251 and 261.

102. *PR* 79.

103. *PR* 215.

104. *PR* 41. Cf. *PR* 149: "The *actual entities* enter into each others' constitutions under *limitations* imposed by incompatibilities of feelings." And cf. *PR* 59, 148, 154, 231, 291, and 445.

105. *PR* 50.

106. *PR* 145.

107. *PR* 7. Cf. *PR* 50: "One role of the eternal objects is that they are those elements which express how any one actual entity is constituted by its synthesis of other actual entities. . . ." Cf. *PR* 56, 190, 206, and 238.

108. *PR* 48. Cf. *PR* 89.

109. *AI* 201.

110. *PR* 238. Cf. *PR* 291.

111. *PR* 230.

112. *PR* 20. Cf. *PR* 27.

113. *PR* 24.
114. *PR* 288.
115. *PR* 28. Cf. *PR* 25: "(xx) That to 'function' means to contribute determination to the actual entities in the nexus of some actual world." And cf. *PR* 230: "Also the more complex multiple nexus between many actual entities in the actual world of a percipient is felt by that percipient." And cf. *PR* 214: ". . . the past is a nexus of actualities." And cf. *PR* 230-231.
116. *PR* 73.
117. *PR* 65. Cf. *PR* 153: "It must be remembered that the objective content is analysable into actual entities under limited perspectives provided by their own natures; . . . ." And cf. *PR* 41, 65, and 67.
118. *AI* 233. Cf. *AI* 236: "No things are 'together' except in experience; and no things *are*, in any sense of 'are', except as components in experience or as immediacies of process which are occasions in self-creation."
119. *PR* 189. Cf. *PR* 190, 309, and *AI* 187. And cf. Victor Lowe, "The Concept of Experience in Whitehead's Metaphysics," *KEP* 125. And cf. Roy Wood Sellars, "Philosophy of Organism and Physical Realism," *LLP-W* 412.
120. *PR* 167.
121. *PR* 166. Cf. *PR* 143: ". . . a final reality is identified with acts of experience." And cf. *PR* 55, 160, and *AI* 190.
122. *PR* 195. Cf. *PR* 24, 186, 193, 257, 261, and 262.
123. *PR* 287. Cf. Burgers, *E* 228.
124. Leclerc, "Some Main Philosophical Issues Involved in Contemporary Scientific Thought," in *Mind in Nature*, p. 104.
125. Shimony, "Quantum Physics and the Philosophy of Whitehead," in *Boston Studies in the Philosophy of Science*, Vol. 2 (1965), p. 325.
126. David Ray Griffin, "Whitehead's Philosophy and Some General Notions of Physics and Biology," in *Mind in Nature*, p. 134.
127. Ibid., p. 134. Cf. Christian, *An Interpretation of Whitehead's Metaphysics*, p. 160: "All the things which ordinary experience finds in nature, and the world itself in any stage of its process, are nexūs." And cf. David L. Miller, *The Philosophy of A. N. Whitehead*, p. 74: "But inasmuch as no single actual occasion can constitute a chair it is certain, from the argument above, that no actual occasion is causally affected by a chair; i.e., by a nexus said to be a unity constituting a chair during an epoch of time." And cf. David A. Sipfle, "On the Intelligibility of the Epochal Theory of Time" in *The Monist*, Vol. 53 (1969), p. 514: "For Whitehead the traffic light is a complex of actual occasions and the particles of which it is composed are historic routes of occasions." And cf. Emmet, *Whitehead's Philosophy of Organism*, pp. 182-183: ". . . Whitehead does not state as clearly as we might wish the relation between the individual concrescent occasion, and the nexus of occasions which forms a 'thing,' or 'organism' in the usual sense, namely of a structured whole of parts organised for a certain end."
128. Ibid., Griffin, "Whitehead's Philosophy," p. 133.
129. *PR* 32. Cf. *PR* 21.
130. *IS* 195.
131. Nathaniel Lawrence, "Time, Value, and the Self," *RW* 157. Cf. Shimony, "Quantum Physics and the Philosophy of Whitehead," in *Boston Studies in the Philosophy of Science*, Vol. 2 (1965), p. 320: "To be sure, Whitehead is reticent about the exact extent of an occasion."

132. Ibid., Lawrence, "Time, Value, and the Self," p. 158.
133. Henry Margenau, *The Nature of Physical Reality*, p. 157. Cf. Capek, *BMP* 266.
134. Ann L. Plamondon, *Whitehead's Organic Philosophy of Science*, p. 65.


PREHENSION

1.   *MT* 191 and 200. Cf. Bohm, *R* x.
2.   *PR* 215 and 41. Cf. *MT* 120.
3.   *SMW* 71.
4.   *PR* 50. Cf. *PR* 159.
5.   *SMW* 71.
6.   *PR* 79. Cf. *IS* 254: "The misconception which has haunted philosophic literature throughout the centuries is the notion of 'independent existence.' There is no such mode of existence; every entity is only to be understood in terms of the way in which it is interwoven with the rest of the Universe." And cf. Albert Einstein and Leopold Infeld, *The Evolution of Physics*, pp. 40-41: "We think of a substance as something which can be neither created nor destroyed."
7.   *PR* 18-19. Cf. *PR* 58, 75, and 222.
8.   *SMW* 180.
9.   *SMW* 157.
10.  *PR* 79. Cf. *PR* 223: "For every actuality is devoid of a shadow of ambiguity: it is exactly what it is, by reason of its objective definition at the hands of other entities." Cf. Bohm, *QT* 161-162.
11.  *PR* 145.
12.  *MT* 177.
13.  *PR* 7. Cf. *PR* xiii, 13, 30, 49-50, 51, 54, 75, 137, 144, 145, 159, 160, 209, and *Prel* in *WhA* 305.
14.  *PR* 222.
15.  *PR* 56.
16.  Milic Capek, "Note about Whitehead's Definitions of Co-Presence" in *Philosophy of Science*, Vol. XXIV (1957), p. 86. Cf. Bohm, *QT* 168.
17.  *PR* 21.
18.  *PR* 22. Cf. *AI* 274: "One principle is that the very essence of real actuality—that is, of the completely real—is *process*."
19.  *CN* 53. Cf. *SMW* 155: "In a sense, all explanation must end in an ultimate arbitrariness."
20.  *PR* 20. Cf. *MT* 67: "The aim of philosophy is sheer disclosure." And cf. *PR* 3 and *AI* 234.
21.  *MT* 208. Cf. *MT* 71.
22.  *PR* 20.
23.  *PR* 21. Cf. *PR* 31 and 164.
24.  *PR* 22. Cf. *MT* 67: "Philosophy is either self-evident, or it is not philosophy." And cf. *PR* 39: "But ultimately nothing rests on authority; the final court of appeal is intrinsic reasonableness."
25.  *PR* 121.
26.  *IS* 195.
27.  *PR* 309. Cf. *PR* 109: "(cf. the way in which the distinction between matter and radiant

energy has now vanished)." And cf. *PR* 238: "In the world there is nothing static." And cf. *AI* 219: "Each actual occasion is in truth a process of activity." And cf. *MT* 188.

28. *PR* 94. Cf. *S* 26: "The conception of the world here adopted is that of functional activity. By this I mean that every actual thing is something by reason of its activity; whereby its nature consists in its relevance to other things, and its individuality consists in its synthesis of other things so far as they are relevant to it."

29. *PR* 309.

30. *MT* 167. Cf. *MT* 228: "It is never bare thought or bare existence that we are aware of."

31. *IS* 262.

32. *MT* 231-232. Cf. *PR* 163: "But even so, the emotional appetitive elements in our conscious experience are those which most clearly resemble the basic elements of all physical experience." and cf. *PR* 116, 163, 315, and *AI* 188.

33. *AI* 176. Cf. *PR* 163: "Thus the primitive experience is emotional feeling felt in its relevance to a world beyond." And cf. *AI* 177.

34. *MT* 158. Cf. *PR* 267: "The simplicity of clear consciousness is no measure of the experience." And cf. *PR* 116, 163, 315, and *AI* 188.

35. *MT* 228. Cf. *PR* 153: ". . . the process is a process of 'feeling.'" And cf. *PR* 113.

36. *PR* 51 and 166. Cf. *PR* 16, 112, 166, and *AI* 179 and 221. And cf. Burgers, *E* 21.

37. *MT* 213. Cf. *FR* 27: "In the course of evolution why should the trend have arrived at mankind, if his activities of Reason remain without influence on his bodily actions?" And cf. *PR* 47. And cf. Burgers, *E* 142-143.

38. *PR* 277. Cf. Lowe, "The Development of Whitehead's Philosophy" *LLP-W* 106-107.

39. *PR* 22. Cf. Lowe, *Understanding Whitehead,* p. 348. The term's "relation" and "relationship" have many meanings, but "prehension" has only Whitehead's. "Prehension" has the advantage in that it more obviously implies time, the time required for an occasion to engage other in relationship.

40. *PR* 41.

41. *AI* 234.

42. Cf. Ramona T. Cormier, "The Understanding of the Past," *TS* 49. And cf. Mary A. Wyman, *The Lure for Feeling in the Creative Process,* pp. 35-36. And cf. Evander Bradley McGilvary, "Space-Time, Simple Location, and Prehensions," *LLP-W* 231. And cf. Nathaniel Lawrence, "Whitehead's Philosophical Development," p1 289. And cf. Rasvihary Das, *The Philosophy of Whitehead,* p. 33. And cf. Burgers, *E* 35. And cf. *SMW* 101.

43. *PR* 40, 49, 52, 117, 146, 154, 155, 275, and *AI* 276.

44. *PR* 164, 219, 231, 275, and *MT* 206.

45. Leclerc, *The Nature of Physical Existence,* p. 271.

46. *PR* 81.

47. *PR* 52.

48. *AI* 236. Cf. *IS* 241: "An occasion is a concretion—that is, a growing together—of diverse elements; that is why each occasion is an organism." And cf. *PR* 51.

49. *PR* 212. Cf. *PR* 79.

50. *PR* 23.

51. *PR* 236.

52. *PR* 221. Cf. *PR* 221: "If we abstract the subject from the feeling we are left with many things."

53. *PR* 154. It is only with respect to subjective forms that Whitehead accepts the subject-

predicate form of language, *PR* 30: "In its development the subsequent discussion of the philosophy of organism is governed by the belief that the subject-predicate form of proposition is concerned with high abstractions, except in its application to subjective forms." Cf. *PR* 232.

54.   *PR* 233.
55.   *PR* 24. Cf. *PR* 256.
56.   *PR* 275. Cf. *PR* 237 and 238. And cf. Burgers, *E* 131.
57.   *PR* 87.
58.   *PR* 232.
59.   *PR* 220.
60.   *PR* 41. Cf. *PR* 227: "It is for this reason that what an actual entity has avoided as a datum for feeling may yet be an important part of its equipment." Cf. *PR* 44.
61.   *RM* 109. Cf. *IS* 251: "Evaluation refers equally to omissions and admissions." And cf. *PR* 26, 45, 112, 148, 238, and 273.
62.   *PR* 23-24.
63.   *PR* 226. Cf. *PR* 26, 41-42, 226, and 237.
64.   *PR* 237.
65.   *IS* 248.
66.   *PR* 28. Cf. *PR* 3: "In other words, it is presupposed that no entity can be conceived in complete abstraction from the system of the universe, and that it is the business of speculative philosophy to exhibit this truth."
67.   *PR* 221. Cf. *PR* 226-227. And cf. Das, *The Philosophy of Whitehead*, p. 36.
68.   *PR* 231. Cf. *PR* 223-224: "This Category of Subjective Unity is the reason why no feeling can be abstracted from its subject."
69.   *PR* 232.
70.   *PR* 231. Cf. *PR* 233: "But conversely, no feeling can be abstracted either from its data, or its subject."
71.   *PR* 235.
72.   *PR* 293.
73.   *PR* 219. Cf. *PR* 19: "In fact, any characteristic of an actual entity is reproduced in a prehension. It might have been a complete actuality; but by reason of a certain incomplete partiality, a prehension is only a subordinate element in an actual entity."
74.   *PR* 222. Cf. *PR* 27.
75.   *PR* 237.
76.   Albert Einstein and Leopold Infeld, *The Evolution of Physics,* pp. 53-54.
77.   *PR* 19. Cf. *PR* 84: "One task of a sound metaphysics is to exhibit final and efficient causes in their proper relation to each other."
78.   *PR* 87.
79.   *PR* 163. Cf. *PR* 116: "The 'datum' in metaphysics is the basis of the vector-theory in physics. . . ."
80.   *PR* 120.
81.   *PR* 151. Cf. *PR* 120 and 177.
82.   *AI* 187-188. Cf. *AI* 188: "The object-to-subject structure of human experience is reproduced in physical nature by this vector relation of particular to particular."
83.   *PR* 231. Cf. *PR* 212.
84.   *PR* 40-41. Cf. *PR* 211.
85.   Einstein and Infeld, *The evolution of Physics,* p. 62.

86. See note 41. Cf. *AI* 234: "This term ['prehension'] is devoid of suggestion either of consciousness or of representative perception."
87. *AI* 233. Cf. *PR* 164: "This word 'feeling' is a mere technical term; but it has been chosen to suggest that functioning through which the concrescent actuality appropriates the datum so as to make it its own." And cf. *PR* 237: "By reason of this duplicity in a simple feeling there is a vector character which transfers the cause into the effect."
88. *AI* 234. Cf. *PR* 12.
89. *AI* 202. Cf. Hans Reichenbach, *The Philosophy of Space and Time*, pp. 136 and 272-273.
90. David A. Sipfle, "On the Intelligibility of the Epochal Theory of Time" in *The Monist*, Vol. 53 (1969), p. 509. Cf. Paul F. Schmidt, *Perception and Cosmology in Whitehead's Philosophy*, p. 105.
91. *IS* 241.
92. *PR* 23. Cf. John Dewey, "The Reflex Arc Concept in Psychology," in *The Psychological Review*, Vol. III, No. 4 (1896), p. 366.
93. *PR* 24.
94. *PR* 46. *PR* 19: "The ontological principle can be summarized as: no actual entity, then no reason." And cf. *PR* 43 and 256. And cf. Kenneth F. Thompson, Jr., *Whitehead's Philosophy of Religion*, p. 34.
95. *PR* 244.
96. *PR* 80.
97. *PR* 75. Cf. *AI* 197: "Thus, 'to be something' is to be discoverable as a factor in the analysis of some actuality." And cf. *PR* 43.
98. *PR* 43, 211, 222, 223, and 225.
99. *PR* 166. Cf. *PR* 32, 43, 166, and *AI* 233.
100. *PR* 4.
101. *PR* 177. Cf. *PR* 41: ". . . by the ontological principle every entity is felt by some actual entity." And cf. Bohm, *QT* 163.
102. *PR* 28. Cf. *PR* 149.
103. *PR* 22. Cf. *PR* 45 and 65. And cf. Burgers, *E* 210.
104. *PR* 28. Cf. *PR* 50 and 166.
105. *PR* 137.
106. *PR* 46. Cf. *PR* 111.
107. *IS* 242. Cf. *PR* 289.
108 *PR* 148. Cf. Richard Schlegel, "Time and Entropy," in *Time in Science and Philosophy*, ed. Jiri Zeman, p. 28.
109. *PR* 350.
110. *PR* 148.
111. *PR* xiv. Cf. *AI* 274: "Thus each actual thing is only to be understood in terms of its becoming and perishing." And cf. *AI* 204.
112. *PR* xiii-xiv.
113. *PR* 25. Cf. *PR* 163: "But the feeling is subjectively rooted in the immediacy of the present occasion: it is what the occasion feels for itself, as derived from the past and as merging into the future."
114. *PR* 85.
115. *PR* 29.
116. *PR* 82. Cf. *AI* 204.
117. *PR* 88. Cf. *AI* 193: "It belongs to the essence of this subject that it pass into objective

immortality. Thus its own constitution involves that its own activity in *self*-formation passes into its activity of *other*-formation."

118. *AI* 176. Cf. *AI* 175. Cf. Das, *The Philosophy of Whitehead*, p. 34.

119. *PR* 210.

120. *PR* 214. Cf. *PR* 150: "According to this account, efficient causation expresses the transition from actual entity to actual entity; and final causation expresses the internal process whereby the actual entity becomes itself."

121. *PR* 128-129.

122. *PR* 47-48.

123. Vere C. Chappell, "Whitehead's Theory of Becoming," *KEP* 71.

124. Ibid., pp. 72 and 73.

125. Ibid., p. 73. Cf. George L. Kline, "Form, Concrescence, and Concretum: a Neo-Whiteheadian Analysis," *SJP* 352: "The epochal theory of becoming can, I think, be defended as cogently in terms of the distinction between concrescence and concretum as in terms of Whitehead's distinction between (microscopic) concrescence and (macroscopic) transition."

126. Griffin, "Whitehead's Philosophy and Some General Notions of Physics and Biology" in *Mind in Nature*, p. 133. And cf. Plamondon, *Whitehead's Organic Philosophy of Science*, p. 24.

127. Leclerc, *Whitehead's Metaphysics*, pp. 127-128. Cf. Robert M. Palter, *Whitehead's Philosophy of Science*, p. 160: "Thus, the immediate appearance of a given drop of water is the apparent character of a certain event and therefore a material object; while the causal character of the same event is an aggregate of 'atomic" entities (or scientific objects) and therefore not a material object."

128. *PR* 203. Cf. *PR* 223: "Each task of creation is a social effort, employing the whole universe." And cf. *RM* 104: "According to the doctrine of this lecture, every entity is in its essence social and requires the society in order to exist." And cf. *PR* 204.

129. *PR* 72. However, not only nexūs may be non-social, but occasions, *PR* 110: "The societies in an environment will constitute its orderly element, and the non-social actual entities will constitute its element of chaos"; and cf. *PR* 206: "There is also an admixture of chaotic occasions which cannot be classified as belonging to any society"; and cf. *PR* 92. Thus, Whitehead has gone back on his dictum that all actual occasions are social. There are chaotic, non-social occasions.

130. *PR* 34. Cf. *PR* 89.

131. *PR* 34, 35, 72, 96-97, 99, and 100.

132. *AI* 203. Cf. *PR* 89 and *AI* 199.

133. *PR* 101.

134. *PR* 89. Cf. *PR* 90: "Thus a society is, for each of its members, an environment with some element of order in it, persisting by reason of the genetic relations between its own members. Such an element of order is the order prevalent in the society." And cf. *PR* 83, 244, and *AI* 203-204. And cf. Burgers, *E* 51 and 197.

135. *AI* 206. Cf. *AI* 206: "For the notion of a defining characteristic must be construed to include the notion of the coordination of societies."

136. *PR* 99. Cf. *PR* 92: "Thus the physical relations . . . are derivative from a series of societies of increasing width of prevalence, the more special societies being included in the wider societies."

137. *PR* 90.

138. *PR* 110. Cf. *RM* 85: "The individual is formative of the society, the society is formative of

the individual." And cf. *AI* 41: "The whole environment participates in the nature of each of its occasions."

139. *AI* 207. Cf. *PR* 99: "For example, we speak of a molecule within a living cell, because its general molecular features are independent of the environment of the cell." Cf. *PR* 103.

140. *PR* 106. Cf. *PR* 99: "Recurring to the example of a living cell, it will be argued that the occasions composing the 'empty' space within the cell exhibit special features which analogous occasions outside the cell are devoid of." And cf. *AI* 41: "But molecules are analysable. Things behave very differently amid a close pack of molecules from their behavior amid the vibrations of so-called empty space." See Chapter 1, note 101.

141. *SMW* 215.

142. *PR* 108-109. Cf. *PR* 339: "It is by reason of the body, with its miracle of order, that the treasures of the past environment are poured into the living occasions."

143. *PR* 339. Cf. *PR* 109: "Owing to the delicate organization of the body, there is a returned influence, an inheritance of character derived from the presiding occasion and modifying the subsequent occasions through the rest of the body."

144. *PR* 109. Here too Whitehead speaks of the intersection of two enduring objects in one actual occasion, *PR* 198-199: "Let us return to the two truly simple enduring objects, *A* and *B*. Also let us assume that their defining characteristics, *A* and *B*, are not contraries, so that both of them can qualify the same actual occasion. Then there is no general metaphysical reason why the distinct routes of *A* and *B* should not intersect in at least one actual occasion. Indeed . . . it is practically certain that . . . intersecting historic routes for *A* and *B* must have frequently come into existence. In such a contingency a being . . . might find A and B exemplified in one actual entity."

145. *PR* 98.

146. *PR* 98.

147. *PR* 98.

148. *PR* 198. Cf. *PR* 34.

149. *PR* 34-35.

150. *PR* 35. Cf. *CN* 72.

151. *PR* 92. Cf. Burgers, *E* 63-64 and 228.

152. *PR* 109. Cf. *AI* 205: "The society, in each stage of realization, then consists of a set of contiguous occasions in serial order. A man, defined as an enduring percipient, is such a society. This definition of a man is exactly what Descartes means by a thinking substance." And cf. *AI* 215: "It is to be remembered also that along the personal succession of the soul's experiences, there is an inheritance of sense-perception from the antecedent members of the personal succession." And cf. *PR* 75, 141, and *AI* 39.

153. *PR* 90. Cf. *PR* 161 and *AI* 208.

154. *PR* 35. Cf. *PR* 35: "An ordinary physical object, which has temporal endurance, is a society." Cf. *PR* 73. And cf. Bohm, *R* 146.

155. *AI* 204. Cf. William P. D. Wightman, "Whitehead's Empiricism," *RW* 350: "If a sequence of such actual entities retains a larger measure of the pattern and modes of objectification of the former we may call it an individual. But its persistence is in part an illusion." What the illusion is here is ambiguous: is it the persistence of a sequence or an individual?

156. *PR* 35. Cf. *PR* 104.

157. *PR* 198. Cf. *PR* 35: "A society may (or may not) be analysable into many strands of 'enduring objects.' This will be the case for most ordinary physical objects."

158. *PR* 63. Cf. Lewis S. Ford, "Kirkpatrick on Subjective Becoming," *PS* Vol. 4, No. 1 (1974), p. 40: "How do we restrict substantial unity to natural compounds? According to

Whitehead's account, all substances interact. If Leclerc, Kirkpatrick, and I mutually interact such that each of us has his opinions modified in the interchange, does that mean we constitute together some overarching compound substance?" Indeed, like the real chair, Ford and his friends conversing together are a corpuscular society, Ford and his friends being some of the enduring objects comprising this "overarching society." And Ford and his own eyes, hands, heart, and limbs are altogether also a corpuscular society, with Ford's own soul, mind, or person being one enduring object contributing to it.

159. *AI* 206. Cf. *AI* 39.
160. *PR* 102. Cf. *PR* 101: "The close association of all physical bodies, organic and inorganic alike . . . suggests that this development of mentality is characteristic of the actual occasions which make up the structured societies which we know as 'material bodies.'"
161. *PR* 99. Cf. *PR* 92 and 101.
162. *PR* 326.
163. *PR* 79.
164. *PR* 36.
165. *PR* 98. Cf. *PR* 323.
166. *PR* 109. Cf. *PR* 102 and 187-188.
167. *PR* 35. Cf. *PR* 36: "Thus, in different stages of its career, a wave of light may be more or less corpuscular."
168. *PR* 36.
169. *PR* 34, 119, and 350.
170. *PR* 83. Cf. *AI* 201: "Thus the term Nexus does not presuppose any special type of order, nor does it presuppose any order at all pervading its members other than the general metaphysical obligation of mutual immanence." And cf. *PR* 291.
171. *AI* 204.
172. *AI* 181.
173. *S* 50.
174. *AI* 191.
175. *PR* 87. Cf. *PR* 220 and IS 241.
176. *PR* 78.
177. *PR* 78.
178. *PR* 78.
179. *PR* 78.
180. *PR* 78.
181. *PR* 78.
182. *PR* 78-79. Cf. Burgers, *E* 14 and 78-79.
183. David Bohm, *R* 111.
184. John W. Lango, *Whitehead's Ontology*, p. 6. Cf. Mason W. Gross, "Whitehead's Answer to Hume: A Reply," *KEP* 65: "Societies of actual entities . . . is Whitehead's term for the macroscopic things in our experience. . . ."
185. Lango, *Whitehead's Ontology* pp. 5-6.
186. Leclerc, *The Nature of Physical Existence*, p. 284. Leclerc continues, p. 291: "In Whitehead's theory, too, in the end the constituents of a body constitute an aggregate."
187. Edward Pols, *Whitehead's Metaphysics: A Critical Examination of Process and Reality*, p. vii. Pols continues, p. 6: "Yet nothing that is an organism in the ordinary sense of that word qualifies as an example of an actual entity. Organisms are in fact *societies* of actual entities." Cf. George L. Kline, "Form, Concrescence, and Concretum: A Neo-

Whiteheadian Analysis," *SJP* 357: "The example is crude and misleading because a living human being is not a concrescence (rather a 'society of societies' of concrescence) and a no-longer-living human being is not a concretum (rather, something like a 'society of societies' of concreta)."

188. Richard H. Overman, *Evolution and the Christian Doctrine of Creation*, p. 197.
189. Ibid., p. 201.
190. Robert M. Palter, *Whitehead's Philosophy of Science*, p. 216. Cf. Abner Shimony, "Quantum Physics and the Philosophy of Whitehead," in *Boston Studies in the Philosophy of Science*, Vol. 2 (1965) p. 313: "All groupings of occasions have derivative status."
191. Donald W. Sherburne, "Whitehead's Psychological Physiology," *SJP* pp. 401 and 402.
192. J. M. Burgers, *E* 57.
193. *PR* 35.
194. *PR* 91. Cf. *PR* 97, 111, 205-206. The cosmic epoch is a "limited nexus," *PR* 288: "But in reference to the ultimate nature of things, [our cosmic epoch] is a limted nexus."
195. Victor Lowe, *Understanding Whitehead*, p. 222 (also *LLP-W* 90). Cf. Ewing P. Shahan, *Whitehead's Theory of Experience*, p. 55.
196. *SMW* 181.
197. Burgers, *E* 41.
198. *RM* 88-90. Cf. Burgers, *E* 19-20, 79, and 106.
199. Bohm, *CC* 153 and 154.


## POTENTIALITY

1. *MT* 136-137.
2. *PR* 23. Cf. *PR* 184, 225, 232, and 236.
3. *PR* 20. Cf. *PR* 29: "Their ingression expresses the *definiteness* of the actuality in question."
4. *PR* 56. Cf. *PR* 89.
5. *PR* 29.
6. *CN* 144. Cf. *PNK* 62-63.
7. *PR* 44.
8. *PR* 48.
9. *PR* 41. Cf. *PR* 164: "Hence, to sum up, there are four modes of functioning whereby an eternal object has ingression into the constitution of an actual entity: (i) as dative ingression, (ii) in conformal physical feeling, (iii) in conceptual feeling, (iv) in comparative feeling."
10. *PR* 25. Cf. *PR* 41 and 23.
11. *PR* 115. Cf. A. D. Ritchie, "Whitehead's Defense of Speculative Reason" *LLP-W* 345.
12. *PR* 227. Cf. *IS* 263.
13. *PR* 257.
14. *PR* 231. Cf. *PR* 236.
15. *PR* 236. Cf. *PR* 58 and 210. And cf. Burgers, *E* 27.
16. *PR* 87. Cf. *PR* 171: "Now it is a primary doctrine that what is 'given' is given by reason of objectifications of actual entities from the settled past." And cf. *PR* 321.
17. *PR* 224.

18.  *PR* 233.
19.  *PR* 152. Cf. *PR* 23: "The term 'objectification' refers to the particular mode in which the potentiality of one actual entity is realized in another actual entity."
20.  *PR* 233. Cf. *PR* 232.
21.  *PR* 238. Cf. *PR* 164 and 309.
22.  *PR* 237.
23.  *PR* 162. Cf. *PR* 115-116, 245, and 291-292.
24.  *PR* 291.
25.  *PR* 291. Cf. *PR* 292.
26.  *PR* 315. Cf. *AI* 183. And cf. Burgers, *E* 197.
27.  *PR* 291. Cf. *PR* 62 and 292.
28.  *PR* 291. Cf. *PR* 24.
29.  *PR* 114. Cf. *PR* 114: "It is possible that this definition of 'sensa' excludes some cases of contrast which are ordinarily termed 'sensa' and that it includes some emotional qualities which are ordinarily excluded." And cf. *PR* 120.
30.  *PR* 61. Cf. *PR* 114: "In sense-reception the sensa are the definiteness of emotion: they are emotional forms transmitted from occasion to occasion." And cf. *PR* 62, 119, 228, 256, and 314-315.
31.  *AI* 246.
32.  *PR* 162-163. Cf. *AI* 246: "The affective tone of perception of a green woodland in spring can only be defined by the delicate shades of the green. It is a strong aesthetic emotion with the qualification of green in springtime." And cf. *PR* 292 and 315.
33.  *PR* 52.
34.  *PR* 52.
35.  *AI* 132.
36.  *AI* 185. Cf. *AI* 39: "An example of [the abstract things which recur] is the shape of a rock."
37.  *PR* 34. Cf. *PR* 89: "This likeness consists in the fact that (i) a certain element of 'form' is a contributory component to the individual satisfaction of each member of the society; and that (ii) the contribution by the element to the objectification of any one member of the society for prehension by other members promotes its analogous reproduction in the satisfactions of those other members. Thus a set of entities is a society (i) in virtue of a 'defining characteristic' shared by its members, and (ii) in virtue of the presence of the defining characteristic being due to the environment provided by the society itself." And cf. *PR* 89.
38.  *PR* 291.
39.  *PR* 291.
40.  *PR* 23. Cf. *AI* 179: "The initial situation with its creativity can be termed the initial phase of the new occasion. . . . It has a certain unity of its own, expressive of its capacity for providing the objects requisite for a new occasion, and also expressive of its conjoint activity whereby it is essentially the primary phase of a new occasion. It can thus be termed a 'real potentiality'." And cf. *PR* 27 and 150.
41.  *AI* 237. Cf. *PR* 84, 189, *AI* 222, *IS* 218, 243, and *RM* 110. And cf. Capek, *BMP* 161.
42.  *AI* 237.
43.  *PR* 88.
44.  *PR* 239. Cf. *PR* 44: "An eternal object is always a potentiality for actual entities." And cf. *PR* 215.
45.  *PR* 220. Cf. *PR* 257: "This is an exemplification of the categoreal principle that the general metaphysical character of being an entity is 'to be a determinant in the becoming of actualities." And cf. *PR* 220: "Any entity, thus intervening in processes transcending itself,

is said to be functioning as an 'object.'" And cf. *PR* 43: "Just as 'potentiality for process' is the meaning of the more general term 'entity,' or 'thing'; so 'decision' is the additional meaning imported by the word 'actual' into the phrase 'actual entity.'" And cf. *PR* 22, 28, and 29.

46. *PR* 52. Cf. *PR* 188-189.

47. *PR* 22 and 28. By "actual" Whitehead means "decision" (see note 45). An eternal object in itself has no possibility for decision and is forever non-actual. But an immortal object is always an actual entity in the generic sense; while it is no longer deciding, yet it is an entity having made decisions and therefore an actual entity. Both objects and subjects are called "actual," *PR* 56 (see Chapter 1, note 17). Cf. *PR* 22, 25, and *MT* 207.

48. *PR* 22. Cf. *PR* 149: "If the term 'eternal objects' is disliked, the term 'potentials' would be suitable." Cf. *PR* 29, and 39-40.

49. *PR* 70. Cf. *PR* 256: "In itself an eternal object evades any selection among actualities or epochs."

50. *PR* 257.

51. *PR* 256. Cf. *PR* 114 and 257.

52. *PR* 239. Cf. 29: "But eternal objects, and propositions, and some more complex sorts of contrasts, involve in their own natures indecision." And cf. *PR* 44 and 149.

53. *PR* 276. Cf. Burgers, *E* 34-35.

54. *PR* 154.

55. *PR* 148. Cf. *PR* 50.

56. *PR* 43. Cf. Burgers, *E* 267.

57. *MT* 229.

58. *PR* 240.

59. *PR* 23, 29, and 114.

60. *PR* 65. Cf. *PR* 86 and 192.

61. *PR* 46. Cf. *PR* 40.

62. *PR* 257. Cf. *PR* 31 and 164.

63. *PR* 40. Cf. *PR* 257: "The general relationships of eternal objects to each other, relationships of diversity and of pattern, are their relationships in God's conceptual realization. Apart from this realization, there is mere isolation indistinguishable from nonentity."

64. *PR* 22.

65. *PR* 257.

66. *PR* 23.

67. *PR* 149. Cf. *PR* 46 and 244.

68. A. H. Johnson, *Whitehead's Theory of Reality*, pp. 43-44. Cf. Richard Rorty, "Matter and Event," in *The Concept of Matter*, p. 517: "The irreducible individuality and novelty of each actual entity is made possible by the inexhaustible array of alternative subjective aims which its pure conceptual prehensions—its prehensions that is, of eternal objects not yet exemplified among its ancestors—make available to it."

69. Rasvihary Das, *The Philosophy of Whitehead*, p. 180.

70. *PR* 93. Cf. *PR* 46: "It is a contradiction in terms to assume that some explanatory fact can float into the actual world out of nonentity. Nonentity is nothingness."

71. Lewis S. Ford, "Genetic and Coordinate Division Correlated," *PS* Vol. 1, No. 3 (1971), p. 206.

72. *PR* 77. Cf. *CN* 78: "This is the concept of an ether of events which should be substituted for that of a material ether."

73. *PR* 224. Cf. Burgers, *E* 267-268.

74. *PR* 308. Cf. *PR* 317: "Mental and physical operations are incurably intertwined; and both issue into publicity, and are derived from publicity." And cf. *PR* 88.
75. *PR* 25. Cf. *PR* 275 and 278.
76. *PR* 224.
77. *PR* 244.
78. *PR* 167.
79. *PR* 150. Cf. *PR* 84.
80. *PR* 244.
81. *PR* 32. Cf. *PR* 31, 34, 87-88, 189, and 257.
82. *PR* 225.
83. *PR* 244. Cf. *PR* 88.
84. *PR* 87. Cf. *PR* 47. See Chapter 1, note 84.
85. *PR* 31.
86. *AI* 198.
87. *PR* 245.
88. *PR* 31.
89. *PR* 164.
90. *PR* 247. Cf. *PR* 40.
91. *PR* 164.
92. *PR* 67.
93. *PR* 88. Cf. *PR* 27, 88, 100, 101, 105, 119, 277-279, and *AI* 201.
94. *PR* 248. Cf. *PR* 245 and *IS* 252.
95. *PR* 88. Cf. *PR* 246: "There is an autonomy in the formation of the subjective forms of conceptual feelings, conditioned only by the unity of the subject."
96. *PR* 47. Cf. *PR* 27 and 255.
97. *PR* 222.
98. *PR* 244.
99. *PR* 224. Cf. *PR* 224: "Each temporal entity . . . derives from God its basic conceptual aim, relevant to its actual world, yet with indeterminations awaiting its own decisions. This subjective aim, in its successive modifications, remains the unifying factor governing the successive phases of interplay between physical and conceptual feelings. These decisions are impossible for the nascent creature antecedently to the novelties in the phases of its concrescence." Cf. Burgers, *E* 41-42.
100. *PR* 87.
101. *PR* 84.
102. *PR* 42.
103. *PR* 211-212. Cf. *PR* 85.
104. *PR* 25-26.
105. *PR* 187.
106. *MT* 207. Cf. *AI* 179: "The creativity is the actualization of potentiality, and the process of actualization is an occasion of experiencing." And cf. *PR* 29, 214, and 308.
107. *SMW* 254. Cf. *PR* 184, 187, and 189.
108. *PR* 149.
109. *PR* 223.
110. *PR* 25 and 85. Cf. *AI* 192.
111. *PR* 154.
112. *PR* 128.
113. Isaac Newton, *Philosophiae Naturalis Principia Mathematica,* p. 6.

114. Ibid., p. 8.
115. *AI* 156.
116. *MT* 199.
117. *PR* 70.
118. Cf. G. J. Whitrow, *The Natural Philosophy of Time*, p. 33 and M. F. Cleugh, *Time and Its Importance in Modern Thought*, p. 104.
119. *SMW* 75 and 85.
120. *MT* 120-121. Cf. Capek, *PICP* 150 and 151.
121. Albert Einstein, *Relativity: The Special and the General Theory*, p. 279.
122. *CN* 71.
123. Milic Capek, *PICP* 51.
124. Ibid., pp. 172-173.
125. Ibid., pp. 384-385. Cf. *PR* 70. And cf. Capek, *PICP* 165 and 136-137.
126. Capek, "The Fiction of Instants," in *The Study of Time*, ed. J. T. Fraser, p. 339. Cf. Capek, *PICP* 221 and *BMP* 96. And cf. *PR* 126, 174, 290, 319, and 489.
127. Newton, *Principia Mathematica*, p. 8.
128. Capek, *PICP* 190-191 and xv. Cf. Capek, *PICP* 328.
129. Hans Reichenbach, *The Philosophy of Space and Time*, p. 110. Cf. Capek, *PICP* 158 and 173, and "The Inclusion of Becoming in the Physical World," *CST* 501-524.
130. Cf. Capek, *PICP* 181 and 185. Cf. Capek, *PICP* 384-385.
131. *MT* 190. Cf. Capek, *PICP* 164 and 181.
132. Capek, *PICP* 168. Cf. Einstein and Infeld, *The Evolution of Physics*, pp. 199-245.
133. *MT* 179. Cf. *MT* 177, 185, 197, and *PNK* 15. Cf. Capek, *PICP* xii-xiii and 181. And cf. Bohm, *R* 50-51. And cf. Burgers, *E* 210.
134. *CN* 71.
135. Einstein, *Relativity: The Special and the General Theory*, p. 149. Cf. Burgers, *E* 80: "Einstein showed that this notion of [absolute] simultaneity cannot be supported by any possible experiment and that it must be considered as a fiction. . . . The notion of an undubitable 'now' valid here and everywhere at the same time is thus lost."
136. Capek, *PICP* 156.
137. *CN* 57.
138. A. S. Eddington, *The Nature of the Physical World*, pp. 46 and 47.
139. David Bohm, *R* 182. Capek describes absolute simultaneity as a "graphical representation," each instant being an "artificial cut across the world process," *PICP* 152-156 and 170.
140. *CN* 56-57.
141. *MT* 207. Cf. Capek, *PICP* 154.
142. *AE* 159. Cf. *MT* 131.
143. *CN* 73.
144. *CN* 72.
145. Das, *The Philosophy of Whitehead*, p. 187.
146. Ibid., p. 79. Cf. Rem B. Edwards, "The Human Self: An Actual Entity or a Society?" *PS* Vol. 5, No. 3 (1975), p. 202: "We are confronted with the dubious notion of a becoming in which everything happens all at once. And this notion of becoming is not made more intelligible by labeling it 'genetic' succession as opposed to 'temporal' or 'logical.'" Indeed, intelligibility is not achieved by labeling alone. And cf. John Robert Baker, "Omniscience and Divine Synchronization," *PS* Vol. 2, No. 3 (1972), p. 201: "Each actual entity has temporal extension, but the temporal extension happens all at once as an indivisible unit."

147. Lewis S. Ford, "Genetic and Coordinate Division Correlated," *PS* Vol. 1, No. 3 (1971), pp. 200-201.
148. William A. Christian, *An Interpretation of Whitehead's Metaphysics,* p. 30.
149. Ibid., p. 30. Cf. The same work, p. 81.
150. Plato, *The Republic,* pp. 501, 503, and 505. Cf. Richard Schlegel, *Time and the Physical World,* p. 10. And cf. G. J. Whitrow, "Reflections on the History of the Concept of Time," in *The Study of Time,* ed. J. T. Fraser, p. 11.
151. Capek, *PICP* 211-212.
152. *PR* 27-28.
153. *CN* 68.
154. *PR* 140.
155. *RM* 109-110. Cf. *RM* 153: "The passage of time is the journey of the world towards the gathering of new ideas into actual fact." And cf. *PR* 40, 59, and 96.


PROCESS

1.   *MT* 192-193. Cf. *MT* 216 and *IS* 195.
2.   *PR* 31. Cf. *PR* 213: "In the metaphysical language here adopted for metaphysical statement, 'passing on' becomes 'creativity', in the dictionary sense of the verb *creare,* 'to bring forth, beget, produce.'"
3.   Ivor Leclerc, *The Nature of Physical Existence,* p. 272. Cf. Harold N. Lee, "Causal Efficacy and Continuity in Whitehead's Philosophy," *TS* 66-67. And cf. Lewis S. Ford, "Kirkpatrick on Subjective Becoming," *PS* Vol. 4, No. 1 (1974), p. 38. And cf. Sheilah O'Flynn Brennan, "Substance Within Substance," *PS* Vol. 7, No. 1 (1977), p. 15: "For one thing, although it is the object that is causally efficacious, nevertheless all activity belongs to the subject. The activity by which the subject relates itself to the object is prehension. The object is not active with respect to the subject. It is merely there." And cf. Gene Reeves, "God and Creativity," *SJP* 380: "And both God and past occasions are, relative to the becoming occasion, inactive. They *have* acted, but are now objects for the becoming occasion." And cf. Robert D. Mack, *The Appeal to Immediate Experience,* p. 39: "Whitehead gives to immediate experience the static character of a 'given,' and to the knower the character of a passive 'spectator.'" On the contrary, *PR* 58: ". . . according to this philosophy, the knowable is the complete nature of the knower, at least such phases of it as are antecedent to that operation of knowing."
4.   *AI* 179.
5.   *AI* 176, 179, 188, *PR* 56, 220, and 231.
6.   *SMW* 214.
7.   *PR* 288.
8.   *PR* 250.
9.   *PR* 50.
10.  Evander Bradley McGilvary, "Space-Time, Simple Location, and Prehensions," *LLP-W* 231. Cf. Paul F. Schmidt, *Perception and Cosmology in Whitehead's Philosophy,* p. 123.
11.  *IS* 242.
12.  *PR* 23. Cf. *PR* 214.
13.  *PR* 211. Cf. *PR* 65: "It must be remembered that the phrase 'actual world' is like 'yesterday' and 'tomorrow,' in that it alters its meaning according to standpoint." And cf. *IS* 242: ". . . there is no well-defined entity which is the actual world. This phrase, 'the

actual world', means the past, present, and future occasions as defined from the standpoint of some present occasion." And cf. *PR* 28 and 284.

14. *PR* 230. Henry Pierce Stapp writes, "Quantum Mechanics, Local Causality, and Process Philosophy," *PS* Vol. 7, No. 3 (1977), p. 176: "Each of [Whitehead's] events prehends (and is dependent upon) not all prior events, but only the events of its own 'actual world'. The actual world of a given event is the set of all actual events whose locations lie in the backward light-cone of its own location." But this "set of all actual events" lying in the causal past of the given event is what is meant by "all prior events" from its perspective, its actual world. There is no other meaning of "all prior events" except this relativistic one that depends upon the standpoint of the given occasion whose past is being considered.

15. *PR* 210.
16. *PR* 210. Cf. *PR* 284: "First, there is the doctrine of 'the actual world' as receiving its definition from the immediate concrescent actuality in question. Each actual entity arises out of its own peculiar actual world."
17. *PR* 22-23. Cf. *PR* 65-66: "According to the modern view no two actual entities define the same actual world."
18. *PR* 211.
19. *PR* 121.
20. *PR* 66. Cf. *PR* 318: "The more important contemporary occasions are those in the near neighborhood. Their actual worlds are practically identical with that of the percipient subject."
21. *PR* 66.
22. *PR* 169.
23. *MT* 121.
24. *MT* 13.
25. *IS* 200. Cf. *PR* 44, 45, and 219.
26. *PR* 153-154.
27. *PR* 231.
28. *PR* 221.
29. *PR* 65. Cf. *AI* 179.
30. *MT* 159. Cf. *AI* 229.
31. *AI* 234.
32. *PR* 235.
33. Frederic B. Fitch, "Combinatory Logic and Whitehead's Theory of Prehensions," in *Philosophy of Science,* Vol. XXIV (1957), p. 332.
34. *PR* 29.
35. *PR* 45.
36. *PR* 43.
37. *PR* 155.
38. *PR* 152.
39. *PR* 233. Cf. *PR* 289.
40. *AI* 194. Cf. Burgers, *E* 194.
41. *PR* 278. Cf. *PR* 27 and 215. And cf. Burgers, *E* 46.
42. *AI* 193. Cf. *AI* 195: "But there are no actual occasions in the future, already constituted."
43. *PR* 215. Cf. Capek, *PICP* 395, and "The Inclusion of Becoming in the Physical World," *CST* 520, and "Relativity and the Status of Becoming," in *Foundations of Physics,* Vol. 5, No. 4 (1975), p. 611.
44. *PR* 215.

45. *AI* 195.
46. Milic Capek, "The Inclusion of Becoming in the Physical World," *CST* 517.
47. *PR* 215.
48. *IS* 242.
49. *AI* 204. This passage also affords examples of rather large scale actual occasions. Millennia are the serially successive occasions comprising the enduring object that is the earth's life-time; a man's days are the occasions which in serial succession comprise his life-time, his life considered as a succession of his days. Clearly, a millennium is rather a vast, large scale actual occasion compared to a day, and a day is even a large scale actual occasion compared to an eye blink.
50. *SMW* 180 and 181.
51. *PR* 85. Cf. *PR* 85, 222, 237, and *AI* 177.
52. *PR* 239-240.
53. *PR* 87. Cf. *PR* 88.
54. *PR* 210.
55. John B. Cobb, Jr., *A Christian Natural Theology*, p. 185.
56. Cf. Rasvihary Das, *The Philosophy of Whitehead*, p. 35: "Concrescence and transition are not two processes, but are merely two aspects of the same process. If transition is the process of objectification, concrescence is the process of subjectification and neither is possible apart from the other." And cf. Donald W. Sherburne, *A Whiteheadian Aesthetic*, pp. 22 and 23: "Whitehead's treatment of the Category of the Ultimate implies *one* process with two distinguishable species. . . . Ontologically speaking, transition and growth are faces of the same coin. . . . At bottom they are inseparable, though distinguishable." And cf. William J. Garland, "The Ultimacy of Creativity," *SJP* 371: "It is my contention that both concrescence and transition can be seen as the two complementary aspects of creativity, which is the ultimate principle behind all process." Cf. *PR* 214.
57. *PR* 211.
58. *PR* 137.
59. Capek, *BMP* 384. Cf. *AI* 177.
60. Bertrand Russell, *The Analysis of Matter*, p. 373. Cf. Edward Pols, *Whitehead's Metaphysics: A Critical Examination of Process and Reality*, p. 105: "We have not merely the problem that there is no time within the development of an entity. . . ."
61. A. H. Johnson, *Whitehead's Theory of Reality*, p. 45. Cf. Burgers, "Comments on Shimony's Paper" in *Boston Studies in the Philosophy of Science*, Vol. 2 (1965), p. 339: "The subjective, interior development of the occasion or process is a phenomenon which cannot be described in physical time." And cf. Burgers, *E* 43.
62. M. K. Haldar, *Studies in Whitehead's Cosmology*, p. 184. Cf. Gordon S. Treash, "Whitehead and Physical Existence: A Reply to Professor Leclerc," *International Philosophical Quarterly*, Vol. 10 (1970), p. 122.
63. *PR* 81. Cf. *PR* 119: "The crude aboriginal character of direct perception is inheritance. What is inherited is feeling-tone with evidence of its origin: in other words, vector feeling-tone."
64. *AI* 237-238.
65. *S* 35. Cf. Hans Reichenbach, *The Philosophy of Space and Time*, p. 270. And cf. Das, *The Philosophy of Whitehead*, p. 134.
66. *PR* 120.
67. William W. Hammerschmidt, *Whitehead's Philosophy of Time*, p. 39.
68. Ibid., p. 66.

69. *IS* 244.
70. *IS* 246.
71. *PR* 68.
72. Das, *The Philosophy of Whitehead,* p. 80.
73. Cf. Dorothy Emmet, *Whitehead's Philosophy of Organism,* pp. 180-181: "The word 'atomism' is an unfortunate one for Whitehead to have used, since it has the connotation of ultimate and enduring particles, in external relation to one another. What he wishes to bring out is presumably that an actual entity is an individualised activity; he is therefore in search of a Monadology rather than an atomism." Cf. *PR* 80.
74. Harold N. Lee, "Causal Efficacy and Continuity in Whitehead's Philosophy," *TS* 65.
75. *PR* 19. Cf. Burgers, *E* 117 and 193.
76. *AI* 177.
77. *PR* 36. Cf. *RM* 97-98: "For an epochal occasion is a microcosm inclusive of the whole universe. This unification of the universe, whereby its various elements are combined into aspects of each other, is an atomic unit within the real world."
78. *PR* 94.
79. Capek, *BMP* 142. Cf. Capek, *BMP* 143.
80. Capek, *PICP* 231. Cf. Capek, *PICP* 240.
81. Ibid., p. 230.
82. Ibid., pp. 234 and 231. Cf. Capek, *PICP* 234: "The chronon theory does not basically depart from this habit of spatialization; it merely substitutes, for the zero intervals, intervals of finite length."
83. Harold N. Lee, "Causal Efficacy and Continuity in Whitehead's Philosophy," *TS* 64-65.
84. *IS* 246.
85. *PR* 283.
86. William P. D. Wightman, "Whitehead's Empiricism," *RW* 349.
87. Nathaniel Lawrence, *Whitehead's Philosophical Development,* p. 73. Cf. Burgers, *E* 125.
88. Henryk Mehlberg, "Philosophical Aspects of Physical Time," in *Basic Issues in the Philosophy of Time,* ed. Eugene Freeman, p. 18.
89. Rem B. Edwards, "The Human Self: An Actual Entity or a Society?" *PS* Vol. 5, No. 3 (1975), p. 198.
90. *PR* 283.
91. *PR* 211.
92. *PR* 283.
93. A. H. Johnson, "Whitehead as Teacher and Philosopher," in *Philosophy and Phenomenological Research,* Vol. 29 (1968-69), p. 363.
94. *AI* 180-183.
95. *AI* 182-183.
96. *AI* 182.
97. *AI* 182.
98. David A. Sipfle, "Critical Studies: Milic Capek, *Bergson and Modern Physics,*" *PS* Vol. 2, No. 4 (1972), pp. 311-312. Cf. Paul F. Schmidt, *Perception and Cosmology in Whitehead's Philosophy,* p. 44. And cf. W. Mays, *The Philosophy of Whitehead,* p. 243. And cf. Andrew P. Uchenko, "The Logic of Events: An Introduction of a Philosophy of Time," in *University of California Publications in Philosophy,* Vol. 12, No. 1 (1929), pp. 140-141.
99. *AI* 183.
100. *IS* 195.
101. *MT* 30. Cf. *MT* 29, 155, 156, 221, and *IS* 195.

102. *IS* 205.
103. *IS* 267.
104. *IS* 203.
105. *FR* 78.
106. Capek, "The Fiction of Instants," in *The Study of Time*, ed. J. T. Fraser, p. 335.
107. *CN* 72. Cf. Capek, *BMP* 199: "Even within one individual consciousness the rate of duration, or, in other words, the temporal span of the specious present, varies according to circumstances."
108. *AI* 226.
109. *PR* 193.
110. *Prel* in *WhA* 310.
111. *MT* 224-225.
112. *IS* 255-256.
113. Francis Seaman, "Note on Whitehead and the Order of Nature," *PS* Vol. 5, No. 2 (1975), p. 132.
114. Rem B. Edwards, "The Human Self: An Actual Entity or a Society?" *PS* Vol. 5, No. 3 (1975), p. 200.
115. Das, *The Philosophy of Whitehead*, p. 41.
116. *PR* 121.
117. Martin Jordan, *New Shapes of Reality*, p. 45.
118. Rem B. Edwards, "The Human Self: An Actual Entity or a Society?" *PS* Vol. 5, No. 3 (1975), pp. 202 and 203.
119. *MT* 222. Cf. *PR* 77, 161, and 267. And cf. Lawrence, "Time, Value, and the Self," *RW* 163: "These processes . . . require larger chunks of time to appear . . . and tend to be discontinuous. The gross cases of such discontinuity are sleep, coma, etc."
120. *AI* 189. Cf. *AI* 205: "But a man is more than a serial succession of occasions of experience. Such a definition may satisfy philosophers—Descartes, for example. It is not the ordinary meaning of the term 'man'. There are animal bodies as well as animal minds; and in our experience such minds always occur incorporated. Now an animal body is a society involving a vast number of occasions, spatially and temporally coordinated." Cf. *PR* 234. And cf. Capek, *BMP* 159.
121. *RM* 109. Cf. *PR* 109 and *MT* 35.
122. *AI* 188. See Chapter 2, note 32.
123. *IS* 257.
124. Capek, *BMP* 224.
125. John B. Cobb, Jr., *A Christian Natural Theology*, p. 29.
126. Donald W. Sherburne, "Whitehead's Psychological Physiology," *SJP* 401. Cf. Capek, *BMP* 305: "Both Bergson and Whitehead claim that matter is constituted by events of very short temporal span."
127. A. H. Johnson, *Whitehead's Theory of Reality*, p. 63. Johnson writes, p. 181: "Whitehead argues that subjects rise and very quickly pass away." Cf. The same work pp. 17, 68, and 187. Cf. Richard H. Overman, *Evolution and the Christian Doctrine of Creation*, p. 173: "Whitehead went ahead to develop his cosmology on the assumption that nature in general is a nexus of brief events or processes, which he called, equivalently, 'actual occasions' or 'actual entities.'" But Overman allows that "brief" can mean anything from infinitesimally short to a quarter of a second, thereby acknowledging that brevity is relative, in the same work, p. 174: "Whitehead supposes that an electronic occasion is completed in the space of a single vibration, and that occasions of human personality may

be completed in something like a quarter to a tenth of a second." And cf. Sheilah O'Flynn Brennan, "Substance Within Substance," *PS* Vol. 7, No. 1 (1977) p. 14: "Although Whitehead's actual entities, being relatively short-lived events, differ radically from Aristotelian substances, they nevertheless have this feature in common: they alone are what exist fully, actually, and as ultimate individual entities."

128. Robison B. James, "Is Whitehead's 'actual entity' a Contradiction in Terms?" *PS* Vol. 2, No. 2 (1972), p. 123.

129. Reiner Wiehl, "Time and Timelessness in the Philosophy of A. N. Whitehead," *PS* Vol. 5, No. 1 (1975), p. 10.

130. Ibid., p. 28. Cf. Rem B. Edwards, "The Human Self: An Actual Entity or a Society?" *PS* Vol. 5, No. 3 (1975), p. 202: "The whole process is supposed to repeat itself many times each second."

131. William W. Hammerschmidt, *Whitehead's Philosophy of Time*, p. 37. Cf. David L. Miller, *The Philosophy of A. N. Whitehead*, p. 43: "Apparently an epoch of time is a duration (concrete slab of nature) of minimum extent."

132. Lewis S. Ford, "Genetic and Coordinate Division Correlated," *PS* Vol. 1, No. 3 (1971), p. 202. Cf. John Robert Baker, "Omniscience and Divine Synchronization," *PS* Vol. 2, No. 3 (1972), pp. 202-203: "Suppose that in all of creation every actual entity has a temporal extension of either $1/5$, $1/10$, $1/20$, $1/40$, or $1/80$ of a second. . . . Suppose that every actual entity in the universe enjoys one or another of 24 temporal extensions, it being understood that each represents a fraction of a second."

133. Rem B. Edwards, "The Human Self: An Actual Entity or a Society?" *PS* Vol. 5, No. 3 (1975), p. 203.

134. Vere C. Chappell, "Whitehead's Theory of Becoming," *KEP* 74.

135. Victor Lowe, *Understanding Whitehead*, pp. 55-56. Cf. Lowe, "The Development of Whitehead's Philosophy," *LLP-W* 73: "[Whitehead's] point is that the idea of spatiotemporal spans, of whatever magnitude, must replace instants and points, if what is observed . . . is to fall within the Concept of the material world."

136. Stephen C. Pepper, "Whitehead's 'Actual Occasion.'" *TS* 82 and 79.

137. Lawrence, "Time, Value, and the Self," *RW* 158.

138. Ibid., pp. 161-162.

139. David A. Sipfle, "On the Intelligibility of the Epochal Theory of Time," *The Monist*, Vol. 53 (1969), p. 511.

## BECOMING AND PERISHING

1. Abner Shimony, "Quantum Physics and the Philosophy of Whitehead," in *Boston Studies in the Philosophy of Science*, Vol. 2 (1965), pp. 307 and 308. Cf. Palter, *Whitehead's Philosophy of Science*, p. 215.

2. Milic Capek, *BMP* 305. Cf. Capek, *PICP* 286.

3. Ibid., p. 305.

4. Ibid., p. 318.

5. Victor Lowe, "The Development of Whitehead's Philosophy," *LLP-W* 90.

6. Robert M. Palter, *Whitehead's Philosophy of Science*, p. 218.

7. Capek, *BMP* 309.

8. *PR* 29.

9. *PR* 84.

10. *PR* 309.

11. Norbert Wiener, "Spatio-Temporal Continuity, Quantum Theory and Music," *CST* 543. Cf. Max Born, *Physics in My Generation*, p. 90.

12. Capek, *BMP* 266.

13. *SMW* 52.

14. *SMW* 187.

15. Rem B Edwards, "The Human Self: An Actual Entity or a Society?" *PS* Vol. 5, No. 3 (1975), p. 197.

16. David Bohm, *CC* 120-121. Cf. Gerald Feinberg, "Philosophical Implications of Contemporary Particle Physics," in *Paradigms and Paradoxes*, p. 35: "Since these early experiments, it has been found that the different forms of matter, or subatomic particles, can be readily created or destroyed, when there is enough energy available." And cf. Mary Hesse, *Forces and Fields*, p. 270.

17. Capek, *BMP* 307 and 215.

18. Capek, *PICP* 391. Cf. Bohm, "The Implicate or Enfolded Order: A New Order for Physics," in *Mind in Nature*, p. 39.

19. Bohm, *QT* 146. Cf. Louis de Broglie, "The Concepts of Contemporary Physics and Bergson's Ideas on Time and Motion," in *Bergson and the Evolution of Physics*, ed. P. A. Y. Gunter, p. 59. And cf. Burgers, "Comments on Shimony's Paper," in *Boston Studies in the Philosophy of Science*, Vol. 2 (1965), p. 334. And cf. R. A. Aronov, "On the Foundations of the Hypothesis of Discrete Character of Space and Time," in *Time in Science and Philosophy*, ed. Jiri Zeman, p. 265.

20. Capek, *PICP* 325, 322, and 323. Cf. Capek, *PICP* 259 and 328. And cf. Bohm, "The Implicate or Enfolded Order: A New Order for Physics," in *Mind in Nature*, p. 39.

21. Bohm, *QT* 168 and 158. Cf. Burgers, *E* 23.

22. Capek, *BMP* 266. Cf. Max Born, *Einstein's Theory of Relativity*, p. 292: "These 'light quanta,' or 'photons,' can be converted into other particles, provided the law of conservation of energy and momentum can be fulfilled." And cf. Mario Bunge, *Philosophy of Phycis*, p. 125.

23. *SMW* 53-54. Cf. *SMW* 196: "The discontinuities introduced by the quantum theory require revision of physical concepts in order to meet them." And cf. Einstein and Infeld, *The Evolution of Physics*, p. 51: "The results of scientific research very often force a change in the philosophical view of problems which extend far beyond the restricted domain of science itself." And cf. Capek, *PICP* 372-373. And cf. Bertrand Russell, *The Analysis of Matter*, pp. 365-366. And cf. *SMW* 24, 55, 93, and 157.

24. Capek, *BMP* 318. Cf. Henry Pierce Stapp, "Quantum Mechanics, Local Causality, and Process Philosophy," ed. William B. Jones, *PS* Vol. 7, No. 3 (1977), p. 174.

25. Capek, *PICP* 290.

26. *SMW* 72-73.

27. Louis de Broglie, "The Concepts of Contemporary Physics and Bergson's Ideas on Time and Motion," in *Bergson and the Evolution of Physics*, ed. P. A. Y. Gunter, p. 51.

28. *SMW* 54.

29. *PNK* 3 and 196.

30. Wiener, "Spatio-Temporal Continuity, Quantum Theory and Music, " *CST* 545. Cf. Capek, *PICP* 378, *BMP* 327, and "The Fiction of Instants," in *The Study of Time*, ed. J. T. Fraser, pp. 339-340.

31. Capek, *PICP* 372-373.

32. *PR* 254. Cf. *PR* 116 and 178.
33. Mary B. Hesse, *Forces and Fields,* p. 272.
34. Albert Einstein and Leopold Infeld, *The Evolution of Physics,* p. 65.
35. Max Born, *Einstein's Theory of Relativity,* p. 371.
36. Max Born, *Physics in My Generation,* p. 96. And cf. Einstein and Infeld, *The Evolution of Physics,* p. 146: "We remember how it was in mechanics. By knowing the position and velocity of a particle at one single instant, by knowing the acting forces, the whole future path of the particle could be forseen."
37. Capek, *PICP* 123. Cf. Capek, *BMP* 104.
38. Ibid., p. 124. Cf. Capek, *BMP* 106, 109, and 111.
39. *AI* 126. Cf. *PR* 256: "This doctrine is the ultimate ground of empiricism; namely, that eternal objects tell no tales as to their ingressions." And cf. *PR* 20 and 230.
40. *MT* 203-204. See Introduction, note 14.
41. *FR* 14, 13, and 16. Cf. Burgers, *E* 9 and 204.
42. *IS* 250.
43. *FR* 30 and 27.
44. *FR* 26. Cf. *FR* 16.
45. *MT* 184.
46. *MT* 225-226.
47. Bohm, *QT* 167. Cf. Mario Bunge, *Philosophy of Physics,* p. 122: "They should not expect to find a kinematics, or theory of motion, in quantum mechanics just because one gives it the misnomer *mechanics.*" And cf. de Broglie, "The Concepts of Contemporary Physics and Bergson's Ideas on Time and Motion," in *Bergson and the Evolution of Physics,* ed. P. A. Y. Gunter, p. 54.
48. Capek, *PICP* 238. Cf. Capek, *PICP* 290 and *BMP* 310. And cf. Burgers, *E* 81.
49. Ibid., pp. 289-290. Cf. Burgers, *E* 70.
50. Max Born, *Physics in My Generation,* p. 28.
51. Capek, *PICP* 154. Cf. *PNK* 8: "Our perception of time is as a duration, and these instants have only been introduced by reason of a supposed necessity of thought."
52. Einstein, "Remarks Concerning Relativity Theory," in *Bergson and the Evolution of Physics,* ed. P. A. Y Gunter, p. 133.
53. Capek, "The Inclusion of Becoming in the Physical World," *CST* 512.
54. Bohm, *QT* 152.
55. Capek, *PICP* 395. Cf. *PR* 284: "Thirdly, it is to be noticed that 'decided' conditions are never such as to banish freedom. They only qualify it. There is always a contingency left open for immediate decision."
56. de Broglie, "The Concepts of Contemporary Physics and Bergson's Ideas on Time and Motion," in *Bergson and the Evolution of Physics,* ed. P. A. Y. Gunter, p. 57. Cf. Capek, *PICP* 340.
57. Bohm, *QT* 146-147.
58. *SMW* 166.
59. Capek, *PICP* 304.
60. Bohm, QT 157. Cf. Burgers, *E* 72.
61. *PR* 203.
62. Bohm, *CC* 88 and 89.
63. *SMW* 185.
64. *PR* 284.

65. Bohm, *QT* 166. Cf. Bohm, *QT* 168. And cf. Capek, *BMP* 220 and *PICP* 306.
66. Ibid., p. 161. Cf. Capek, *BMP* 159. And cf. Burgers, *E* 128.
67. Ibid., pp. 166 and 167. Cf. *AE* 153: "The changes in motion of each electron depend entirely on the resultant field in the region it occupies." And cf. Bohm, *QT* 153 and *CC* 109.
68. Bohm, *R* 228.
69. Evander Bradley McGilvary, "Space-Time, Simple Location, and Prehensions," *LLP-W* 236-237.
70. *PR* 170.
71. *IS* 246. Cf. R. A. Aronov, "On the Foundations of the Hypothesis of Discrete Character of Space and Time," in *Time in Science and Philosophy*, ed. Jiri Zeman, p. 269.
72. de Broglie, "The Concepts of Contemporary Physics and Bergson's Ideas on Time and Motion," in *Bergson and the Evolution of Physics*, ed. P. A. Y. Gunter, p. 54.
73. *PR* 77.
74. *PR* 73 and 35.
75. Isaac Newton, *Philosophiae Naturalis Principia Mathematica*, p. 11.
76. Capek, "The Inclusion of Becoming in the Physical World," *CST* 511. Cf. Einstein, *Relativity: The Special and the General Theory*, p. 26. And cf. Reichenbach, *The Philosophy of Space and Time*, p. 219. And cf. John Dewey, "The Reflex Arc Concept in Psychology," in *The Psychological Review*, Vol. 111, No. 4 (1896), p. 365.
77. Capek, *PICP* 327.
78. *PR* 80. Cf. *PR* 73: "It is sufficient to say that a molecule in the sense of a moving body, with a history of local change, is not an actual occasion; it must therefore be some kind of nexus of actual occasions."
79. *PR* 79. Cf. *PR* 73: "The fundamental meaning of the notion of 'change' is 'the difference between actual occasions comprised in some determinate event.'"
80. *IS* 240.
81. *PR* 73.
82. *PR* 80.
83. *PR* 238. Cf. *PR* 136-137, *SMW* 183 and 193. And cf. Burgers, *E* 11-12.
84. *PR* 220.
85. *PR* 351. Cf. *PR* 149-150 and 225.
86. Reiner Wiehl, "Time and Timelessness in the Philosophy of A. N. Whitehead," *PS* Vol. 5, No. 1 (1975), p. 13. Cf. Edward Pols, *Whitehead's Metaphysics: A Critical Examination of Process and Reality*, p. 48: "What should have emerged from the remarks on the epochal character of time is the awareness that when one speaks of the various 'phases' in which conceptual and physical feelings are integrated, the question of the reality of these 'phases', except in regard to the divisibility of the physical pole, must be raised." And cf. Donald W. Sherburne, *A Key to Whitehead's Process and Reality*, p. 38: "But if this is the case, then it seems strange to speak of one phase of concrescence as prior to another when the passage from phase to phase is not in physical time." And cf. Rem B. Edwards, "The Human Self: An Actual Entity or a Society?" *PS* Vol. 5, No. 3 (1975), p. 202: "There are passages in Whitehead in which the priority and posteriority of these phases to others involves succession and clearly has a temporal import and other passages in which such succession and temporal import is denied. These passages contradict one another." And cf. Lewis S. Ford, "On Genetic Successiveness: A Third Alternative," *SJP* 424-425: "A notion of genetic temporality, rigorously defined to fit in with the epochal character of occasions, could go a long way to illuminate the obviously temporal connotations of Whitehead's

talk of 'earlier' and 'later' phases of concrescence." And cf. John S. Lawrence, "Whitehead's Failure" *SJP* 430, note 4: "Whitehead articulates a general principle of 'philosophical muddles' which possibly applies to his employment of temporal language to describe non-temporal quantized development." And cf. Vere C. Chappell, "Whitehead's Theory of Becoming," *KEP* 74: "Whitehead indeed seems to be aware of this difficulty, for he seems to be pulled in two opposite directions in speaking about the process of concrescence." And cf. Robert Neville, "Genetic Succession, Time, and Becoming," *PS* Vol. 1, No. 3 (1971), p. 194: "One of the most important problems is whether the genetic process within an actual occasion from initial data to satisfaction involves some kind of real or temporal succession."

87. *PR* 26, 56, 58, 84, 86, 117, 149, 154, 163, 164, 165, 168, 172, 212, 213, 215, 221, 224, 240, 248, 249, 261, 321, 350.

88. Vere C. Chappell, "Whitehead's Theory of Becoming," *KEP* 73 and 75. Cf. Rem B. Edwards, "The Human Self: An Actual Entity or a Society?" *PS* Vol. 5, No. 3 (1975), p. 202: "The epochal theory of time must be given up because the doctrine of the successive, i.e., 'earlier' and 'later,' but nevertheless coexisting, *phases* in the internal development of an actual occasion is utterly unintelligible, and even perhaps outright self-contradictory."

89. David A. Sipfle, "On the Intelligibility of the Epochal Theory of Time," *The Monist*, Vol. 53 (1969), pp. 512 and 518.

90. Ibid., p. 512 and 518.

91. Ibid., p. 518.

92. *PR* 69-70.

93. *PR* 240.

94. *PR* 33.

95. *AI* 245. Cf. *PR* 56.

96. *RM* 114. Cf. *PR* 239.

97. *PR* 23. Cf. *PR* 220.

98. *PR* 283.

99. *PR* 212.

100. *PR* 239.

101. *PR* 212. Cf. *PR* 248.

102. *PR* 248.

103. *PR* 248.

104. *PR* 248.

105. *PR* 289.

106. Edward G. Ballard, "Kant and Whitehead, and the Philosophy of Mathematics," *TS* 19-20.

107. Donald W. Sherburne, *A Key to Whitehead's Process and Reality*, p. 39. Cf. John S. Lawrence, "Whitehead's Failure," *SJP* 431.

108. *PR* 235.

109. *PR* 227.

110. *PR* 233. Cf. *PR* 115 and 275.

111. *PR* 283.

112. *PR* 4.

113. *PR* 228.

114. *PR* 260-264, 271-273.

115. *PR* 153.

116. *IS* 193.
117. *PR* 56. Cf. *PR* 85.
118. *PR* 187. Cf. *PR* 270-272 and 193.
119. *PR* 256. Cf. *PR* 160 and 361.
120. *PR* 113.
121. *PNK* 14.
122. *PR* 69, 284, and 292.
123. *PR* 84. Cf. *PR* 87. And cf. Burgers, *E* 132.
124. *PR* 85. Cf. *PR* 82.
125. *PR* 238.
126. *PR* 84.
127. *PR* 128. Cf. *PR* 278 and *SMW* 53-54.
128. *SMW* 197.
129. *PR* 85.
130. *PR* 108. Cf. *PR* 28, 113, 115, 117, 154, 186.
131. *PR* 108. Cf. *PR* 248.
132. Robert Neville, "Genetic Succession, Time and Becoming," *PS* Vol. 1, No. 3 (1971), pp. 196-197. Cf. Nathaniel Lawrence, "Time, Value, and the Self," *RW* 157: "A substantial portion of *PR* is devoted to showing that within the actual occasion, the temporal pattern and the qualitative content are given 'all at once'. . . . It will submit to mathematical, i.e., conceptual, dissection without limit; however, genetically, that is in point of its genesis, its parts do not exhibit any priority to one another. They are simultaneous (not instantaneous) with one another in the act of becoming. Whitehead's own use of the notions of 'earlier' and 'later' in the analysis of the phases of the actual occasion is such a conceptual device, one which may mislead the hasty critic."
133. John Dewey, "The Reflex Arc Concept in Psychology," *The Psychological Review*, Vol. 111, No. 4 (1896), pp. 362-363.
134. *PR* 32.
135. *PR* 68.
136. *PR* 69.
137. G. E. L. Owen, "Zeno and the Mathematicians," in *Studies in Presocratic Philosophy*, Vol. 11, ed. R. E. Allen, p. 157.
138. *PR* 68-69.
139. *PR* 68. This passage also shows that Whitehead intends his actual entity or *res vera* to refer to anything, any "something" whatsoever since he explicitly identifies it with "something" here.
140. *PR* 68.
141. *PR* 69.
142. *SMW* 183.
143. *SMW* 186. Cf. *SMW* 198: "Also if this concept of temporalisation as a successive realisation of epochal durations be adopted, the difficulty of Zeno is evaded."
144. *SMW* 183.
145. *IS* 246.
146. *SMW* 184.
147. *SMW* 185.
148. *SMW* 184-185.
149. *Prel* in *WhA* 342. Cf. Palter, *Whitehead's Philosophy of Science*, p. 109.
150. *PNK* 65.

151. John W. Lango, *Whitehead's Ontology*, pp. 97, 38, and 37. Cf. John B. Cobb, Jr., *A Christian Natural Theology*, p. 29.
152. Lewis S. Ford, "Genetic and Coordinate Division Correlated," *PS* Vol. 1, No. 3 (1971), p. 201. Cf. Vere C. Chappell, "Whitehead's Theory of Becoming," *KEP* 71: "The fundamental fact to which the epochal theory alludes is the indivisibility of actual occasions, i.e., the indivisibility of the processes or acts of becoming of which actual occasions are constituted."
153. Reiner Wiehl, "Time and Timelessness in the Philosophy of A. N. Whitehead," *PS* Vol. 5, No. 1 (1975), p. 25. Cf. Mason W. Gross, "Whitehead's Answer to Hume: A Reply," *KEP* 69: "Within each occasion different elements are discriminable and can be labeled past, present, and future in respect of the nature of their causal relations to one another."
154. *PR* 224.
155. William W. Hammerschmidt, *Whitehead's Philosophy of Time*, p. 28. Cf. Lewis S. Ford, "Genetic and Coordinate Division Correlated," *PS* Vol. 1, No. 3 (1971), p. 201: "Whereas all occasions earlier than a given one lie in its past, and all occasions later than it lie in its future, this is not true of the genetic phases of a single occasion. Here earlier and later phases are all equally co-present as constituting that occasion's present becoming."
156. William A. Christian, *An Interpretation of Whitehead's Metaphysics*, p. 81.
157. Vere C. Chappell, "Whitehead's Theory of Becoming," *KEP* 77-78. Chappell continues, p. 78: "And Whitehead's basic reason for holding that actual occasions are indivisible unities, atomic drops of process, is, I think, his doctrine that they are finally caused, which doctrine is in no way required by or even related to the Dichotomy argument of Zeno."
158. Bohm, *QT* 144. Cf. Bohm, *QT* 625: "The system of quantum concepts involves the assumptions of incomplete continuity, incomplete determinism, and the indivisible unity of the entire universe." And cf. Capek, Bergson's Theory of Matter and Modern Physics," in *Bergson and the Evolution of Physics*, ed. P. A. Y. Gunter, p. 307.
159. Gerald Feinberg, "Philosophical Implications of Contemporary Particle Physics," in *Paradigms and Paradoxes*, ed. Robert G. Colodny, p. 45.
160. Victor Lowe, *Understanding Whitehead*, p. 36.
161. G. J. Whitrow, "'Becoming' and the Nature of Time," *CST* 527.
162. Capek, *PICP* 175.
163. *IS* 246.
164. *MT* 129. Cf. Bohm, *CC* 157-158.
165. Abner Shimony, "Quantum Physics and the Philosophy of Whitehead," in *Boston Studies in the Philosophy of Science*, Vol. 2 (1965), p. 317. Cf. Capek, *PICP* 306.
166. *PR* 64.
167. *PR* 88. Cf. Das, *The Philosophy of Whitehead*, pp. 108 and 186.
168. *PR* 154. Cf. *PR* 45: "This evaporation of indetermination is merely another way of considering the process whereby the actual entity arises from its data." And cf. *PR* 232.
169. *PR* 154.
170. *PR* 212.
171. Rasvihary Das, *The Philosophy of Whitehead*, p. 80. Cf. Frederic B. Fitch, "Sketch of a Philosophy," *RW* 96: "Each primary occasion is a spatio-temporal unit in the sense that there is no meaning to speaking of spatio-temporal parts of it. If space-time is simply the relatedness of primary occasions, there can be no meaning to the notion of spatio-temporal parts of a primary occasion." And cf. David A. Sipfle, "On the Intelligibility of the Epochal Theory of Time," *The Monist*, p. 508: "The process of concrescence is not divisible into parts with temporal extension."

172. *PR* 21. Cf. *Prel* in *WhA* 323 and 324: "We are interested in equality because diversity has crept in. . . . The important use of equality is when there is diversity of things related and identity of character. This identity of character must not be mere identity of the complete characters. For in that case, by the principle of the identity of indiscernables, the equal things would be necessarily identical." Cf. Capek, *BMP* 327.

173. *PR* 66.

174. Dorothy Emmet, *Whitehead's Philosophy of Organism*, p. 178.

175. *PR* 116. Cf. Henry Pierce Stapp, "Quantum Mechanics, Local Causality, and Process Philosophy," *PS* Vol. 7, No. 3 (1977), p. 174: "Whitehead has proposed a theory of reality that provides a natural ontological basis for quantum theory." See note 32.

176. *SMW* 166. Cf. Bohm, *R* 125: "And now it seems likely that current elementary particle theory, along with quantum mechanics, will be shown to be false, in the sense of being approximations to some as-yet-unknown theory of a new kind that is still more general."

177. *SMW* 198. Cf. *PR* 239 and 309.

178. J. M. Burgers *E*, 20.

179. *PR* 244.

180. Robert Neville, "Genetic Succession, Time, and Becoming," *PS* Vol. 1, No. 3 (1971), p. 197.

181. *SMW* 106. Cf. *AI* 199: "The whole Universe is the advancing assemblage of these processes."

182. Jerome Ashmore, "Diverse Currents in Whitehead's View of Time," *PS* Vol. 2, No. 3 (1972), p. 198. Cf. Das, *The Philosophy of Whitehead*, pp. 182-183. And cf. Harold N. Lee, "Causal Efficacy and Continuity in Whitehead's Philosophy," *TS* 64.

183. *MT* 75. Cf. Burgers, *E* 38.

THE EXTENSIVE CONTINUUM OF OCCASIONS

1. *SMW* 173.

2. Milic Capek, *BMP* 326. Cf. Albert Einstein, *Relativity: The Special and the General Theory*, p. 56: "Pure 'space-distance' of two events with respect to a co-ordinate system K results in 'time-distance' of the same events with respect to K¹."

3. Capek, "The Inclusion of Becoming in the Physical World," *CST* 515. See Chapter 3, notes 131 and 132. And cf. Capek, *PICP* 384.

4. *AI* 150.

5. *PR* 76. Cf. *PR* 72. See Chapter 3, notes 117 and 120.

6. *SMW* 96.

7. *PR* 73. Cf. *PR* 80: "Newton, in his treatment of space, transforms potentiality into actual fact, that is to say, into a creature, instead of a datum for creatures." And cf. *PR* 70: "The alternative doctrine, which is the Newtonian cosmology, emphasized the 'receptacle' theory of space-time, and minimized the factor of potentiality." Here Whitehead is using the term "receptacle" synonymously with "container" and not in its Platonic sense. Cf. Robert R. Llewellyn, "Whitehead and Newton on Space and Time Structure," *PS* Vol. 3, No. 4 (1973), p. 239. And cf. Stephen C. Pepper, "Whitehead's 'Actual Occasion,'" *TS* 72.

8. *AI* 150. This is the answer to Evander Bradley McGilvary's question in "Space-Time, Simple Location, and Prehensions," *LLP-W* 239: "Where among the categories of existence does the extensive continuum find a place? Is it an 'eternal object?'"

9. G. J. Whitrow, "'Becoming' and the Nature of Time," *CST* 529.

10. *PNK* 45-46. Cf. Robert M. Palter, *Whitehead's Philosophy of Science*, p. 165. Cf. Louis

de Broglie, "The Concepts of Contemporary Physics and Bergson's Ideas on Time and Motion," in *Bergson and the Evolution of Physics*, ed. P. A. Y. Gunter, p. 47.

11. Robert M. Palter, *Whitehead's Philosophy of Science*, p. 31.

12. Victor Lowe, *Understanding Whitehead*, p. 54.

13. *SMW* 149 and 191. Cf. *SMW* 195. And cf. Bohm, *QT* 153 and 161.

14. *PR* 163. Cf. *PR* 36. And cf. Bohm, *CC* 109 and Bohm, *QT* 159: "Thus an individual electron must be regarded as being in a state where its variables are actually not well defined but exist only as opposing potentialities. These potentialities complement each other, since each is necessary in a complete description of the physical processes through which the electron manifests itself."

15. *PR* 80.

16. *MT* 188 and 189. See Chapter 2, note 27.

17. *SMW* 151. Cf. *PR* 80 and 124. And cf. Gerald Feinberg, "Philosophical Implications of Contemporary Particle Physics," in *Paradigms and Paradoxes*, p. 39. And cf. Henry Pierce Stapp, "Quantum Mechanics, Local Causality, and Process Philosophy," ed. William B. Jones, *PS* Vol. 7, No. 3 (1977), pp. 174-175.

18. *PR* 148. Cf. *MT* 151.

19. *SMW* 186. Cf. *CN* 53: "The relations of other events to this totality of nature form the texture of time." And cf. *Prel* in *WhA* 314.

20. *AI* 156-157. Cf. *SMW* 72: "By simple location I mean . . . that material can be said to be *here* in space and *here* in time, or *here* in space-time, in a perfectly definite sense which does not require for its explanation any reference to other regions of space-time." And cf. *MT* 179.

21. *MT* 199.

22. *AI* 158.

23. *PR* viii and *SMW* 77.

24. *IS* 22.

25. Capek, "Bergson's Theory of Matter and Modern Physics," in *Bergson and the Evolution of Physics*, ed. P. A. Y. Gunter, p. 302.

26. *Prel* in *WhA* 335. Cf. *SMW* 180: "Each relationship enters into the essence of the event; so that, apart from that relationship, the event would not be itself. This is what is meant by the very notion of internal relations. It has been usual, indeed, universal, to hold that spatio-temporal relationships are external. This doctrine is what is here denied."

27. *AI* 157.

28. John W. Blyth, *Whitehead's Theory of Knowledge*, p. 40.

29. *IS* 201.

30. *AI* 157. This passage shows clearly that Whitehead does not make a special ontological case of electrons or any other subatomic entities as the sole actual occasions of the universe. Clearly he does not regard them as the only "physical things" and the only possible focal regions of space-time." He has simply included subatomic entities among his list of "physical things" or actual occasions, a list that names "stars, planets, lumps of matter, and molecules" along with them. The passage shows also that Whitehead does not regard the subatomic entities as completely simple. He regards "electrons, protons, and quanta of energy" as having a "divergent stream of influence throughout the utmost recesses of space and time" just like everything else. Such an influence would not be possible but that it is a complex system of real potentialities. Cf. *PR* 67: "For each process of concrescence a regional standpoint in the world, defining a limited potentiality for objectifications, has been adopted."

31. *MT* 192. Cf. Bohm, *QT* 162 and 167: "At the quantum level of accuracy, the universe is an

indivisible whole, which cannot correctly be regarded as made up of distinct parts. . . . Even in the classical limit, we recognize that the separation between object and environment is an abstraction." And cf. Burgers, *E* 128.

32. *PR* 72. Cf. *CN* 78: "It is therefore a consequence of this doctrine that something is always going on everywhere, even in so-called empty space. This conclusion is in accord with modern physical science which presupposes the play of an electromagnetic field throughout space and time." And cf. Einstein, *Sidelights on Relativity,* pp. 22 and 23.

33. *PR* 72.

34. *AI* 158.

35. *PR* 66.

36. *PR* 62. Cf. *PR* 69. Cf. Capek, "The Fiction of Instants," in *The Study of Time,* ed. J. T. Fraser, p. 341.

37. *PR* 67-68. Cf. *PR* 67: "Actual entities atomize the extensive continuum. This continuum is in itself merely the potentiality for division; an actual entity effects this division." And cf. *PR* 288.

38. *PR* 77. See Chapter 1, note 82.

39. *PR* 77. Cf. *PR* 124.

40. *PR* 67.

41. *PR* 66.

42. *PR* 289. Cf. *PR* 67.

43. *PR* 35.

44. *SMW* 197.

45. *PR* 289. See Chapter 4, notes 90 and 92.

46. *IS* 246.

47. J. M. Burgers, *E* 79.

48. *PR* 80.

49. *MT* 166. Cf. Bohm, *R* 197. And cf. Capek, *BMP* 196: "Let us consider the visual sensation of redness. . . . It has a certain duration and, what is even more surprising, it is simultaneous with *an enormous number of successive events in the physical world.* To one second of our sensation of redness corresponds, in the realm of matter, the succession of about four hundred billions of electromagnetic vibrations."

50. David Bohm, *R* 208 and 210. Cf. Capek, *BMP* 134 and 159.

51. *PR* 76. Cf. *PR* 40. And cf. *PR* 76: "[The extensive continuum] provides the general scheme of extensive perspective which is exhibited in all the mutual objectifications by which actual entities prehend each other." And cf. Lowe, *Understanding Whitehead,* p. 54.

52. *PR* 72. Cf. *PR* 288: "But, for our epoch, extensive connection with its various characteristics is the fundamental organic relationship whereby the physical world is properly described as a community." And cf. Burgers, *E* 26.

53. *PR* 66. Cf. Lowe, *Understanding Whitehead,* p. 54.

54. Henry Pierce Stapp, "Quantum Mechanics, Local Causality, and Process Philosophy," ed. William B. Jones, *PS* Vol. 7, No. 3 (1977), p. 176. Cf. *PR* 67: "With the becoming of any actual entity what was previously potential in the space-time continuum is now the primary real phase in something actual." And cf. Michael Whiteman, *Philosophy of Space and Time,* p. 48.

55. *PR* 66.

56. *PR* 289.

57. *PR* 67. Cf. Bohm, *QT* 157-158. And cf. McGilvary, "Space-Time, Simple Location, and Prehensions," *LLP-W* 230 and 231.

58. *MT* 188. Cf. *PR* 80: "This amounts to the assumption that each actual entity is a locus for the universe." And cf. *MT* 75: "In process the finite possibilities of the universe travel towards their infinitude of realization."
59. *PR* 310.
60. *PR* 308-309. Cf. *PR* 288.
61. John W. Lango, *Whitehead's Ontology,* p. 34.
62. *PR* 215.
63. *PR* 290.
64. *PR* 309. Cf. *PR* 88 and 160.
65. *PR* 120. Cf. *PR* 62-63.
66. A. H. Johnson, *Whitehead's Theory of Reality,* p. 177.
67. William A. Christian, "Whitehead's Explanation of the Past," *KEP* 98.
68. Everett W. Hall, "Of What Use Are Whitehead's Eternal Objects," *KEP* 109. Cf. Lucio Chiaraviglio, "Whitehead's Theory of Prehensions," *KEP* 87: "Indeed, the ontological principle, the cornerstone of the philosophy of organism, does not mention eternal objects."
69. *SMW* 172-173. Cf. *SMW* 131: "The Subjectivist position has been popular among those who have been engaged in giving a philosophical interpretation to the recent theories of relativity in physical science." And cf. P. Frank, "Is the Future Already Here?" *CST* 388.
70. *PR* 212, *MT* 141, and *S* 45.
71. Capek, *PICP* 154.
72. *PR* 190.
73. *PR* 50.
74. Nathaniel Lawrence, *Whitehead's Philosophical Development,* p. 302.
75. Ibid., p. 296. Cf. Bohm, *QT* 160: "The continuous and discontinuous aspects of the transition of an electron between discrete energy levels are complementary in the sense that both are needed for a complete description of the process, despite the fact that the complete precision of definition of either is incompatible with that of the other." And cf. R. A. Aronov, "On the Foundations of the Hypothesis of Discrete Character of Space and Time," in *Time in Science and Philosophy,* ed. Jiri Zeman, p. 271.
76. Ibid., pp. 301 and 302. Lawrence allows himself to reason from experience but not Whitehead. Lawrence writes, p. 299: "Whitehead's argument is apparently that, since time is an abstraction from what is realized and what is realized is realized atomically, time must inherit the atomicity of the duration from which it is abstracted. The force of this argument, at least as thus presented, evades me. I see no reason why Whitehead's analysis drives him to the assumption that time is atomic." Then the force of Lawrence's own argument by way of abstraction from experience should escape himself. Lawrence emphatically declares, p. 300: "*Time as a feature of some concrete experience.*" which is Whitehead's view also; yet Lawrence sees no reason in Whitehead's view.
77. Ibid., p. 300. Cf. Rem B. Edwards, "The Human Self: An Actual Entity or a Society?" *PS* Vol. 5, No. 3 (1975), p. 200.
78. Ibid., p. 302.
79. Mario Bunge, *Philosophy of Physics,* p. 117. Cf. Alfred Lande, *New Foundations of Quantum Mechanics* (Cambridge: Cambridge University Press, 1965), p. 17.
80. *AI* 183. See Chapter 3, note 26.
81. A. S. Eddington, *The Nature of the Physical World,* p. 48.
82. Capek, "The Inclusion of Becoming in the Physical World," *CST* 511. Cf. Bohm, *R* 156.

83. Capek, "The Myth of Frozen Passage: The Status of Becoming in the Physical World," in *Boston Studies in the Philosophy of Science*, Vol. 2 (1965), p. 453. And cf. Mario Bunge, "Time Asymmetry, Time Reversal, and Irreversibility," in *The Study of Time*, ed. J. T. Fraser, p. 128.

84. *PR* 237. Cf. *IS* 244: "The irreversibility of time follows from this doctrine of objective immortality."

85. Capek, "The Myth of Frozen Passage: The Status of Becoming in the Physical World," in *Boston Studies in the Philosophy of Science* Vol. 2 (1965), p. 452.

86. Capek, "The Inclusion of Becoming in the Physical World," *CST* 520.

87. *PR* 61.

88. Capek, "Note about Whitehead's Definitions of Co-Presence," in *Philosophy of Science*, Vol. XXIV (1957), p. 85. Cf. Hans Reichenbach, *The Philosophy of Space and Time*, p. 145.

89. Ibid., p. 85. Cf. Bohm, *R* 54. And cf. Burgers, *E* 217.

90. *AI* 195. Cf. *PR* 123 and 124. And cf. Capek, "The Inclusion of Becoming in the Physical World," *CST* 511. And cf. Hans Reichenbach, *The Philosophy of Space and Time*, pp. 113 and 136. And cf. Bertrand Russell, *The Analysis of Matter*, pp. 377-378.

91. *AI* 195-196.

92. *AI* 196.

93. Capek, "The Inclusion of Becoming in the Physical World," *CST* 516. Capek continues: "In Robb's formulation, 'an instant cannot be in two places at once.'"

94. Capek, "Note about Whitehead's Definitions of Co-Presence," in *Philosophy of Science*, Vol. XXIV (1957), p. 84.

95. Henri Bergson, "Remarks Concerning Relativity Theory," in *Bergson and the Evolution of Physics*, ed. P. A. Y. Gunter, p. 131.

96. Martin Jordan, *New Shapes of Reality*, p. 57.

97. Ibid., p. 99.

98. Filmer S. C. Northrop, "Whitehead's Philosophy of Science," *LLP-W* 172.

99. Ibid., p. 200. Cf. William W. Hammerschmidt, *Whitehead's Philosophy of Time*, p. 39: "Whitehead means by 'nature' that which is immediately posited in sense-awareness or directly known."

100. Ibid., p. 200.

101. *PR* 176. Cf. *PR* 113 and 163, IS 253, *MT* 150-151, and *S* 44.

102. William W. Hammerschmidt, *Whitehead's Philosophy of Time*, p. 99.

103. Burgers, *E* 27.

104. Bohm, *R* 1. Cf. P. Frank, "Is the Future Already Here?" *CST* 388.

105. Capek, *PICP* 321. Cf. Capek, *PICP* 334, 337, and 340.

106. Capek, "The Inclusion of Becoming in the Physical World," *CST* 508. Cf. Hans Reichenbach, *The Philosophy of Space and Time*, p. 204. And cf. Bertrand Russell, *The Analysis of Matter*, p. 352. And cf. Stephen C. Pepper, "Whitehead's 'Actual Occasion,'" *TS* 80.

107. Albert Einstein and Leopold Infeld, *The Evolution of Physics*, p. 127. See Chapter 3, note 116.

108. Elizabeth M. Kraus, *The Metaphysics of Experience: A Companion to Whitehead's Process and Reality*, p. 129.

109. Ibid., pp. 127 and 135.

110. *IS* 218.

# Selected Bibliography

PRIMARY SOURCES

Whitehead, Alfred North. *Adventures of Ideas*. New York: The Macmillian Company, 1933. Free Press, 1967.
———. *The Aims of Education*. New York: The New American Library, 1957.
———. *An Anthology*. Selected by F. S. C. Northrop and Mason W. Gross. Cambridge: Cambridge University Press, 1953.
———. *The Concept of Nature*. Cambridge: Cambridge University Press, 1964.
———. *An Enquiry Concerning The Principles of Natural Knowledge*. Cambridge: Cambridge University Press, 1955.
———. *Essays in Science and Philosophy*. New York: Philosophical Library, Inc., 1947.
———. *The Function of Reason*. Boston: Beacon Press, 1967.
———. *The Interpretation of Science: Selected Essays*. Edited by A. H. Johnson. New York: The Bobbs-Merrill Company, Inc., 1961.
———. *Modes of Thought*. New York: G. P. Putnam's Sons, 1958.
———. *Process and Reality: An Essay in Cosmology*. Corrected Edition, Edited by David Ray Griffin and Donald W. Sherburne. New York: The Free Press, A Division of Macmillan Publishing Co., Inc., 1978.
———. *Religion in the Making*. Cleveland, Ohio: The World Publishing Company, 1954.
———. *Science and the Modern World*. New York: The Macmillan Company, 1925.
———. *Symbolism: Its Meaning and Effect*. New York: G. P. Putnam's Sons, 1959.


SECONDARY SOURCES

### BOOKS

Allen, R. E. and David J. Furley (eds.) *Studies in Presocratic Philosophy*, Vol. 11. London: Routledge and Kegan Paul, 1975.
Blyth, John W. *Whitehead's Theory of Knowledge*. Millwood, New York: Kraus Reprint Co., 1973.
Bohm, David. *Causality and Chance in Modern Physics*. Princeton: D. Van Nostrand Company, Inc., 1957.
———. *The Special Theory of Relativity*. New York: W. A. Benjamin, Inc., 1965.
———. *Quantum Theory*. Englewood Cliffs: Prentice-Hall, Inc., 1951.
Born, Max. *Einstein's Theory of Relativity*. New York: Dover Publications, Inc., 1965.
———. *Physics in My Generation*. New York: Springer-Verlag, Inc., 1969.
Bunge, Mario. *Philosophy of Physics*. Boston: D. Reidel Publishing Company, 1973.

Burgers, J. M. *Experience and Conceptual Activity.* Cambridge, Mass: The M.I.T. Press, 1965.

Capek, Milic. *Bergson and Modern Physics.* Dordrecht, Holland: D. Reidel Publishing Co., 1971.

———. *The Philosophical Impact of Contemporary Physics.* Princeton: D. Van Nostrand Company, Inc., 1961.

———. (ed.) *The Concepts of Space and Time.* Boston: D. Reidel Publishing Company, 1976.

Carnap, Rudolf. *Philosophical Foundations of Physics.* New York: Basic Books, 1966.

Christian, William A. *An Interpretation of Whitehead's Metaphysics.* New Haven: The Yale University Press, 1967.

Cleugh, M. F. *Time and its Importance in Modern Thought.* New York: Russell and Russell, 1970.

Cobb, John B., Jr. *A Christian Natural Theology.* Philadelphia: The Westminster Press, 1965.

———, and David Ray Griffin. (eds.) *Mind in Nature.* Washington, D.C.: University Press of America, 1977.

Colodny, Robert G. (ed.) *Paradigms and Paradoxes: The Philosophical Challenge of the Quantum Domain.* Pittsburgh: University of Pittsburgh Press, 1972.

Das, Rasvihary. *The Philosophy of Whitehead.* New York: Russell and Russell, 1964.

Eddington, A. S. *The Nature of the Physical World.* Cambridge: Cambridge University Press, 1929.

Einstein, Albert. *Relativity: The Special and the General Theory,* trans. Robert W. Lawson. New York: Crown Publishers, Inc., 1961.

———. *Sidelights on Relativity,* trans. G. B. Jeffrey and W. Perrett. London: Methuen and Co. Ltd., 1922.

——— and Leopold Infeld. *The Evolution of Physics.* New York: Simon and Schuster, 1938.

Eisendrath, Craig R. *The Unifying Moment.* Cambridge, Mass.: Harvard University Press, 1971.

Emmet, Dorothy. *Whitehead's Philosophy of Organism.* New York: St. Martin's Press, 1966.

Fraser, J. T., F. C. Haber, and G. H. Muller (eds.) *The Study of Time.* Vol. I. New York: Springer-Verlag, 1972.

Freeman, Eugene and Wilfred Sellars (eds.) *Basic Issues in the Philosophy of Time.* La Salle, Illinois: The Open Court Publishing Co., 1971.

Gunter, P. A. Y. (ed.) *Bergson and the Evolution of Physics.* Knoxville: The University of Tennessee Press, 1969.

Haldar, M. K. *Studies in Whitehead's Cosmology.* New Delhi: Atma Ram and Sons, 1972.

Hammerschmidt, William W. *Whitehead's Philosophy of Time.* New York: King's Crown Press, 1947.

Hartshorne, Charles. *Whitehead's Philosophy.* Lincoln: University of Nebraska Press, 1972.

Hesse, Mary B. *Forces and Fields.* Westport, Conn.: Greenwood Press, 1970.

Johnson, A. H. *Whitehead's Theory of Reality.* New York: Dover Publications Inc., 1962.

Jordan, Martin. *New Shapes of Reality.* London: George Allen and Unwin Ltd., 1968.

Kline, George L. (ed.) *Alfred North Whitehead: Essays on his Philosophy.* Englewood Cliffs: Prentice-Hall, Inc., 1963.

Kraus, Elizabeth M. *The Metaphysics of Experience: A Companion to Whitehead's Process and Reality.* New York: Fordham University Press, 1979.

Lango, John W. *Whitehead's Ontology.* Albany: State University of New York Press, 1972.

Lawrence, Nathaniel. *Whitehead's Philosophical Development.* Berkeley: University of California Press, 1956.

Leclerc, Ivor. *The Nature of Physical Existence.* London: George Allen and Unwin Ltd., 1972.

------. *Whitehead's Metaphysics.* New York: The Macmillan Company, 1958.

------. (ed.) *The Philosophy of Leibniz and the Modern World.* Nashville: Vanderbilt University Press, 1973.

------. (ed.) *The Relevance of Whitehead.* New York: The Macmillan Company, 1961.

Lowe, Victor. *Understanding Whitehead.* Baltimore: The Johns Hopkins Press, 1962.

------, Charles Hartshorne, and A. H. Johnson (eds.) *Whitehead and the Modern World.* Boston: The Beacon Press, 1950.

Lucretius, Titus Carus. *De Rerum Natura,* trans. W. H. D. Rouse and revised by Martin Ferguson Smith. Cambridge: Harvard University Press, 1975.

Mack, Robert D. *The Appeal to Immediate Experience.* Freeport, New York: Books for Libraries Press, 1945.

Mays, W. *The Philosophy of Whitehead.* New York: The Macmillan Company, 1959.

Margenau, Henry. *The Nature of Physical Reality.* New York: McGraw-Hill Book Company, Inc., 1950.

McMullin, Ernan. (ed.) *The Concept of Matter.* Notre Dame: University of Notre Dame Press, 1963.

Miller, David L. and George V. Gentry. *The Philosophy of A. N. Whitehead.* Minneapolis: Burgess Publishing Company, 1938.

Newton, Sir Isaac. *Philosophiae Naturalis Principia Mathematica,* trans. Andrew Motte 1729, revised by Florian Cajori. Berkeley: University of California Press, 1960.

Northrop, F. S. C. *Science and First Principles.* New York: The Macmillan Company, 1932.

Overman, Richard H. *Evolution and the Christian Doctrine of Creation.* Philadelphia: The Westminster Press, 1967.

Palter, Robert M. *Whitehead's Philosophy of Science.* Chicago: The University of Chicago Press, 1960.

Plamondon, Ann L. *Whitehead's Organic Philosophy of Science.* Albany: State University of New York Press, 1979.

Plato. *The Republic,* Vol. II, trans. Paul Shorey. Ed. E. H. Warmington. Harvard University Press, 1970.

Pols, Edward. *Whitehead's Metaphysics: A Critical Examination of Process and Reality.* Carbondale: Southern Illinois University Press, 1967.

Reichenbach, Hans. *The Philosophy of Space and Time,* trans. Maria Reichenbach and John Freund. New York: Dover Publications, Inc., 1958.

Russell, Bertrand. *The Analysis of Matter.* New York: Dover Publications, Inc., 1954.

Schilpp, Paul Arthur. (ed.) *The Philosophy of Alfred North Whitehead.* New York: Tudor Publishing Company, 1951.

Schlegel, Richard. *Time and the Physical World.* New York: Dover Publications, Inc., 1968.

Schmidt, Paul F. *Perception and Cosmology in Whitehead's Philosophy.* New Brunswick: Rutgers University Press, 1967.

Seeger, Raymond J. and Robert S. Cohen. (eds.) *Philosophical Foundations of Science.* Boston: D. Reidel Publishing Company, 1974.

Shahan, Ewing P. *Whitehead's Theory of Experience.* New York: King's Crown Press, Columbia University, 1950.

Sherburne, Donald W. *A Key to Whitehead's Process and Reality.* New York: The Macmillan Company, 1966.

------. *A Whiteheadian Aesthetic.* New Haven: Yale University Press, Inc., 1961.

Suppes, Patrick. (ed.) *Space, Time, and Geometry.* Boston: D. Reidel Publishing Company, 1973.

Whiteman, Michael. *Philosophy of Space and Time*. London: George Allen and Unwin Ltd., 1967.

Whitrow, G. J. *The Natural Philosophy of Time*. London and Edinburgh: Thomas Nelson and Sons Ltd., 1961.

Wyman, Mary A. *The Lure for Feeling in the Creative Process*. New York: Philosophical Library, Inc., 1960.

Zeman, Jiri. (ed.) *Time in Science and Philosophy*. New York: Elsevier Publishing Company, 1971.

## PERIODICALS

(i) *Tulane Studies in Philosophy*, Vol. X, 1961.

Ballard, Edward G. "Kant and Whitehead, and the Philosophy of Mathematics," 2-29.
Brinkley, Alan B. "Whitehead on Symbolic Reference," 31-45.
Cormier, Ramona T. "The Understanding of the Past," 47-58.
Lee, Harold N. "Causal Efficacy and Continuity in Whitehead's Philosophy," 59-70.
Pepper, Stephen C. "Whitehead's 'Actual Occasion,'" 71-78.
Whittemore, Robert C. "The Metaphysics of Whitehead's Feelings," 109-113.

(ii) *The Southern Journal of Philosophy*, Special Issue on Whitehead, Vol. 7, No. 4, Winter 1969-70.

Ford, Lewis S. "On Genetic Successiveness: A Third Alternative," 421-425.
Garland, William J. "The Ultimacy of Creativity," 361-376.
Kline, George L. "Form, Concrescence, and Concretum: A Neo-Whiteheadian Analysis," 351-360.
Lawrence, John S. "Whitehead's Failure," 427-435.
Neville, Robert. "Whitehead on the One and the Many," 387-393.
Reeves, Gene. "God and Creativity," 377-385.
Sherburne, Donald W. "Whitehead's Psychological Physiology," 401-407.
Whitehead, Alfred North. "Unpublished Letter from Whitehead to Kemp Smith," 339-340.

(iii) *Process Studies*

Ashmore, Jerome. "Diverse Currents in Whitehead's View of Time," Vol. 2, No. 3, 1972. 193-200.
Baker, John Robert. "Omniscience and Divine Synchronization," Vol. 2, No. 3, 1972. 201-208.
Bennett, John B. "Unmediated Prehensions: Some Observations," Vol. 2, No. 3, 1972. 222-225.
Brennan, Sheilah O'Flynn. "Substance Within Substance," Vol. 7, No. 1, 1977. 14-26.
Cobb, John B., Jr. and Donald W. Sherburne. "Regional Inclusion and the Extensive Continuum," Vol. 2, No. 4, 1972. 277-295.
Edwards, Rem B. "The Huamn Self: An Actual Entity or a Society?" Vol. 5, No. 3, 1975. 195-203.
Ford, Lewis S. "Genetic and Coordinate Division Correlated," Vol. 1, No. 3, 1971. 199-209.
———. "Critical Studies and Reviews: Ivor Leclerc, *The Nature of Physical Existence*," Vol. 3, No. 2, 1973. 104-118.
———. "Kirkpatrick on Subjective Becoming," Vol. 4, No. 1, 1974. 37-41.

Fowler, Dean R. "Whitehead's Theory of Relativity," Vol. 5, No. 3, 1975. 159-174.

Garland, William J. "Critical Studies: John Lango, *Whitehead's Ontology,*" Vol. 3, No. 1, 1973. 44-55.

James, Robison B. "Is Whitehead's 'actual entity' a Contradiction in Terms?" Vol. 2, No. 2, 1972. 112-125.

Llewellyn, Robert R. "Whitehead and Newton on Space and Time Structure," Vol. 3, No. 4, 1973. 239-258.

Mason, David R. "Time in Whitehead and Heidegger: Some Comparisons," Vol. 5, No. 2, 1975. 83-105.

Neville, Robert. "Genetic Succession, Time, and Becoming," Vol. 1, No. 3, 1971. 194-198.

Nobo, Jorge Luis. Whitehead's Principle of Process," Vol. 4, No. 4, 1974. 275-284.

Seaman, Francis. "Note on Whitehead and the Order of Nature," Vol. 5, No. 2, 1975. 129-133.

Sipfle, David A. "Critical Studies: Milic Capek, *Bergson and Modern Physics,*" Vol. 2, No. 4, 1972. 306-316.

Stapp, Henry Pierce. "Quantum Mechanics, Local Causality, and Process Philosophy," ed. William B. Jones. Vol. 7, No. 3, 1977. 173-182.

Wiehl, Reiner. "Time and Timelessness in the Philosophy of A. N. Whitehead," trans. James W. Felt, S. J. Vol. 5, No. 1, 1975. 3-30.

(iv) Other Articles

Burgers, J. M. "Comments on Shimony's Paper," *Boston Studies in the Philosophy of Science,* Vol. 2 (1965), 331-342.

Capek, Milic. "The Myth of Frozen Passage: The Status of Becoming in the Physical World," *Boston Studies in the Philosophy of Science,* Vol. 2 (1965) 441-463.

———. "Note about Whitehead's Definitions of Co-Presence," *Philosophy of Science,* Vol. XXIV (1957) 79-86.

———. "Relativity and the Status of Becoming," *Foundations of Physics,* Vol. 5, No. 4 (1975) 607-617.

Dewey, John. "The Reflex Arc Concept in Psychology," *The Psychological Review,* Vol. III, No. 4 (1896) 357-370.

Fitch, Frederic B. "Combinatory Logic and Whitehead's Theory of Prehensions," *Philosophy of Science,* Vol. XXIV (1957) 331-335.

Johnson, A. H. "Whitehead as Teacher and Philosopher," *Philosophy and Phenomenological Research,* Vol. 29 (1968-69) 351-363.

Shimony, Abner. "Quantum Physics and the Philosophy of Whitehead," *Boston Studies in the Philosophy of Science,* Vol. 2 (1965) 307-330.

Sipfle, David A. "On the Intelligibility of the Epochal Theory of Time," *The Monist,* Vol. 53 (1969) 505-518.

Treah, Gordon S. "Whitehead and Physical Existence: A Reply to Professor Leclerc," *International Philosophical Quarterly,* Vol. 10 (1970) 118-128.

Uchenko, Andrew P. "The Logic of Events: An Introduction to a Philosophy of Time," *University of California Publications in Philosophy,* Vol. 12, No. 1 (1929) 1-180.

*Upon those that step into the same rivers different and different waters flow: it scatters and gathers, it comes together and flows away, approaches and departs.*

Heraclitus


*Nor is it divisible, since it is all alike; nor is there more here and less there, which would prevent it from cleaving together, but it is all full of what is. So it is all continuous; for what is clings close to what is.*

Parmenides

# Index of Names

# Index of Terms